D1544927

THE FROOD

THE AUTHORISED AND VERY OFFICIAL HISTORY OF

DOUGLAS ADAMS

& THE HITCHHIKER'S GUIDE TO THE GALAXY

Also by Jem Roberts

The Fully Authorised History of I'm Sorry I Haven't a Clue

The True History of the Black Adder

THE FROOD

THE AUTHORISED AND VERY OFFICIAL HISTORY OF

DOUGLAS ADAMS

& THE HITCHHIKER'S GUIDE TO THE GALAXY

JEM ROBERTS

preface

Published by Preface 2014

2 4 6 8 10 9 7 5 3 1

Copyright © Jem Roberts 2014

Jem Roberts has asserted his right under the Copyright, Designs
and Patents Act 1988 to be identified as the author of this work

This book is sold subject to the condition that it shall not, by way of trade or
otherwise, be lent, resold, hired out, or otherwise circulated without the
publisher's prior consent in any form of binding or cover other than that in
which it is published and without a similar condition, including this condition,
being imposed on the subsequent purchaser

The author and publisher gratefully acknowledge the permission granted to
reproduce the copyright material in this book. Every effort has been made to
trace copyright holders and to obtain their permission. The publisher apologises
for any errors or omissions and, if notified of any corrections, will make suitable
acknowledgement in future reprints or editions of this book

First published in Great Britain in 2014 by
Preface Publishing
Random House, 20 Vauxhall Bridge Road,
London SW1V 2SA
An imprint of The Random House Group Limited

www.randomhouse.co.uk

Addresses for companies within The Random House Group Limited can be found at
www.randomhouse.co.uk/offices.htm

The Random House Group Limited Reg. No. 954009

A CIP catalogue record for this book is available from the British Library

Hardback ISBN 9781848094376
Trade paperback ISBN 9781848094383

The Random House Group Limited supports the Forest Stewardship Council®
(FSC®), the leading international forest-certification organisation. Our books
carrying the FSC label are printed on FSC®-certified paper. FSC is the only
forest-certification scheme supported by the leading environmental organisations,
including Greenpeace. Our paper procurement policy can be found at
www.randomhouse.co.uk/environment

Designed and typeset by Carrdesignstudio.com
Printed and bound in Great Britain by Clays Ltd, St Ives plc

For Janet, Sue, Jane, James and Polly

In memory of Peter, Geoffrey –
and The Frood

CONTENTS

* These extracts are referenced in the main text by their number in
the Appendices

DO NOT READ
THIS INTRODUCTION

You can if you like, but you don't have to. I hardly ever read the introductions to books, and suffer from occasional twinges of anxiety about it, just as I still sometimes do if I step on the cracks in the pavement. Do not worry. You can skip the introduction entirely, if you like, and the bears will not get you.

I've been asked to try out a wonderful new machine which interviews authors automatically and means that journalists won't need to bother to leave the bar at all in future. The inventor tells me that the job of programming it turned out in the end to be a lot simpler than he had anticipated. He had at first gone to all the trouble of devising elaborate parsing routines to analyse all the questions that journalists might ideally ask, select them, merge them, and arrive thereby at a kind of quintessential synthesis – the perfect author interview.

When this unexpectedly turned out to consist of complete silence he had to pause and reconsider his criteria. Perhaps perfection was too noble an objective, and so a little pragmatic workaday-ness was introduced into the program. A little too much, in fact. When the machine was at length prised out of the local pub and sobered up with a couple of quick zips through the Sieve of Eratosthenes, it announced that it had lost patience with the whole silly exercise since it should be perfectly clear to any idiot (though not, it admitted, to its inventor, who was a genius and therefore easily fooled) that journalists all asked exactly the same questions anyway. The program should be as simple as possible.

So the inventor rewrote the program along the simplest possible lines (simple, that is, by his standards – remember, we are speaking here of genius), until the machine seemed satisfied with itself. Yet the inventor remains anxious. He suspects the machine of having got a kind of satirical glitch from somewhere but, like all malfunctioning machines, it only goes

1

wrong whenever anybody capable of putting it right is not watching. He has asked me to field test it and treat it very gently, as it's a prototype. I have agreed, but I don't like the way the thing looks at me at all. Luckily I am prepared …

INTERVIEWING MACHINE: Well, Douglas. I thought that instead of asking the same old obvious questions, we'd do something a little different and get back to basics. So tell me – where did you first get the idea?

DOUGLAS: Er, well, it's interesting you should ask that, interviewing machine. The story goes that I first thought of the idea in 1971 while lying drunk in a field in Innsbruck …

IM: So you thought it all up just like that, lying in a field in Spain?

DOUGLAS: Well, not all of it, no. Just the title. It was Innsbruck, actually, in Austria.

IM: Are you surprised by its success?

DOUGLAS: Um, it's hard to say, interviewing machine. It's been growing since 1978. It's difficult to say you've been surprised gradually over a period of seven years.

IM: Seven years? Well, it's come a long way since that field in Spain. Has it made any difference to your life?

DOUGLAS: Er, yes. I think it was in Austria in fact. That was in 1971. I just thought of the title then. I didn't start writing it till the end of 1976. And yes, if I hadn't been doing this continually for the last seven years,
I would have been doing something different. Since I don't know at all what that would have been it's not easy to say what the difference is.

IM: Where do you get all your ideas from?

DOUGLAS: I wish I knew, interviewing machine. The dull truth is that you just have to sit there and think of them. If you can't think of them you just have to sit there – or think of an excuse for doing something else. That's quite easy. I'm very good at thinking of reasons for having a quick bath or a Bovril sandwich …

IM: Which planets do you visit most often?

DOUGLAS:	I beg your pardon?
IM:	It's a whacky question. You can answer it in a whacky way. Just say something crazy. It will be fun.
DOUGLAS:	What?
IM:	Have you always been funny?
DOUGLAS:	Er, well ... that is ...
IM:	Say something funny now.
DOUGLAS:	Er ...

And so on.

There is a large number of Questions I've been asked about *Hitchhiker*. Or to be more precise, a small number. The large number is how often I've been asked them, and is the reason why I now find it hard to remember the answers any more.

Of course, it's a complete fallacy that ideas are the sort of things that pounce on you in fields, or rather, that that's all there is to it. Inventing catseyes is a lot simpler. Once you've thought of the little glass beads stuck in a bit of rubber, you can presumably pat yourself on the back, pour yourself a stiff one, and take the century off. An idea is only an idea. A script is hundreds of ideas, bashed around, screwed up, thrown into the bin, fished out of the bin an hour later and folded into a wad to stop the table wobbling.

So where do the ideas actually come from? Mostly from getting annoyed about things. Not big issues so much (I'd love to be able to construct a joke that would let us blow away the very idea of nuclear armaments in howls of derisive laughter, but I can think of nothing more patently absurd than the situation we actually are faced with, so what can you do? Answers, please, on a postcard. I'm keen to know) as the little irritations that drive you wild out of all proportion. Any time I have any dealings with the gas board or credit card companies are usually a very fertile period.

To try and explain how an idea comes about is actually long and boring and doesn't make for bright snappy interviews. However, it doesn't matter being boring in a book introduction because nobody ever reads them anyway.

DOUGLAS ADAMS, Islington, circa 1985

THE FROOD

Most humbly we beseech your honours, with your accustomed favour in all godly and just causes, to hear and to judge of our matters. We have received the charge, as loyal and faithful men, to instruct and teach our people in the way of life ...

Arthur Dent, *The Plain Man's Pathway to Heaven* (1601)

The whole series of my life appeared to me as a dream; I sometimes doubted if indeed it were all true, for it never presented itself to my mind with the force of reality.

Mary Shelley, *Frankenstein* (1818)

He felt that his whole life was some kind of dream, and he sometimes wondered whose it was and whether they were enjoying it.

Douglas Adams, *The Hitchhiker's Guide to the Galaxy* (1979)

FIT THE FIRST

CREATOR

"I Seem to be Having Tremendous Difficulty With My Lifestyle."

Coincidence is a subject upon which *The Hitchhiker's Guide to the Galaxy* is dismissive. This is unsurprising because a Universe of such Infinite Possibility – and indeed a fair degree of Improbability – is a virtually limitless playground for the laws of cause and effect. Consequentially the strangest things can – and more often than not, do – happen ...

– The Book

The word 'lunch' has never sat well as a verb. Taken from the Germanic term for a midday drink, *luncheon* is an honest noun. To the metropolitan mover and/or shaker, however, lunching is not just a verb, but a way of life. Particularly in the pre-austerity media world of the last quarter of the twentieth century, restaurants were the battlegrounds where deals were done, empires were built, dreams were pitched and throat-narrowingly expensive drinks were drunk. What tales the eateries of London W1 could tell, of the luxuriant skulduggery carried out within by executives, producers, publishers and publicists, and the artists they suffered. The governing of the United Kingdom at the turn of the millennium was even hammered out years in advance by two ambitious politicians in a restaurant in Islington.

A specific hospitality within staggering distance of the BBC Light Entertainment offices behind Broadcasting House in West London, operating in the late 1970s as a Japanese restaurant, provided the lunch that changed the life of our hero. From our conceptual vantage point in the 21st century, we can glance over to see a breathtakingly tall, impressively-nosed youth, gratefully accepting an invitation to dine on BBC expenses. This struggling almost-25-year-old comedy writer is called Douglas Adams, and he is our

Frood – although right now he is not what you would call 'an amazingly together guy'. His friends would describe the enormous dark-haired chap's entry into any room as electrifying – largely because of the certainty that something was about to get accidentally broken. His story begins quite simply, on 18th February 1977, with a midday sushi break and an outpouring of frustrated ambition and imagination.

Although a celebrated writer in his own right, and the second key figure in giving life to the comedy titan which would come to be known as *The Hitchhiker's Guide to the Galaxy*, the friendly-faced, less ceiling-hogging figure accompanying our Frood need not be too invasively scrutinised. In time, he would give up the glamour of Light Entertainment production to create the sitcom *After Henry*, and by 1975 had already written his first novel to star the popular crime-solving thespian Charles Paris. But at the age of 32 for the duration of the lunch in question, First-class English graduate and Surrey native Simon Brett was something of an LE golden boy, having put in several years' good service in the BBC's radio comedy powerhouse since receiving a tap on the shoulder from Humphrey Barclay after an Oxford revue up at the Edinburgh Fringe.

In those pre-Comedy Store times, Brett has since suggested, there was nowhere besides Oxford and Cambridge which sprang to the minds of any of the Oxbridge BBC brethren as a place to harvest educated, ambitious comic talent. Barclay and the now sadly only legendary David Hatch had received their own taps on the shoulder from Peter Titherage when part of the most successful Footlights show of all, 1963's *Cambridge Circus*, alongside John Cleese, Tim Brooke-Taylor, Jo Kendall and others, and when in turn the gifted producer Barclay made Brett his own offer at the end of that decade, the debutant had timing on his side, with some of his earliest paid work including the job of helping to pad out Bill Oddie and Graeme Garden's scripts for that team's radio home – the hottest (certainly the noisiest) comedy show on the wireless, *I'm Sorry I'll Read That Again*.

Getting to write for *ISIRTA* would in itself have made Simon Brett a luminary to goggle at for his dining partner that Friday lunchtime in 1977, but after his years in the BBC Radio LE department, as the staff evolved from the crusty demob generation of producers to Hatch's bright young (but, of course, still male) Oxbridge gang, Brett was marked out for special things. He enjoyed a spell honing and producing *ISIRTA*'s panel-game-spoofing spin-off *I'm Sorry I Haven't a Clue* and, at the time of the sushi-sharing we are concerned with, was skipper of the only real successor to Radio Prune's anarchy.

Adams – the enormously eager sketch-writer and performer who we can safely picture expressively whirling his arms around and possibly causing sundry breakages as he shares his ideas with the visibly amused BBC insider – was certainly thankful not just for the lunch invite, but for the material which had been already accepted by Brett for dastardly clever cult sketch show *The Burkiss Way,* and he would have a further sketch under contract by the end of lunch. But the main function of the luncheon, far from being about friendship or nutrition, or the enjoyment of raw fish, was for the young arm-twirler to finally have his own stab at getting his very own format broadcast by the BBC. The producer knew he had something; this was a final attempt to really get to grips with whatever it was.

The comedy Adams had been trying to crowbar into the existing radio programmes rarely seemed to fit the formats, and his ideas needed their own separate home ... Or, if there really was no room for his ideas in the radio schedules, the desperate writer felt it was finally time for him to call it quits, get a proper job, and accept that the Really Wild Things in his head would just have to stay there. This wasn't just a lunch to Douglas Adams, this was his last chance at being the comedy star he had always wanted to be. If we can dare to impose the suggestion of a sheen of perspiration on this Frood's brow as he enthusiastically pitches shows to his lunch partner, it would neatly convey just how far he is from realising that he is a few sips of sake away from the defining green light of his life.

The Most Improbable Tale

We are all, naturally, the results of streams of coincidences stretching back to the primordial soup, but few people have revelled in their own personal coincidences as often and as publicly as Douglas Noël Adams, from his very first appearance at the Mill Road Maternity Hospital, Cambridge on 11th March 1952, mere months before the official discovery in that city of his initial namesake DeoxyriboNucleic Acid by Crick and Watson – coincidence or nominative determinism, it's an origin story Adams described as 'completely meaningless, but I am terribly proud'. Cambridge is fenland, misty with mystery and folklore – a sign at the Cambridge Museum states 'Many fenmen told "tall" or improbable tales and in some villages the local blacksmith struck a medal which was awarded to the man who, in the listeners' opinion, had told the most improbable tale'. Had this tradition thrived, the spring of 1952 would have seen the birth of the all-time champion.

The string of coincidences which went into the delivery of this unusually large, gangling baby (said by maternity witnesses to resemble some sort of beached ocean mammal – or, when dressed in his nappy, a to-scale Gandhi) were researched as far back as the 18th century by Nick Webb for his in-depth biography, *Wish You Were Here*. The paternal line of uniformly tall high-achievers can be traced to the eminent Edinburgh physician, lecturer and writer Dr. Alexander Maxwell Adams (1792–1860), who, among a whole raft of distinctions, had narrowly escaped a lynching when unjustly fingered for involvement in the Burke & Hare murders. This, however, would be an ignoble remembrance of a great man. This Dr. Adams was not only a celebrated and humane medic, leading the field in what were then termed 'Female Complaints', he even found time to write a novel: *Yamhaska, or Memoirs of the Goodwin Family*. This first known spurt of literary talent in the Adams line was to be the last for many generations, but others showed some glint of fascination with topics embraced by their descendant – Alexander's son Dr. James Maxwell Adams (1817–99) was both the inventor of the widely used 'Adams Inhaler', and a fierce early promoter of animal rights, penning a laceration of the practice of lion taming.

To skip a generation or two, it was perhaps our Frood's grandfather Douglas Kinchin Adams MB, ChB, MA, BSc, MD, FRCP (1891–1967) who set the bar highest, not least for his son Christopher. This Adams fought in the navy during the Great War before returning to Glasgow, where he became an internationally renowned lecturer on all manner of medical issues, winning the Bellahouston gold medal for his thesis on Generically Disseminated Scleroses, and becoming one of the first to recognise the serious nature of conditions such as MS. Born in 1927, Christopher Adams grew to be a giant of a man – at 6ft 4in only an inch shorter than his own son would reach – and was intelligent, swarthily bearded and trifled with by few. But it's possible that his father's success was something to which Christopher could never quite reconcile himself. He broke the mould of the Adams line by eschewing medicine and science for theology, and it was immediately after graduating from St. John's College, Cambridge at the start of the 1950s, beginning studies for a post-grad in Divinity at Ridley College with every intention of taking holy orders, that young Christopher met and wooed a nurse at the Addenbrookes Hospital, Janet Donovan.

Conforming considerably to the norms of her profession, widely considered to be as caring and warm as her first husband is remembered as somewhat opposite, it's possible that Janet felt out of her depth when the lofty theologian swept her off her feet. Douglas Adams would describe his mother as 'a great lady, somebody who is always at her best dealing with anybody else's problems – and can never deal with any of her own'. But the daughter of Irish immigrants brought her own apt exoticism to the union, being the great-niece, on her maternal line, of Benjamin Franklin Wedekind (1864–1918), a hugely influential German actor-director, sexual-boundary-breaking pioneer of the Theatre of the Absurd, and star of satirical cabaret. Genetically, Douglas would ultimately and unconsciously follow his Wedekind ancestry, though he would often regret not diligently following the Adamses' scientific successes. Curiously, Douglas' physical resemblance to the great Wedekind is as uncanny as his inheritance of the Adams nose and stature; it was almost like an experiment to create the most Douglassy Douglas imaginable.

Their passion having lit the blue touchpaper that would result in an internationally renowned comic author, Adams and Donovan were married in 1951, just in time to escape the pursed lips of post-War disapproval, and after a sojourn in Hackney, they set up home in Essex, as Christopher abandoned his religious ambitions and began to earn a crust as a teacher.

This is a story about many things, examined from many different angles, but viewed from almost any direction, this is a story about money: the sudden avalanche of it, the boundless spending of it, the obligation to it, and at the start of Douglas Adams' worldly awareness, it is undeniably about the absence of it. It's not possible to gauge the extent to which the infant Douglas was truly conscious of the problems the shortage of these green pieces of paper caused his parents, but it seems fair to suggest that among his earliest memories, the fraught rows about where it all went must have featured. He was hardly from a poverty-ridden background, but the family resources clearly failed to reach the accustomed requirements of the Adams clan.

It feels singularly unfair to over-analyse the negative aspects of Adams Senior, decades after his death, but he rarely comes out of the story of Douglas' childhood well. Janet and Christopher found it extremely hard to make ends meet, particularly after the arrival of their daughter, Susan, and yet the Master of the House was used to his luxuries, and rows about, for instance, his refusal to economise on tobacco, could not have made for the happiest of nests. Their elder child was three years old at this time, and reportedly showed some signs of not-quite-normality even at such an early stage, being a silent, 'neurotic' child, constantly weighing up his place in the world within his own head, unable to pronounce any slight judgement: 'I was the only kid who anybody I knew has ever seen actually walk into a lamp-post with his eyes wide open,' he recalled. 'Everybody assumed that there must be something going on inside, because there sure as hell didn't seem to be anything going on on the outside!' The child was even taken for tests to see whether it was his hearing or mental ability that made him such a closed-off oddity. At last, at the age of four, a visit from a local clergyman coincided with young Douglas' struggles to communicate – 'Da, Ma, Ma, Da, Ma...' – would it be 'Dada' or 'Mama'? Janet recalled that the ecstatic cries of 'DAMN DAMN DAMN!' failed to please either party, or the aforementioned startled cleric.

As if Adams Senior's attitude to familial harmony wasn't problematic enough, while his son was still only tiny, Christopher had retreated to an isolated island off Iona with two Cambridge friends, a physicist and a cleric, to perform some arcane metaphysical experiment, the details of which were taken to the grave by all three, but which left Adams a nervous wreck for some time. Allegedly some form of group hallucination was experienced, but Christopher never discussed any details, preferring instead to write an epic poem, 'A fusion between mysticism and science and the eternal battle between good and evil', which has long since disappeared. This unpredictable behaviour surely did little to alleviate Janet's struggles as a homemaker, and the marriage was not one that either party seemed willing to allow to drag on too far beyond the boundaries of bearability.

Few decisions could be more painful to take, but finally Janet was to flee to her parents' house in Brentwood, Essex, taking the children with her, and thus began a less than idyllic childhood which Adams would describe as being a 'shuttlecock kid', split between two families only ten miles apart and, at his lowest ebbs, not feeling particularly wanted by either of them. 'It's amazing the degree to which children treat their own lives as normal,' he was to reflect. 'But of course it was difficult. My parents divorced when it wasn't remotely as common as it is now, and to be honest I have scant memory of anything before I was five. I don't think it was a great time, one way or another.'

Nonetheless, Adams' new surroundings would swap one major biographical theme – Money – with a far more positive one: Zoology. His Irish grandparents' household was a far more hectic and furry one than he had grown used to. Grandfather Donovan reportedly took to his bed on his retirement, declaring 'I've done my bit!' and stayed there until his death seven years later, while his wife enjoyed being Brentwood's answer to St. Francis of Assisi, the local RSPCA lady offering homes to all four-legged or otherwise friends and foes that needed one: savage but toothless dogs, cats who would inspire a lifetime of feline sadism in Douglas' comedy, myriad rabbits and a resident pigeon, known as 'Pidge', who perched above a doorway lovingly nurturing a china egg, a permanent symbol of futile optimism. And amid this Ark roll-call was the diminutive Frood, sneezing violently, at his own estimation, about once every fifteen seconds: 'There are those who say that I tend to think and write in one-liners, and if there is any truth to this criticism, then it was almost certainly while I lived with my grandmother that the habit developed.'

Even from a small boy, these sneezes must have been resonant – his first exposure to a peer group at Miss Potter's private primary school on Primrose Hill brought it home to Douglas that he was likely to spend his life standing out from the crowd in at least one regard: 'My mother has a long nose and my father had a wide one, and I got both of them combined. It's large ... As a boy, I was teased unmercifully about my nose for years until one day I happened to catch sight of my profile in a pair of angled mirrors and had to admit that it was actually pretty funny.' This wise acceptance of his amusing features came just in time for his first taste of big school, as he was accepted into Brentwood Prep at the age of seven, and continued to grow at an alarming rate.

The cost of public (i.e. private) education was not something the Donovan family would have considered, but the fees would be taken care of, thanks to his father. One year after his arrival at prep school, Douglas received a new stepmother, an RAF widow of independent means, Judith Stewart, née Robinson, who married Christopher Adams in July 1960. They moved into an impressive country home, Derry, in Stondon Massey near Brentwood, Christopher took ownership of his dream Aston Martin, and Douglas and Susan had to get their small heads around the gulf between their homes, ten miles apart – the madness at Grandma's interspersed with opulent weekends at Stondon Massey. Within two years, they were to welcome a half-sister, Heather, in addition to new stepsisters Rosemary and Karena, who were just a few years older. Douglas' complex family tree would continue to blossom, but very shortly it would be the order and comradeship of Brentwood School that would provide him with perhaps the most defining home of his childhood. What he needed, above all, was a peer group.

An Unearthly Child

Brentwood was a traditional 'minor public school' in many clichéd ways, but luckily for Douglas Adams, it came with little pressure to rule the world like an Etonian. There was the usual emphasis on cricket, rugby and religion – Adams himself worked his way up to being the Chaplain's assistant, or Sacristan, and won a special prize for service in the chapel – but the relatively undemanding academy allowed its alumni to prepare for any number of careers. Old boys included Jack Straw, Noel Edmonds and, a year below Douglas, Griff Rhys Jones, plus a number of computer-programming pioneers, but Douglas was to insist, not unproudly, that the records of achievement boasted 'a major lack of archbishops, prime ministers and generals'.

Adams – he effectively signed away his Christian name for the duration of his education – was only a day boy in Heseltine House when he first arrived at Brentwood, to his chagrin: 'When I left school at four in the afternoon, I always used to look at what the boarders were doing rather wistfully. They seemed to be having a good time, and in fact I thoroughly enjoyed boarding. There is a piece of me that likes to fondly imagine my maverick and rebellious nature. But more accurately I like to have a nice and cosy institution that I can rub up against a little bit. There is nothing better than a few constraints you can comfortably kick against.'

There was little or no kicking in his four years of prep, as he started out as top of the class, and began working his way up to Junior Remove B and the eleven-plus entry into 'big school' – the closest he got to kicking would be the occasion on which the patently unsporty lad somehow managed to break his already problematic nose on his own knee during his first rugger match. Adams was a far from unpopular pupil, but although he would for a time be Captain of his House Junior Second XI cricket team, he predictably had little affinity for the boisterousness of the playing fields, being one of the cerebral clique who invested considerable time in finding inventive ways to get off games.

A six-footer in no time, Adams towered over several teachers, and his form master felt no compunction to spare the shy boy from being singled out, allegedly telling the class on school outings to 'meet by Adams', as the most unmissable landmark in the vicinity. The awkwardness the boy felt at this physical prominence was magnified ten times when his mother's plea to the headmaster for permission for him to wear long trousers was not just denied – when he *was* finally allowed to progress to covered knees, the uniform suppliers had none in his size, so he had to be the only pupil in class still wearing shorts, suffering 'four weeks of the greatest humiliation and embarrassment known to man or, rather, to that most easily humiliated and embarrassed of all creatures, the overgrown twelve-year-old boy. We've all experienced those painful dreams in which we suddenly discover we are stark naked in the middle of the high street. Believe me, this was worse, and it wasn't a dream.'

Thankfully, his size would not be Douglas' defining attribute at school, due in no small part to his English teacher, Frank Halford. Adams' infant silence had remained a problem, and he admitted, 'They could never work out at school whether I was terribly clever or terribly stupid. I always had to understand everything fully before I was prepared to say anything.' But Mr. Halford was to coax something new out of the reticent boy: 'I immediately warmed to his friendly, enthusiastic manner and instinctively trusted him.'

The story of Adams and Halford must surely be one of the most celebrated examples of teaching inspiration on record. Halford took Adams for English Composition class, and one Thursday morning, 7th March 1962, just before lunch, the famously stringent teacher's red pen recorded a unique score for a pupil's work, top marks, 10/10, for a now lost adventure story about hidden treasure which Halford remembered being 'technically and creatively perfect; a remarkable piece of work for a boy of that age'. On one hand, this early vote of supreme confidence nudged the delighted pupil on a long and occasionally winding road which would lead to much agonisation in his life, but the confidence it gave Douglas would remain a permanent touchstone: 'when I have a dark night of the soul as a writer and think that I can't do this any more, the thing that I reach for is not the fact that I have had best-sellers or huge advances. It is the fact that Frank Halford once gave me ten out of ten, and at some fundamental level I must be able to do it.' Douglas and Frank would regain contact and become friends in later life, and Halford would never again reward such top marks to a pupil.

Adams was already known for his imaginative flair amongst his friends thanks to his inventive post-lights-out ghost stories starring school spectre 'The Blue Lady' which had kept many of his dormitory chums from slumber. That it was an adventure story which first marked out Douglas' skill with language was not surprising, though: this was a new era of 'Boy's Own' adventures, and the Ripping Yarns of yore were popularly stoked with a less traditional ingredient: Science Fiction. The genre had of course been defined decades earlier in the wake of Wells, Verne and Burroughs, and pulp heroes like Philip Francis Nowlan's Buck Rogers had been around for years in many formats – the first science fiction saga to appear in comic and radio-serial form. Although happy to curl up with American offerings from DC Comics and Marvel, Adams' taste was more towards the stiff-upper-lipped school of space lore – where once Africa and the Empire provided unexplored worlds to inspire hearty juvenile minds, many British authors now looked to the stars as the new frontier in imagination, and Adams listed E.C. Elliott's *Kemlo* novels, following the antics of a space-station schoolboy, among his favourites. 'I didn't read as much, looking back, as I wish I had done,' he was to admit. 'And not the right things, either. (When I have children I'll do as much to encourage them to read as possible. You know, like hit them if they don't.) I read *Biggles*, and Captain W. E. Johns' famous science fiction series – I particularly remember a book called *Quest for the Perfect Planet,* a major influence, that was.' In that futuristic yarn Professor Lucius Brane took his crew on a jaunt around the galaxy to find a safe new home for humanity, coming across different bizarre ecosystems in each one.

The most addictive source of boyhood reading thrills in the period, however, was the *Eagle* comic, which had been launched at the start of the 1950s by a Lancashire vicar, but was at its zenith in Adams' most impressionable years. The greatest success within its pages was of course Frank Hampson's *Dan Dare: Pilot of the Future* (boasting Arthur C. Clarke as 'science advisor'), in which the lantern-jawed star-skipping Tommy took on Venus' iconically dome-headed hordes: 'It was brilliantly drawn and had really good stories and he was seminal throughout the whole generation of kids. The Mekon was just the most wonderful, exotic villain ever. I used to spend ages just drawing the Mekon.'

At the age of thirteen, bolstered by Halford's perfect mark, Adams was inspired not just to hungrily gobble up the *Eagle*'s stories every week, but to turn the comic into an interactive entertainment, by writing for it. As M.J. Simpson notes, in one sense Adams' very first piece of writing to be edited and published was a report on the school's Photographic Society's development in developing, written for *The Brentwoodian* when he was only ten ('Some of the results were hilarious, such as Buckley's attempt, which turned green!'), and he continued to see pieces in the periodical, when he handed them in on time – one item began 'I confess and worthily lament that laziness and lethargy on my part deprived these columns of an account of that worthy body the Chapel Choir in the January edition … To all the choir's avid followers I present my humble apologies.'

However, the sight of his carefully chosen words within the hallowed pages of the *Eagle,* dated 23rd January 1965, was something else:

Dear Editor,
The sweat was dripping down my face and into my lap, making my clothes very wet and sticky. I sat there, watching. I was trembling violently as I sat, looking at the small slot, waiting – ever waiting. My nails dug into my flesh as I clenched my hands. I passed my arm over my hot, wet face, down which sweat was pouring. The suspense was unbearable. I bit my lip in an attempt to stop trembling with the terrible burden of anxiety. Suddenly, the slot opened and in dropped the mail. I grabbed at my *Eagle* and ripped off the wrapping paper.
My ordeal was over for another week!
D. N. Adams (12), Brentwood, Essex

Merely a letter, maybe, but besides gaining huge kudos from his class-mates, Adams was to boast that the ten shillings he received for it could at that time have practically bought him a yacht. He also felt, in very little time, that he could do better, and within one month his second moment of fame was to come, a proper printed narrative:

SHORT STORY

"'London Transport Lost Property Office' – this is it," said Mr. Smith, looking in at the window. As he went in, he tripped over the little step and almost crashed through the glass door.

"That could be dangerous – I must remember it when I go out," he muttered.

"Can I help you?" asked the lost-property officer.

"Yes, I lost something on the 86 bus yesterday."

"Well, what was it you lost?" asked the officer.

"I'm afraid I can't remember," said Mr. Smith.

"Well, I can't help you, then," said the exasperated officer.

"Was anything found on the bus?" asked Mr. Smith.

"I'm afraid not, but can you remember anything about this thing?" said the officer, desperately trying to be helpful.

"Yes, I can remember that it was a very bad – whatever-it-was."

"Anything else?"

"Ah, yes, now I come to think of it, it was something like a sieve," said Mr. Smith, and he put his elbows on the highly polished counter and rested his chin on his hands. Suddenly, his chin met the counter with a resounding crack. But before the officer could assist him up, Mr. Smith jumped triumphantly into the air.

"Thank you very much," he said.

"What for?" said the officer.

"I've found it," said Mr. Smith.

"Found what?"

"My memory!" said Mr. Smith, and he turned round, tripped over the step and smashed through the glass door!

That this first published fiction had more in common with a Music Hall quickie than the adventuring tales which otherwise filled the comic was both portentous and natural, as science fiction had no monopoly within the pre-pubertal Adams mind: 'When I was a kid I used to hide under the bedclothes with an old radio I'd got from a jumble sale, and listen enraptured to *Beyond Our Ken*, *Hancock*, *The Navy Lark*, even *The Clitheroe Kid*, anything that made me laugh. It was like showers and rainbows in the desert … I just loved all those early radio programmes. I thought there was something tremendously important about being funny, but I wasn't really funny for a while and I gradually learned it, in a sense.' These earlier shows would soon make room for a youthful new sound, as the surreal, saucy radio antics of the *ISIRTA* team moved from Footlights into a wireless hit more aimed at the ears of youth than any other. This true progenitor of *Monty Python* would go on to inspire not just Adams, but Marshall & Renwick and a whole wave of comedians.

Adams' appreciation of the generation of laughter would overtake even the fascination for perhaps his greatest science fiction inspiration of all. Despite it being aired twice in the autumn of 1963, Douglas claimed to have missed the first *Doctor Who* adventure, but he recalled that from the Doctor's second outing in the TARDIS – particularly the first-ever cliffhanger introducing the Daleks in all their terrifying metallic villainy – *Doctor Who* became the one programme that he dared not miss, literally appointment viewing in the school's shared television lounge. In the years to come, the BBC's esoteric blend of educational historical drama and space capering would develop in ways to make any lively child's mind broaden, as the crotchety old humanoid in a police box clashed with villainous forces throughout space and time, introducing a number of tropes that would embed themselves in Adams' mind for further use – ludicrous green monsters, faraway spaceships, and impossible perils or cliffhangers (which could usually be overcome either with unintelligible techno-babble or the famous phrase 'I'll explain later'). And yet, the first documented reaction to *Who* from the schoolboy was to send it up – armed with the flashy gadgetry of a new tape recorder, he sat down and wrote a whole episode of the thrilling caper *Doctor Which* – featuring the Doctor's struggle against a race of Daleks unaccountably fuelled by Rice Krispies – and played the result to the rest of Barnard House at 1964's Christmas festivities. At the age of only twelve, the strapping six-footer had taken his first step towards creating science fiction comedy in audio, and above all, had written something that made all his friends laugh.

This wasn't the only element of school life which would have echoes for Douglas' work later on – as a fixture within the Debating Society, M.J. Simpson notes that Adams would have had to choose a side on the motion proposed in October 1965: 'This House thinks that the Brentwood bypass will not benefit the people of Brentwood.' Throughout the 1950s and beyond, Britain's green and pleasant land was being carved up by motorways and covered in concrete to the horror of many, and whichever

side of the argument Adams fell on, it can be presumed that 'You've got to build bypasses!' would never settle the matter.

No One I Think Is In My Tree

Comedy and science fiction were, it seems, the two most crucial fuels to Adams' burgeoning creativity in those sponge-like formative years, but neither was the most important to him. The early 1960s bloomed with new ideas in both artforms, but that was nothing compared with what the arrival of The Beatles did to a whole generation, and to no child more intensely than Douglas Adams. It was The Shadows who first thrilled him to the soul-shaking properties of the guitar, leading to further lamp-post-denting anecdotes as he blissfully walked along miming to the Hank Marvin riffs in his head. But from the first ear-splitting squeal of John Lennon's mouth harp, nothing else would compare. 'I vaguely remember my schooldays,' he said. 'They were what was going on in the background while I was trying to listen to The Beatles.'

Adams was an apt pupil when it came to music lessons, and as a member of the church choir he was already developing a separate worship for the intricate wonders of J.S. Bach, but from '63 onwards, like so many other kids the world over, except with a fiery passion few could equal, Douglas was a devout Fab Four disciple. Holed away within the confines of school, he had to risk severe punishment to keep up with the band – playing truant to purchase 'Can't Buy Me Love' on its first day of release, he scraped his knees breaking into Matron's quarters to play the record, and received a sound thrashing with a slipper into the bargain, but with that music washing around his head, he didn't care. Beatlemania was rife at Brentwood – when one poor lad bragged about having heard 'Penny Lane' before anyone else, Douglas and friends bullied him outright until he could hum an even passable rendition of what the next step forward from Lennon/McCartney sounded like: 'The Beatles planted a seed in my head that made it explode. Every nine months there'd be a new album which would be an Earth-shattering development from where they were before.' It was to be a life-long obsession, despite his regrets: 'A friend of mine at school once had some studio tickets to see David Frost's show being recorded, but we ended up not going. I watched the show that night, and The Beatles were on it playing "Hey Jude". I was ill for about a year. Another day that I happened not to go to London

after all was the day they played their rooftop concert in Savile Row. I can't
– ever – speak about that.'

This was not just a wild teenage mania, but a developing obsession
with sound. As the decade progressed, no act would push the boundaries
of sound reproduction as much as George Martin and the band, and the
stereophonic effect of *Sergeant Pepper's Lonely Hearts Club Band* in 1967
was to turn Adams into a lifelong technological audiophile, the friend of
electrical-store owners the world over, never happy with his staggeringly
pricey Hi-Fi set-up until it felt as if Ringo was using his head as a hi-hat.
When the band tore themselves apart at the end of the decade, although he
claimed Lennon's *Plastic Ono Band* to be the greatest album ever recorded,
Adams would switch allegiance to those he considered to be carrying on
The Beatles' work, pushing back the boundaries of recorded music, and
inspiring Douglas and his friends to see how much hair below the school
uniform collar they could get away with. Chief among these progressive
artists was Pink Floyd, who had been lucky enough to record at Abbey Road
alongside The Beatles, and picked up a few tips for their intergalactic new
direction, as Syd Barrett slipped into the Total Perspective Vortex. Roger
Waters' 'Set The Controls For The Heart Of The Sun' was a particular inspiration, one of a variety of chemically influenced musical looks to the sky,
designed to spark a million late-night adolescent debates about Life on
other planets, and the future of the human race (with or without the sixth
formers' own chemical influence, beer and tobacco aside). In that same year,
Douglas' 'perfect day' had been realised, when he and a friend slipped out
of school to attend a Simon & Garfunkel show in London – and prefaced it
with a trip to the cinema to see Kubrick's *2001*, which branded itself deeply
in Douglas' imagination.

Bach, The Beatles and Pink Floyd may be said to be Adams' greatest
musical hang-ups, besides his love for Donovan, Procol Harum, Dire Straits
and others – artists who would often be generically branded 'Dad Rock'
in decades to come but who were, at this stage, exciting, progressive, and
new. In his Brentwood adolescence, Adams had also been fortunate to
catch early performances from 'David Bowie & The Lower Third', who
were booked to play the school's Christmas dance in 1965, a fair while
before 'Space Oddity' would make David Jones of South London an alien
icon around the planet. Even more significantly, just over a week before
that dance, the Brentwood Folk Club had booked a visiting American

balladeer to play at the school, and Paul Simon's performance would inspire Adams, more than any other act, to make music himself: 'When I learnt to play the guitar, I was taught by Paul Simon. He doesn't know this. When I was a kid I would sit and play the same record over and over and over again, dropping the needle in the groove, then bringing it back and dropping it in the same groove ... until I'd worked out every single note and every finger position and so on.' Douglas' life-long admiration of Simon sadly never led to a meeting between the two, despite his eventual fame allowing Adams to befriend many of his heroes. Just before a US rendezvous could be nailed down, the singer's 'people' enquired about Douglas' height, and on being assured that Simon could easily fit inside the enormous Adams like a Russian doll, the correspondence became suddenly icy. Nevertheless, Simon didn't just inspire Douglas to pick up a guitar, but also, in a way, his attitude to writing: 'He's not someone who has a natural outpouring of melody like McCartney or Dylan, who are just terribly prolific with musical ideas. He obviously finds that very difficult, and I can identify with that, because I find writing very difficult. He is an incredibly clever, literate musician, but he always makes it sound terribly simple. I like the feeling that he's had to work hard for what he's got and has then been modest enough to disguise it.'

The failed meeting with his musical idol was long after Adams had devoted himself to a lifetime of finger-picking at his own left-handed guitar (of which he would eventually amass a mighty forest), at first taking lessons from a local blind player, David James, but in time settling on the exact same painstaking by-rote technique he used to master Simon & Garfunkel numbers. He also took piano lessons alongside Paul 'Wix' Wickens, who would go on to be one of the most admired keyboardists in the world as Paul McCartney's right-hand man for live shows throughout his solo career, and would also leave his mark on the *Hitchhiker* oeuvre. Adams' piano skills couldn't have been meagre, as he also helped another Brentwood boy, future comedy anarchist Keith Allen, with his lessons (as well as inadvertently getting Keith expelled by loudly crediting him with the whizzo scheme of switching the school organ pipes before one memorable assembly).

The guitar remained his constant companion, however – his elevated position at chapel allowed him to perform 'Blackbird' as part of prayers on one occasion, though 'Eleanor Rigby' was vetoed. A lad from the year below Douglas, Griffith Rhys Jones, was to record that his last memory of Douglas before he left Brentwood was of the older boy obsessively plucking at a Donovan song on a shadily lit platform in the Memorial, with 'so many self-conscious twiddles in his guitar-picking technique' that the lighting crew ran out of different coloured gels to accompany the marathon performance.

A short while earlier, young Griff had been a prole chanting 'Ave Caesar!' towards Adams' greatest theatrical triumph, playing the title role in *Julius Caesar*, 'strutting about with a double bedsheet over his shoulder and his huge conk in the air', but Douglas too was well used to taking supporting roles in school plays. Griff had been Rosencrantz while Douglas played Hamlet's father, but Adams' only other juvenile role of note was starring in the curious *Insect Play* by Josef & Karel Čapek (the latter being the sci-fi writer who first coined the term 'robot' for a humanoid automaton in 1920), in which Douglas' Tramp had a deathly dream featuring a series of strange insects each displaying some satirical facet of human behaviour, who then engaged in curious audience participation. *The Brentwoodian* saluted his performance, calling it 'ably played ... adequately sympathetic for the audience to realise their involvement, no easy task'.

Not for the last time in his life, Adams often had to create his own opportunities to share his talents with his friends, as he had with *Doctor Which*. On one hand, he co-founded Artsphere, an artistic group which published high-minded student magazine *Broadsheet* and was quickly labelled 'Fartsphere' by most of the boys, though Douglas tried to liven it up with humorous pieces. Adams' co-founder was budding poet Paul Neil Milne Johnstone, but the latter's earnest versifying ambitions and apparent total lack of a sense of humour were to ensure that the two never really got on. For many years, memories of Paul's morbid poetry readings involving dead swans in stagnant pools would cause Douglas to crease up. Adams could mix with the intellectual crowd, and towards the end of his time at Brentwood he was invited to join Milne Johnstone and others at the school's exclusive literary club, Candlesticks. Members had to write and perform a poem about a candle to gain entry, and by a stroke of luck a spot of spring cleaning at Brentwood School in 2014 turned up efforts from both Griff and Douglas, the latter's dated January 1970, *A Dissertation on the Task of Writing a Poem on a Candle and an Account of Some of the Difficulties Thereto Pertaining*:

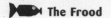

I resisted temptation for this declamation to reach out to literary
* height*
For high aspiration in such an oration would seem quite
* remarkably trite*
So I thought something pithy and succinct and clever was exactly
* the right thing to write.*
For nights I sat musing, and musing ... and musing whilst
* burning the midnight oil;*
My scratchings seemed futile, my muse seemed quite mute, while
* my work proved to be barren toil.*
I puzzled and thought and wrestled and fought 'till my midnight
* oil was exhausted,*
So I furthered my writing by dim candle lighting, and found, to
* my joy, this of course did*
The trick, for I flowered, my work – candle-powered – was
* inspired, both witty and slick ...*

Douglas went on to describe the candle burning the work of genius, requiring the replacement doggerel he was reciting – which just shows that by this stage the teenager had developed a major inability to take such things particularly seriously. He was far more at home writing and performing sketches for house revues, inspired by his greatest influence of all: John Cleese.

As one of the generation of young listeners tuned in to Radio Prune on *ISIRTA*, Adams would soon become aware of Cleese's anarchic radio persona, John 'Otto' Cleese, interchangeably laconic and manic, when he joined the show in March 1966. However, by the time Cleese hit the airwaves he had already been broadcast live to the nation televisually in the first-ever *Frost Report*, which debuted on the first day of the month. The effect of first seeing this monochromatic young lantern-jawed stranger on the screen was as electrifying for young Douglas as the sound of The Beatles had been a few years previously. With a leap of logic, he announced to his friends, 'I can do that! I'm as tall as he is!'

Perhaps inspired by the white-hot progress of science reflected in the sci-fi comics and shows he loved, as well as annual visits to the Royal Institution Christmas Lectures for Children, hitherto Adams' avowed ambition landed strongly on one side of the arts/science divide: 'At the age when most kids wanted to be firemen, I wanted to be a nuclear physicist. I never made it because my arithmetic was too bad – I was good at maths conceptually, but lousy at arithmetic, so I didn't specialise in the sciences. If I had known what they were, I would have liked to be a software engineer ... but they didn't have them then.' But from the spring of 1966, he insisted, 'I wanted to be a writer-performer like the Pythons. In fact I wanted to be John Cleese and it took me some time to realise that the job was taken.'

Later in life he was to rail against this way of labelling children, complaining, 'It was that decision you have to make when you're fifteen or sixteen about which A levels you're going to do. It always haunts me – did I take the right decision? It's a great flaw in our educational system – you divide into these two cultures from that age on: the arts on the one side, the sciences on the other, regarding each other with a mixture of contempt and loathing.' But as he passed his O levels (well, all of them except Greek) and moved into the sixth form, everything became geared towards following in the considerably silly and widely paced footsteps of Cleese.

The debut of *Monty Python's Flying Circus* in October 1969 only heightened the feeling of urgency: '*Monty Python* started when I was 17. Right from the word go, it just had a huge impact on me. Those of us who wanted to watch *Python* would congregate in the television room, just to make sure everybody agreed that we were going to watch *Python* ...' Most teenage lads from the turn of the '70s have tales of discovering the *Flying Circus* and fighting for control of the three TV channels on offer, and in Adams' case, during the first series, some broadcast of footling football highlights seriously threatened to keep BBC1 off Brentwood's communal television screen. Faced with the terror of missing that week's half-hour of increasingly mind-expanding comedy, Douglas and his friends escaped the school grounds and ran a mile or so to his grandmother's house just in time to switch desperately to BBC1 and collapse in a sweaty, hysterical heap. Nothing mattered more now than *Monty Python* – except, of course, The Beatles, who George Harrison insisted had passed on a torch to the Python mob in the first place. Adams saw both cultural giants as 'messages out of the void saying there are people out there who know what it's like to be you'.

The sketch show had already won Adams as a devoted viewer, but the young science fiction fan was not prepared for something completely different when the seventh episode aired at the end of November – after a typically silly preamble, the episode 'You're No Fun Any More' suddenly completely changed direction, to become an extended narrative about an alien invasion, when a race of interstellar blancmanges put into action their plan to change the population of Britain into Scotsmen, so they could land on Earth and become Wimbledon champions. There was nothing new in British comedy spoofing sci-fi – Pete & Dud had their own run-in with alien counterparts in *Not Only But Also* – but Python's mixture of zany sketch comedy and sci-fi cliché was exactly what Douglas had been obsessing about since his early teens, and his heroes had got there first.

There was clearly a crisp kind of logical silliness to Cleese's humour, combined with a withering hatred of the easy laugh which inspired the young comic to coin his own (selectively followed) rule of comedy: 'No puns, no puns and no puns.' This elitism instantly found favour with Douglas – so much so that he refused to take part in a House revue because it failed to come up to Cleeseian standards. He was beginning to take his authorial ambitions seriously – after a fashion: 'I used to spend a lot of time in front of a typewriter wondering what to write, tearing up pieces of paper and never actually writing anything,' he told Neil Gaiman. 'I don't know when the first thoughts of writing came, but it was actually quite early on. Rather silly thoughts, really, as there was nothing to suggest that I could actually do it. All of my life I've been attracted by the idea of being a writer, but like all writers I don't so much like writing as having written. I came across some old school literary magazines a couple of years ago, and I went through them to go back and find the stuff I was writing then. But I couldn't find anything I'd written, which puzzled me until I remembered that each time I meant to try to write something, I'd miss the deadline by two weeks.'

Adams learned that Cleese – not to mention Graham Chapman and Eric Idle – had been at Cambridge, just like his father, and that all of them had been stars of the Footlights Club, like Peter Cook and Jonathan Miller before them. That, he concluded, with no shadow of doubt, was where he was headed after Brentwood.

Ultimately this new plan could have been derailed by his unimpressive A level results – his first real girlfriend, Helen Cutler from the nearby Convent School, providing a worthy distraction from his studies. But fortunately, an essay on the 18th-century religious poet Christopher Smart (which managed to crowbar in comparisons with John Lennon) was to win Douglas an Exhibition to his father's college of St. John's, beginning in October 1971. 'For years Smart stayed at Cambridge as the most drunken and lecherous student they'd ever had,' Adams said. 'He used to do drag revues and drank in the same pub that I did. He went from Cambridge to Grub Street, where he was the most debauched journalist they had ever had, when suddenly he underwent an extreme religious conversion and did things like falling on his knees in the middle of the street and praying to God aloud. It was for that that he was thrust into a loony bin, in which he wrote his only work, the *Jubilate Agno*, which was as long as *Paradise Lost*, and was an attempt to write the first Hebraic verse in English.' The zealously eccentric Smart was an apt study for Adams, his meagre output also including odd odes to his cat Jeoffry's fleas – and coincidentally, if you're of a superstitious bent, as Nick Webb pointed out, line 42 of *Jubilate Agno* reads 'For there is a mystery in numbers ...'

Not This Story Again

Safe in the knowledge that his place studying English Literature at St. John's College was secure for the following autumn, Adams was free to indulge in that great near-necessity for middle-class teenagers at this time: the Gap Year. Much of his time was spent saving up his wages from jobs as a chicken-shed cleaner or a porter at Yeovil General Hospital, where he admitted to pangs of guilt about not following the family calling: 'I kept working in hospitals ... and I had the feeling that, if there is Anyone Up There, He kept tapping me on the shoulder and saying, "Oi! Oi! Get your stethoscope out! This is what you should be doing!" But I never did.' These were just student jobs, as he worked towards finally getting to see a bit more of the world – the cheap way.

The act of hitchhiking almost seems as archaic a remnant of a lost society as student grants, or Sir Clive Sinclair's digital watches which could only be operated by holding down a button. Of course there are still plenty of brave hitchers out there holding up their patches of cardboard pointing towards Glastonbury (and a fair few charitable ex-hitchers happy to pick them up once in a blue moon), but there is still a greater taboo surrounding some kid thumbing a lift from a random stranger today than there was forty-two years ago. Life on the road, thumb out, nonetheless exemplified the height of bohemian behaviour when Douglas caught the hitching bug – Kerouac's influence still reigned ten years on, and hitching was a way of life for the dispossessed and the philosophical, as well as for those unable to stump up the train fare.

Douglas got his first taste of thumbing his way across the UK at a particularly impressionable age, thanks to further developments within his fractured family. In 1964 his mother Janet had fallen in love with a warm-hearted local vet with the pleasingly Dickensian moniker of Ron Thrift, and by the time of the arrival of their first child, Jane, in 1966, the Thrift family had moved far south-west to Stalbridge in Dorset, where their son James would be born two years later. This completed the widespread bough on Douglas' family tree, and Douglas was overjoyed to have a new sister and brother and an affectionate stepfather, but the distance down to Dorset made his heart sink. His own father was never far away from Brentwood, but Janet and Ron's household, and his mother's loving but amusing fuss (family catchphrases for Janet included 'It'll all end in tears!', 'Right! Who said that?' and 'Don't panic!') made Dorset more of a home for Adams, no matter what the distance. And so, when the holidays arrived, he hitched. He was underage, but of course, being the size of an amateur giant, nobody would ever take young Douglas for a schoolboy, and few would dare to mess with him, despite the friendly personality that hid behind his intimidating outer shell.

There was another aspect to Adams' maturing views of life at this stage, besides hitching and the growing length of his hair, and although it's a rite of passage many of us undergo in our teenage years, for Douglas it was one which would crucially free his mind to explore all the dimensions of reality he could in his later work. As he told *American Atheist* in 2001, 'As a teenager I was a committed Christian. It was in my background. I used to work for the school chapel, in fact. Then one day when I was about eighteen I was walking down the street when I heard a street evangelist and, dutifully, stopped to listen. As I listened it began to be borne in on me that he was talking complete nonsense, and that I had better have a bit of a think about it …' Experience would send Adams on a slow progression through shades of agnosticism for most of his career, only arriving at outright atheism relatively late in life. 'I used to love the school choir and remember the carol service as always such an emotional thing,' he continued. 'Life is full of things that move or affect you in one way or another. The fact that I think Bach was mistaken doesn't alter the fact that I think the B-minor Mass is one of the great pinnacles of human achievement. It still absolutely moves me to tears to hear it. I find the whole business of religion profoundly interesting. But it does mystify me that otherwise intelligent people take it seriously.'

By July of 1971 Douglas had saved up a few quid, he had an enormous coat, he had his left-handed guitar, and he had his copy of *The Hitchhiker's Guide to Europe* by Australian writer Ken Welsh (borrowed and never returned, which he admitted 'counts as stolen'). This snarky guidebook was the slightly cheaper option for any freewheeling traveller looking to explore the Continent with only a few dollars a day – its appeal can be summed up by its entry for Albania as a hitching proposition, which simply read: 'FORGET IT.' 'I went to Austria, Italy, Yugoslavia and Turkey, staying in youth hostels and campsites,' Adams said, 'and supplemented my diet by going on free tours round breweries. Istanbul was particularly wonderful, but I ended up with terrible food poisoning and had to return to England by train, sleeping in the corridor just next to the loo. Ah, magical times ...'

Douglas initially made his way to Austria, earning a few schillings by playing his guitar in bars along the way, but his funds were already low by the time he reached Innsbruck. He was to recall, 'So much of my memory of hitchhiking, which is really vivid, was really "How am I going to survive? How do I get through this day?" I'd get to a youth hostel and ask for half a meal because it was all I could afford ... There were periods where it really was rotten, because you don't know what's going to happen to you in the future ...' He wandered Innsbruck for hours trying to ascertain directions to a handy address, incapable of making himself understood by any of the locals he happened to flag down. When he realised that he had been asking directions from visiting members of an organisation for the deaf and dumb, he gave up, spent his last coins on a couple of pints of lager, and went to find himself a field, to bed down under the stars.

This is the anecdote which Douglas told to interviewers so many thousands of times throughout his life that it became more famous for his claim not to actually remember whether it was even remotely true than it ever was in its own right. However, as the kernel is hardly an improbable tale to swallow, revisionism would be pointless here – this is how it happened; it was simply the constant repetition of the tale that removed all attachment to the moment for Adams.

The story abides, that in a field in Innsbruck now reputed to be nothing but a stretch of autobahn, Douglas lay gazing up with beer goggles at a particularly astounding vista of twinkling constellations. Half of his day had been spent at the roadside scanning the horizon for a handy lift to a new situation, and as his perspective took a shift from the horizontal to the vertical, it seemed that much the same desire applied, and he pondered for the very first time what it really would be like to stick out his thumb and hitchhike not just across Europe, but the entire Milky Way: 'I was lying drunk in a field in Innsbruck ...' the anecdote would usually begin. 'Not particularly drunk, just the sort of drunk you get when you have a couple of stiff Gössers after not having eaten for two days straight, on account of being a penniless hitchhiker. We are talking of a mild inability to stand up ... Night was beginning to fall on my field as it spun lazily underneath me. When the stars came out ... I thought, "Oh, it looks much more interesting up there." A title fell out of the sky: *The Hitchhiker's Guide To The Galaxy*. It seemed like a book that somebody ought to write, but it didn't occur to me that I should be the one to do it ... If only someone would write it then I for one would be off like a shot. Having had this thought I promptly fell asleep and forgot about it for six years.'

More Differed From Than Differing

Being housed within an ancient finishing school for the great and the good like Cambridge, it's no wonder that the Footlights should have had a constant stream of high achievers pass through its conceptual portals – but on the other hand, despite the generations of famous comedians who did serve their term with the club, it has to be said that the majority of generations disappear immediately into obscurity. For every *Cambridge Circus* or *The Cellar Tapes*' ready-made showbiz gang, the records show several, a dozen, years of comic hopefuls whose time in the lights would be brief and forgettable. When Douglas finally swapped the familiar traditions of Brentwood School for the hotbed of hair-growing which was Cambridge in late '71, he had to admit to being disappointed with the Footlights Club of the day – and not just because they wouldn't let him join.

There is a notable hiatus in the Footlights' golden roll-call, from the mid-1960s of Eric Idle, Germaine Greer and Clive James, to Adams' strata, where household names begin to crop up once again – albeit none of them in any hit revues, until the Thompson, Fry & Laurie bunch at the turn of the 1980s. Nonetheless, Adams had programmed himself to become a budding Python, and with his outstanding appearance and creativity, he felt that maybe he could be the one to turn the club's fortunes around. He would reportedly only complete and hand in three essays throughout his three years, but study was just a marginal hindrance; what mattered was making audiences laugh. There was absolutely no doubt in his mind that Footlights was where he belonged, from where he would set off on the road to fame, and his overgrown-puppyish enthusiasm and self-belief were two of the main things which would put people on their guard against him on first contact. In his first week, he was to bump into his contemporary Jon Canter, a similarly lanky, curly-mopped law student from Gonville & Caius college, and quickly informed him as they ambled across the quad that he was going to be President of Footlights – an assertion vehemently pooh-poohed by Canter, as he already planned to take the job himself in his third year.

There was nothing new about ambitiously signing up to Cambridge purely for the Light Entertainment possibilities even then – Graham Chapman had done precisely the same thing a decade earlier – but, to Adams' chagrin, joining Footlights wasn't just a question of signing a piece of paper; first you had to be invited, and then you had to impress – and to impress a bunch of theatricals who cast an instant sneer at young Douglas' ambitions, and equally failed to impress him one bit: 'My first experience was very off-putting because I found everybody rather grand and aloof, rather cold and unencouraging,' he was to admit – though John Lloyd would sum up that Footlights committee more succinctly as 'a bunch of wankers'. So, like many a Footlights rebel in the past, Douglas turned his back on the smug club and joined the Cambridge University Light Entertainment Society, having seen their revue *Funny, Bloody Funny* early in his first term.

Despite sharing many great alumni, CULES never had the cachet of Footlights, and after only one show, where the whole cast was booed off stage at Chelmsford Prison, Adams was determined to go through with Plan A. On reflection, he would charitably admit that the club had certain restrictions: 'Footlights had a very traditional role to fulfil: it had to produce a pantomime at Christmas, a late-night revue in the middle term, and a spectacular commercial show at the end of every year (May Week), as a result of which it couldn't afford to take any risks.' But he soon learned that most of the really inventive Cambridge comedy was lucky to ever make it into one of the few Footlights productions, while the real mortar of the University's humorous output was created at regular college 'smokers', late-night arenas where there was far more freedom to try material out, and shove a few boundaries around in a less snooty environment. They were far more akin to Brentwood's house revues, and the frustrated fresher was soon more at home.

Adams' first close friend on campus was a Northern Irish history student (now Professor) Keith Jeffrey, and in no time at all Douglas convinced Keith to form a duo for an audition, with an impersonation of a fountain which involved Jeffrey pumping Douglas' arm up and down, triggering a jet of water, spat out into the front row. This failed to impress many of that generation's Footlighters, but luckily the club's 'Victualler' was most amused, and his name was Simon Jones. Decades later, he was to insist that the water-spouting business was 'funny – much more so than the pseudo-intellectual crap I'd had to endure ...' A shade older at 21, the smart Wiltshire-born actor (son of the Earl of Suffolk's estate manager and blessed with crystal-clear clipped tones Noël Coward would have envied) soon became Adams' major supporter within Footlights, and an instant friend. Douglas decided that he was 'totally unlike the rest of the Committee, actually friendly and helpful, all the things the others weren't ... He encouraged me, and from then on I got on increasingly well in Footlights.'

He might have gained access to the club, but that was still a far cry from actually being cast in any revues – the best he would manage was to cameo as Torquemada in a Ken Russell spoof filmed in a nearby chalk pit, designed to plug a gap in the '72 revue *Norman Ruins*, featuring Simon Jones and future Radio 4 sitcom queen Sue Limb. Undaunted, just as at Brentwood, Douglas decided he had to take the initiative, and put on his own shows. He happened upon fellow English scholar Will Adams and his Economics student comedy partner 'bloody Martin Smith from Croydon' – the former tall and hairy, the latter slight and bespectacled – at his first documented smoker, the cornily titled *Prepare To Drop Them Now*, towards the end of his first year. The bitter-sweet event was to mark the passing of the Footlights' Falcon Yard venue, a long room in the centre of town, in Petty Cury, which smelt of gas and fish due to the Mac Fisheries warehouse below, but which had, over the years, housed early flourishes of genius from Cook, Cleese and others – and was now to be demolished to make way for a shopping arcade. This was just a performing gig for Douglas, and the sketch before his own debut was a Smith/Adams original which amused Douglas enough for him to approach the writing partnership a week later, at a special lunch to mark the close of the clubroom – they were so amused by his swaggering assurance that it would probably be good for their comedy careers to join up with him, that they did.

His first year was drawing to a close with very little to show in the way of bathing in an audience's adoring laughter – in fact, one of the highlights of the whole period came not at Cambridge, but Warwick University, where Douglas had hitched down to visit his girlfriend Helen, guitar in tow, and ended up in a late-night student halls jam with a pre-fame Mark Knopfler. Nevertheless, Adams did not panic, he simply built up relationships and prepared himself for a busy second year packed with hilarity.

Do You Want To Come Back To My Place?

This plan got off to a good start when Sue Limb cast him as the violent Irishman Sir Lucius O'Trigger in her production of Sheridan's *The Rivals*. This was, however, to give Douglas' friends a first taste of his sheer danger as a performer – as Sir Lucius, sword drawn, Adams had a lethal reach and lack of coordination that made his fellow cast members recoil from the stage for fear of their lives. 'I was a slightly strange actor,' he admitted. 'There tended to be things I could do well and other things I couldn't begin to do. I couldn't do dwarves, for example; I had a lot of trouble with dwarf parts.' Limb still appreciated the ungainly actor's comic powers enough to give him and Keith Jeffrey two slots in a smoker *LSO In Flames* a few weeks later, performing lost sketches 'Post Offices Prefer Bombs' and 'Trees Afoot', and a solo spot for Adams, 'The Serious Sketch'. This was Jeffrey's last comic outing, as Douglas began to collaborate more with the other Adams and Smith – but the friends would remain close, sharing a palatial residence at 69 Bridge St., thanks to Jeffrey's captaincy of the Boat Club. Those handsome quarters were a dream party venue, and Douglas' natural skills as a host ensured that Keith and he were at the centre of many a memorable evening.

The Smith/Adams writing duo always worked closely together, incorporating Douglas' work into their own. They remarked that their eager new collaborator was particularly adept at *starting* sketches, and would race up the hill to their college, Fitzwilliam, and sit the pair down with a grinning impatience to share his inspired opening monologues – such as 'Beyond The Infinite', a show-opening *2001*-inspired monologue from 1974 about Space's entry in the Guinness Book of Records for being so damn BIG. The audience were plunged into darkness as a deep voice intoned:

> Far out in the depths of the cosmos, beyond the furthest reach of man's perception, amidst the swirling mists of unknown galaxies, where lost worlds roll eternally against the gateway of

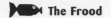

infinity; inexorably on through millions of light years of celestial
darkness we call Space … Space – where man dares to brave
indescribably elemental horrors, Space, where man boldly splits
infinitives that no man has split before … I can't begin to tell you
how far it is – I mean it is so far. You may think it's a long way down
the street to the chemist, but that's just peanuts to Space …

However, it would usually then be Will and Martin's job to decide where
all this was leading. A collaborator at heart, Douglas needed approval on an
almost atomic level, and would share material of which he was proud with
such a keen eye for the intended effect of every joke, that to get right to
the end of a sketch, or a page, or a sentence, without breaking off to test
it on friends, seemed almost impossible. Although the famous 'peanuts to
Space' line is now a beloved *Hitchhiker* quote, it's slightly bemusing to see
just how obsessed Douglas Adams was with it, crowbarring the phrase into
a number of non-sci-fi contexts before it slotted into its final home. It was
admittedly an early sign of his great gift for tripping up magisterial intergalactic hyperbole with a kind of awkward bathos, but above all, it clearly
had a *rhythm* that was pleasing to the writer, and so he could not let it
lie. This would not be the last gag or idea that was to nag away at Adams
until it found a permanent place in his work, and recycling would remain an
important ecological element of his craft.

This practice was not strictly limited to his own comedic earworms either
– in one early smoker Jon Canter took to the stage as an aged flat-capped
Northerner with a face like thunder and began a miserable monologue with
the words 'Life? Don't talk to me about life …' This was another phrase which
refused to budge from Douglas' consciousness – although of course he was
quick to ask Jon for permission to recycle the line, and would give him full
acknowledgement for coining it at every possible opportunity (conversely,
he never bought Clive Anderson's claim to have thought up the 'I wish I'd
listened to what my mother told me …' gag). Adams' comedy colleagues
all agree that, just as Douglas finding his own jokes amusing was somehow
endearing, to be the one to make him laugh – and Adams was a very voluble,
animated laugher – was one of life's pleasures. That he remembered and
envied Canter's line was a source of pride for the originator.

Prior to formally forming the renegade comedy outfit Adams-Smith-
Adams – 'a sort of guerrilla group' – in the spring of 1973 Will and Martin

staged their own smoker *The Heel-Fire Club*, with Douglas appearing only in a couple of minor roles. They had been inspired by a golden couple one year above who were equally placed on the fringes of the Footlights, the talented Mary Allen and her boyfriend, freshly indoctrinated into the club despite his misgivings, John Hardress Wilfred Lloyd. In time, Adams' friendship with the dashing polymath Lloyd would become one of the closest and most complicated in a lifetime of intense friendships, but at Cambridge the two were not close, merely fellow members of a sprawling network of sketch performers.

Adrift from his partnership, Douglas had turned to musical comedy as an outlet for his material, and John and Mary had booked him for their own smoker in February, *I Don't Know – I've Never Looked*, performing one of his own compositions, 'A Song For Stupid People'. Accompanied by his folky finger-picking (although not the greatest singer post-puberty), Douglas specialised in rambling lyrics which were a blessing for any subsequent sketch which required much setting up, such as his 'Talking Blues', otherwise known as 'Backdated':

> *I was walking down the street today, or maybe it was yesterday,*
> *   it may in fact have been last week ... Yes, it probably was last*
> *   week ...*
> *I was walking down the street, when who on Earth should I*
> *   chance to meet? Yes, who on Earth did I meet that day, which*
> *   was yesterday? Or the day before yesterday ...*
> *Yes, now I remember the time, I mean, it was yesterday at 2.15,*
> *   no, 3.15, two weeks ago, I really would quite like to know,*
> *   because next time I can get on to the interesting bit.*
> (Turns and walks off, frustratedly.)

Despite being, as ever, an unmissable landmark on the Cambridge comedy scene, and although the cast would boast friends like Canter and fresh Footlighter Rhys Jones, yet again that year's crucial May Week revue would pass Adams by. Or rather, the approach of *Every Packet Carries A Government Health Warning* would prove anathema to his comic tastes, despite Lloyd and Allen being the driving forces behind it. Lloyd and Co.'s distaste for the pretentions of the previous generation led to a back-to-basics approach of pun-slinging wackiness that consciously harked back to the similar Music Hall theme of 1963's *Cambridge Circus*. At this stage,

Douglas was still firmly under the pun-shunning influence of his idol, John Cleese, who might have been part of the *Cambridge Circus* team but openly expounded about having loftier comedic ambitions than his anything-for-a-laugh friends. Adams explained, 'Python sketches would create a new world with a new set of rules – that really was the line I was taking: "Let's start out with a world that has certain rules, and just see where that goes in the long run." Something that starts out as a silly idea actually has to have consequences in the real world.'

By this stage, the undergraduate could claim the towering Python star to be not merely an idol but an acquaintance, if not a friend-in-waiting. One famous instance of Douglas' proudly displayed ambitiousness (seen as careerism and putting a few noses out of joint at Cambridge) was a fortuitous bumping into Cleese on a trip down to London, to see a show at the Roundhouse. There was The Man Himself, at the bar just inches away, all parallel six-foot-five of him, and as Adams refused to dither or to play the fanboy, he sidled up to his teenage hero and introduced himself respectfully, but with a forthrightness which disarmed the famous comic. As with so much in his life, Adams simply cordially assumed that his rightful place in life was way up high, rubbing shoulders with the best, and as he behaved in this way, subconsciously assuring people 'you haven't heard of me yet' (and of course quickly proving himself to be outstanding in one way or another), he *became* successful.

In his very first term, Adams had been courageous enough to introduce himself to one comedy performer who was affability itself when he was booked to chair a charity auction at his college – veteran comic Peter Jones, star of *The Rag Trade* on TV and *Just a Minute* on radio: 'I was terribly impressed with him,' Douglas said. 'I'd seen him on television and heard him on the radio, but he'd never made a particular impression on me. He has this very amiable, slightly lost persona, but it was extraordinary, seeing him work an audience for about three hours off the top of his head, and continually giving the appearance of being slightly out of control and uncertain of what was going on, but obviously being an absolute professional as far as what he was doing.'

In the case of Cleese, although the Python didn't exactly take the student to his bosom, they struck up a respectful rapport which would gain Adams and a few friends regular trips to BBC TV Centre to see *Monty Python's Flying Circus* being recorded, and first of all, an invitation to the home of John and his wife Connie Booth to conduct an interview for the Cambridge magazine *Varsity*. Adams' assumption of being at one with Cleese is implicit in the one-page article which resulted, where he observed, 'The hard aloof Cleese is a figment of the box; privately he is quiet, unassuming and very friendly, and I was aware of talking to somebody else from Cambridge rather than a television star. He gets a little embarrassed if people expect him to behave like a funny man.'

Another handy result of approaching John was that Douglas gained permission to perform one of his favourite *ISIRTA*-cum-*The Frost Report* sketches, 'Butterling', in which Cleese's exasperated Zoo Keeper held Tim Brooke-Taylor's terrified and inept trainee to account for losing an entire menagerie in one day (Cleese would return to the idea for his *Fish Called Wanda* 'equal' *Fierce Creatures*). The already classic two-hander (credited to 'Otto', after Cleese's radio persona) was slotted into the first show master-minded by Adams-Smith-Adams, designed to cock a snook at Lloyd's official May Week offering. *Several Poor Players Strutting and Fretting* debuted after closing time on 14th June 1973 at St. John's ancient venue The School of Pythagoras, just a short cycle ride from where the other Footlighters were performing dance routines at the ADC Theatre. For 30 new pence Footlights renegades fresh out of the official show could enjoy 'something completely different' – a late night of logically constructed whimsy courtesy of the trio, assisted by actresses Stefanie Singer and Rachel Hood – and packed houses did just that. Adams-Smith-Adams were the talk of the town as they strode from college to college drumming up publicity in fancy dress, Adams leading the way as a seven-foot-tall turkey, and they quickly established themselves as the real Alternative to Footlights.

Not that they were truly opposed to the club, of course (Martin and Will received writing credits for *Every Packet ...* as did Simon Jones) and when they returned to start their third year in the autumn, all three apparent rebels were given places on the committee – with Adams as PR Officer. Jon Canter, on the other hand, finally won his initial argument with Douglas, and became President.

Shaving The Cat

As piracy and parrots were another of Adams' discernible lifelong preoccu-pations, we can presume that many Long John Silver impersonations were performed for friends when he returned to Cambridge on crutches that autumn, having spent a considerable amount of his summer in Yeovil Hospital – only this time as a patient. There had been no hitching down to Warwick for the summer break, as he and Helen had gone their separate ways – indeed, he had fallen for a fellow Cambridge student in his second year, but was beaten to her wooing by new friend Michael Bywater, who would compound his offence by marrying the girl in question. Bywater was famous at Cambridge for turning up late for a Footlights rehearsal with the killer excuse, 'Sorry, I've just crashed a plane.'

Spending the summer of '73 with his mother's young family, Douglas found himself a summer job helping to build barns down in the West Country, and lost control of a tractor on a steep hill, breaking his pelvis – although he did as much damage to the road as to himself. Yet another unsettling coincidence was noted here by Nick Webb, in that a very similar accident occurred on the exact same spot twenty years later, this time proving fatal – the victim being another 'Douglas Adams'.

'Mr Adams' pelvis by Yeovil District Hospital' ran a credit in the programme for the first Adams-Smith-Adams presentation of the new term, *The Patter Of Tiny Minds*, which ran from 15th to 17th November, once again at The School of Pythagoras. It was, as ever, fuelled by sketches tried out at earlier smokers, including *Duplicator's Revenge* and *Nostalgia's Not What It Was*. John Lloyd provided some material and remarked on the pleasing chemistry of the three performers, with Martin in the straightest role, trying to keep order David Hatch-like, Will earning the audience's affection in a Tim Brooke-Taylor vein, and Douglas, of course, channelling 'Otto' Cleese to the best of his ability. The most significant offering of the evening was a song inspired by the local headlines surrounding the building of the Cambridge bypass that threatened the building of the University's £2 million radio telescope. In 'How To Plan Countries', a man learns that his idyllic cottage is planned for demolition to make way for a motorway, and is powerless in the face of blind bureaucracy. Although co-written, this idea would form another nagging blockage in Adams' creative brain, just begging to be developed in some other form. Douglas may not have written the lyrics, but the first verse could be sung by Arthur Dent without changing a syllable:

> *I bought a little cottage in the Garden of England,*
> *Thatched roof and roses round the door;*
> *Every morning waking up to birdsong by my window,*

Perfect peace, and who could ask for more?
And then the country planner came along
With his country planning schemes;
He showed me his maps and his Irish navvy chaps
And shattered all my dreams.

Hot on the heels of this first outing for *Tiny Minds* came that year's Footlights pantomime, *Cinderella*, and Adams must have been content that he was now a lynchpin of the club, bagging the plum role of 'King Groovy', the positively horizontally laid-back father of Prince Charming. Now being resident within St. John's itself (Room K6) sharing with friends Nick Burton and Johnny Simpson, for this role he drew on the behaviour of the latter, of whom Adams would recall, 'He had that nervous sort of hyper-energetic way of trying to appear relaxed. He was always trying to be so cool and relaxed, but he could never sit still.' There was a certain transatlantic post-hippy idea of cool shared by this generation of undergraduates, and in a few years Douglas was happily admitting Zaphod Beeblebrox's debt to Johnny's studied louche grooviness.

As that year's May Week show drew ever nearer, Adams-Smith-Adams must have felt confident that their contributions would be considerable, and they continued to build up their profiles, taking the unusual step in mid-January of hiring a London venue, the Bush Theatre in Shepherd's Bush, for a special production of their latest show. This time, Mary Allen – opting to take the stage name 'Adams' for Equity purposes – filled the female roles, and Lloyd, who was less than two weeks into his new job as a junior producer at BBC Radio Light Entertainment, found time to complete the cast under the pseudonym of 'John Smith', forming the troupe 'Adams-Smith-Adams-Smith-Adams'. The group gelled so well that letterheads were ordered under the moniker of 'Tiny Minds', with a view to launching the line-up as a full-time sketch outfit.

Although Douglas would make a memorable appearance as a mad pirate called Mr. Y-Fronts Silver, giving a terribly urbane TV interview from a hijacked London bus he was running as a pirate ship, the main theme of the evening was cat-shaving. Where the Monty Python team were happy to dispense with punchlines, a number of the Bush Theatre show's sketches, far apart enough for the motif to catch the audience off guard, tended to close on a suggestion of the irresistible, sensuous temptation to deprive a feline of its fur, culminating in the torch song 'Sheer Romance', performed by Mary 'Adams':

> 'Well, babe, it often seems, I've always known you in my dreams,
> You came to me beneath the moon, that starry night in early June.
> Well, babe, I think I love you, you make my heart go pitter-pat,
> Feeling so romantic, Think I'll go and shave the cat ...'

It was a one-night-only show, but the cast made a very handy £25 each, and enjoyed the theatrical patronage of dancer Lindsay Kemp, whose show preceded their own late-night slot. (They would also find him in the cinema, when the 'Tiny Minds' gang took a break from rehearsals to see *The Wicker Man*, with Kemp as the camp landlord MacGregor.)

The revue's heady mix of music and absurdism was a success on its London date, and particularly with one comedy-writing duo in the stalls. Not every schoolboy in Britain who had been inspired by *ISIRTA* and *Flying Circus* had set course for Footlights, and meeting the grammar-school lads David Renwick and Andrew Marshall after the final bow gave Douglas and Co. their first meeting with ambitious non-Oxbridge comedians. Renwick had embarked on his writing career as a journalist for the *Luton News,* but on joining the rudimentary writing team for *Week Ending*, the infamously material-hungry satirical sketch show devised by David Hatch and Simon Brett, he had quickly bonded with the Lowestoft-born Marshall, as two of the few writers in the building who had not attended one of the top universities – they would also have a short run in revue at the Little Theatre, persuading Brett out of retirement to perform with them. Lloyd would subsequently get to know the pair well as he took over the reins of *Week Ending*, but for Adams-Smith-Adams their one night of metropolitan success was over, and it was time to head back up to the shire to face their final exams – or rather, after two more successful smokers, *Late Night Finale* and *In Spite Of It All* (each packed with collaborative efforts from Jon, John, Griff, Will, Martin and Clive), to prepare for their moment in the Footlights limelight.

It was a painful shock when they learned from the director of that year's revue *Chox* (Robert Benton, another Brentwood boy, from the year above Douglas), that only Martin Smith was welcome to join the cast. The trio's material, Benton was at pains to point out, was beyond reproach, and badly needed for the show (their sketches made up nearly half the running time), but their performance skills were not. What the director could not quite bring himself to say was that Adams was something of a liability on stage, and many of his closest friends had to admit that his inability to keep a straight face when delivering a funny line, the contorted 'moue' which Canter recalls flashing across Douglas' lips every time he had a zinger to deliver, was often off-putting for cast and audience. It was merely Douglas' unfettered enthusiasm, his sheer joy at performing sketches like his Python heroes, but it was a drawback for any director putting together a killer comedy cast. This was all irrelevant to Adams, though; he insisted that those who thought up the funny ideas should always be the ones to get the laughs: 'The writer-performer was the lynchpin of all the Python lot when they were at Cambridge. By my time there, it was the director who would decide what to do. To my mind, that always produced very artificial results ...' he was to complain. 'It is something I still get upset about, because I think Footlights should be a writer-performer show. But, in my day, Footlights became a producer's show – who's going to be in it, who he wants to write it, they are appointed and the producer calls the tune. I think that's wrong. My year in Footlights was full of immensely talented people who never actually got the chance to work together properly ...' He added, 'Somehow there was this creeping quasi-professionalism that came in, "No, what you do is get the best people to write it and the best people to perform it." To me, there's a logic there that doesn't quite work, because the best performers aren't necessarily the best people to perform the stuff that somebody else has written from their own point of view.'

To make matters worse, besides law student Clive Anderson, the cast was studded with students from the year below who had not even paid their dues, like Rhys Jones and his contemporary, Geoffrey McGivern – a former head boy of Archbishop Holgate's School in York, who had been feted as the thespian du jour on his arrival at Cambridge, the darling of the Marlowe Society, and reportedly he was well aware of his acclamation. Adams' perceived displacement seemed to fuel gossip in *Varsity* when it whispered 'at this term's Footlights party Douglas Adams had a slight altercation (punch up) with Geoff "Goldenego" McGivern'. In reality, however, Geoff admitted to being worse for beer and simply took an unconnecting swing at Douglas for being pompous – there was no retaliation besides a gigantic pratfall from the Frood.

Adams' three essays bagged him an indifferent BA in English Literature that June which would ultimately see him sighing, 'I did have something of a guilt thing about reading English. I thought I should have done something useful and challenging. But while I was whingeing I also relished the chance not to do very much. If I had known then what I know now I would have done Biology or Zoology.' And that seemed to be the end of his three years at Cambridge, all that momentum fizzling out with the death of his long-held dream to dazzle in a Footlights revue. What chance did he now stand of kick-starting the next Monty Python?

Hang The Sense Of It

Fortunately for our Frood, he was shortly to experience intense *Schadenfreude*, with a side order of apparent dream fulfilment, when *Chox* faced the glare of the London media for its glittering West End debut on 15th July 1974, promoted by hip theatrical impresario Michael White. Besides the critics, the cream of modern British comedy were there – including the whole Monty Python team, keen to check out the young pretenders – and the cast had already been snapped up for a BBC2 broadcast of the revue in August. Had the BBC anticipated the show's lacklustre reception and critical mauling, they might have saved themselves the effort of drawing up the contracts. The closest thing to a positive reaction to the show was possibly *The Times*' even-handed insistence that 'a person or persons called Adams Smith Adams contribute the best and the worst material' – even hidden behind a presentation deemed 'faintly pervy' by John Lloyd, 'all top hats and tights', Adams' ideas stood out one way or another, and luckily his sketches wouldn't be damned by association with the disastrous production, which was fated to close after just a few weeks.

Newly arrived in the capital, Adams was there for that first night, of course, as was Lloyd, to whom he would grow increasingly close, post-graduation. If nothing else, attending that first night would give them the chance to happily agree with the generally damning verdicts on the entertainment from their comedy heroes, including Graham Chapman, who only enjoyed one sketch – an Adams-Smith-Adams original.

Finding a niche in the capital was tough for any graduate making their own way in the world, but with Will moving in with his wife-to-be, Douglas had found an affordable and frilly billet with Martin in Earl's Court, let by a pair of genteel ladies who resented their tenants, if not the rent that they paid. His first arrival coincided nicely with a whole host of paid writing credits, thanks to a collection of his best sketches catching on with BBC insiders like Lloyd's new colleague Simon Brett. Even before they left Cambridge, they had managed to convince Brett to squeeze some Adams-Smith-Adams material into *Week Ending,* phoned in from St. John's to Lloyd at the BBC. The first Adams sketch written for radio made use of the show's regular 'Brain Teaser' spot, as the Watergate scandal unfurled:

NIGEL REES   This week's Brain Teaser. Imagine a man in front of two doors - one leads to the White House, and the other to jail. One guard is Mr. Nixon who always tells lies, and the other is Mr. Ford who alternately tells the truth, and tells a lie and then contradicts himself twice. What you have to do is work out how many Nixon aides can be rowed across the river before the boat sinks, and the fox is set amongst the ones who chickened out and sold their apples for three years, each pleading executive privilege. Then complete the sentence 'Nixon is a ...' in not more than fifteen deleted expletives, and send your entry on blank tape to the Senate Watergate committee. Members of the President's family are not allowed to enter unless they can lie very convincingly, and the President's decision is subpoena.

Forty-five seconds' worth of airtime did not equal a long evening in the pub, but – it was a broadcast! A palpable broadcast, and on Radio 4 too! The following week, a short skit about the Giant Flying Panda, marking London Zoo's new arrivals from China, gave all three of the 'Tiny Minds' a chance to hear their words on the air, but they weren't to prove prolific. Writing to topical order did not suit Douglas, though they did manage to shoehorn in some less ephemeral material, in this case a thoroughly sick spin on the growing cult of Marilyn Monroe – the sketch would become better known once it was recycled for a 1975 album release, becoming a great deal sicker in the process ...

```
INTERVIEWER   Carl, we're all a little mystified by your claim
              that your new film stars Marilyn Monroe ...
CARL          It does, yes.
INTERVIEWER   ... Who died over ten years ago?
CARL          Er, that's correct.
INTERVIEWER   Are you lying?
CARL          No, no, it's just that she's very much in the public
              eye at the moment.
INTERVIEWER   Does she have a big part?
CARL          She is the star of the film.
INTERVIEWER   And dead.
CARL          Well, we dug her up and gave her a screen test - a
              mere formality in her case - and ...
INTERVIEWER   Can she still act?
CARL          Well ... she still has this enormous, er, kind of
              indefinable, er ... no.
```

One of many many producers to helm *Week Ending* was of course John Lloyd. Although he was dismayed to see the media (and Flying) circus surrounding *Chox*, John was quickly honing his craft at BBC Radio LE, and while the younger Footlighters were crashing and burning on TV, he was learning the ropes of radio production by formulating and starring in a programme developed from his own revue, entitled *Oh No It Isn't*, which would of course make use of available material from Adams-Smith-Adams, while the cast included Allen, Canter and the growingly ubiquitous young Rhys Jones. Lloyd could have had no finer mentor for the job than the department's leading young producer, Brett, who had come across the talented new Footlights breed, Adams included, when up in Cambridge the previous year – nobody could be better placed to recapture the silliness of Radio Prune. The sketch show they created did well enough to be offered a second outing by the BBC, but by that stage John felt that his performing days were over, and he was happy to see it canned at one series.

That show did however boast one sketch which would do Douglas' reputation a great deal of good (not to mention the royalty payment which supplemented the £100 he had banked for the BBC2 show), and it would even be included on the *Douglas Adams at the BBC* release, while every other minute of *Oh No It Isn't* was consigned to eternal obscurity. The two-hander between Jon and Griff was a favourite at smokers, but the similarities with the 'Butterling' sketch written by Cleese are glaring, being positively written to the same template, albeit with an incongruous philosophical bent:

GRIFF   Ah, Pritchard. I, er, I understand the 8.45 to Basingstoke was late again, Pritchard? ... Very, very, very late. Three days late, Pritchard!

JON   Yes, well, we were having a tea break in the signal box, sir, and that kettle does take an unconscionable long time to boil.

GRIFF   What did you say, Pritchard?

JON   I said 'an unconscionable long time', sir.

GRIFF   And what should you have said?

JON   'A <u>bloody</u> long time'.

GRIFF   That's better.

JON   I've been meaning to see you about that, sir. I want to put in for a vocabulary rise ... I want to use words like 'existentialism' on duty, sir!

GRIFF   Existentialism? In a signal box? It hardly seems relevant, Pritchard.

JON   Existentialism informs all areas of life, sir!

GRIFF   Yes, but does it explain why the 8.45 to Basingstoke was three days late?

JON   ... Well, it was existentialism that did it, sir! ... It was on account of not being able to use the actual word that it all happened. You see, I was trying to explain it to my mate Bob, and I had to do it by some sort of a charade ... to give him the basic idea of existentialism, I left all the points open over the entire Western region.

GRIFF   So it was you! Do you realise that your existential points system has caused hundreds of trains not only to be derailed, but to go leaping over each other like copulating caterpillars?!

The *Chox* sketch which impressed the indulgent elder statesman Chapman, however, as he explained to Douglas in between alleged attempts to kiss John Lloyd, was one which would be known under a number of titles

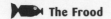

as it was recycled time and again for sketch shows and charity concerts, from 'The Hole In The Wall Club' to 'The Committee':

CLIVE   Now, before I formally open this meeting, there's something very important I have to say. As yet I don't know who to point the finger at, but I know it is somebody here. What they have done, they have done in such a cunning, secretive, furtive sort of way, carefully covering their tracks, that not only do I not know which of you has done it, I'm not sure what it is they have done yet exactly. But be warned, I am on my guard. Mr. Secretary, possibly you could start this meeting by reading the minutes of the last meeting?

GRIFF   Certainly. The minutes of the 42nd meeting of the Crawley & District Paranoid Society ... The meeting was duly convened and Mr. Smith gave us a very spirited talk about the holes which his next-door neighbours have been drilling in his wall. Then he went on to say . .. here, somebody's been tampering with these notes!

If Adams-Smith-Adams had any one calling card, it was the Paranoid Society sketch. It would be brought out of mothballs for a number of disparate revues for years to come, culminating in an all-star performance over ten years later as part of a cancer charity fundraiser, *Comedians Do It On Stage*. It was just the kind of simple but barking concept which appealed to Chapman's sensibilities, and the admission that he wished he had written it himself must have sent Adams' spirits soaring – they must have then soared into the stratosphere when he felt Graham's home address being pushed into his hand, with an open invitation to pop round for gin and sketch-writing.

Jynnan Tonnyx All Round Then!

As was explained to the graduate when he called at the good doctor's home in Highgate, North London which he shared with his partner David Sherlock and a wine cellar stocked to the ceiling with bottles of gin, the reason for Chapman's invitation was as distressing as it was thunderingly exciting. With a fourth, shorter run of the Python sketch show under contract, and having been reluctant to carry on since the second series, John Cleese had officially declared himself finished with TV sketch comedy, and was leaving the five other Pythons to labour on as best they could. Although Graham had enjoyed many writing partnerships in his career, particularly with legendary gag merchant Barry Cryer and 'belligerent Scotsman' Bernard McKenna, Cleese's exit left him particularly exposed within the group. It's a common routine for writing partners to have one grafter and one pacer – the first diligently typing up the material while their partner throws out ideas – and Chapman was a born pacer. Or rather, he tended to sprawl languidly with a G&T and throw utterly unpredictable comedic spanners into the works – such as, most famously, suggesting that a faulty toaster is less funny than a dead Norwegian parrot. Perhaps, he suggested, the eager young Adams could become his new grafter? Douglas had after all been weaned on Python humour, and knew how it ticked: 'I felt what happens with Python is you have some aspect of the world that's twisted and you follow the logic of that twist and see where it leads; either it leads somewhere very funny, or gives you a few good laughs and then you veer off into something else ...' This was a technique he would similarly cling to throughout his career.

You can imagine the young Cleese fan's dismay at realising that his favourite show was coming to an end without his hero, but on the other hand ... to be invited to *write* for the renamed show *Monty Python*, taking the place of the man whose shoes he had always planned to squeeze into, was an offer which must have confirmed to Douglas that even if there was no such thing as Fate, then life surely did a very good impersonation of it, and it was on his side. Chapman's offer was almost unspoken, he just needed help and Adams eagerly agreed to give it, and was working on a sketch for series four before the ice in his first G&T had melted. Quite fittingly, this was a medical skit created by Michael Palin and Terry Jones, but Dr. Chapman had decided to give it another go, with Adams' help.

DOCTOR	Well, do take a seat. What seems to be the trouble?
WILLIAMS	I've just been stabbed by your nurse!
DOCTOR	Oh dear, well I'd probably better have a look at you, then. Could you fill in this form first?
WILLIAMS	... Couldn't I fill it in later, doctor?

DOCTOR	No, no. You'd have bled to death by then. Can you hold a pen?
WILLIAMS	I'll try.
DOCTOR	Yes, jolly good, it's a hell of a nuisance, all this damn paperwork, really it is … It really is a hell of a nuisance. Something ought to be done about it … Well let's see how you've done, then. Oh dear, oh dear, that's not very good, is it? Look, surely you knew number four! It's from 'The Merchant of Venice' - even I know that!

The idiocies of British bureaucracy have provided material for countless comedians, and it was always a Python touchstone, along with all manner of potshots at authority, from the Ministry of Silly Walks to the housewife who has to gas herself to ensure delivery of her new gas cooker. This sketch, 'Patient Abuse', was a particularly good lesson for Adams in the art of ridiculing red tape, and although he would only receive credit for adding one 'Silly Word' when the sketch was finally broadcast in the last episode that December, he had still seen his dream become reality. His brainstorming sessions with Chapman were recorded, and he delighted in playing the tape to his friends, ecstatically sharing – without any real intention of flaunting – his comedic good fortune. As an extra vote of confidence in the newbie, Palin & Jones also reworked the Marilyn Monroe sketch for inclusion on *The Album of the Soundtrack of the Trailer of the Film of Monty Python and the Holy Grail*. For his music and a series of cameos, former Bonzo Dog Band star Neil Innes has been granted the honorary title of 'Seventh Python' (which he would surely more accurately concede to Carol Cleveland), but Adams' unique sketch writing credits should grant him at least 'Ninth Python' status, even though in time the association would become slightly embarrassing for all.

Before long Douglas and Martin had moved to a house in the undesirable area of Kilburn, which was shared with a confusing array of transitory graduates and oddballs – one exception to the latter being Mary Allen, no longer going out with John, but starting her career with a saucy role in the West End production of *The Rocky Horror Show*. The house was not exactly luxurious, and was infested with mice, which the residents agreed had to be dealt with. Douglas did not demur against the plan to poison the rodents, but he did spend a joyfully procrastinatory amount of time making a small poison restaurant for the doomed pests out of matchsticks, with a tiny sign reading 'HAUTE CUISINE THIS WAY!' Allen recalls Douglas once opening a cupboard only to have a mouse fall on him, sending his enormous frame thudding to the ground in a melodramatically energetic fight for survival as the tiny rodent pawed at his neck.

Adams found himself a number of temping jobs, including a nightmarish time as an inept filing clerk, but he refused to follow the example of Martin and Will and sign up for anything more taxing: 'The two of them felt it was a good idea to get a day job to support themselves while writing, but I thought if you did that you'd end up doing the day job and not doing the writing, so I simply got the odd office job now and then for a few weeks to pay the rent. And they ended up, just as I thought, doing their day jobs, so I went ahead on my own.' This was retrospective bravery – at the time, Adams was afraid that an accounting career or something similarly ghastly was in store for him, and had gone out and bought a tie as a kind of symbolic acceptance of his fate. The one thing that gave him strength to leave it on the rack was Chapman's support, and particularly the important step of signing contracts with his first agent Jill Foster, who had most of the Pythons on her books. Nonetheless, Adams-Smith-Adams prevailed for some time, with gently dwindling energy, signing off from Cambridge theatre with *Cerberus: The Amazing Three-Headed Revue*, which debuted at the Arts Theatre in early November '74 – though their sketches would crop up in Footlights shows and smokers for the rest of the decade. *Cerberus* was originally to also feature Geoff McGivern, proving that any nastiness over *Chox* was already history – although he caused them further trouble by dropping out at the last minute.

Will Adams would eventually move into publishing while Martin Smith built a successful career in advertising, but the three of them cooked up a whole host of projects throughout the 1970s, besides their live shows, using their 'Tiny Minds' headed paper. In 1974 the trio joined forces on a historical mockumentary designed for TV, which may well have sown a few ideas in John Lloyd's head, sprouting years later on *Blackadder*. *Earls (Of Warwick)* was a pilot for a quirky take on *World In Action*, in which the modern-day descendants of Warwick the Kingmaker run a business that actually creates history. Travelling through time, their team of epochal troubleshooters had been on hand to sway causality in the direction we know it, as a kind of legendary marketing board, with testimonies from William the Conqueror, Richard III and Queen Victoria, and case studies including the torching of London in 1666, and the design of the Wars of the Roses, which two camp artists from the Earls' Aesthetic Department insisted were supposed to be tangerine and mauve. A whole series of mockumentaries were planned, reusing sketch ideas to focus on the problems of bus piracy, and of course, the shame of cat-shaving, but somehow this brilliantly prescient idea slipped through TV commissioners' fingers.

Despite his distrust of a cosy billet career-wise, Douglas had already started a sort of day job – a pattern was established on most days whereby he would rise at a decent hour and travel up to Highgate to begin attacking the typewriter, with Chapman at his shoulder spewing out silliness. However, this being the mid-1970s, with Graham's alcoholism flailing awkwardly towards crisis point, this plan rarely went much further than opening time, before noon, whereupon the Chapman entourage would decamp to his local, The Angel, and all bets would be off. Sometimes McKenna would be with them, often even Lloyd would make it up the hill in his lunch break, and the procrastinating collective would sink drinks and polish off the broadsheet crosswords with little perspiration. 'Everybody drank all day,' Adams admitted, 'so by the end of the day everybody was completely pissed, or Graham was pretty pissed. I was too young and inexperienced; I didn't know how barmy this all was, or to know what to do about it being that barmy.' Propping up bars with Chapman made for stunning future anecdotes about the great man banging his penis on the bar for service, or dangling it into strangers' drinks just for the reaction, but Adams was to find that collaborating with a man who drank an average of two bottles of gin a day was no apprenticeship: 'He was an extraordinary man, obviously an enormous talent in writing, even if he became a bit undisciplined and self-indulgent. He commanded an enormous amount of real affection and loyalty, from a very wide and eclectic bunch of people who just thought he was wonderful, strange – and exasperating ... Again, in our work he was the subversive one, but instead of subverting a group of his peers, he was giving *me* a hard time, as the sort of wet-behind-the-ears guy who didn't know anything ... I think if I had more experience at that time and was better able to stand up to him, or to know for sure what to stand up to him about – in other words, if I had more grip on my own craft – then I think we could have fared better. But in the end it was not a marriage of equals.'

The last dregs of TV Python provided a stronger framework, though there was some muttering on Adams' visits to script meetings, with Terry Gilliam admitting to an uncharacteristic suspicion of the interloper, and Douglas himself had to admit, 'It's rather like being a passing taxi driver who's asked to play the tambourine on a Beatles record.' The lack of Cleese also gave the ever-enthusiastic Terry Jones a far freer hand in shaping the programmes, with the result that each episode became increasingly plot-led, presaging the team's move into movies. It was with Jones that Adams would form the most lasting friendship, the two bonding over a shared love of real ale.

There was more excitement to come for Douglas when he was invited to join the group for location shooting over in Exeter, allowing him the further honour of actually appearing in the show. Between donning a surgical mask to play up to the camera as 'Doctor Emile Konig' during a lengthy opening montage for 'The Light Entertainment War' (which was, entirely coincidentally, episode 42), and walking across the street in drag to place a missile on a scrap cart, Adams' on-screen time amounted to a little less than fifteen seconds, but it was yet another honour – particularly to be squished into women's clothing to become an honorary 'pepperpot', Python's breed of insane frumpy women. This chance came with an extra glaze of pleasure for Adams, as it was for the episode 'Mr. Neutron' – the team's second attempt at an all-out science fiction narrative, in which Chapman's extra-terrestrial beefcake has the ability to destroy the Earth with a glance of his laser eyes. If the death and misfortune of others provided age-old comic fuel, Douglas learned, then you could go for no bigger laugh than staging planetary apocalypse – the ultimate slapstick: 'I think people find it easier to pass off a cataclysm with a joke. It's a Pythonesque form of acceptance, drawing on a higher absurdity.'

Destruction closer to home was narrowly averted when the extra took the wheel of his mother's camper van on the journey home after that day's filming. Chauffeuring the Python gang through foggy roads after a pleasant evening at a local restaurant, Adams was just peering uncertainly into the gloom when Eric Idle wisely pointed out to him that they were travelling not on a slip road, but the motorway itself – and going in the wrong direction. Douglas' desperate U-turn prevented a head-on collision by mere seconds, and a tragically precipitate end of the Monty Python legend.

It Don't Come Easy

With their TV show finally coming to a stop, the individual Pythons were busily preparing solo projects: Palin & Jones sowing the seeds of *Ripping Yarns*, Gilliam making in-roads into film-making, and busiest of all was Idle, industriously laying the ground for *Rutland Weekend Television* – on which Douglas and Martin Smith were invited to perform, only being stymied by not being members of the acting union Equity. It was left to Adams to facilitate Chapman's own break-out comedy offering, but before the pair could really learn how to work together there were other projects calling out for their shared skills. And as if Douglas hadn't had enough wishes fulfilled, the most pressing (and silliest) project to hand came from a real-life Beatle.

Ringo Starr had been feted as the clown of the group very early on, and cemented this by making a lazy cameo as himself in the last episode of *Monty Python,* stepping in for John Lennon, who was recovering from a car crash. It was inevitable that Ringo and Graham would hit it off, both at this stage being hardened boozers, and sharing similarly thirsty friends in Harry Nilsson and Keith Moon, with whom Starr had recently stumbled through the filming of an Apple Films production, *Son of Dracula* – originally *Count Downe*. Ringo was a diehard horror and sci-fi fan, and masterminded the film as a Nilsson musical, starring the singer as Dracula's reluctant inheritor, fighting against the Wolfman, Baron Frankenstein with his monster, and a whole gang of hideous ghoulies determined to make him their King, while Van Helsing aided him in turning his back on vampirism and experiencing human love. Starr played Merlin, the Dracula family's adviser, for no apparent reason besides the possibility that the costumiers only had a wizard costume left. The original screenplay by actress Jennifer Jayne barely held together Nilsson's musical set pieces, and his flat performance, alongside Ringo's famously guileless delivery, did not augur well for a hit release, so it was quickly withdrawn from circulation.

It was less eccentric than it sounds, therefore, that Ringo and a few Apple bods were to call at Graham's house and set up a Steenbeck editing suite showing the film, inviting their host, abetted by Adams and McKenna, to improvise a funnier soundtrack. The trio tried to argue themselves out of a pay cheque, Douglas recalling his protest, 'It's not necessary because the movie is not bad, it's actually quite good, and this is the way to really destroy it – this is an exercise that can't possibly work!' But they laboured on with the renamed *Dracula's Little Boy*, with Chapman doing his best Ringo imper-sonation, filling the story's clunking longueurs with Pythonesque prattlings until a finished and transcribed track had been created – whereupon Ringo's people thanked them, and placed the fruits of their labours in a legendary Apple archive to rot. The film never surfaced again. 'That's what you get for working with rock stars,' Adams sighed.

Theoretically, a far more positive run-in with rockers presented itself for Graham and Douglas on 5th July, when the Python was invited to share the bill at the Knebworth Rock Festival with Adams' heroes Pink Floyd, plus Captain Beefheart and others. The chance to be in full Gumby garb, backing up Chapman's anti-silly Colonel character as he filled in between bands, was a dream for the young fanboy – but although memories of that day are hazy, it is recalled that the comic interludes were all but bottled off by the rowdy crowds.

Another disappointment was to come with Ringo's next commission for Chapman & Adams in 1975 – the script for a TV special to tie in with his latest album, *Goodnight Vienna*, which had been recorded with many of the same musicians as *Son of Dracula*'s soundtrack, and had similarly geeky overtones – this time, being pure science fiction. Seizing the opportunity to realise his ambition of writing a long-form sci-fi comedy, Douglas worked with Graham to develop the concept hinted at on Ringo's album cover – Starr's head superimposed on the body of the alien Klaatu in a famous still from the 1951 flying saucer movie *The Day The Earth Stood Still,* standing alongside the mighty robot Gort. As a framework on which to hang some of Ringo's latest hits, the fledgling partnership (under the pseudonyms of Nemona Lethbridge and Vera Hunt) decided that Ringo's UFO adventures could provide broad scope for silliness, and coincidentally allow Adams to make use of a plot idea which had been turned down by the *Doctor Who* bosses the previous year.

Adams' experience with Python had emboldened him to attempt to realise another ambition, and he began submitting ideas and treatments to the *Who* production office rapidly after arrival in London. The idea he felt most strongly about was a satirical comment on the mediocrity of modern society, akin to his all-encompassing contempt for red tape and mediocre authority figures, in which a planet solves its overpopulation problems by jettisoning all of its middlemen – 'The advertising executives, P.R. men, film producers, deodorant manufacturers, South Africans, the Osmonds, David

Frost, politicians, bunny girls ... career advisors, telephone sanitisers; that sort of person' – and sending them off in a 'B-Ark' in the belief that the 'A-Ark' of great artists, thinkers and leaders and the 'C-Ark' of people who actually do things would follow shortly; but as the Doctor was intended to discover, the shallow space crew are destined to crash into a sun, and good riddance to them all. This plot outline elicited the first of many rejection letters from his favourite sci-fi show, but now Ringo had given Adams the chance to prove them wrong, and also a chance to set up the proceedings with a very resonant introduction:

```
NARRATOR    Once upon a time ... a long time ago in a far, far land,
            I mean a really long way, I mean you may think it's
            a long way down the road to the hardware store, but
            that's just peanuts to this sort of distance ...
```

```
Through a hole we see an enormous metallic foot, which then
shrinks and we see it belongs to a silver ROBOT ... ROBOT walks
through the wall, atomising GIRL #3 as she runs off.
```

```
RINGO    Oh well, I didn't like her anyway. Good afternoon.
ROBOT    Are you Rinog Trars?
RINGO    No, but it's close.
ROBOT    Rinog Trars, I have been sent by our masters in the
         galaxy of Smegmon to pass on to you the ancestral
         powers of your race, the Jenkinsons.
RINGO    I think you've got the wrong bloke.
ROBOT    My circuits are infallible, there can be no error ...
         It's near enough, I've had a hard day. Come with me! ...
WOMAN    What on earth was that?
MAN      Must be the telephone sanitisers.
WOMAN    Oh, I'd forgotten it was Tuesday.
```

The idea of a 'telephone sanitiser' may be rather meaningless today, but Adams certainly had it in for them in the mid-1970s – he had also written a sketch, 'The Telephone Sanitisers of Navarone', in which a gang of diehard rebels storm a fort and cleanse their earpieces. Telephone sanitising was the chosen profession for the underdog hero of this TV special, until his sulky

new robot friend mistakenly presents him with a whole new way of life, and
a portfolio of incredible abilities:

```
RINGO       Any other powers?
ROBOT       Yes, you can go into nightclubs.
RINGO       Good!
ROBOT       You can write television situation comedy.
RINGO       (DOUBTFULLY) Hmmmmmm ...
ROBOT       And you can do quite nice flower arrangements.
RINGO       That'll be useful.
ROBOT       And merely by doing this (HE WAVES A HAND), you can
            destroy the entire Universe.
RINGO       What, just that?
```

He starts to wave his hand. The screen shakes.

After a number of adventures taking in Ancient Rome and a filthy
old garage claimed by its owner (a role marked for Keith Moon) to be a
spaceport, at last Ringo and the Robot arrived on an unfamiliar vessel ...

They are in an area with a curved floor which suggests a
centrifuge. Dotted around it are futuristic sarcophagi, each with
its own elaborate life-support systems - like 2001.

```
RINGO       There must be a notice somewhere ... (READING OUT
            PLAQUE, EMPHASISING THE WORD 'RON') Starship Ron -
            B-fleet unit 3 - Pod 7 - Telephone Sanitiser Class 4.
            That's funny, I once had a mate called that ... Pod.
            He was a strange bloke ... He wasn't christened Pod -
            his real name was Lonsdale Cowperthwaite. I never
            found out why.
```

They are grabbed from behind by paramilitary guards. One of
them touches ROBOT's arm, which lights up again with the words
'erogenous zone'. ROBOT's face glows red again ... By now they have
arrived on the bridge of the starship ... The CAPTAIN is sitting in a
chair, of which we only see the back ...

```
NUMBER 3    Captain, the intruders are here.
CAPTAIN     Well, gin and tonics all round, then.
NUMBER 3    Shouldn't we interrogate them first?
CAPTAIN     Why? Don't they like gin and tonics? Perhaps they'd
            prefer something else.
RINGO       No, gin and tonic's fine.
ROBOT       That would be very nice...
```

Then the CAPTAIN swings his chair round and we see him dressed as
a very large and realistic turkey.

Between the Captain's predilection for gin and tonic and the turkey costume, the jobbing comedy writers seemed to be aware of which ark they were likely to be booked onto. But there was to be no resolution to the recycled *Doctor Who* concept here – Ringo's rambling space odyssey concluded with the Robot knocking back the gin, his metal heart broken by a space crab, before the arrival of the real Rinog Trars triggered the total annihilation of the entire Universe, via a single wave of his hand.

The first draft which survives obviously lacks cogency – it was essentially a series of links for Ringo's songs – but it was still one of the best things Chapman & Adams wrote together, a very solid dry run for *Hitchhiker*, and effortlessly funnier than Ringo's eventual US TV special, which repeated the doppelganger concept. Chapman was to complain that it foundered because TV executives failed to get the jokes, and thought it was too rude, but Adams placed the blame elsewhere – on one of his four greatest heroes of all time: 'It was not made, partly through Ringo's various difficulties – he lost interest in it – partly because the deal fell through from one angle or another. It could then have gone on further if he'd wanted to deal with the hassles. He didn't.'

The End Of The Road Show

Almost unique among the Chapman/Adams projects, having actually been made and broadcast, was a mere bread-and-butter half-hour for the second series of Humphrey Barclay's sitcom *Doctor On The Go* for LWT, 'For Your Own Good', in which Dr. Dick and his pals' lives are turned upside down by the arrival in the ward of the obnoxious wealthy father of one of the lads. Even that was a struggle to get to screen, the only one of a number of scripts co-written for the series to be accepted, notwithstanding loyal friend Bernard McKenna's job as Script Editor. With the radio version of Richard Gordon's *Doctor* series being successfully produced by David Hatch, Graham's other old Cambridge pal Barclay's TV incarnation made good use of Cleese & Dr. Chapman as the ideal sitcom adaptors, alongside Bill Oddie & Dr. Graeme Garden and others. A financial upset, however, meant that Cleese had decided to start writing on his own even outside of Python, leaving Chapman high and dry, and eager to present young Douglas with the same incredible power to write situation comedy as Ringo Trars. An ITV sitcom in which the stethoscope-swinging cast wink at the camera in every opening sequence was hardly fecund Adams territory, but Chapman at least showed his protégé how he could pay a few bills with 25 minutes of mildly lairy medical antics. It's moot whether Adams' medical ancestry or summer job experiences were advantageous, but the resultant episode did at least get broadcast in February 1977, with Adams even sticking around for rehearsals, seeing the script through to the screen.

However, what mattered most at this time, and what was being pieced together and redrafted numerous times, was the great Chapman solo vehicle. The other Pythons' solo plans were advancing admirably, and Graham could not afford to fall behind – Adams had, however, lucked his way into the pilot recording of the new sitcom from his hero Cleese and Connie Booth, *Fawlty Towers*, and confidently declared it a total shambles, full of wobbly sets and with no chance of success. This drubbing would have been some kind of comfort for any competing Python, if Douglas' verdict hadn't been so drastically wrong. Graham's ambitions were simpler, though – Chapman & Adams had a whole raft of ideas left over from a hoped-for fifth Python series, and he had no great desire to explore his talents beyond TV sketch comedy at that time. In the main, Graham wanted to carry on somewhat as 'normal', except, naturally, with him now centre stage.

Despite the now almost indispensable Adams habit of beginning with an ominous science fiction narration from far out in the universe, Chapman's vision for *Out of the Trees* – originally entitled *The End of the Road Show* – was more down to Earth, with the idea being that each sketch would spin off from the musings of two travelling linguists, but the only episode to be made (which Chapman had intended to be the second of a series) often showed more signs of his junior partner's style throughout, despite McKenna

stepping in at the last minute to corral the material into shape, controversially (and ungrammatically) beginning and ending with the word 'than':

Stock film of galaxies etc. Followed by planets, followed by the earth.

V/O   Than the Universe, a multitude of mighty galaxies,
        within each galaxy a myriad of mighty star systems,
        within each star system a multiplicity of mighty
        planets and in one of these mighty planets the mighty
        British Rail electric train...

This train contains what would have been the series' repertory company, which Douglas had ensured contained his great defender Simon Jones, as half of a gooey-eyed young couple, and, as a surly waiter, a Footlights graduate of a slightly earlier vintage, Mark Wing-Davey, the son of actress Anna Wing, who would get little time to prove himself on-screen but would forge an important friendship with Adams during production. So many sketches of the Python school in one way or another dealt with the petty hurdles that life erects in our way, traditionally involving two stock characters – a blithely uncooperative antagonist, and an increasingly desperate protagonist. Without this eternal comic dialogue, of desperation and obstruction, *Hitchhiker* would have been about ten minutes long. This first meeting of Jones and Wing-Davey on videotape, although an undeniably tawdry dispute, showed that both were perfect for the trad roles, with one outburst from the frustrated Jones previewing a perfect Arthur Dent delivery:

YOUNG MAN   I'd like a sandwich too, please.
WAITER   Thought you wanted coffee?...I wish you'd make up your
            mind.
YOUNG MAN   What sort of sandwiches have you got?
WAITER   Well, there's, er, cheese and tomato...
YOUNG MAN   Yes, and what else?
WAITER   What d'you mean, 'else'?
YOUNG MAN   Well, I mean, other than cheese and tomato sandwiches?
WAITER   I thought you wanted a sandwich?...

YOUNG MAN	<u>Look, will you please listen, it's very very simple!</u>
WAITER	I have been listening, mate, you go and get your own coffee and sandwiches, I got a job to do, you load of tits!

The commuters' conversations link into the show's numerous sketches, which would all have fitted perfectly into a Python framework, with one notable historical spoof of which Adams was clearly proud: 'My favourite bit from that show was a lovely sketch about Genghis Khan; who had become so powerful and important and successful as a conqueror he really didn't have any time for conquering any more, because he was constantly off seeing his financial advisors and so on – it was partly a reflection of what one heard Graham muttering about the other members of Monty Python ...' Both writers were strangely coy about the target here, but without question Khan was a direct and pointed ridiculing of Cleese's high-handed and world-weary attitude to diary-keeping. From the start of his career, Cleese's collaborators had to learn to steel themselves against his detailed schedule, insistence on regular 'R&R', and repeated angst about never having time for himself. *Out of the Trees* arguably contains a number of pokes at the other Pythons (there's a boy scout with verbal diarrhoea who seems designed for Palin), and having so recently seen himself written out of his ex-partner's schedules, it's no wonder Chapman was ready to turn his old friend into a cathartic source of mirth:

Khan enters his yurt.

KHAN	Oh dear, which battle was that?
OGDAI	The Battle of Samarkand, O Khan!
KHAN	Oh dear, I really can't tell the difference any more. Did we win?
OGDAI	Yes, O Khan, it was a mighty victory!
KHAN	After twenty years of these half-hour battles, I really get the feeling there ought to be something more important to life ...
OGDAI	We must push forth to Persia, and then we shall be poised to take over the whole world!
KHAN	... When?
OGDAI	Tomorrow!

```
KHAN      Ah, now, look, tomorrow's a bit difficult, you see, because
          I was going to give a lecture on carnage techniques in
          Bokhara next week, and I thought I'd use tomorrow to
          prepare it.
OGDAI     Well, can't you put that off?
KHAN      Well, not really, you see, they've paid me quite a lot for
          it, so I am a bit committed.
OGDAI     Wednesday?
KHAN      Well, I haven't got anything down, but I'm sure I'm meant
          to be doing something, so better count that out ... I think
          I'm free about four, but I was hoping to get away early
          for a long weekend, so let's see ... no! R&R I'm afraid.
OGDAI     What?
KHAN      Rest & Recuperation, that's one thing I do insist on ...
```

Perhaps the most memorable sketch in the half-hour (not least thanks to the BBC wiping the tapes, so only the filmed inserts survived until a copy recorded by Chapman himself was donated to the National Film and Television Archive) was 'The Peony Incident', which again featured Jones' young lover, plus Adams in another faceless cameo as a mugger. Inspired by a genuine contretemps experienced by Graham and his boyfriend David Sherlock one evening, Jones' girlfriend's careless plucking of a flower arouses the violent ire of the local constabulary, triggering emergency piled on hysterical emergency, until an all-out international nuclear strike seems to be the only solution:

Stock footage of explosions, missile launches, devastation.

```
V/O           (Simon) Hold on, the world seems to be ending!
```

A long red spaceship, as in Gerry Anderson's 'UFO', approaches the smoking earth. Two aliens in space suits are inside.

```
ALIEN 1       We are too late! We are too late! They have severed
              the peony! Mission has failed! Impossible to effect
              peony severance prevention!
```

The earth explodes.

Even by 1970s BBC science fiction standards, the special effects for the show were staggeringly rudimentary, but the modest budget did not hamper the comedy, which Adams described as 'only semi-brilliant', and it was a shame that no series was to follow. 'It was good in parts – it was excellent in parts ... it was also dreadful in parts,' Douglas said. 'No more got made simply because then the Pythons started up all over again with films ... and Graham got involved with that.' That this period was the epicentre of Chapman's struggle with the booze could not have helped – *Out of the Trees* was recorded in the autumn of 1975, a few months after his frighteningly dipsomaniacal experience playing King Arthur in *Holy Grail*, and he knew he had to dry out at last – or die. Partly due to the fact that he was working with another collaborator, David Yallop, there was some confusion as to whether another one or two further episodes of the programme had been scripted, but Adams recalled, 'The second episode was never made, although there was some nice stuff in it. My favourite sketch was called "A Haddock at Eton", about a haddock given a place at Eton to show the place was becoming more egalitarian. It got terribly bullied ...'

Between numerous temp jobs and, of course, his own determination to break through as a solo writer, Douglas simply could not afford to be kept on standby by Graham much longer, Python or not. The final straw proved to be Chapman's wild medley of memoir and fantasy, *A Liar's Autobiography Volume VI*, which was begun with Adams but ultimately had a total of four co-writing credits, and besides a fleeting appearance from a spaceship shaped like a cigarette and a name-check for Stalbridge as a red herring for Chapman's birthplace, there are few traces of Adams within its pages. Very early in the book's production, the agonised young collaborator had been forced to break off his professional association with Chapman by letter, as reproduced in the official Python autobiography:

> I gather from Jill that once again you feel unable to work for the rest of this week. This situation has been carrying on for so long now and so very little has actually been achieved that I can only assume that the book project comes very very low on your priority list. Since it has become totally impossible for me to believe you when you say we'll start tomorrow or we'll start next week or at any time at all, I've had to commit myself to a job that I couldn't afford to turn down ... I'll have the occasional day off which I will

be prepared to spend getting raw material down on tape with you which I can then work over at home. If that doesn't suit you then it'll have to wait till September – I know that's late, but I've been ready and willing to work for a very long time and nothing's got done. At the same time I'm trying to launch my own career and the constant frustration and anti-climax of endless cancelled or wasted days makes this very difficult to concentrate on. If you really do want to do this book then let's arrange a definite time to do it later in the year, and if you don't want to do it than that's your decision. Hope the drying out goes alright. Love, Douglas.

The letter was undated, but presaged a general winding down of their always lackadaisical association towards the end of '75. 'We virtually came to blows about Graham's autobiography,' Adams said. 'He actually went through about five co-writers, of which I was the first, and really I didn't think it was going anywhere because I didn't think it was the sort of thing you could do as a pair. I think there's one very bad section which was the bit that he and I co-wrote.'

At first, he admitted, 'I thought, "Good God, this is fantastic, this is wonderful!" But Graham, at that stage – which is well documented, so it's not being disloyal – was going through a fairly major drink problem, and at the end of the year an awful lot of good ideas got wasted, and not much had actually been achieved ... When we went our separate ways we had a row. I can't quite remember even what it was about, but we were definitely on bad terms for a few weeks or months or something. Though we repaired relations after that, we were never that close again.' One particularly odd October day saw an extraordinary meeting between lyricist Tim Rice, animator Bob Godfrey and an almost amnesically plastered Graham, Bernard and Douglas. Thanks to a chain of complicated movie rights, taking in industry giants Beryl Vertue and Robert Stigwood, a screenplay was required for a movie adaptation of *The Guinness Book of Records*, and Chapman was pencilled in to pen it, but he was as uninterested as he was drunk. McKenna recalled Adams slurring his undying love to Chapman in the taxi home, and getting very annoyed when everyone burst out laughing. Those kind of lost days could not go on forever.

Still keenly following his planned route to writer-performer stardom, Adams had too many irons in the fire to sit around any more – and above all, he had finally found a collaborator who he could work with as an equal, and moreover one with the same obsession with quality, and who would not fuel his immense capacity for procrastination with gin and crosswords.

I Might Just Stun The World One Day

Although they had only been mildly friendly at Cambridge, as their shared comedic social circle in the capital increasingly brought them together, hanging out at The Angel or burger bar Tootsies in Notting Hill, Douglas Adams and John Lloyd were to develop a fraternal closeness perhaps unparalleled in their personal and professional lives. In 1975, maybe at one of those drunken pub lunchtimes, Bernard McKenna offered the youths rooms in a house he owned in the relatively upmarket locale of Greencroft Gardens, West Hampstead (just about), and it wasn't long before his scruffy new tenants – the ones who played extremely loud rock music and never seemed to open their curtains – started to find their own way of hammering jokes into the typewriter together: a relative luxury for Adams after the nursemaid role of working with Chapman. One of the things which most bonded the pair was the realisation that both were passionate sci-fi lovers – in fact, Lloyd was more well-read and passionate about both science fact and fiction at this stage, but the pair would argue and muse over the theoretical quirks of the Universe and existence long into the night.

A crucial difference between the two friends was that it was rarely necessary for Douglas to have to set his alarm for the morning, while John would have to be off bright and early to work at the BBC's LE department where he was rapidly establishing an unprecedented reputation as a producer with a golden ear, particularly for painstaking editing. He hadn't entirely abandoned performing, but since being inspired by David Hatch into the 'comedy cleaning lady job' of Producer, Lloyd's natural aptitude, combined with an intense work ethic, had set him on the road to being one of the most prolific and successful programme makers in the history of the corporation, enlivening *Just a Minute* and piloting long-running shows like *The News Huddlines* and *The News Quiz* to greatness. Ever the grafter, John also directed that year's Footlights offering, *Paradise Mislaid*, which once again made use of a few scraps of Adams-Smith-Adams material, although it would pass without making any great impression – though at least escaping the high-profile drubbing of *Chox*.

Meantime, when he wasn't wasting precious working days at The Angel, Adams also continued to work in revue, and a new show with Martin and Will was lined up for an autumn debut at a small West End venue, now languishing as Stringfellows but then known as the Little Theatre. This wasn't Adams-Smith-Adams, however, but the first and last creation of Renard-Adams-Smith-Adams. Gail Renard was a sparky and ambitious redhead from Canada who had also written for *Doctor on the Go*, finding a home on the books of Jill Foster with support from Cleese rather than Chapman, and the decision to bring her in as a full member of the A-S-A line-up was not a tricky one. As the quartet put together their revue *So You Think You Feel Haddocky* (the terrible title got a free pass as it came directly from Chapman) the poor ambitious comics all mucked in, clubbing together to share desperately precisely divided miniscule meals and packet soups as they rehearsed, all young enough to hope for their project to become The Next Big Thing.

Renard was also a passionate Beatlephile, famously managing to bag an interview with John and Yoko when she was a teenager, and it's unlikely that this heady mix of beauty, ambition, Fabness and borderline malnutrition did not have a potent effect on Douglas, but any attempt to make something of it was certainly rebuffed. According to Gail, one clumsy move by Adams did result in the two of them not speaking for some considerable time, even while the revue was running. Another exchange recalled by Renard came upon Douglas' return from his summer 1975 jaunt to Greece – yes, he was broke, but holidays, particularly to the Greek Islands, tended to be more important than food to Douglas, and were of course partly possible on his budget due to hitching. Arriving at his first rehearsal since landing, Adams stretched out his full six feet five inches with a yawn and asked the company whether they had ever considered the benefits of hitchhiking around the galaxy? That idea was clearly never as deeply buried in his subconscious as he often claimed.

Haddocky changed nobody's lives, and although the quartet continued to make some attempts to break through as a comedy outfit, these went no further than a few meetings about a possible children's TV show, and the group eventually folded – the very end of the road for the rebelliously formed Adams-Smith-Adams trio, although that famous sketch credit would surface from time to time, with the 'classics' being brought out for the 1981 *Who Dares Wins*-presaging album *An Evening Without* (not to mention in the associated Radio 4 show *Injury Time*) and reworked for 1989's *The Utterly Utterly Definitive and Pretty Damn Amusing Comic Relief Revue Book*.

A return to reality of a sort called for Adams, as he accepted an unexpected but gratefully debt-easing job as a bodyguard to an Arab sheik and family who were so overwhelmingly wealthy that they could afford to order everything on the menu at the Dorchester Hotel every evening to see what they fancied, before sending out for McDonald's. All the naturally pacific but physically prepossessing Adams had to do was sit outside the family's suite for twelve hours at a time, and look imposing – at any sign of danger, of course, he wouldn't have had the slightest idea of what to do, except perhaps hone a suitably cutting remark. It was sheer drudgery – all through the night, he perched with a book, attempting to keep sane as every computerised lift in the building randomly 'tinged' his attention, stopping at every floor and opening with a guileless preprogrammed desire to serve, blasting the bored bodyguard with muzak before moving on to another floor. One memorable dawn, an exhausted escort sauntered down the corridor towards him, and complained that at least he could read 'on the job'. When he could bear no more, Douglas passed the job on to the similarly impecunious Griff, but he was still barely making pocket money with his comedy.

Another temp job, more in line with Adams' ambitions at this time, was a few days as a prop buyer for one of John Cleese's Video Arts training films – in this case, on accountancy. This brief job would barely be worth mentioning were it not for the fact that the beleaguered abacus-fingerer played by Cleese was faced with a struggle to come up with the answer to an irritating sum – and it had to be an amusing number. A certain amount of debate broke out over the tea break, about what actually was the funniest two-digit number. Cleese maintained that he and Chapman had once decided that there was no number funnier than 42, and so that had to be the one.

Amid temp jobs, Lloyd and Adams had a number of ideas on the burner, some being just the sketchiest ideas for sitcoms – *Knight & Day* was a rather straight suburban concept unconsciously nabbed from Gilbert & Sullivan, in which 'the original odd couple' share a single-bed flat, with one chap working nights, and the other working days, with potentially hilarious results, and then there was Douglas' idea about the two warring lighthouse keepers who split their living quarters down the middle, *Steptoe & Son*-style.

These concepts were combined into a far more solid basis for a sitcom, originally a comic play, again featuring a mismatched male duo – *Sno 7 and the White Dwarfs*, which no doubt was developed further due to its mix of comedy and sci-fi enthusing the two writers. High up in the Arctic Circle, two astronomers, the anally tidy Nigel and laid-back scruff Simpson – uncanny prototypes for *Red Dwarf*'s Rimmer and Lister – spend their days gazing at the stars and getting on each other's nerves:

NIGEL   Simpson … do you remember when we both left Cambridge? You were tipped as being potentially the greatest astronomer of our generation - you remember that?

SIMPSON   (LAUGHING DISMISSIVELY) Well, someone may have said that.

NIGEL   Well, what <u>are</u> you doing?

SIMPSON   Well, at least I'm not getting a knighthood, that's one consolation. Though I might do one day, you never know. I might just stun the world one day. Or I'll fold up and vanish into nothing - I don't really mind either way so long as it's fun …

NIGEL   Everything you do is deliberately calculated to annoy me!

SIMPSON   No! Every time I do something you just calculate how to be annoyed by it!

The scientists' situation could have provided the set-up for a whole host of scientifically themed plots, including one where they discover that intergalactic advertising executives have earmarked our sun as the final stop on their supernovae-based campaign which would spell out the fizzy-pop-flogging slogan 'THINGS GO BETTER WITH BULP!' across the Universe (another idea coincidentally echoed in the first *Red Dwarf* novel). There was also a sequence involving a machine designed to analyse any object and which kept insisting that Nigel's hamster was a sausage, but the writing duo were disappointed to meet an astrophysicist at a party who told them that they did actually have such a machine.

None of these projects came to anything – the BBC's stock line for any idea involving space was that sci-fi was, quote, 'too fifties', which in retrospect has more than a ring about it of Decca's insistence to Brian Epstein that 'guitars are on the way out' a generation earlier. John and Douglas got a lot further by taking on Chapman's abandoned – or rather, not even attempted – *Guinness Book of Records* project. Given a free hand, they proposed a very silly intergalactic face-off, in which a villainous fleet of invading extra-terrestrials challenge the Human Race – the General Secretary of the UN being John Cleese – to a contest for the very survival of humanity, in which every kind of sport, race, long or high jump or athletic feat of any kind is effortlessly won by the genetically superior aliens, but the humans win the day via their greater prowess in the egg-and-spoon race, gherkin-eating, walking backwards, or any number of a thousand pointlessly bizarre record-breaking stunts. The movie project fell through just as the writing duo were hoping to blag a free exotic writing holiday out of it, which would have been a double blow to Adams' morale, while of course Lloyd always had his day job to return to. Adams was learning to predict the perennial complaint that there was 'no market for science fiction'.

Another thing John had which seemed to elude Douglas was a girlfriend – in this case, Griff's sister Helen Rhys Jones – and a little into 1976 the couple decided to find a place to live together. They found an eccentric shared place in Roehampton, a house of cobwebbed gentility let by an old lady who retained its dolly-festooned chintz throughout – and, of course, Douglas came with them. Lloyd remembers this as a relatively happy time. He would come home from his hard day at the office, often bringing dinner with him – the usual routine was that he would buy, say, a couple of ducks for roasting, one of which would be a decoy purely for the ravenous Douglas to eat while he was setting the table for the three of them. The happy homestead was only marred for John when they advertised for a fourth tenant, and an American with acute obsessive-compulsive issues moved in and ended up ripping up all the carpets for being 'smelly', and attacking the garden with a chainsaw because it was all too untidy.

Douglas' memories of Roehampton were not so rosy, and indeed the house – particularly his strange bedroom, which was a maze of wardrobes, seven in total – would provide the backdrop for the struggling writer's downward spiral, as the daily torture of being left at home with no paying work on the horizon, and nothing flowing from his pen or typewriter ribbon, began to take its toll. Famously, his one pleasure, combining procrastination, comfort, and providing an alleged source of inspiration, was a nice hot bath:

or rather, numerous hot baths, every single day. Adams was a smoker from quite a young age, only escaping tobacco's clutches intermittently, and having such psychedelic influences it's no shock to learn that his tobacco was often mixed with stronger stuff (albeit he only admitted on record to smoking weed 'half a dozen times a year', otherwise claiming to be 'a clean-living boy'). He joked that he briefly tried cocaine merely as a gambit to destroy his septum, as his infamously mangled nose was little more than decorative anyway, while alcohol and fast cars would perhaps go on to be slightly more addictive vices once he was rich enough to afford them. But more than any other indulgence, baths were something else – he was perfectly capable of filling the tub first thing in the morning and spending the entire day making a prune of himself, only intermittently replacing the water and padding around in his bathrobe until it was time for the next soak, where he would lie, zoning out, waiting for something to happen. 'I was convinced I had my best ideas in the bath,' he said, 'so I would get up in the morning, get in the bath and lie there until I had an idea. And of course, by the time I'd got out, towelled myself dry and got dressed and so on, I would have forgotten what it was, so I would have another bath to remind myself.'

When Lloyd returned home in the evening, greeting his scrupulously clean housemate with the established term of semi-endearment 'Vast Creature', he would usually find that nothing of any note had been written, and he would have to engage his own buoyant work ethic to start the evening shift together. This wasn't the only way in which the undeniably dishy 'Johnny' unintentionally played havoc with Adams' growing inferiority complex. Throughout his life, rich or poor, Douglas had no trouble getting girlfriends, but he could not contend with Lloyd, who when he was not in a relationship was believed by his friends to be constantly juggling dates with beautiful women, sandwiched in between his hugely busy schedule of comedy shows and production duties, and his own writing and performing. It's not wise for any work of comedy history to get too snagged on prurient matters, but there's nothing new about sexual competitiveness between two close male friends in their early twenties, and Douglas and John were undeniably competitive, whether it was on paper, between the sheets or on the Scrabble board. But where Adams was more the kind to play both sides of a Pink Floyd album to a date and try and dazzle her with philo-sophical wit, Lloyd, being tall but not ungainly, and having piercing blue eyes where Douglas' were brown and mournful, had a higher success rate with the opposite gender, and this clearly bothered the hormonally charged Adams. A particularly painful example of this immature roistering was tactfully recalled by Mary Allen in *Wish You Were Here*: Douglas had taken a shine to one female acquaintance and unsubtly arranged for her to join his close group of friends on the famous Corfu holiday which inspired the *Liff* books. Douglas' romantic plans required a clumsily self-conscious juggling of bedrooms … which all came to naught when John got off with the desired guest in question after all. Details seem unseemly, but such episodes definitely fed into Adams' powerfully competitive friendship with his closest collaborator, and he was not the type ever to forget or wholly forgive a single kink in his armour placed there by John Lloyd.

The Plain Man's Pathway To Unpleasantness

In mid-1976 Douglas was temporarily buoyed to get a chance to top John, when he was picked from a shortlist of potential ex-Footlighters to return and direct that year's May Week revue, a consciously punky effort entitled *A Kick In The Stalls*. Although his election for the role largely came because the vote was held very shortly after the single broadcast of *Out of the Trees*, for our Frood it was a form of delayed vindication after the deep disappointment of *Chox*, and he decamped to his alma mater determined to put together a show worthy of his own lofty standards, for once.

As was usual, the name and design of the revue was not Adams' domain – as a lover of Prog, the growing trend for Punk at the time held little fascination for him, but he could work with the graffitied bovver-boy title, eventually illustrated on the poster with a threatening cast line-up, fists to the fore, with 'OH, HOW WE LARFED' tattooed across their knuckles. He was aiming to make the meat of the show itself more intricate, intelligent and subversive than ever before – what he was not prepared for was the sheer lack of enthusiasm from that year's talent. His determination that the show should always be run by writer/performers suffered from a lack of either, and he found himself actually knocking on doors trying to press-gang undergraduates into taking part. That year's President, Chris Keightley, was too busy with his PhD in biochemistry to perform, but worked closely with the director on the script at regular meetings at the home of club Treasurer Dr. Harry Porter – a well-loved veteran lecturer who would become Footlights' greatest archivist. Keightley was pleased to find Adams a keen

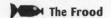

pupil of the sciences – where most Footlighters were positively antagonistic to his subject, Douglas would avidly debate matters of astrophysics, atomic structure and quantum mechanics, in between trying to think of gags.

Two key pieces of the *Hitchhiker* puzzle would fall in Adams' lap in this time. The more controversial of the two concerned an original 17th-century manuscript which was on clear display in Porter's lounge, a dry Puritan work, *The Plain Man's Pathway to Heaven,* by a zealous Cambridge graduate of four centuries previously, called Arthur Dent. Douglas never recalled picking the precious book up at any stage, though Porter did admit to an uncomfortable reaction from him when the subject was brought up many years later – it seems fairest of all to put this down not as coincidence, but as yet another example of Adams' ability to file away influences imperceptibly. Certainly, his amusement was genuine when some poor researcher sent him a long dissertation on the (entirely mistaken) parallels between Dent's work and Adams' – it was a 'joke' the writer never intended.

Of far more material benefit to Douglas was a book that Keightley had picked up, *I Was a Kamikaze* by Ryuji Nagatsuka, which by its very nature was written by something of a failure. Monty Python had written their own kamikaze sketch, involving lots of enthusiastically suicidal Scotsmen, but the 'Butterling' format, of having an inept Japanese pilot explaining himself to his superior, was a rich seam for the pair to mine:

```
Wild flurry of flamenco music which continues for some time.


VOICE    Japan 1945...


Set consists of a bench in a briefing room on which sits one
kamikaze pilot with his gear and headband on. On the bench
are laid out the headbands of many other presumably deceased
kamikaze pilots. A commander stands to address the 'meeting'.


COMM     Now, you all know the purpose of this mission... Your
         sacred task is to destroy the ships of the American
         fleet in the Pacific. This will involve the deaths of
         each and every one of you. Including you.
PILOT    Me, sir?
COMM     Yes, you... What are you?
```

PILOT   A kamikaze pilot, sir.

COMM   And what is your function as a kamikaze pilot?

PILOT   To lay down my life for the Emperor, sir!

COMM   How many missions have you flown on?

PILOT   Nineteen, sir.

COMM   Yes, I have the reports on your previous missions here
         ... Let's see. Couldn't find target, couldn't find target,
         got lost, couldn't find target, forgot to take headband,
         couldn't find target, couldn't find target, headband
         slipped over eyes, couldn't find target, came back with
         headache ...

PILOT   Headband too tight, sir.

This proved to be the highlight of a multi-threaded revue comprised of self-referential interlocking sketches centred on the Russian annexation of the state of 'Bogoffia' – which was worked on assiduously by Adams and his team, with a cast including ambitious freshers Charles Shaughnessy, Nonny Williams and Jimmy Mulville and extra material from Jimmy's writing partner Rory McGrath, Will and Martin and Jon Canter. The director's ambitious aims did not, however, translate into a successful night at the theatre that June. His role as director had been promoted to some extent, and he had even enjoyed his first ever interview (albeit as 'Doug Adams'), with the *Cambridge Evening News* happily stressing the Monty Python connection, despite his protestations – he admitted to being 'extremely lucky', but the show's press release humbly described him as 'part-time under-assistant spelling-mistake corrector to the Monty Python team'. His biography in the programme went further, having fun with a few of his already infamous foibles:

> Douglas is larger than the average family and wears two pairs of trousers on each leg. This year's director, he was unable to do the show last year, because he became suddenly tall at the last minute and had to go into hospital to have his clothes burnt off. He is very sensitive about his enormous nose ... He has an unending supply of witty stories, which keep everyone amused until long after they've fallen asleep. This doesn't matter however, as he comes round first thing in the morning to tell you what you've missed. Recently he worked with members of the Monty Python team, but

on the completion of the M62, he returned to a less demanding
job. Always a generous person, he rarely carries money in case he
gives it away. Favourite sport: flicking elephants onto their backs
and watching them struggle. Possible last words: 'Well, basically I
think that the basic basis of this is basically rubbish, actually.'

But reportedly the nigh-on-three-hours which audiences were presented
with both in Cambridge and on tour through Oxford, Southampton and the
Robin Hood Theatre, Nottinghamshire drew the wrong kinds of howls from
the stalls. The local paper had to follow up their puff-pieces with the verdict
that *A Kick In The Stalls* was 'crushingly unfunny and woefully over-long ...
an almost total lack of originality', and other reviewers tended to concur. It
would be gradually honed, and the 'Kamikaze Briefing' sketch was always
singled out for praise, but while Douglas was in charge, there were problems.
Simple practicalities of staging had apparently been ignored with Douglas'
characteristic single-mindedness, with the result that one sketch about the
ascetic hermit St. Simeon Stylites, who lived for years at the top of a pole
trying to commune with God, took longer to set up than it did to perform,
with stage hands desperately nudging the heavy platform into place in the
interminable blackout.

One young punter bemused by these ineptitudes while appreciating
the genuinely funny sketches studded through the long dark evening was
Oxford graduate Geoffrey Perkins, who was there for the opening night.
Although a star of the Oxford Revue just a year previously, Perkins had made
the mistake of taking a sensible job with a shipping company in Liverpool,
but was still clearly doggedly interested in comedy – and learning how not
to mess it up. Within a year, Simon Brett would have sponsored his entry
into BBC Radio LE. But back in June '76, Perkins' first impression of his
future collaborator Adams was of the giant director unnecessarily standing
on a rickety chair to give a post-show speech to his cast and crew, with
barracking from a bibulous Mulville. 'It was plain,' Perkins was to write, 'that
here was someone prepared to stick his neck out further than most people,
someone who would carry on in the face of adversity, and someone who
would shortly fall off a chair. I was right on all three counts.'

A Kick In The Stalls would undergo dramatic surgery before arriving in
Edinburgh that August, performed to considerable approval by new director
Rhys Jones and utterly rending all of Adams' carefully embroidered sketch

links and callbacks, but at least bringing the curtain down before midnight. This indignity, added to the sting of the reviews, did no good at all for Douglas' sagging ego, and seemed not to have helped his prospects one iota. As he admitted, 'the final show had some good bits, but they were few and far between, and the whole experience was pain and agony. I had to conjure something out of nothing. At the end of the show I was completely demoralised and exhausted.' There were only two further sources of comfort for him that summer.

The first was an interlude – but one which would give him one of his most polished and repeated anecdotes in a life tent-poled by them, which would be crowbarred into a novel, sampled by Jeffrey Archer for a short story, and ultimately become a powerful international urban myth, still claimed by folk the world over to have really happened to them. It happened, however, to Douglas Adams one April day at Cambridge train station. Having arrived early for his departure, Douglas bought *The Guardian*, a cup of coffee and a small packet of digestive biscuits, and sat down to wait, at the same table as a thoroughly unremarkable city-gent type. It was Adams' consternation which always sold the story as real, on the realisation that his perfectly respectable-looking neighbour had picked up his, Douglas', packet of biscuits, opened them, and taken one. With necessarily American terms, he was to write about the realisation being 'the sort of thing the British are very bad at dealing with. There's nothing in our background, upbringing, or education that teaches you how to deal with someone who in broad daylight has just stolen your cookies.' Nonetheless, young Douglas' reaction was, after a respectable recovery period, to reach over and take the second biscuit, marking his territory very clearly – to similarly affronted looks, and another biscuit subsequently snaffled by the city gent. And so it continued, each stubbornly sticking to the same gambit as the packet slowly emptied, whereupon Douglas' nemesis arose, exchanged 'meaningful looks' with him, and departed, to the wronged writer's relief. It was, of course, just a few minutes later that his own train arrived, he picked up his newspaper, and discovered his own unopened packet of digestives right there on the table. 'The thing I like particularly about this story,' he was to say, 'is that somewhere in England there has been wandering around for the last quarter-century a perfectly ordinary guy who's had the same exact story, only he doesn't have the punchline.'

The other potential source of comfort was his own show, a brand new revue for Edinburgh that would be up against Griff's decimated staging of *Stalls*. With Martin and Will no longer treading the boards, the former 'Tiny Minds' line-up was to be fortified with a different partnership – David Renwick & Andrew Marshall. As two of the strongest gag-pitchers on *Week Ending*, Marshall & Renwick had hit it off not just with Lloyd, but also fellow writer John Mason, and along with Mason were offered their own sketch vehicle on Radio 3 in 1975 – a spoof educational programme, *The Half-Open University*. By the summer of the following year, however, Mason had decided to train as an actor, leaving the other two to move over to Radio 4 with *The Burkiss Way*, similarly produced by Brett, giving free rein to their unapologetically Python-inspired brand of clever silliness, constantly mangling the audience's expectations. In time the show would become a raucous cult hit in the vein of *ISIRTA* (with comparisons more glaring after Jo Kendall joined the line-up of Fred Harris, Chris Emmett and Nigel Rees), but in the summer of 1976 Renwick, Marshall and Brett's creation had not actually reached the airwaves, and the writers were keen to head up to Edinburgh for a chance to perform their own material. It was Mason who booked the venue, a tiny Masonic hall named for the infamous criminal Deacon Brodie – hence the Dorothy L. Sayers-referencing name, *The Unpleasantness at Brodie's Close*. As one of the 'Brodie's Close Rollers', John even had a T-shirt printed to advertise the revue, so that rather than flyering, he could saunter round delivering the slogan 'I've been unpleasant at Brodie's Close'. Douglas tended to stick close to him, to keep the context of his own T-shirt, which read 'So have I'.

I Think You Ought To Know …

Although the two writing partnerships worked together well, Marshall was compelled to pull out of performing once the script had been stitched together, due to prior teaching commitments, but he had become a particular friend of Douglas, despite making himself singularly difficult to get close to. As a young Lowestoft lad, three years Adams' junior and suddenly surrounded by braying Footlighters, Marshall claimed that his alleged moroseness was simply due to shyness, even though he was also tall and broadly built, with a hugely imposing presence. Douglas told interviewers, 'It used to be that you'd be terribly nervous about introducing Andrew to everybody. You'd be with a bunch of people in the pub and Andrew would come in and you'd say, "Andrew meet John, meet Susan …"'

Everybody would make introductions, and Andrew would stand there. And once everybody had come to a finish in whatever they were saying, Andrew would then say something so astoundingly rude that it would completely take everybody's breath away. In the silence that was to follow, he would stalk off to a corner of the pub and sit there, nursing a pint. I would go over to him and say, "Andrew, what on Earth was the point of saying that?" And he would say, "What would be the point of not saying it? What's the point of anything? ... Including being alive at all? That seems particularly pointless to me."' Despite glum first impressions, Marshall was not just extremely funny, providing the Chapman-esque lunacy to Renwick's Cleeseian logic, he proved to be a good friend. As another science fiction nut he and Adams could talk about the genre all night, particularly when Douglas was in need of company. Despite his reputation, Andrew was rarely the one who needed the cheering up – there's more than an element of projection in Adams' public naming of Marshall as the original Marvin the Paranoid Android.

As an irresistible aside, the book which Andrew recalls enthusing about with Douglas until dawn was *Dimension of Miracles*, a curiously philosophical humorous romp across space and time written by New Yorker and eccentric sci-fi author Robert Sheckley in 1968. It tells the story of unsuspecting space traveller Tom Carmody, who wins a dubious prize requiring him to be whisked across the Universe to collect it – and is subsequently left to find his own way home. With funny sci-fi a major preoccupation of Adams', he recalled, 'People kept saying, "If you write this stuff you must know the work of Robert Sheckley?" So I finally sat down and read *Dimension of Miracles*, and it was quite creepy. The guy who constructed Earth ... it was completely fortuitous. There are coincidences, and though they're very tempting to people there are after all only a small number of ideas. I felt what I did was more akin to Sheckley than Vonnegut.' The latter was still a particular favourite, but Douglas had to stress, 'I get embarrassed by people trying to draw comparisons between him and me – on one very, very superficial level, it's an easy comparison: he writes stuff that is a) funny, and b) uses science fiction to make its points, and I write stuff that is funny and uses science fiction to make its points. But Vonnegut is essentially a deeply serious writer who uses comedy to make his points, and I am essentially a comic writer who occasionally tries to slip a point about something or other "under the counter," so to speak, and so from that point of view, I find the comparison embarrassing because he's a great writer, and I think I'm essentially a frivolous one, I'm afraid.'

Despite his preoccupation with sci-fi as a genre, Marshall and Lloyd were far bigger fans than Adams. He said, 'I've read the first thirty pages of a tremendous amount of science fiction. One thing I've found is that, no matter how good the ideas are, a lot of it is terribly badly written. Years ago, I read Asimov's *Foundation* trilogy. The ideas are captivating, but the writing! I wouldn't employ him to write junk mail! I loved the film of *2001*, saw it six times and read the book twice. And then I read a book called *The Lost Worlds of 2001* in which Clarke chronicles the disagreements between himself and Kubrick – he goes through all the ideas left by the wayside, "Look at this idea he left out, and this idea!" and at the end of the book one has an intense admiration for Kubrick … What's good? Vonnegut, he's great, but he's not a sci-fi writer. People criticise him for saying it, but it's true. He started with one or two ideas he wanted to convey and happened to find some conventions of sci-fi that suited his purpose. It's funny, people make this comparison, and I'm always incredibly flattered, because I don't think it's a fair comparison.'

Returning to Sheckley, over the years some have accused Adams of a certain degree of plagiarism – and he did himself few favours by giving Neil Gaiman the impression that he had never read *Dimension of Miracles* until after making it big with *Hitchhiker*. But as the fact that the two men met later in life, became friendly and almost worked together suggests, it's nonsense to suggest any impropriety. Any *Hitchhiker* fan can get a kick out of noting parallels between Tom Carmody's adventure and Arthur Dent's – the totally unheroic hero's quiet home life is disrupted by a sassy alien and he's quickly zapped into outer space and subjected to comical torture; he picks up his prize, which acts as a crucial source of exposition Guide-style (though this prize mutates into all sorts of odd forms with each materialisation), meets the professional planet designer who created the Earth, and visits the planet during its prehistoric period. It's funny, and packed with clever ideas, but from page to page, distinctly different from anything that Adams ever wrote:

> A moment later there was a clap of thunder and a flash of lightning from the middle of the living room … a man appeared in the middle of the brilliance. (He) was of medium height, stocky, had curly blond hair and wore a golden-colored cloak and orange leggings. His features appeared normal except that he had no ears. He took two steps forward, stopped, reached into the empty air

and plucked forth a scroll, tearing it badly as he did so. He cleared his throat – a sound like a ball bearing failing under a combination of weight and friction – and said, 'Greetings! ... We are come as the fortuitous respondent of an ineffable desire. Yours! Do any men? No so, then! Shall it?'

The stranger waited for a reply. Carmody convinced himself by several proofs known only to himself that what was happening to him was indeed happening to him, and replied on a reality level:

'What in God's name is this all about? ... Who are you?'

The stranger considered the question, and his smile faded. He muttered, half to himself, "The fog-mined squirms! They have processed me wrong again! I could mutilate myself from sheer mortification. May they haunt themselves unerringly! Never mind, I reprocess, I adapt, I become ...'

The stranger pressed his fingers to his head, allowing them to sink in to a depth of five centimeters. His fingers rippled like those of a man playing a very small piano. Immediately he changed into a short dumpy man of average height, balding, wearing an unpressed suit and carrying a bulging briefcase, an umbrella, a cane, a magazine, and a newspaper.

Douglas was happy to admit, 'When I read a collection of Robert Sheckley stories for the first time I really felt my nose well-and-truly put out of joint because I thought, "This is precisely what I wanted to try and do and he's done it a great deal better."' But then, with reference to any more serious accusation, he rightly thundered, 'It's funny how eager people are to assume, when they see things that have some vague similarity in one book/movie/ etc. and another, that it must be the result of deliberate copying, as if there is an infinite number of wholly distinct ideas in the universe and it is absolutely inconceivable that two or more people might have come up with something similar to each other.' *Dimension* and *Hitchhiker* are excellent companion pieces, almost like a transatlantic adaptation so dramatically altered as to bear only the slightest resemblance to each other, but no more than that.

The indispensable linking device for the sketches in *The Unpleasantness at Brodie's Close* was inspired by *Brief Encounter*, with John Mason and his girlfriend Becky playing lovers trying to complete an intensely romantic private rendezvous but being regularly interrupted by the eruptions of very silly sketches. Adams provided a sketch about a cereal manufacturer with a great plan to boost sales by putting dead jellyfish in packets, and once again reprised his bus pirate (a theatrical experience which terrified audiences into silence until he was told to shave off the thick swarthy beard he had been perfecting – Douglas' piratical bulk was, it seemed, simply too much at close range, and the beard added insult to injury), as well as a barman with a chip on his lofty shoulder, sneering at customers' lack of verticality: 'I bet the women can't keep off you, being "averagely heighted" like that.' Despite none of the team being undergraduates any more, it was a joyful period of making do and mucking in. The venue had no lighting besides the switch on the wall, and no wings or changing rooms, with the result that Douglas' rear end made an unplanned cameo in several sketches as he bent over behind a tatty curtain trying inconspicuously to change his trousers. The quality of the material shone through any production shortfall, and business was so brisk that they added two further dates, all leaving Edinburgh with at least a fiver each in their pockets, which is an achievement of which most modern comedians could only dream.

Whatever ebullience the project instilled in Adams, however, was short-lived. Marshall & Renwick's new series was starting on Radio 4, Lloyd had his job to go back to, and what did he have? The 'Groundhog Day' of waking up in a maze of wardrobes, waiting for the phone to ring, and all that bathwater gurgling down the plughole. His earnings as a writer that year were somewhere around the £200 mark, but his overdraft was nearing £2,000. He was, simply, a failure.

Martin and Will always functioned perfectly well as a duo, and they were both *Week Ending* writers by this point, but Douglas found it increasingly impossible to confine himself to the show's topical-quickie strictures – Lloyd coached him when he was in charge, trying to get him on the team, but an effort to write a sketch about Lord Lucan's coffin came in at fifteen minutes long. Similarly, the producer worked hard at trying to craft gags for mainstream shows like *The Two Ronnies*, but nothing could have been further from Adams' scope. He kept trying, and got a few quickies accepted eventually for *The News Huddlines* – but only two and a half of the twelve minutes of material he supplied made it to air. Why didn't these people realise what he was capable of? When would anyone with the power to make things happen see that mixing science fiction with humour was rich, uncharted territory, and give him a chance to prove it?

The sizzling hot summer of '76 was over, and the incessant dull monsoon that succeeded it reflected the struggling writer's frame of mind all too well. His agent Jill Foster could time her watch by his plaintive daily 10 o'clock phone calls, but there simply wasn't enough work to keep his sizeable body and soul together. Above all, he was simply all out of self-belief: 'I totally lost confidence in my ability to write, or to perform, or to do anything at all ... and went into a catatonic spiral of depression,' he was to tell Danny Danziger of *The Independent* in 1991. 'I suppose because of my background, having grown up as the child of divorced parents, a typical sort of shuttlecock kid, when I get depressed I tend to feel superfluous, that the world is actually better off without me, and is not interested in my welfare at any level. When I was in this state of depression, I kept trying to find activities that would stop my brain going round and round. One day I decided to learn German, got myself a pile of 'Teach Yourself German' books, and spent every single waking hour poring over those books. And by a strange coincidence, at the end of the month I happened to wander into the garden, and there was a woman looking for someone who used to be in the flat, and she was a German. So I sat and talked in German with her and discovered that I had done incredibly well. But since then I've never spoken German, and I don't think I remember a word.'

He applied for more 'proper jobs' – a familiar threat to his friends and himself, but a dramatic move this time, as it was with finance and trading houses in Hong Kong and Japan. But this was just an indication of his desperation. Shortly after, he found himself 'spending an entire day crouched behind the sofa, crying. I mean, it was that extreme. I think that was probably the closest I ever came to killing myself.' Above all, Douglas had made the lethal error of comparing his progress with that of his heroes, telling himself: '"I am completely and utterly washed up. Nothing has worked, nothing is going to work, I haven't got anywhere, everything I've tried to do has been an abject failure." And what really bugged me,' he continued, 'what really made that intolerable, was the fact that George Harrison, who was the youngest of The Beatles, had been 24 when they made *Sergeant Pepper*. And that really was a problem to me ...' The first thing anyone dealing with depression must learn: never compare yourself with George Harrison.

One evening John and Helen came home from work to find their 'Vast Creature' a sobbing wreck, and he told them it was time for him to move out. At the grand old age of very nearly 25, all of his lucky strikes, the wishes

that had come true after graduation, had failed him – or he had failed himself. Either way, he admitted his defeat, and was lovingly scooped up by his mother and stepfather, and ferried home to the bosom of his maternal family in Stalbridge, Dorset.

The Christmas Redemption

'My mother was terrific,' he insisted. 'I must have been hellish to be with at that stage, because I was completely immobile, and just overwhelmed with depression. But my mother was very, very supportive, and I have always been very grateful for that.' Being at home in the run-up to Christmas, with a little brother and sister aged eight and ten, provided a thoroughly different environment for Douglas, but it could not silence the voice of disappointment in his head – he was a Cambridge graduate, but not even able to make a living in the capital without being bailed out by his Mum. On the other hand, the sheer humiliation of the experience could give him a new creative impetus, and he was aware of his need to turn things around: 'Because I had got rather fat and unwell, I started to make myself run round the country lanes. Outside the house was a hill, and I remember the first time I tried it, I managed just about 100 yards up the hill, and thought, "This is absolutely going to kill me," which made me feel even more depressed. But I stuck at it, and after a while I was running five miles two or three times a week. And that eventually played a very, very major part in the psychological battle to get myself up and functioning.' Throughout his life, Douglas would be prone to expanding widthwards to complement his 'dwarf-scaring' length, regularly punishing himself with blasts of intense exercise to try and keep things in proportion. In a similarly manic mode, long periods of frenetic activity often called for even longer periods of absolute recovery in bed – not just in the typical depressive sense, but simply as a physical side effect of the exertion of his huge frame. He also had a notoriously fragile back – John Lloyd applauded the sheer achievement of Douglas once throwing his back out for a week just from buttering a slice of bread.

It wasn't as if Adams was totally devoid of work, and deadlines to hit, even if he had decamped to the sticks. Simon Brett had been aware of Douglas' singular comic invention since the Footlights days, and needed no great convicing when Marshall & Renwick suggested him as an excellent supplier of additional material, for when the second series of *The Burkiss Way* came around. The first commissions were due to be posted from Stalbridge in time for a 5th November deadline, destined for use in the first episode, but Douglas' first-ever solo material failed to reach Brett until six weeks later, just before Christmas. The programme began as a spoof correspondence course led by a Professor Emil Burkiss, but was soon just a playground for Marshall & Renwick to explore all the possibilities of audio comedy, wrong-footing listeners (and some announcers) by weaving believable lampoons into an extremely silly and experimental framework which changed from week to week – and as a result, the format (or lack of it) gave Adams plenty of scope to write what he liked. The unashamedly Pythonesque tone of the show was a bonus.

Of course, his first desire was to poke fun at science fiction – or rather, reputed science fact, rubbishing the 'aliens were our forefathers' theorising of *Chariots of the Gods* author Erich von Daniken, in a sketch performed by Fred Harris (as Melvyn Bragg) and Chris Emmett in the fifth episode of series two, eventually broadcast in mid-January:

BRAGG   Good evening, and tonight on 'This Programme Is Way Above Your Level' we talk to Erik Von Kontrik, author of such best-selling books as 'Spaceships of the Gods', 'Some More Spaceships of the Gods', and 'It Shouldn't Happen To Spaceships of the Gods'. Now, Professor Von Kontrik, one of the most interesting things about your series of books, in which you claim that mankind is descended from beings from outer space, is that they all seek to prove exactly the same thing, using exactly the same evidence. Now, why is this?

KONTRIK   You sink zey are all ze same? Have you read zem all?

BRAGG   Well, yes, I have, that's why I...

KONTRIK   So vat does it matter if zey are all ze same, if you read zem all? I mean to say, zat is ze whole purpose of ze exercise...

BRAGG   Oh, I see, so you are only in it for the money. Does this mean that you don't actually believe what you say? That man is descended from extraterrestrial life forms?

KONTRIK   How can I not believe it? Ze evidence is
           incontrowertible!

BRAGG   And do you use that same evidence again in your new
           book, coming out next week?

KONTRIK   No no no, I use entirely new evidence, zat I have
           manufactured - er, discovered! Discovered! Only last
           year ...

BRAGG   This is incredible ...

KONTRIK   That's the point! It's incredible! I've got a new
           kiddies' book coming out too! Zat is based on incon-
           trowertible proof zat Mankind is descended from
           little fluffy kittens. And also, a natty little
           number for ze lonely housefrau, proving zat Mankind
           is descended from Sacha Distel. A lovely chapter on
           primeval slime in zat one!

GRAMS   EERIE MUSIC

FX   A ROCKET SOUND, THE CEILING FALLS IN

BRAGG   Just a minute, what was that?

KONTRIK   And I've worked out zat ze ant book will get me a new
           yacht, ze fluffy kitten book vill get me a couple of
           zose nice Lagondas ...

BRAGG   Shh! Something's going on, um ...

ALIEN   Erik Von Kontrik!

KONTRIK   Ja?

ALIEN   I am Oolummmm-Bbbbbbb of the race of your forefa-
           thers, from the galaxy of Smegmon! We've come for our
           cut!

Having repeated the alien greeting from the Ringo Starr script, the sketch concludes with a growing mania, as the Earth is invaded by fleets of ants, fluffy kittens, and Sacha Distel. The silliness of the situation fitted seamlessly alongside Andrew and David's material, and three episodes later Adams saw fit to provide perhaps the most Pythonesque concept in the entire series – albeit one which equally lampooned Python itself once the action switched to '42 Logical Positivism Avenue', a series of reports on attempted comedy sketches, which ran throughout the eighth episode.

FX	BIRDS TWEETING
FRED	Hello, well, here we are outside Number 23 Gungadin Crescent, in Sawbridgeworth, where we've had a tip-off there might well be a sketch happening sometime today. But I must say, if anything droll is going to happen here, it's certainly belied by the calm, suburban exterior of this thoroughly ordinary house. Though there is a slight air of expectancy, one or two passers-by have already stopped to look. Derek, do you think we're going to get a sketch here today?
CHRIS	Well, I must say, David, there's little doubt in my mind. To me, the house looks exactly right - semi-detached, small bay window, neat little garden at the front. I think we can expect something fairly surreal, a Viking at least ...

Turning in this work just before Christmas, however, did not wholly extinguish the inferiority complex that had taken root in the once-swaggering writer. The *Burkiss* team had made complimentary noises, and Douglas' younger siblings idolised him as a sophisticated metropolitan writer, but the threat of the tie in his wardrobe still lingered – until, that is, he was finally talked around by his former Footlights rival, Jon Canter. Douglas invited Jon across to snowy Dorset for the festivities – Canter's Jewishness causing a momentary flap from Janet Thrift, as she had no idea how to cater for a kosher Christmas – and that 25th December, Jon sat Douglas down and made him see that there was still hope. Jon knew exactly what it was like to struggle as a comic writer, and equally knew that what Adams had in mind was not an impossible dream. He was just about paying his rent on a shared house in Arlington Avenue in the up-and-coming (soon to become truly snooty) North Central London borough of Islington, sharing with two couples including Cambridge contemporary Johnny Brock and his wife Clare. They all knew of Douglas' plight, and would be happy for him to make use of their (thankfully voluminous) sofa while he got back on his feet. With the New Year a week away, Douglas was glad to take the words of his auld acquaintance to heart – and had the good fortune to find a reason to act on the invitation just a few weeks later, when Simon Brett, emboldened by the *Burkiss* material which had tickled both him and his boss John Simmonds, called Adams and invited him across to the metropolis to discuss further ideas.

Time Is An Illusion. Lunchtime, Doubly So

And so it was, on the penultimate Friday of the following February, that Douglas Adams travelled nervously up to the BBC Light Entertainment office to meet up with his potential benefactor, who shortly suggested a bite to eat at a nearby Japanese restaurant. One positive outcome was arrived at with little difficulty – a heavily revised version of the 'Kamikaze Pilot' sketch was commissioned for the twelfth episode of the current run of *Burkiss Way* shows. But Brett had invited Adams down to see whether his unique brand of comedy could find a broader canvas, as Marshall & Renwick's had. Cautiously, Douglas outlined a few relatively simple ideas, knowing that every science fiction pitch he had ever made had led to a cold shoulder: 'I came up with various ideas and various permutations of people living in bedsits and this sort of thing, which seemed to be what most situation comedy these days tends to be about. And he said, "Yes yes yes, that might work, that might not work ..."'

This went on for the bulk of lunch, but Brett was not so impressed with these everyday ideas, no matter how expansive Adams' gestures were as he outlined them. What happened next, like so much else in the *Hitchhiker* story, for ever has one foot in myth and one foot in history, but in Adams' own memory Simon leaned back and dreamily mused that what he had always *really* wanted to try was a science fiction comedy.

Adams' claim to have then fallen off his chair we can certainly put down to anecdotal decoration, but the effect on young Douglas was clear enough. Once his jaw was able to do anything but sag, he admitted to Brett that yes, he had a few ideas along those lines himself. How about, he pondered, a series of separate stories, each of which concludes with the total annihilation of Planet Earth, if not the Universe? Brett was amused by the idea of *The Ends of the Earth*, but how many ways of blowing up the planet had Douglas thought of? As the idea pinged back and forth, Brett paid the bill and the two enthused diners left the restaurant to give the idea a thorough going-over back in Brett's office, Adams still excitedly brainstorming as the door closed behind them.

FIT THE SECOND

CREATION

"Excitement and Adventure and Really Wild Things."

"Don't Panic."
"I'm not panicking!"
"Yes, you are."
"All right, so I'm panicking, what else is there to do?"
"You just come along with me and have a good time.
The Galaxy's a fun place ..."

– Ford Prefect and Arthur Dent

It all began so very simply. When Douglas Adams returned to his family in Dorset, he had a commission for his own vehicle, 'a science fiction comedy adventure in time and space, which weaves in and out of fantasy, jokes, satire, parallel universes and time warps' – and at first, he didn't even have a deadline to fear. Once the Kamikaze sketch had been recorded, however, Brett had the leverage to make the offer official, with John Simmonds' okay – the writer would earn £165 for the pilot, half to be paid on delivery, and the rest after the recording. The pilot script would be one of those few writing projects that required no extension – the contract was signed on 10th March, and the script delivered less than four weeks later.

At last, Douglas had a definite goal to drive him as he thundered around the country lanes, puffing his way back home for a bath, a Bovril sandwich and a crafty smoke. Perfecting the thirty minutes that would launch him to the world would trigger an upswing that would not falter in its trajectory for a long time. Having started from a position of utter misery, he told an interviewer after publication of his first novel, 'In *Hitchhiker* there's an element of writing myself back up out of that. I was surprised and delighted to find a lot of letters from people in the early days would say, "I was terribly depressed and upset until I sat down and read your book. It's really shown me the way up again." I wrote it to do this for myself, and it's seemed to have the same effect on a lot of other people. I can't explain it. Perhaps I've inadvertently written a self-help book.'

It's hardly surprising that the initial story Adams was to tell came together so quickly, as he had expanded on it enthusiastically in Simon Brett's office after lunch. There were just so many ideas constipatedly fermenting in his brain, it was more a case of picking and choosing. He was happy to say, 'If a thing was going to get thrown away, you'd use it. You never waste anything. You suddenly find there's something you wrote when you were ten that will actually fit – it hasn't been published, so you'll use it. All sorts of ideas float around at the back of your mind, and you keep on wanting to use them, and they never fit, and then one day you have a situation, you're looking for an idea, and you think "Oh! That thing I thought of when I was ten would fit here!"' A perfect example of this was the 'memory like a sieve' gag – first published when the writer was twelve, it was recycled for the character Professor Chronotis when Adams was 27, and then again at the age of 35.

Would It Save Time If I Just Went Mad Now?

Demolition was a hot topic in Dorset at this time – an old glove mill which loomed over the Thrift home was in the local news, as the owner of the attached listed building, Silk Hay, had a fight on her hands to fend off town planners hell-bent on knocking the whole lot down for new flats, while Janet Thrift bemoaned the destruction of the view, grumbling that all the plans had been left locked away in the council's bottom drawer, in a cellar, in another town. From Douglas' improvised 'desk' – a piece of wood balanced in the corner of his bedroom – he could see the JCBs actually moving in, and got to know the workmen. At the time they were temporarily defeated and the mill had a short reprieve, but the same could not be said of a pigsty in the back garden a few yards to the left – that was reduced to rubble as Adams typed. His hero would be one of those brave Britons who chained themselves to railings to prevent this sort of thing – except, in Adams' world, a bigger danger lurked in the sky. Douglas always had in mind that the first of his six planned stories would take the familiar idea of protesting against motorway construction to an intergalactic level, but once he realised that it would be difficult to tell the story if all the Earthlings involved were ignorant of what peril was approaching them from beyond orbit (admittedly the original draft claimed 'Only two people on the surface of the planet were aware of it. One was a deaf and dumb lunatic in the Amazon basin who now leapt off a fifty-foot cliff in horror, and the other was Ford Prefect'), his magpie memory began to stir – his human hero would need an alien guide, and how about making them a roving researcher for that most desirable tool, 'The Hitchhiker's Guide to the Galaxy'?

Once his retentive brain had fished out the 'Hitchhiker's Guide' concept from the ether, it was clear that the self-contained apocalypse concept of *The Ends of the Earth* was not needed – with this ideal form of interstellar space travel, he could take the listening audience anywhere he wanted: 'When you're a student or whatever, and you can't afford a car, or a plane fare, or even a train fare, all you can do is hope that someone will stop and pick you up. At the moment we can't afford to go to other planets ... but it's nice to think that one could, even here and now, be whisked away just by hitchhiking ... There really is no reason why we should have to wait until we can build our own long-distance spacecraft before being able to travel around the Universe. I rather like the idea of being able to hitch a ride on somebody else's.' He explained to Neil Gaiman, 'the more I thought about it, the more that seemed to be a promising idea for a continuing story.'

Although an alternative outline[1] had the hero originally living above a village shop before escaping into a universe torn apart by war between a benevolent force known as 'Mrs Rogers' and a malign Chinese takeaway known as 'The Naughty One', Douglas and Simon soon agreed on a synopsis which followed that famous first half-hour much more closely – the major difference in both outlines being the name of the protagonist, 'Aleric B' (sic):

ALERIC	Good grief. Is this really the interior of a flying saucer? It's a bit squalid, isn't it?
FORD	What were you expecting?
ALERIC	Well, I don't know. Gleaming control panels, flashing lights, computer screens.
FORD	This is a working ship, squalid but solid.
ALERIC	Trusty but rusty.

Why Adams chose the name – perhaps for its misleading alien qualities – he never disclosed, but equally mysterious was the rather speedy pencilling-in of the better name: Aleric, no, *Arthur* Dent. We already know that Harry

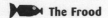

Porter's library was not forefront in Douglas' mind, and he later rationalised the decision: 'I wanted the name to be, on the one hand, perfectly ordinary, but on the other hand, distinctive. "Arthur" is a name like that – it's not like Dominic or Sebastian or something obviously very odd or even affected. It's a solid, "olde English" name that's perfectly ordinary, but not many people actually have it. There was a character at school called Dent. It just seemed to have the right ring. And also, I suppose, because Arthur was very much somebody to whom things happened – somebody who reacted to things that happened to him, rather than being an instigator himself – he seemed to be a "Dentish" sort of character, and that was partly in my mind ...'

The model of car in question may be less prevalent on UK roads now, but the joke that named Arthur's saviour was obvious at the time. However, Ford Prefect needed to be more than just an exposition-spouting E.T., and to Douglas, Dent's partner was primarily 'a reaction against Doctor Who, because the Doctor is always rushing about saving people and planets and generally doing good works, so to speak; and I thought the keynote of the character of Ford Prefect was that given the choice between getting involved and saving the world from some disaster on the one hand, and on the other hand going to a party, he'd go to the party every time, assuming that the world, if it were worth anything, would take care of itself. So that was the departure point for Ford. He wasn't based on any particular character but come to think of it, aspects of Ford's later behaviour became more and more based on memories of Geoffrey McGivern's more extreme behaviour in pubs.' Ford doesn't tell Arthur 'Come with me if you want to live', but 'Come along with me and have a good time'.

Another drastic difference with the original outline was that it was unequivocally designed not to be a humorous sci-fi serial but a sitcom, with Ford and Arthur hitching their way into self-contained half-hour plots every week, on different planets and in different dimensions. The multi-dimensional nature of Earth – famously situated in the notoriously tricky sector of ZZ9 Plural Z Alpha – which would go on to be central to the *Hitchhiker* novels, was clearly mapped out by Ford in the first draft, before being excised and left out of the radio show altogether, with a few lines craftily kept back for recycling:

```
FORD      I rescued you from the Earth ... it just boiled away into
          space.
```

ARTHUR   Look. I'm a bit upset about that.

FORD   Yes, I can understand. But there are plenty more Earths just like it.

ARTHUR   Are you going to explain that? Or would it save time if I just went mad now?

FORD`   ... The Universe we exist in is just one of a multiplicity of parallel universes which co-exist in the same space but on different matter wavelengths, and in millions of them the Earth is still alive and throbbing much as you remember - or very similar at least - because every possible variation of the Earth also exists.

ARTHUR   Variation? I don't understand. You mean like a world where Hitler won the war?

FORD   Yes. Or a world in which Shakespeare wrote pornography, made a lot more money and got a knighthood.

One week seemed to be inspired by Douglas' bodyguard experience, with the two heroes caught in an Impossible Journey to shepherd food through a rich alien's digestive system while war rages in his intestine, and in another plot idea too good to be forgotten, they were to discover that dolphins were a superior race to humanity. The Swiftian parallels in the way that the hitchers' experiences on strange worlds would reflect satirically on our own society were explicitly stated in the pitch: 'In a way, *Hitchhiker* is a kind of *Gulliver's Travels* in space. One goes out into space, one leaves the world and comes across all sorts of extraordinary people who behave in extraordinary ways and one discovers that the more things change, the more they stay the same. One sees human foibles played out on a grand scale really ... The advantage of science fiction is managing to look through the other end of the telescope, see things in a totally different perspective.'

Many fans could argue that for the programme to be seen as a 'situation comedy' in some way diminishes it – but even worse would be the suggestion that Adams was writing something that could be described as a 'spoof'. When it comes to deciding where to land on the subject of whether *Hitchhiker* is spoof or parody, or the preciously delineated 'science-fiction-with-humour', we find ourselves bogged down in an area of nomenclature-wrangling which ultimately serves little purpose. As a continuing comedy with characters in a situation, the programme could take a place somewhere on the outer edges

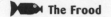

of sitcom as we know it anyway, but this age-old humbug about *Hitchhiker* not being a genre spoof needs more attention. Douglas Adams himself was quoted as denying almost any element of spoof – but then this was in an interview with diehard science fiction fans who he knew would not take kindly to being reminded that they had invested so much devoted fandom in a joke. With reference to the *Star Trek* gag recycled from Cambridge days, as recited by Peter Jones in episode three:

```
Far back in the mists of ancient time, in the great and
glorious days of the former Galactic Empire, life was
wild, rich, and on the whole tax free ... men were real men,
women were real women, and small furry creatures from
Alpha Centauri were real small furry creatures from Alpha
Centauri. And all dared to brave unknown terrors, to do
mighty deeds, to boldly split infinitives that no man had
split before, and thus was the Empire forged ... Many men of
course became extremely rich, but this was perfectly natural
and nothing to be ashamed of because no one was really poor
- at least, no one worth speaking of ...
```

Adams commented, 'I never saw myself as actually sending up science fiction. There is only one thing that I can think of where I deliberately "sent up" something from the science fiction genre, which was the thing about "to boldly split infinitives that no one has split before". It was just one of those things where I thought, "I can't think of anything better – I'll go with that." But otherwise, as far as I was concerned, I wasn't sending up science fiction, I was using science fiction as a vehicle for sending up everything else.' Which isn't too dissimilar to an arsonist saying 'I didn't intend to be an arsonist, I simply started a fire on the hearthrug ...'

It does have to come down ultimately to a question of snobbery. The innocent terms 'spoof', 'pastiche', 'parody' and 'lampoon' have over the years been tainted with a number of stains, which have rendered their usage somehow offensive and reductionist to some minds, whereby anything which contains elements of any of the above can only be frivolous, silly, or profane. A quick nip to dictionary.reference.com would clear this matter up, compelling any reasonable observer to admit that if *Hitchhiker* was not initially a science fiction spoof, then it wasn't very much at all. It may not be as shallow and wacky a spoof as Mel Brooks' *Spaceballs* from 1987, but it's inescapable, by getting laughs from known science fiction traditions, concepts and memes, that 'spoof', 'pastiche', 'parody' and 'lampoon' are the essential building blocks of the series – the saga-triggering concept itself was at its heart *Carry On War Of The Worlds* via Monty Python, and Python was of course packed with silly spoofs of all kinds, while still managing to comment intelligently on any number of subjects: *Life of Brian* functions as a spoof of religious epics, but nobody would claim that it had nothing to say. A supposed 'low' form of humour need not flee from embracing matters of great import, and *Hitchhiker* would become an excellent example of this fact.

Despite the raging wars between fans of *Hitchhiker* as a comedy and as science fiction, real devotees know perfectly well that it is ultimately a glorious example of both. But either way was to be entirely gravy for Adams, who laughed, 'I've inadvertently done something quite clever, in that I've done a show which science fiction fans like because they think it's science fiction, and which people who don't like science fiction like, because they think it's knocking science fiction'. Above all, he said, 'I just wanted to do stuff I thought was funny. But on the other hand, whatever I find funny is going to be conditioned by what I think about, what my concerns or preoccupations are. You may not set out to make a point, but points probably come across because they tend to be the things that preoccupy you, and therefore find a way into your writing.'

There hadn't been a great deal of note in the field of sci-fi comedy by 1977 – the odd US screwball comedy series like *My Favourite Martian* (which was simultaneously inspiring a new kooky alien sitcom, *Mork & Mindy*, via *Happy Days,* as Douglas sat down to work), and cartoon invaders like Warner Bros' Marvin the Martian, who debuted in 1948. More in Adams' line, of adult, ideas-based silly science fiction, was Woody Allen's *Sleeper* in 1973, and John Carpenter's rookie low budget spaceship farce *Dark Star* which was released a year later, and starred a stir-crazy deep-space crew dealing with a naughty alien and a sentient bomb. Quite forgotten then, let alone now, was a 1970 prime-time ITV sitcom based on Cervantes' greatest work, *The Adventures of Don Quick,* with a pair of astronauts meeting strange species around the galaxy, but strangest of all, in 1977 purveyors of cosy nostalgia sitcom David Croft and Jimmy Perry were already working on their own spaceship farce for BBC1, *Come Back Mrs Noah*, which would be a notorious flop. Despite all this, while Adams worked away on zapping his heroes out into the madness of space, he certainly felt like a pioneer.

Besides a 1973 BBC adaptation of Isaac Asimov's epic *Foundation* series (another fiction to be directly lampooned by *Hitchhiker*, the Guide itself specifically cocking a snook at Asimov's dusty 'Encyclopedia Galactica'), there hadn't even been a notable radio sci-fi series in the UK since 1953's *Journey Into Space,* a hugely influential and popular tale of British astronauts coming up against the hazards of space and time travel. But of course no medium could be more perfect for exploring outlandish concepts on a minimal budget, as the listener would be providing all the sets, costumes, make-up and special effects in the mind's eye. Adams had to explain to interviewers in years to come, 'To be absolutely honest the reason I did it on radio to begin with was because I was at that point too junior to do television, if you like. But that was the best thing that could possibly happen to me, because I discovered what a wonderful, extraordinary medium radio was, and it's still in many ways my favourite.' It was a steep learning curve for a writer who had largely just adapted sketches for the sound-only medium in the past. As he explained, if on TV or in the cinema your character finds themself in a volcano, 'you may then go on to talk about vegetables, but you can see he's still in a volcano, whereas in radio you have to keep on saying "It's very curious, the fact that I'm talking about the price of vegetables whilst I'm in this volcano ..."'

Of course, he had found a sneaky way of simplifying this challenge – his third main character, the eponymous Guide itself, which on one hand he felt 'should allow for the almost unlimited development of freewheeling ideas whilst at the same time retaining a fairly simple and coherent shape and purpose'. But, even more importantly, 'The Book' could also function as a charming, subversive and notoriously unreliable narrator – not that Adams wanted to make things easy for himself: 'One of the things I think you learn,' he once said, 'is to get the characters to tell the story. You have to, because there's nobody else. There's a tendency when you write books for you as the author to stand in the middle of stage wittering on while your characters are sort of sitting in the wings rapping their fingers on the table wondering when they're going to be allowed on. But then there are areas where you're simply going to have to have somebody saying those things that can't emerge from the dialogue, so we had to have a narrator. Now, the Narrator figure is interesting, because, having decided there was going to have to be a Narrator, I knew I didn't want him to be saying what was happening, because that would be dull, so he ended up describing a lot of things that *weren't* happening.'

The first episode would be written relatively quickly, but this first attempt at writing a long-form comedy on his own would lead Douglas to a hugely pedantic approach to writing – undeniably paying dividends quality-wise, but ultimately becoming a millstone around his neck when deadlines bore down on him: 'Trying to put in the Narrator's pieces, both information and jokes simultaneously, was quite a tall order. Usually what happens is the jokes and the information are pretty much mutually exclusive, so you end up with a first draft of a Narrator's speech five pages long, and it'll take half the programme to read, therefore you have to start cutting – and this is where you learn that one of the most creative parts of writing is when you've got some sort of rough stuff on a piece of paper, and you start to cut it, hone it – chip away at this little bit, that little bit, get rid of every word that isn't absolutely essential, that isn't doing some vital job. And when you've done all that, you begin to find that the meaning has shifted very slightly, and maybe has acquired some kind of tone or undertone, and you think "That's interesting, let's develop that a bit ..." You end up with something about a tenth the length that you started with.' This reductionist, perfectionist attitude to crafting text would be both the key to Douglas' success, and a source of ulcers to anyone who ever needed him to deliver material.

Is This You Continuing?

The basement of the Rex House building in Lower Regent Street, W1 is now one of ten billion gyms packed into that dense area of London, but for most of the 20th century it was the Paris Theatre, an intimate studio space where an average of 400 punters enjoyed the recordings of radio shows from *Round the Horne* to *ISIHAC*, or performances from The Beatles and The Stones in the 1960s. Simon Brett booked the venue for the recording of the *Hitchhiker* pilot for Tuesday, 28th June 1977 – but with the unusual proviso that no audience would be needed. This was the first of many battles that Brett had to win with his BBC bosses, as he tried to communicate the unique nature of the programme they had tentatively green-lit, and luckily it was an easier battle, due to the sheer logic of not boring an audience to death as tricky special effects were put in place to bring Adams' creation to life. From the very beginning, the writer was concerned that his show should sound like no other before it, and as Canter promised, the giant sofa at Arlington Avenue was there for him as he made regular trips across to the capital to work with Brett on getting it right.

With a vehemence that only somebody who insisted on listening to Pink Floyd albums with the very best headphones could muster, Adams was adamant that *Hitchhiker* would have a decidedly epic audio impact: 'Though it was now ten years since *Sergeant Pepper* had revolutionised the way that people in the rock world thought about sound production, it seemed to me, listening to radio comedy at the time, that we still hadn't progressed much beyond "Door Slam A, Door Slam B, Footsteps On a Gravel Path and the odd Comic Boing". This wasn't so much lack of imagination, as a perfectly reasonable worry that an over-indulgence in sound effects easily creates irritating mish-mash, which detracts from a strong script and fails to disguise a weak one. Also it took time, which, it was felt, could be better used making more programmes ... I felt you could do a great deal more with sound than I had heard being done of late. The people who were exploring and exploiting where you could go with sound were people in the rock world – The Beatles, Pink Floyd, and so on ... I had the idea of scenes of sound. That there would never be a moment at which the alien world would let up, that you would be in it for half an hour. I'm not saying we necessarily achieved that, but I think that what we achieved came about as a result of striving after that ... I wanted the voices and the effects and the music to be so seamlessly orchestrated as to create a coherent picture of a whole other world – and I said this and many similar sorts of things and waved my hands around a lot, while people nodded patiently and said, "Yes, Douglas, but what's it actually *about*?"'

Douglas' own cosmic record collection was crucial to creating this alien soundscape – the experimental twiddlings/wailings of two composers being particularly prevalent, Californian Terry Riley and Transylvanian Gyorgy Ligeti. But of course, the chief priority was to find the right theme music to introduce *Hitchhiker* to the listener. 'I figured as it was set in space it should have something spacey with synthesisers on it,' he said. 'And since it was funny it should have something to show it wasn't too serious, like banjo music. So I went through my record collection looking for something with synthesiser and banjo ...' The 1975 Eagles album track 'Journey of the

Sorcerer' had been written by Bernie Leadon just before he left the group – and before they really hit the big time with 'Hotel California'. Far from lending an air of frivolity, the song's sparse jangling banjo, the sound of the lonely space hobo, would come to exemplify the series' sense of alienation, an ominous sound from the dark side of the Universe, creating a suitably serious tone for the ensuing silliness to undermine.

The most important element of the soundscape, naturally, came from the actors, and Adams had very clear ideas about casting. McGivern was clearly long forgiven for any previous punch-up, and was the ideal Ford – but above all, Douglas wanted to repay the kindness shown to him by Simon Jones and make him the star of the show – Jones' career since Cambridge had also, fittingly, included a stint in the *Doctor Who* stage play. Adams rang his old friend, allegedly promising him a part 'which is pretty much you', although for years to come he had to insist, 'Arthur wasn't *based* on Simon Jones. Simon is convinced I've said this at some point, whereas what I've said was that I wrote the part with him in mind. Which is a very different thing to say about an actor. But there's only the slightest echo of Simon himself in it. He isn't based on Simon, but he is based on what I thought Simon's strengths as an actor were. Nor, by the same token, is it autobiographical ... having said that, Arthur Dent is not so remote from myself that it's impossible to use things which have happened to me in writing about him.'

Since leaving Cambridge, Simon's acting career had got off to a good start, with a plum role in a musical ITV series that would employ a whole host of performers crucial to *Hitchhiker* – *Rock Follies*. The cultural history of the 1970s has of course been endlessly and handily streamlined for subsequent generations by decades of documentaries that tell us that the be-caped dinosaurs of Prog Rock were swept away in 1976 by marauding hordes of Punks, and that was that. But for those, like Adams, who were less inclined to taper their trousers, life went on, and other music was available. The rock musicals of Lloyd-Webber, Rice and Richard O'Brien, not to mention ABBA, Queen, and a whole rash of disco reworkings of classical pieces (Adams' favourite Bach particularly) that stemmed from American synth pioneer Wendy Carlos and her dystopian soundtrack to 1971's *A Clockwork Orange*, provided a bridge between Glam or Prog Rock and the nebulous New Wave of Kate Bush, Elvis Costello, Squeeze, and others, while the rise of the vocoder-heavy synthesiser sounds pioneered by Kraftwerk would soon become central to the *Hitchhiker* sound. The Thames TV show *Rock Follies* was a popular mainstream hit no matter what Punk was about to unleash, and it featured Jones as pretentious waiter Juan, but he was intrigued by the role Douglas had created for him, and signed up without demur – though, of course, he had to stress that he wasn't in the least bit like Arthur.

Besides *ISIRTA* and *Burkiss Way* heroine Jo Kendall, playing the subsequently superfluous role of snooty local dignitary Lady Cynthia Fitzmelton, proud to begin the vandalism of Arthur's village of 'cruddy Cottington', there were roles for two more Footlights luminaries, with the barman played by David Gooderson (shortly to embody Davros), while sometime Peter Cook collaborator and subsequent *Blackadder* irregular Bill Wallis stepped in at the last minute to take the dual roles of demolition foreman Mr. Prosser and his interstellar equivalent, the Chief Vogon – not identified at this time as Prostetnic Jeltz. It would have been too easy to make the pilot's alien antagonists truly villainous, in the vein of the Mekon or the Daleks, and so Adams stipulated, echoing his own European guidebook's opinion on hitching in Albania:

```
Here is what to do if you want to get a lift from a Vogon:
forget it. They are one of the most unpleasant races in the
Galaxy - not actually evil, but bad-tempered, bureaucratic,
officious and callous. They wouldn't even lift a finger to
save their own grandmothers from the Ravenous Bugblatter
Beast of Traal without orders signed in triplicate, sent in,
sent back, queried, lost, found, subjected to public inquiry,
lost again, and finally buried in soft peat for three months
and recycled as firelighters. The best way to get a drink out
of a Vogon is to stick your fingers down his throat, and the
best way to irritate him is to feed his grandmother to the
Ravenous Bugblatter Beast of Traal.
```

Prosser and Dent's dispute was far longer and more exhaustingly Pythonesque in its pedantry in the original draft – a later dramatic sting was also annotated 'SHRUBBERY!' with reference to *Holy Grail* – and you can't get much more Pythonesque than the famous punchline 'Beware Of The Leopard!' For Adams, bureaucracy simply had to be the most powerful danger in the Universe, and by directly linking the petty red tape of the local council with the magnitude of an alien invasion, he provided a perfect entry into his Universe, giving BBC bosses and eventual listeners a strong idea of what was to come, and how his space adventures could directly comment on life on Earth.

On the subject of spoofery, once Ford and Arthur were zapped up by the Vogon spaceship, the vicious torture which would be threatened for the hero in traditional sci-fi serial cliffhangers was sent up by replacing lasers or razors with bad poetry (via, of course, the audacious introduction of the Babel fish, a painstakingly crafted solution to the Galaxy's language problem), in a way that allowed Douglas to have some fun at the expense of an old acquaintance. The series would be thick with references designed to be picked up on by Douglas' close friends, though he protested, 'there are bits and pieces that go in which are sort of little personal jokes, but they're usually very, very tiny – you can't put in something that most of the audience will feel "There's something here I don't understand, and I have the feeling I wasn't meant to understand it." That's a very arrogant way to treat your audience. So if I put in a detail just to amuse a couple of people or myself, then it's usually something where there would have to be something there anyway – as a little bit of background colour.' The background colour here was to cause great ructions with his fellow Artsphere founder P. N. M. Johnstone: 'This character used to share a room with me at school. Kept me awake all night scratching this awful poetry about swans and stuff. When it was on radio, there was a section about Vogon poetry, which was the third-worst in the Universe. And somebody asked me what the first-worst was, and I couldn't think and I said, "Well, it's Milne Johnstone, isn't it?" He ignored it for a while and then when the book and the album appeared, he started to wax litigious. We ended up getting this bloody letter and it turned out that although he hadn't published anything, he had gone on to edit all these poetry mags and organise various festivals.' Johnstone's perfectly reasonable legal request was to have the name changed, for the sake of his own reputation, and so most book printings and the TV series would ridicule the verse of 'Paula Nancy Millstone Jennings', with a dragged-up Douglas even illustrating the section on TV. The ICA Theatre adaptation threw caution to the wind and named Paul, as he had been an apparently less than easygoing press officer for the venue, and it does seem apparent that the poor slandered poet had an infamous lack of any sense of humour – which, of course, was the exact reason that Douglas could not resist the ribbing in the first place. The two never made the slightest peace with each other, and Johnstone died three years after his comic tormentor.

The last and most crucial part to be cast was, of course, the title role. Adams and Brett agreed that the outlandish and often outrageous extracts from the Guide would be best served by a crisp and comforting Radio 4 voice, which Douglas soon identified as being 'Peter Jones-y'. Early suggestions included Michaels Hordern and Palin – of the latter, twenty years later Adams told fans on his forum: 'Michael reminded me the other day that I had originally asked him to do the voice of the Guide, and he wondered how differently his career would have gone if he had accepted. Pretty much exactly the same is my guess.' After much anguished argument, he recalled, 'eventually Simon Brett's secretary got very annoyed hearing us talking on and on like this and not spotting the obvious. She said, "What about Peter Jones?" I thought, "Yes, that would be a way of achieving it, wouldn't it?" So we asked Peter, he was available, and he did it.'

Jones was confident enough with the script to travel all the way up from his home in Cornwall, but at first Douglas was not sure that the old Salopian, who arrived looking more than ever like a bank manager on his lunch break, had a clue what the job entailed: 'When he first came for the read-through of the script, and peered at it as if it was an application for a loan to buy an ostrich farm in Shrewsbury, I nervously leapt in and tried desperately to explain things. You can imagine: "There's this kind of fish, you see, they have to wear in their ears and it absorbs brainwave energy" or "It's this vicious race of alien poets, you understand!" ... and he sat there, saying "Yeees ...?" And finally, a terrifyingly long time after I'd finished explaining: "Hmm. I see." Another pause. And then at last, a very slight chuckle, and: "Yes, I like that. That's quite funny."' Adams seemed to have forgotten that Peter Jones had his own experience of pushing the boundaries of radio comedy, having abetted Peter Ustinov in an early example of comedy improv, *In All Directions*, two decades earlier. Naturally, 'Peter was extraordinary. He always affected not to understand what was going on at all, and managed to transmute his own sense of "I don't know what this is about" into "I don't understand why this happened", which was the keynote of his performance. He's never had the recognition he should have had. He's terribly good. He rarely met the other actors at all, because he'd be doing his bits completely separately. It was like getting session musicians in on a multi-track rock album, sitting alone in a studio doing the bass part.'

And so, with all of the parts in place for what seemed like an interstellar breakthrough for Radio 4, but was in fact hugely simple in comparison to what was to follow, for the very first time, Arthur Dent lay down in the mud to save his cottage, and the forces of bureaucracy converged to change his puny Earthling life for ever:

```
NARRATOR      (Over music. Matter of fact, characterless voice.)
              This is the story of The Hitchhiker's Guide to the
              Galaxy, perhaps the most remarkable, certainly the
              most successful book ever to come out of the great
              publishing corporations of Ursa Minor …
```

The introduction always seemed set in stone, but the opening dialogue went through copious redrafts, with many exchanges not even making it into the famously exhaustive script books:

```
FX            GENERAL ROAD BUILDING NOISES. BULLDOZERS, PNEUMATIC
              DRILLS, ETC.
```

(The following conversation is carried out over this noise. The man from the council, Mr. Prosser, is being dictatorial through a megaphone, and Arthur is shouting his answers rather faintly in the distance.)

```
PROSSER   Come off it, Mr. Dent, you can't win, you know. There's no
          point in lying down in the path of progress.
ARTHUR    I've gone off the idea of progress. It's overrated.
PROSSER   But you must realise that you can't lie in front of the
          bulldozers indefinitely.
ARTHUR    I'm game, we'll see who rusts first …
PROSSER   Mr. Dent, will you please be realistic …
ARTHUR    Look, I'm fine. I'm beginning to quite enjoy it down here.
          The bulldozers keep the wind off, the mud's nice and
          warm - it's a way of life I could easily adapt to.
PROSSER   I'm afraid you're going to have to accept it. This bypass
          has got to be built, and it's going to be built. Nothing
          you can say or do …
```

ARTHUR   Why's it got to be built?

PROSSER   What do you mean, why's it got to be built? It's a bypass, you've got to build bypasses ...

ARTHUR   Didn't anyone consider the alternatives?

PROSSER   There aren't any alternatives. The volume of traffic ...

ARTHUR   You could demolish the cars instead of the houses. Bet you didn't think of that.

PROSSER   It's not a particularly nice house, anyway.

ARTHUR   I happen to rather like it.

PROSSER   I am empowered by the council ...

ARTHUR   And I think it's got used to me.

PROSSER   I am empowered by the council ...

ARTHUR   If I let you knock it down, I don't think another house would ever trust me again. They can tell, you know.

PROSSER   I am empowered by the council ...

ARTHUR   I bet your house doesn't trust you ...

PROSSER   Will you allow me to continue?

ARTHUR   Yes, all right.

PROSSER   I am empowered by the council ...

ARTHUR   Is this you continuing?

PROSSER   Yes! I am empowered by the council ...

ARTHUR   Ah, I'm sorry, it's just it sounded like you saying the exact same thing.

The rough edit of the day's recording was expertly licked into shape by BBC Radiophonic Workshop legend Paddy Kingsland, with Simon and Douglas on hand to ensure that the finished edit matched the sound in the writer's head, and they even managed to knock off early for a celebratory drink at The Dover Castle. Chief among Kingsland's duties was of course to destroy the Earth, as outlined in the script:

FX   A LOW THROBBING HUM WHICH BUILDS QUICKLY IN INTENSITY AND PITCH. WIND & THUNDER, RENDING, GRINDING CRASHES. ALL THE NIGGLING LITTLE FRUSTRATIONS THAT THE BBC SOUND EFFECTS ENGINEERS HAVE EVER HAD CAN ALL COME OUT IN A FINAL DEVASTATING EXPLOSION WHICH THEN DIES AWAY INTO SILENCE.

This effect was realised with a blend of numerous trad SFX – thunderclaps, explosions, train crashes, but it more than did the job even when mixed down and broadcast on tinny radio speakers, and was considered 'the technical highlight of the show'. The way in which this fictitious finale seemed to suggest an auspicious start, filling Adams with confidence as he made his way back to Dorset, was as misleading a signifier of the road ahead as Arthur Dent's waking belief that particular Thursday, that he would spend the day doing a bit of reading and brushing the dog.

You Don't Want To Take Over The Universe, Do You?

Simon Brett served Douglas' vision well. On 12th July he played back the finished pilot to his bosses, who sat in stony silence for the full half-hour. At the end of the playback a puzzled Con Mahoney, old-school Head of LE, could only turn to the producer and ask, 'But Simon, is it funny?' Brett assured the bigwigs that it certainly was, and thankfully his great track record was enough for them. 'Simon was playing quite a deep political game,' Douglas said, 'positioning it so it could sort of get on. For instance, we were told that you could not do comedy in stereo – the audience wouldn't know which speaker the punchline was going to come out of! So for a little brief moment in *Hitchhiker*'s history it was officially a drama, just to get us through that little wrinkle in the system … it was through knowing the right buttons to push at the right moment, so to speak.'

Thanks to Brett's belief in Adams, the BBC finally gave the official go-ahead to *Hitchhiker* on the last day of August, at the rate of £180 for each of the remaining five episodes. Sadly, by this time, neither Simon nor Douglas were in a position to get back to work – the former because he had taken the big decision to leave Radio 4 and follow Humphrey Barclay to LWT, and the latter because he found himself realising another childhood dream – at last, he had been invited to pitch his own *Doctor Who* adventure.

The journey of the *Hitchhiker* pilot through the BBC system had taken so long, and Adams' positivity was too fragile to stand the suspense as summer wore on, and so, armed with the script for his very own Radio 4 sci-fi show, he thought that perhaps the time was right to try the *Who* production office yet again, with a fresh idea. He had made a second assault on the department only the year before, with a convoluted film proposal entitled *Doctor Who and the Krikkitmen*, in which an army of ruthless automatons modelled on a cricket team (but whose galactic campaigns actually inspired the sport itself, thanks to 'one of those curious freaks of racial memory') will stop at nothing to re-form the wicket-shaped key to free their Krikkit masters from the time envelope preventing them from destroying all life in the Universe besides themselves. Only the Doctor and Sarah-Jane Smith can stop them, having initially failed to prevent the murderous robots taking the Ashes during a game at Lord's cricket ground. Although Adams might have dimly recalled a sequence from the William Hartnell adventure *The Daleks' Master Plan* which involved the sport, the prime influence here was the Brentwood chaplain Tom Gardiner, who once delivered a memorable sermon on 'If visitors from Mars came down on the First XI cricket pitch, how would you deal with them?' which surely commanded young Douglas' full attention. Cricket itself actually held very little appeal for the writer – it was even described as 'an incomprehensibly dull and pointless game' in his pitch – and he admitted, 'I am not a great cricket fan. I just came across an article about the history of the Ashes – a cricket stump which was burnt in Melbourne in 1882. I happened to read it in a daydreamy mood and it went from there. There was no deep significance to it.' In 1976, the then script editor Robert Holmes' reaction to this plot was allegedly a dispiriting 'We'd like to see more evidence of talent than this' – apparently the *Hitchhiker* pilot fulfilled that criteria.

In July, Adams travelled from his spot on the Arlington Avenue sofa to the BBC, and met Holmes, new script editor Tony Reed, and producer Graham Williams, armed with a story involving the dark secret of the Time Lords' immoral mining activities, and a Gallifreyan renegade who finds a way to jump across the Universe in a hollow planet to the Time Lords' home, bent on revenge. Douglas was to describe this as 'probably the best worked-out plot I'd ever done', but his epic pitch apparently forced the *Who* bosses lower and lower in their seats, provoking an aggrieved 'Now I know how Kubrick felt!' from the producer when it was over. Nevertheless, Adams was sent away to work on it, and returned with a script which was 'much too long – on paper it was twice as long as it should have been. It started out as quite a simple story but it had to arch its back to get round several problems and weave past a couple of things that were in the pipeline. The whole script actually did make sense from beginning to end – in fact they were astonished that it did. But by the time it had been cut to the proper length, large holes had begun to appear. The whole plot eventually hinged on eternal life, which actually is a bit dull, but originally it had involved a drug-pushing analogy. I had envisaged a fly-by-night company which went around looking for those people that were most afraid of dying and sold them "time-dams" which would hold up time, making it go slower and slower, until the people were into the last few seconds of their lives ...' After numerous wranglings with Reed, including the need to crowbar in the 16th series story arc, involving 'The Key to Time' (uncannily similar to Adams' own Krikkit key quest), *The Pirate Planet* bore little resemblance to the writer's original outline, even if it did allow him to have fun with a favourite cliché, by featuring a boorish space pirate complete with robotic parrot. On this occasion, however, clinging to perfectionism wasn't important – what mattered was that the story was commissioned, paid for, and eventually made.

With the formal commission arriving in late October for completion first thing in 1978, Adams' writing duties were beginning to stack up, having at least five hours of entertainment to script – and he was already six weeks into trying to find out what happened next to Ford Prefect and Arthur Dent. Back home in Dorset, a strict regime of running and writing was established, as his Mum served sandwiches and cups of tea. The forbiddingly rigid structure of *Who*, fifteen years into The Show's original run, with perhaps its most beloved and iconic Doctor at the helm – the mercurial and irrepressible Tom Baker – suited Adams' logical instincts as a writer, compared to the positively dizzying freedom of *Hitchhiker*, but he was aware of the schizophrenic nature of writing both programmes at once: 'Oddly enough, I found *Doctor Who* quite liberating to do. At one point I was writing both simultaneously, and in many ways, even though people assume there was some cross-fertilisation, in fact they inhabit such entirely different universes, there really wasn't. But I did notice one odd thing: I was writing episodes of *Hitchhiker* which all seemed to happen in corridors, and writing episodes of *Doctor Who* which called for huge, enormous, impossibly elaborate sets. I thought, "I've got this the wrong way round."' This unrealistic level of visual ambition was to show in the finished *Pirate Planet* when it was broadcast the following year. Legendarily, no TV show in history has been as mocked for its superseded special effects quite as mercilessly as classic *Who*, often unfairly, but Adams' debut was particularly compromised by basic visual production – he would learn in time to keep within the programme's scope, and most importantly, to make up for any effects shortfall with brilliant concepts and sharp dialogue. Certainly, every *Who* fan watching that first Adams adventure would have detected an increase of cheek in the Time Lord's badinage:

```
DOCTOR      ... Newton's revenge ...
ROMANA      Newton? Who was Newton?
DOCTOR      Old Isaac! Friend of mine on Earth. Discovered
            gravity. Well, I say he discovered gravity, I gave
            him a bit of a prod.
ROMANA      What did you do?
DOCTOR      Climbed up a tree.
ROMANA      And?
DOCTOR      Dropped an apple on his head.
ROMANA      Ah, and so he discovered gravity?
DOCTOR      No, he told me to clear off out of his tree.
            I explained it to him afterwards at dinner.
```

Humour was always a crucial part of The Show's DNA, certainly since the debut of Patrick Troughton in the title role, but perhaps the crossover with his own ongoing comedy writing made Adams' scripts all the more irresistible to the naturally comic Baker. Tom was known to snarl at many a fresh script, hurling them across the room and reducing writers to jelly, but being presented with Douglas' work only triggered that famous toothy grin, and gave the star something to really work with. The two developed a rare rapport, and Douglas enthused, 'Tom is really one of a kind. One of those people who oscillate between being one of the most wonderful, awesome, engaging people you have ever met to someone you would gladly shove off a cliff!' To his chagrin, however, the writer felt the levity on The Show could go too far – he derided the phrase 'tongue in cheek', which he insisted simply meant 'we're not going to do it properly', and went on to reflect, 'It shouldn't have been so overtly funny or jokey as it was. I wrote it with a lot of humour, but the point is, when you do that it very often gets played to the hilt. I felt there was too much: "Oh, the script's got humour in it. Therefore we've got to wheel out the funny voices and the silly walks," which I don't think does it a service.'

His real comedic playbox was currently stalled with his two heroes in the clutches of the Vogons – 'Either die in the vacuum of space, or tell me how good you thought my poetry was!' – and although he had carefully set up a departure point for further adventures (the revelation that Earth was deemed no more than 'Mostly Harmless' being enough to convince Arthur to join Ford on whatever adventures lay ahead), Douglas had to admit that he had very little idea of what actually was going to happen next.

I Can Work Out Your Personality Problems To Ten Decimal Places

Adams' workload through the autumn of 1977 surely proved to his Mum, stepfather and siblings that he was not kidding himself about his ambitions, and yet the threat of normality still hung over the ambitious lad as his typewriter clattered away and he tried to rack up pages advancing the adventures of both Arthur Dent and the Doctor. In his worst anxieties, he left notes for himself pinned to the wall: 'If you ever get the chance to do a proper, regular job ... take it. This is not an occupation for a healthy, growing lad ... This is not written after a bad day. This is written after an average day.'

Where could he begin, faced with the first blank page following his successful pilot? Well, there was always one handy gambit that had never stopped nagging away at him: it would get the typing fingers warmed up at least:

```
NARRATOR    The Hitchhiker's Guide to the Galaxy is a truly
            remarkable book. The introduction starts like this:
            'Space,' it says, 'is big. Really big. You just won't
            believe how vastly, hugely, mind-bogglingly big it
            is. I mean, you may think it's a long way down the
            street to the chemist, but that's just peanuts to
            space. Listen ...' And so on.
```

This Old Familiar, however, would not prove useful until his two heroes were flushed into the wastes of space with only thirty seconds of air in their lungs. Before that, there had to be the English graduate's poetry criticism face-off with the Vogon Captain, and the lampooning of sci-fi clichés with the guard whose empty life is largely based around the repeated yelling of 'Resistance is useless!' Douglas' eventual kicking-off point, after many a redraft, brought him back to that undying theme of money, and how the movement of 'small green pieces of paper' were incapable of making ape-descended life forms happy – a notably incisive observation from a young man without very much of it. The nonchalant mention of the Girl in the Café in Rickmansworth was just one example of how throwaway ideas would eventually grow into major plot points.

But, almost immediately, he found himself stuck. Less than half an hour off the planet, he had navigated his unheroic duo to almost certain death, in his words, 'just to see what would happen. Unfortunately, of course, if anything was going to happen, I was going to have to think of it ... Every way out of the corner seemed to amount to nothing more than "with one bound Jack was free" – which was a cop-out. There's no point in making a big song and dance about what a terrible predicament your characters are in if you just cheat your way out of it. I began to think that maybe we should just finish the series there and perhaps play light music for the remaining four and a half episodes which would save a lot of time and headaches all round, but not – and here was the crunch – pay my rent. They had to be rescued. The problem was the sheer *improbability* of every solution I came up with ...'

Defeated, he gave up for the day and turned on the TV, to find a judo demonstration in full swing: 'If you have a problem,' said the instructor on the programme, 'the trick is to use this problem to solve itself ...' Using an opponent's weight against them is a well-known martial arts technique, but in Douglas' case, 'I thought – if my problem is one of improbability, let's use Improbability to solve the problem, so just for the heck of it I invented the Infinite Improbability Drive, and gave myself a whole new thing to write about.' Despite the tea-infused technobabble which explained away the existence of a spaceship which could do absolutely anything the writer required to get onto the next piece of paper, sci-fi fans, authors and even the most highly educated technicians and theoretical physicists have marvelled at and argued over the invention which drives the starship *Heart of Gold*, how it works, what weight the theory holds ... but like so much else in the *Hitchhiker* Universe, the device was simply that: a brilliant bare-faced-cheek of a tool, to get on with the story, the first of many *deus ex machinas* – or rather, *scientia ex machina*. Adams was hardly alone in wanting to cut to the chase and get on with the story rather than writing a lengthy essay on theoretical physics: Kurt Vonnegut's second novel *Sirens of Titan* was a particular favourite of his, complex and multi-threaded, but its plot is lubricated constantly by a substance called The Universal Will To Become, an exposition-saving pinch of 'magic' which just allowed the unbelievable to lose the 'un'.

Improbability, then, allowed Adams' jaunt to get back on track – but where to now? This new starship, a gleaming Roddenberry-style futuristic craft to contrast with the deliberately pathetic gloom of the Vogon vessel, had to be manned by somebody. Luckily, the closest thing to a Captain had already been nominated in the pilot script during the passage about alcohol which introduced another all-time fan favourite – 'The man who invented this mind-pummelling drink also invented the wisest remark ever made, which was this: "Never drink more than two Pan Galactic Gargle Blasters unless you are a thirty-ton elephant with bronchial pneumonia." His name is Zaphod Beeblebrox and we shall learn more of his wisdom later.' This aside, however, was edited out before broadcast. This President Beeblebrox was clearly a hell of a guy, not just a satirical comment on the kind of dude who would want to run the Galaxy, but now he had to come in from the wings and stop being just a silly name.

Douglas kept a notepad next to his typewriter and would often scribble down odd names and ideas which appealed to him, playing with sounds and anagrams like any good crossword-lover, but it seemed to him that the name 'Zaphod Beeblebrox' had just appeared there one day, without his having any memory of writing it down. In his typically sarcastic manner, however, he was happy to put any fans off reading anything meaningful into his work by explaining, 'I sat and stared out of the window for a while, trying to think of a good name for a character. I told myself that, as a reward, I would let myself go and make a Bovril sandwich once I'd thought of it ... Zaphod was definitely a three-sandwich idea. Arthur came quite easily after a couple of biscuits and a cup of tea. Vogon poetry I remember was a tough one, and only came after several miles of rampaging round the country lanes of Stalbridge in a tracksuit trying to work off the effects of thinking up the Babel fish (six slices of toast and peanut butter, a packet of crisps and a shower).'

Ford and Arthur's saviour was originally intended to be the rich American whose guts they would be hired to explore and protect, but this whole plot strand was soon dumped, with confirmation that the ship would actually be skippered by the totally reprehensible President of the Galaxy, and a girl ('oh yes, yes please, someone really lovely, and smashing'). Exacerbated by the ownership of two heads (one of which was originally intended to speak French), a regular facet of Zaphod's story in all versions of *Hitchhiker* is his inability to grasp the motives for his own actions, and what his ultimate goal is – Adams felt his ship had to somehow be a money-making scam, perhaps he would fleece the rich American? The actual reason for Zaphod's nebulous motivation for anything he does is that Adams then decided that the three-armed egomaniac was an interstellar Beatles bootlegger, carrying a complete set of the band's recordings saved from the destroyed Earth, with which he planned to become rich beyond all imagination, selling the greatest music ever recorded to all life forms – this also explained his stop-off on our planet in the guise of a human called 'Phil'. When this Fab plan was scuppered (to avoid huge copyright complications if nothing else) the writer was left with a charismatic character still in search of a mission.

Increasingly, life at Stalbridge was proving a lonely experience for the gregarious youth – being in a friendless part of the world, he kept his little brother and sister up well past their bedtimes – and so the Islington sofa developed a more marked Douglas-shaped imprint as the year wore on, the indulgent household regularly being kept awake by their guest's voluble late-night typing – and having to clear spaces between his strewn effects and discarded shoes the size of almost serviceable canoes.

As Arthur's universe infinitely expanded, the second episode rapidly filled with event and character, Adams ransacking his experiences for inspiration. Sirius Cybernetics' smugly satisfied sighing doors and obsequious upholstery were a dream-like extrapolation of the seemingly sentient lifts that had plagued his late-night bodyguard duty, while Johnny Simpson was still in Adams' mind as the prototype for his groovy Galactic President. And then, of course, there was the Paranoid Android (who was not especially paranoid, but it sounded good), his new comically perverted take on the generic service mechanoid, who showed the full ramifications of mindless corporations like Sirius creating 'Genuine People Personalities' – unsubtly at this stage named 'Marshall'. The morose robot's unnatural melancholia clearly built on Douglas' view of Andrew, but also made good use of Canter's 'Life? Don't talk to me about life', and added shades of Woody Allen at his most hypochondriac in the machine's martyrdom to the diodes down his left-hand side. The clashing homespun chirpiness of Eddie the Computer's alternate personality, meanwhile, had its roots in Janet Thrift's matronly buoyancy.

The 1999 short film *George Lucas In Love* made sport of the idea of the *Star Wars* creator being entirely inspired by real life, like Shakespeare in the similarly named hit movie, but a similar take on the creation of *Hitchhiker* would need far less invention – in many ways Adams was surrounded by his inspirations. And yet, from Zaphod's preoccupation with cool to Ford's with partying, and above all, the flip side which was the Paranoid Android's defining depression, all could equally be seen as projections of the writer's own personality. 'There is a sense in which every character you write comes from you,' he said, 'because you only have your own experience to go from, and your own experience of other people is only *your* experience of other people, so every character actually comes from you. But I suppose I would have to own up and say Arthur Dent was the closest to me. One of the things that seems to be crucial about his character is everybody thinks he's a bit dim, but he's actually cleverer than you think he is. The reason he appears to be a little bit slow on the uptake is things genuinely are more complicated and more puzzling than most other people see ... To begin with, I only had a sense of "This is somebody to whom things are happening", and then gradually his tone of voice begins to assert itself.' Often, Adams would have problems identifying which character suited which half of a dialogue, but he was to learn, 'Any writer will tell you that after a while, if a character is working, it'll start telling you what it wants to do, rather than vice-versa. And any time you're sitting there trying to put words into a character's mouth, the character isn't working.' The new voices added to the cast, though only intended to be passing characters in an episodic odyssey, greased the gears of Douglas' imagination, and his confidence grew.

The remaining figure on the bridge of the *HoG*, of course, was Tricia McMillan – although the names Goophic or Smoodle were floated for a while, until 'Trillian' came to mind. 'Her name was a sort of feeble little twist, actually,' Adams admitted. 'When she is introduced to the audience you think, "Trillian – she must be an alien!" Then later you realise it was just a nickname, and that she was actually from Earth. It's a feeble surprise, isn't it?' As the one notable female role in the entire first series, it rather adds insult to injury that the character was originally planned to be just another guy: 'I thought it would be useful to have somebody else from Earth so that Arthur could have somebody that he could have some kind of normal conversation with, otherwise he is going to be totally lost, and the reader/viewer/listener/whoever will be utterly lost as well. There has to be someone who will understand when Arthur mentions something Earth-specific, therefore there must be someone else who survived Earth. But in fact that wasn't really necessary, because obviously Ford fulfils that function, so I'm afraid the main problem with Trillian is that the part wasn't really required … Everyone always asked me, "Why is Trillian such a cipher of a character?" It's because I never really knew anything about her.' She was of course immensely intelligent and intuitively correct – only travelling the Galaxy to avoid the dole queue like all the other qualified astrophysicists – and, in that obviously overcompensating way in which so many male authors draw their women, she was effortlessly superior to the more interestingly flawed men. Adams continued, 'I always find women very mysterious anyway – I never know what they want. And I always get very nervous about writing one as I think I'll do something terribly wrong. You read other male accounts of women and you think, "He's got them wrong!" and I feel very nervous about going into that area.' Douglas may have gone to a single-sex school, but he was hardly a clueless virgin, and strong female figures were prevalent in his life. Nonetheless, it would take a long time for his one heroine to develop any real depth, and her intro-duction in prose spoke volumes – 'She was slim, darkish, humanoid, with long waves of black hair, a full mouth, an odd little knob of a nose and ridiculously brown eyes' – as the 'fullness' of the men's features were not so lovingly detailed. The oblique admission that she was 'based on an old girlfriend' who kept gerbils spoke volumes about the object of Arthur's hopeless desire: 'beautiful, charming, devastatingly intelligent, everything I'd been saving myself up for …'

It's an amusing trait of science fiction that many fans are always looking for inconsistencies, and in just the second episode Douglas was creating problems for himself on that score. The coincidence of the ship picking up the guy who had been yearning for Trillian for six months and Zaphod's semi-cousin could be explained away with the IID, but that Beeblebrox instinctively knew Ford by the name he had mistakenly assumed on Earth – his birth name eventually being revealed as something akin to 'Ix' – caused many a scoff, and repeated nit-picking at conventions and author events eventually led to Adams sarcastically offering, 'It was very simple. Just before arriving he registered the new name officially at the Galactic Nomenclaturoid Office, where they had the technology to unpick his old name from the fabric of space/time and thread the new one in its place, so that to all intents and purposes his name always had been and always would be Ford Prefect. I included a footnote explaining this in the first book, but it was cut because it was so dull.' In the *Hitchhiker* Universe, there is a pleasingly mad explanation for absolutely everything, making any 'inconsistency' nothing of the sort – but fans still liked to make the creator sweat to provide it. In addition, throwaway jokes at this stage would lead to oceans of stress and technological quandaries years down the line, particularly in connection with the groovy President's extra arm and head: 'The two heads, three arms was a one-off radio gag. If I'd known the problems it was going to cause ... I've had lots of rationales for where the extra head and arms came from, and they all contradict each other. In one version I suggested that he had always had two heads, in the other I suggest he had it fitted. And I suggested somewhere he had the extra arm fitted to help with his ski-boxing.'

There is a certain level of disingenuousness in Douglas' claim to have written his serial entirely on the hoof, as every episode now foreshadowed the following week's development, and no sooner was the *HoG*'s crew in place than Eddie was announcing their arrival at the legendary planet of Magrathea. Adams had originally scoured a star atlas to try and establish his series with some kind of astronomical verisimilitude, but he soon relented and let his imagination have free rein: 'Magrathea ... essentially, it's not so much that it sounds "spacey", but it does sound like a real name ... You believe this is the name of a place. Oddly, a lot of real stars do have extremely silly names. A lot of people assumed that I invented the name "Betelgeuse".'

With sketch-writing still forefront in the writer's mind, it was a blessing that the Guide allowed him to break off on any tangent which tickled him, and the writer's starting point every day was to list the concepts which he would hopefully get round to before the day was through, in a scrapbook bearing the legend, in schoolboy block writing, 'The Hitchhiker's Guide to the Galaxy by Douglas Adams (with bits by John Lloyd)'. Having reached Magrathea, hoping to arrive at some kind of showdown, Douglas' frustration was unmistakable. Besides a suggestion that a couple of American tourists would show up somehow believing they were in Amsterdam, Adams had a whole host of half-developed, contradictory ideas, presaged by gloom:

What I'm about to say now is deeply shocking, so I've started a new book to say it in. Here is the deeply shocking thing I'm about

to say: SCRAP THAT PLOT ON ACCOUNT OF IT STINKS, AND
IT'S A MILLSTONE ROUND EVERYONE'S NECK, MOST OF ALL MY
OWN.

So where are we? At the beginning of another brand new day
and no further forward. Terrific.

Ford meets and discusses with Slartifarst the Failure ... He also
has Marvin with him.

The gerbils have an enormous bank account, I suppose. Lucky
bastards.

I suppose we ought to mention the fact that Zaphod is going
to be bootlegging Beatles, but it doesn't seem to be relevant at the
moment. It's a fucking red herring. Never mind.

Do they get the Girl from Rickmansworth? Well I don't bloody
know, do I? Let's wait till we get to that bit.

What do I need? A villain I think. Definitely a villain would
help.

Some silly details about previous planets which the Magratheans
have built. Meeting some more Magratheans - Garkbit and
Bwootlething.

Flying saucer - tea urn.

The Vogons have come to demolish Magrathea as well. Some
terrible comeuppance for having been so arrogant as to create
worlds. Complaint from someone who didn't like his world has been
waiting for them all this time ...

Zaphod has made a deal with the mice that they will find
the question and save all the money they were going to spend on
making the New Earth. He gets them drunk on PGGBs and they
eventually go off and do holographic chat shows. So our four get
paid a fat commission to go and find the question: 'Well it doesn't
have to be <u>the</u> question, but I'm sure we can think of a good one.'

So - with the promise of a lot of money they go off to the
Restaurant at the End of the Universe. Arthur can be commissioned
to do the question finding because he once went past Rickmansworth
on the A40.

The way of dealing with all notorious or undesirable people is to
put them on chat shows.

The celebrated philosophical skit starring the tragic Whale and the exasperated Bowl of Petunias was another concept which came directly from switching on the TV – in this case, an episode of the American cop show *Cannon*: 'Some guy who was probably one of the henchmen of the baddies got shot and his only function in the story was to get shot. I began to think, "Well, who is he, where did he come from?" He must have grown up and had a mother and a father who sent him off to school and were very proud of him, and suddenly he gets shot on the street and no one's even noticed. That sort of mindless, meaningless violence which nobody even notices ... I get almost unnaturally upset about it. I thought I'd write in a character whose sole function was to be killed for the sake of it ... I received quite a number of letters saying how cruel and callous this section was – letters I certainly would not have received had I simply mentioned the whale's fate incidentally and passed on. I probably wouldn't have received them if it had been a human either.'

On Magrathea, Adams could not help being inspired by *Dimension of Miracles* when he decided to introduce a disappointingly commercial Creator of Earth, but he was after all writing for an entirely different medium, and besides, Slartibartfast (originally pencilled in as 'Maviviv') was an entirely unique planet-maker. 'I thought that this character should be a dignified, elderly man, weighed down with the burden of a secret sorrow. I wondered what that sorrow should be, and thought perhaps he might be sad about his name. So I decided to give him a name that anybody would be sad to have. I wanted it to sound as gross as I possibly could, while still being broadcastable. So I started with something clearly unbroadcastable, "Phartiphukborlz", and simply played around with the syllables until I arrived at something which sounded that rude, but was almost, but not quite, entirely inoffensive.' Douglas would repeat this trick with the Deep Thought programmers Lunkwill and Fook. Famously, the other reason for the outrageous name was a private joke at the expense of the poor producer's secretary who was forced to painstakingly type it out several times in the script despite the mysterious figure's admission to Arthur, 'My name is not important.'

Adams and his friends had often tired the moon drunkenly debating the Ultimate Questions of 'Life, the Universe and Everything', small talk be damned, so the overtly philosophical theme of Arthur's journey was understandable, particularly since the writer was still actively concerned with his own emotional rehabilitation:

ARTHUR   You know, all this explains a lot of things. All through my life I've had this strange unaccountable feeling that something was going on in the world, something big, even sinister, and no one would tell me what it was.

SLARTY   No, that's just perfectly normal paranoia. Everyone in the Universe has that.

ARTHUR   Well ... perhaps that means that somewhere ... outside the Universe ...

SLARTY   Maybe. Who cares? Perhaps I'm old and tired, but I always think that the chances of finding out what is really going on are so absurdly remote that the only thing to do is say hang the sense of it and just keep yourself occupied. Look at me - I design coastlines. I got an award for Norway. Where's the sense in that? None that I've been able to make out. I've been doing fjords all my life ... for a fleeting moment they become fashionable and I get a major award ... What does it matter? Science has achieved some wonderful things, of course, but I'd far rather be happy than right any day.

ARTHUR   And are you?

SLARTY   No. That's where it all falls down, of course.

ARTHUR   Pity, it sounded like quite a good lifestyle otherwise ... I seem to be having this tremendous difficulty with my lifestyle ...

Further ideas not to make the grade concerned what happened to the Magrathean after his dismissal by the mice:

Slartibartfast coming to the end of his life, sad, disillusioned, worried about whether fjords were just easy self-indulgence, falls under the influence of a cultish sect who preach that man cannot allow himself the luxury of action, of impingement on matter, he must leave the Universe the way he found it. He is therefore revisiting all the worlds he created whilst he was a Magrathean engineer, being terribly nice, being feted because he's such a lovely old bloke, and then quietly destroying them and going on his way, not sorrowfully or triumphantly or anything, just quietly and surely. He is serene to have discovered something he can sink his whole being in. As he is dying he discovers that the cult leader was a fraud and a charlatan. No one knows how he reacted to this knowledge because he died soon afterwards.

And a possible story arc that would draw the home of the Guide itself into an apparently profitable terrorist atrocity:

The *Hitch Hiker's Guide to the Galaxy* is the first publishing concern ever to be hit by an interstellar ballistic attack. Subsequently one or two of their rivals such as 'The Crab Nebula on Twenty Grutfoos a Day' or 'The Hrung Varquethzon Hypercluster on the Cheap' and 'Where to Get Laid in Antares' did suffer minor guerrilla raids within the next few weeks, but most of these were perfunctory affairs, almost certainly put-up jobs arranged by the companies themselves in an attempt to undercut the massive publicity kudos that the Hitch Hiker company had gained from this totally bizarre and inexplicable attack.

Then there was the 'Wisheteria' – a concept which led on the one hand to the Nutrimatic machine, and also, eventually, the Dish of the Day confrontation at Milliways:

Ideas to be jotted down before I go and forget them.
WISHETERIA. They are waiting for a lift somewhere and go into the wisheteria, the ultimate in self-service cafes - you get the menu, and wish very hard for whatever it is you want which then materialises in front of you, and at the same moment, money dematerialises in your pocket. It gets round trades description problems because who's to say you didn't get exactly what you wished for?
'I didn't wish for that! I didn't wish for it to be all greasy!'
'I'll have main wish of Vegan Rhino cutlet with a side wish of ...'
'Look buster, you wanna eat me, you eat me, you don't wanna eat me you get the hell out of here and let me lie in this grease for a while. I haven't felt this good since I was a foetus.'
'I'm not staying for this! I'm not going to have my food talking back at me'

'You've got a lot to learn about Vegan cuisine. So long schmuck'
'Look shut up you cutlet, or I'll stab you with this fork'
FX STABS IT
'Ooooorrrr, that feels great'
'Look, can we get out of here, I want to be sick'
'You shouldn't say things like that in a Wisheteria'
'Now he tells me ... Yeeuulgggghhhh ...'

Despite the ideas left on the wayside, after a sluggish start, Douglas always remembered these first four episodes zooming off his typewriter. Of course, it was never that simple – the ink, ribbons and paper he was working with obviously did not allow him to cut, flesh out or re-edit as word processors would subsequently allow, and he still had to regularly break off to return to *The Pirate Planet*, which was due for delivery in instalments, and so by the time the *Hitchhiker* recordings came round in November, there was still much work to be done. He had in mind a good reason for Slartibartfast's creation of the Earth, and knew it involved Trillian's gerbils (subsequently altered to mice by the show's incoming producer) but with production under way, he would just have to perfect as he went along. Worrying news for Geoffrey Perkins.

Come In, Perkins!

Simon Brett had specifically nominated his protégé Perkins when leaving the Corporation, rescuing him from wasting his comic talents on the shipping industry, but although he was about to take the reins of panel-game spoof *ISIHAC* (acting as nursemaid to the popular game Mornington Crescent), Geoffrey was still the most junior producer in the department, and had to pitch for the job of continuing Brett's work on *Hitchhiker*. Once successful, the softly spoken, bashful-seeming young Turk took Douglas for a Greek meal and openly admitted that he had no idea what he was doing, but thankfully, the writer came clean that he was equally at a loss, making it up as he went along, and so they were perfectly suited. A more experienced producer would almost certainly have minimised any writer's interference, but as everybody at the department was aware, this was no ordinary comedy series.

Further changes in personnel were necessitated by the loss of Paddy Kingsland to children's programming, but Dick Mills and Harry Parker were to provide Radiophonic backup at the BBC's studios – a former ice rink in Maida Vale – along with legendary sound engineer Alick Hale-Monro and his 'crack team of hardened drinkers' in the back room, plus production secretary Anne Ling, studio manager Colin Duff, and the trusty Lisa Braun. The chief concern, however, was casting the new characters. Adams and Simon Jones had of course already worked with Mark Wing-Davey – he presumed they were aware of his lingering reputation for long-haired sartorial eccentricity at Cambridge, which might have helped him to the part of an intergalactic show-off – but it was his turn as a disreputable media trendy in the Cambridge-based TV drama *The Glittering Prizes* which inspired Adams to nominate him for Beeblebrox. As Peter Jones was an old friend of his family, Mark asked his advice and was inspired to sign up with the glowing referral 'It's all right, I suppose.' Zaphod's paramour was to be played by budding voice actor Susan Sheridan, with the more seasoned audio thespian David Tate playing Eddie and a whole host of minor roles every week, Adams dubbing him the backbone of the show: 'I like the Eddie bits. But one of my favourite parts of the whole thing is the Galactic News report: "A big hello to all intelligent life forms everywhere. And to everyone else out there, the secret is to bang the rocks together, guys!"' Eddie was of course the first of many computers to be ridiculed by Adams, but 1977 also saw his first step towards a change of heart when it came to machines he initially saw only as trumped-up calculators: 'I remember the first time I ever saw a personal computer,' he said. 'It was at Lasky's, on the Tottenham Court Road, and it was called a Commodore PET. It was quite a large pyramid shape, with a screen at the top about the size of a chocolate bar. I prowled around it for a while, fascinated. But it was no good. I couldn't for the life of me see any way in which a computer could be of any use in the life or work of a writer. However, I did feel the first tiniest inklings of a feeling that would go on to give a whole new meaning to the words "disposable income".'

Stephen Moore was just as keen as Tate to muck in with silly voices, but his identification with Marvin (renamed at Perkins' insistence, to avoid the military connotations of 'Marshall') would be a cornerstone of a long and successful career. Another player poached from *Rock Follies*, the forty-year-old Londoner's performance as a morose boyfriend in that show was what caught the producer's eye, but as the show wore on, his range expanded to include The Man In The Shack and of course, that unfortunate Whale. The last of the primary roles was filled by veteran sitcom player

Richard Vernon as Slartibartfast, who was well known for his bluff and/or dreamy aristocratic characterisations (he would personify Blandings Castle's Lord Emsworth on radio in the 1980s), but Vernon was presumably primarily exciting casting for Douglas due to his cameo as the old square on the train in The Beatles' *A Hard Day's Night*.

It would be fair to say that the cast were assembled at the Paris studio for the first recording of the series on 23rd November, but the audio effects often required most actors' contributions to be recorded separately for precise sonic tinkering, in a technique defined by Wing-Davey as 'cupboard acting' – Moore insisted that he for one didn't get to meet his co-performers for several hours, having been stuffed into a closet moaning as Marvin for much of the day. The flaw in this practice was underlined in the second series, when the beloved elderly actor Richard Goolden was left in his cupboard for hours, too polite to request his freedom, after completing his part as Zaphod's great-grandfather. A further unusual move for a Radio 4 comedy was the movie-style decision to record scenes out of sync, making the most of whatever talent was on hand at the time. Sheridan recalls withdrawing to the BBC Club at lunchtime with Peter Jones, both agreeing that they didn't understand a word of what they were performing, but that there was clearly something special about it …

The creation of the first series of *Hitchhiker*, nobody knowing precisely what they were doing and where they were heading, but everyone committed to working their brains to the nub to get it right, was one of the most electric periods of Adams' life, even if it was 'nerve-racking': 'Were we doing something extraordinary, or were we simply going mad? It was mostly very hard to tell. Because the BBC Light Entertainment Department had simply never attempted anything like this before, we were largely having to invent the process by which we worked as we went along … I can remember sitting in the subterranean studio auditioning the sound of a whale hitting the ground at 300 miles an hour for hours on end, just trying to find ways of tweaking the sound. After hours of that, day after day, you do begin to doubt your sanity. Of course, you have no idea if anybody's going to listen to this stuff, but there was a real sense that nobody had done this before. And that was great; there's a great charge that comes with that.' Slightly disconcertingly, Moore's performance as the existentially racked sea mammal was mysteriously wiped and re-recorded twice before it made it to air – while Perkins noted how fitting it was that the tape loop for Marvin's lumbering mechanical walk was always lying around on the floor, getting stuck to the bottom of people's shoes. Today an entire series of *Hitchhiker* could be put together with a modest folder of audio files – in 1977, it was a case of analogue experimentation not much more technologically advanced than the tape-loop breakthroughs of The Beatles' 'Tomorrow Never Knows' over a decade previously. Hours were spent at Maida Vale just finding out what all the gadgetry could do, and synthesised effects were at first added via a rudimentary muzak machine, the ARP Odyssey. As the recordings rapidly spun off-schedule, being a week behind in no time, Perkins had to play careful political games to ensure maximum studio time with the minimum of overtime payment (*Hitchhiker* often posed as other programmes to poach just a few hours), but luckily, when ordered to stop work by studio managers, the crew were so immersed in creating Adams' world that they carried on working for free. Perfectionism against the clock is rarely conducive to a relaxed workplace, and Adams' habit of retyping entire pages because of a misplaced semicolon did not help – nor did his habit of inserting hugely ambitious directions into the script, such as the IID effect:

```
FX      THIS IS REALLY A WILD FLURRY OF SOUND WHICH QUICKLY
        DIES AWAY INTO THE BACKGROUND, AS THE DIALOGUE BEGINS.
        SOON AFTERWARDS A SLOW QUIET WASH OF SOUND BUILDS UP
        BEHIND THE VOICES, PARTLY REFLECTING WHAT THEY SAY
        THEY CAN SEE AROUND THEM, BUT ALSO WITH MANY RANDOM
        ELEMENTS WITH AN UNREAL DREAMLIKE QUALITY, NOT UNLIKE
        PARTS OF REVOLUTION NO. 9 FROM THE BEATLES' WHITE ALBUM.
        ALL THE SOUNDS CHANGE IMPERCEPTIBLY BEFORE IT'S REALLY
        POSSIBLE TO HEAR EXACTLY WHAT THEY ARE, SO FOR INSTANCE
        THE SOUND OF THE WASHING OF SEA WAVES COULD ALMOST BE
        ASTHMATIC BREATHING INSTEAD, AND THE SOUND OF TRAFFIC
        IN THE STREET COULD ALMOST BE GALLOPING HOOVES BUT
        ISN'T

(NB: It's worth spending a little time getting the tape right
because it will be useful on occasions in the future.)
```

The team dutifully spent an entire day on just this one effect – and, of course, it was never used again. Such manifest experimentation had to result in a certain number of missed targets, such as Marvin's early attempts to hum 'Shine On, You Crazy Diamond', 'Rock & Roll Music' and 'Also Sprach Zarathustra' which never quite came across on broadcast, and caused rights issues with Pink Floyd when it came to commercial releases – despite Douglas' eventual personal friendships with most of the band (albeit not with Roger Waters, who wrote the song).

As 1978 drew nearer, the writer needed a more permanent base in the capital, and serendipitously Jon Canter was compelled to leave Arlington Avenue as the Brocks were expecting their first child, and needed more space – a lot more space, with Douglas gone from their sofa. Adams would not forget their hospitality, however, not just dedicating his first book to the household, but also immortalising their phone number as the rate of Improbability at which Arthur and Ford had been saved by the *Heart of Gold*: 2267709 (albeit the probability was rapidly changed for every iteration following, after bored fans began calling the number asking for Marvin). One year on from giving Douglas the confidence to return to writing, Jon found a small affordable flat on Kingsdown Road, N19, and the pair took up residence in January. It was far too small for two such sizeable youths – they had to take it in turns to squeeze into the kitchen – and the house was less than a bundle of laughs, the two regularly feeling imprisoned for fear of running into creepy neighbours, but it was to be an otherwise memorably happy period for them both – and particularly for Douglas, once his ambitious creation was finally revealed to the world.

The first outside feedback – and the most important, for Douglas – came when the opening episodes were completed, and he asked Michael Palin and Terry Jones to stop by and give them a listen. Geoffrey and particularly Douglas watched the comic heroes with obsessive attention to every nuance of amusement, and would have kept them captive for hours if they hadn't protested that they had a dinner date. Finally allowed to go free, Palin and Jones raised worried eyebrows at each other, fearing that while what they heard 'wasn't that bad', the Python protégé might be headed up a blind alley.

What Do You Get If You Multiply Six By Nine?

Thanks to the lapsed schedule, the final recordings of the series were looming ever closer, with the scripts still to be written, triggering the most controversial personnel development of all: 'My writing muscles were so tired that even though I had a rough idea of what was supposed to be happening in the last two episodes, I had quite simply run out of words. Since John Lloyd nearly always beat me at Scrabble I reckoned he must know lots more words than me and asked him if he would collaborate with me on the last couple of scripts. "Prehensile", "anaconda" and "ningi" are just three of the thousands of words I would never have thought of myself.' The change in living arrangements hadn't weakened the friendship between John and Douglas at all, and they could often be found playing snooker together until 5 a.m. in one of London's numerous drinking clubs, in those days of strict licensing laws. Accompanied by studio manager (and later Perkins' wife) Lisa Braun and Helen Rhys Jones, they were also among the first audiences in the UK to be present for the birth of a whole new era of sci-fi mania, when *Star Wars* previewed at the end of 1977. When subsequently contacting producers for work, Adams was quickly forced to clarify: 'The show has some terrible revelations to make about the origins and purpose of the human race, but is otherwise ... well, a comedy, I suppose. Everyone's going to say of course that we're jumping on the *Star Wars* bandwagon, so I would just like to put in a small plea of mitigation – I'd been hawking my idea of sci-fi comedy for years and only managed to sell it six months ago.'

Lloyd's devotion to sci-fi was greater than his occasional writing partner's, and for a while he had been meticulously constructing his own humorous space novel, *Gigax* – named partly with reference to the creator of 'Dungeons & Dragons', Gary Gygax, but in Lloyd's universe, fittingly for the future creator of *QI*, the word signified the entire scope of human understanding, microcosm to macrocosm – not too dissimilar to the Guide itself. John generously showered Douglas with pages of notes and rough drafts, and gave him carte blanche to plunder what he wanted to meet his deadlines.

The two of them had developed a new writing regime, with John at the keyboard while Douglas specialised in pacing up and down, in a garage attached to the posh Knightsbridge home of their friend Alex Catto, where the industrious Radio 4 producer was laying his head. Adams had already written nearly all of the fourth episode, which would reveal the meaning of Life, the Universe and Everything – but some details were open to discussion. 'There's a story on one Procol Harum track of someone going off to find enlightenment and there's a bathetic answer,' Douglas said. 'So it occurred to me that you take the question and build it and build it and build it and the answer is a number – completely banal. It should be a number of no significance, part of the joke.' Thus was the ten-million-year research programme concerning the porn-referencing computer Deep Thought conceived by Douglas – but the question of precisely when and how the ultimately disappointing Ultimate Answer, 42, was arrived at, is one which would take longer to finally settle. We already know that the number was agreed upon as comedically perfect by the Pythons, and Adams had followed their lead a few times here and there, with the Paranoid Society's 42nd meeting and the sketch commentary at 42 Logical Positivism Avenue, but the insertion of the number at such a critical juncture in the *Hitchhiker* story was not arrived at without much deliberation, with John central to the proceedings, just as he would go on to aid *Blackadder* to such linguistic perfection with his endless pedantic 'plumpening' of scripts, abetted by the cast. Griff is on record as saying that he was in the vicinity when the crucial punchline was set in stone, and the debate was lively, but everyone was happy with the multiple of seven on which they finally agreed.

It was a relatively minor decision which would plague Adams for the rest of his life, with endless conspiracy theories put forward concerning the number's significance, which he had to endlessly bat away: 'If you're a comedy writer working in numbers you use a number that's funny, like 17¾ or whatever. But I thought to myself that, if the major joke is the answer to Life, the Universe and Everything and it turns out to be a number, that has got to be a strong joke ... What is the most ordinary, workaday number you can find? I don't want fractions on the end of it. I don't even want it to be a prime number. And I guess it mustn't even be an odd number. There is something slightly more reassuring about even numbers. So I just wanted an ordinary, workaday number, and chose 42. It's an unfrightening number. It's a number you could take home and show to your parents.'

You could fill a book with all the lunacy written about this two-digit number, 101010 in binary – and at least one person has. In ancient Egypt, the fate of the dead was supposed to be decided by 42 demons, there's a 42-armed Hindu god, 42 is sacred in Tibet, there are 42 generations from Abraham to

Jesus, and multiplying six by nine does equal 42 – in base thirteen, to which Adams indignantly responded, 'I may be a sad case but I don't write jokes in base thirteen!' Peter Gill shared one of those pleasing and meaningless *Hitchhiker* coincidences in his book *42* when he noted that the relevant page in Ken Welsh's original European guidebook suggested to Australians that the UK 'offers the solution to the most puzzling question of all: where did our families come from? Plenty of people find the answer a little disappointing.' There was a degree of excitement when some scientists claimed that the number was the value of an essential scientific constant determining the age of the Universe – but they soon found that it wasn't quite so constant. In fact, the greatest answer to 'Why 42?' was probably given by Terry Jones on an exhausted Douglas' behalf when a foolish journalist brought it up yet again at a press junket, to general sighs – 'Shall I take this one, Douglas? IT'S JUST A FUCKING FUNNY NUMBER! NEXT QUESTION!'

The majestic Deep Thought sequence was to prove so popular that it formed the centrepiece of many an iteration of *Hitchhiker*, but in the original radio series it was just one mad step on Arthur's journey, and shortly after his easy escape from the mice, and the showdown with sensitive cops Shooty and Bang-Bang (surely also inspired by the generic henchmen in *Cannon*), episode five, with Lloyd's help, took the *HoG* crew to the Restaurant at the End of the Universe.

The art of dining is as ubiquitous a theme in *Hitchhiker* as wealth, philosophy, tea and bureaucracy, and the final episode of the series would kick off accordingly:

```
The History of every major Galactic civilization has gone
through three distinct and recognizable phases - those of
survival, inquiry and sophistication, otherwise known as the
How, Why and Where phases. For instance the first phase is
characterized by the question "How can we eat?", the second by
the question "Why do we eat?" and the third by the question
"Where shall we have lunch?"
```

Therefore it was inevitable that the ultimate place to 'do' lunch would figure somewhere. In this case, the inspiration came yet again from Procol Harum: 'Whenever I'm writing, I tend to have music on in the background, and on this particular occasion I had "Grand Hotel" on the record player.

This song always used to interest me because while Keith Reid's lyrics were all about this sort of beautiful hotel – the silver, the chandeliers, all those kinds of things – suddenly in the middle of the song there was this huge orchestral climax that came out of nowhere and didn't seem to be about anything. I kept wondering what was this huge thing happening in the background? And I eventually thought, "It sounds as if there ought to be some sort of floor show going on. Something huge and extraordinary, like, well, like the end of the Universe ..."' The idea had originally been to perform the sequence to sync with the track, but this was one of those ideas that Geoffrey had to veto in the studio. In fact, although the writer would of course be the oracle for any decision, halfway through the recording schedule Perkins did have to diplomatically order Adams out of the editing booth, due to his unrealistic ambitions and desire to give every other scene one more go, long after the perfect take was down on tape and their time was up. 'Geoffrey was a very crucial and central part of it,' Adams told Neil Gaiman. 'When I was writing the script, he was the person I would go and argue with about what I was going to have in it and what I wasn't. I'd do the script and he'd say, "This bit's good and that bit's tat." He'd come up with casting suggestions. And he'd come up with his own ideas about what to do with bits that weren't working. Like throw them out. Or suggestions about how I could rewrite. I'd be guided by him, or by the outcome of the argument. When we were in production I'd be there, but at that point it was very much a producer's show. The producer gives instructions to the actors, and generally if you have anything you want to say, or suggestions or disagreements or points you want to make, then you'd say it to Geoffrey, and he'd decide whether or not to ignore it. Very rarely do you as a writer actually start giving instructions to the actors; it's protocol. To be honest, I'd sometimes step over it, but you can't have more than one person in charge. When I wrote the script I was in charge, but when it was made, Geoffrey was in charge, and the final decisions were his, right or wrong.'

The *HoG* crew's visit to Milliways was far simpler on radio – the infamous 'Dish of the Day' sketch was to be written specially for the third theatrical adaptation, and even its eventual spot was heavily cut for time, losing the following:

ARTHUR   Do you do Take-Aways?

GARKBIT   Ah ha, no sir, here at Milliways we only serve the
very finest in Ultracuisine.

ZAPHOD   (With disgust) Ultracuisine? Don't give me head pains.
Look at this ... Algolian Zylbatburger smothered in a
hint of Vulcan Dodo spit.

GARKBIT   Saliva, sir, saliva. The salivary gland of the Vulcan
UltraDodo is a delicacy much sought after.

ZAPHOD   Not by me.

From Arthur and Co.'s explosive arrival to the end of all existence itself (realised on radio with a gurgle recorded in the Maida Vale toilets), Milliways was another hugely successful sequence, not least due to the performance of radio legend Roy Hudd as the compère, which compelled the funnyman to busk sci-fi gobbledegook until he was literally rolling on the floor begging to stop.

Adams knew that he wanted to end the series with his old B-Ark plot recycled from both Ringo's show and the failed *Doctor Who* pitch, but it was how his heroes got from one scenario to another which defeated him, with the clock ticking away. This was where Lloyd stepped up to the plate, not just writing some celebrated Guide extracts with indistinguishable style (a crucial producer's skill that he would repeat in *Blackadder*, creating the third series' beloved 'rotten borough' scene), but introducing the Haggunenons – an alien race with such impatient chromosomes they were in a constant state of chameleonic evolution, and were very bad news for any species which wasn't. It was a brilliant idea straight out of *Gigax*, and of course any slight towards Douglas' creation within the dialogue on their introduction was purely affectionate:

ARTHUR   What was the name the second-in-command said?
Haggunenon. Why don't we look it up in the book?

TRILLIAN   What book?

FORD   The Hitchhiker's Guide to the Galaxy.

ZAPHOD   Oh, that hack rag.

As Adams' odyssey was a series of loosely linked concepts, this is the one section which has always been clearly a Lloyd creation, and though the attack from the shape-shifting villains (repayment for Zaphod and Co. stealing their Admiral's ship in the Milliways car park) allowed Douglas to separate his original duo from the new characters and move on to the telephone-sanitiser-baiting, the stress of getting the scripts in the cast's hands on time was perhaps beginning to show in the facetiously unhelpful FX directions, once Zaphod, Trillian and Marvin are eaten by a Haggunenon posing as a Bug-Blatter Beast:

```
FX         HUGE ARM SWEEPS DOWN AND PICKS THEM UP. THE
           MONSTER ROLLS HIS EYES WHICH TURN RED, GREEN, THEN
           A SORT OF MAUVY PINK. IT RUNS ITS TONGUE AROUND ITS
           LIPS, BLINKS A COUPLE OF TIMES AND THEN MENTALLY
           REGISTERS THAT IT HAS JUST REMEMBERED WHAT 10
           ACROSS IN THE GALACTIC TIMES CROSSWORD WAS TODAY,
           MAKES A MENTAL NOTE TO WRITE IT IN WHEN IT'S NEXT
           GOT A COUPLE OF MINUTES
CAST       (Shouts, etc. ...)
MARVIN     (Resigned) Ouch ... Oh dear, oh dear ... My arm's come
           off.
```

With Arthur and Ford replacing the Beatles drummer and his robot friend, the B-Ark business provided a relatively easy march towards some kind of conclusion, with Lloyd and Adams jointly developing the concept to leave the Earthman and Betelgeucian stranded on prehistoric Earth – including an irresistible Scrabble reference. In hindsight, the hiring of Sir David Jason to play the bath-bound Captain seems impressive, but at that stage he was a regular voice on Radio 4, a good friend of David Hatch with his own show, *The Jason Explanation*, and regular appearances on *Week Ending* (on which he played politician David Owen, who, oddly coincidentally, was also usually found in the bath). This was five years before he accepted the role of Delboy Trotter in *Only Fools and Horses* which would make him a household name – and also coincidentally, the original choice for that role, Jim Broadbent, had already recorded his own contributions to *Hitchhiker*, as Vroomfondel and Shooty.

The B-Ark's crash-landing on Earth allowed the writers to develop the attacks on its cargo of shallow middlemen – who, of course, turn out to be the progenitors of mankind – and bring the otherwise relentlessly facetious series to a close with a rather unexpected sense of sincere wonder at our beautiful planet, as Louis Armstrong's 'What A Wonderful World' reached a crescendo. Douglas held forth to the production team at length on the need to convey in sound a kind of epic cinematic pull-back from Ford and Arthur as they make their way in the new world. Geoffrey Perkins listened attentively, and then simply achieved the desired effect by pushing the fader down slowly. One year on from the original commission, the series was complete.

Life's Bad Enough As It Is Without Wanting To Invent More Of It

It was a dark and not notably stormy night when *The Hitchhiker's Guide To The Galaxy* was finally unleashed upon the British public, on BBC Radio 4 at 10.30 p.m., Wednesday, 8th March 1978. As Arthur Dent lay down in the mud for the very first time, the schedules of other radio stations and the three available TV channels in the UK were almost devoid of interesting competition, but thanks to what he described as 'a huge blaze of no publicity at all', Adams' estimation of the listening audience was cynical: 'Bats heard it. The odd dog barked.' Despite his misgivings, he was his usual puppyish self when he happened to run into Simon Brett two days later, and wondered whether there had been any good reviews? Brett had to laugh, as the review coverage of any mid-week Radio 4 debut was as good as zero, but he was to be proved wrong – the unique nature of *Hitchhiker* had already caught the ears of a couple of radio critics for the Sunday papers, and to Adams' delight, they were cautiously approving, with *The Telegraph* noting that Adams' 'previous experience seems to indicate a talent for the surreal', and the even more discerning *Observer* critic commenting that the programme 'began promisingly with that difficult trick, a lunatic plot used with conviction ... This just might be the most original radio comedy show for years.'

Despite this auspicious criticism, the audience figures that Perkins was receiving for each episode were about as close to 0.0 as could be imagined, and the proud cast and crew could be forgiven for presuming they had made a brilliant failure. Famously, the tide didn't turn until the producer noted what was happening in the post room. In addition to lending his production expertise for *Hitchhiker*'s soundscape, and showing his skill with casting and comic direction, Geoffrey was the one who took charge of the regular silly announcements for announcer John Marsh to intone after the closing credits, such as 'And that programme will be repeated through a time warp on the BBC Home Service in 1951', or 'Zaphod Beeblebrox is now appearing in *No Sex Please, We're Amoeboid Zingat-Ularians* at the Brantersvogon Starhouse'. One week's announcement that listeners could send off for their own 'Hitchhiker's Guide' by writing to 'Megadodo House, Megadodo Publications, Ursa Minor' triggered a flurry of cheeky requests, which reached Perkins via well-informed postal employees, who had the nous to write 'Try BBC!' on the envelopes. The ratings for that first run remained minimal, and yet Perkins estimated that by the fourth week they were receiving an average of twenty letters a day from fans hooked on Arthur Dent's adventures – perhaps the very definition of a 'cult hit'.

Hitchhiker was picked up by Radio 4's showcase programme *Pick of the Week*, and once even the sceptical BBC bosses had realised the devotion of the show's fans, it was scheduled for an instant repeat two weeks after the last episode had been broadcast, and then again six months later – a bizarre distinction for any UK radio comedy. However, glorious though all this kudos unquestionably was for Douglas' bruised but ebullient ego, none of it provided any immediate financial benefit for a man still struggling to slice away at a monstrous overdraft. David Hatch's offer, therefore, for Adams to sign up for a full-time job as a producer in BBC Radio LE, alongside John, Geoffrey, Jimmy and Griff, was something of a no-brainer from Douglas' point of view – and a total non-brainer in the views of his friends and colleagues.

John Lloyd and Geoffrey Perkins would become two of the greatest comedy producers in the history of British entertainment, and both were in accord that nobody was less suited to the producer's role than their curious giant friend. Even with the infamous entry-level job of producing *Week Ending* he risked a walk-out from the amicable cast with his heavy-handed directions – 'Could you try that line a bit more like John Cleese would do it?' – and his irritating habit of keeping his finger down on the control room talkback button so the offended cast couldn't actually reply to any of his outlandish requests. On that occasion Perkins had to step in and soothe the situation, and it wasn't surprising that Adams only lasted five weeks, in between Rhys Jones' tenures. He was delighted to be dismissive: 'Well, everybody's produced *Week Ending* – I mean *everybody* has. The Queen hasn't produced *Week Ending*, I know that. Not that she hasn't been asked, of course, but she was busy.'

Besides this satirical sideshow, Douglas was inevitably a very different employee from the industrious Lloyd and Perkins. John asked him to set the odd question for his new topical panel game *The News Quiz*, plus a few bits for *The News Huddlines*, there was a sketch about Harrods written for radio show *Not Now, I'm Listening,* and to his disdain he was sent out to interview old-school entertainers like Des O'Connor and Max Bygraves for a one-off documentary about practical jokes. In fact, the greatest benefit of the job was that Lloyd was in the neighbouring office at the BBC's LE building round the back of Broadcasting House, so the two of them could happily moonlight on their own projects when nobody was looking.

Their most fondly recalled job was a children's cartoon which in its own way chimed with elements of many of Douglas' interests, particularly *Doctor Who* and ecology, and had the extra benefit of dropping right into their lap. The British creator of *Doctor Snuggles*, Jeffrey O'Kelly, had tuned in to *Hitchhiker*, and was so impressed by the ingenuity in the air that the writers were tracked down and specifically asked by him to come up with some new adventures for his cuddly hero. John and Douglas claimed that they were won over by the amusing surnames of the Dutch production team – Visch, Oops, and Plinck – but the promise of £500 per script may also have inspired the two friends to find time in their busy days at the BBC to script a couple of episodes, allowing animation to give their imaginations carte blanche. In *The Remarkable Fidgety River*, the cuddly tea-obsessed philanthropist (voiced by Peter Jones' old partner in improv, Peter Ustinov) and his friends Dennis the Badger and Nobby Mouse try to convince a paranoid waterway to flow into the sea, but find out that huge chunks of the ocean are missing. A trip out into the show's smiley colourful galaxy in his Heath Robinson-esque spaceship the *Dreamy Boom Boom* leads the gang to a distant water planet inhabited by aliens called 'Sloppies':

SNUGGLES	(V/O) We easily recognised the Grand Master of the Water Planet.
MASTER	Hullo! What can we do for you?
SNUGGLES	Good afternoon, I am Doctor Snuggles from Earth. Er, have you been taking water from our seas?
MASTER	This water, you mean?
SNUGGLES	That looks like it, yes …

```
MASTER        (Indicating litter and old tyres in the chunks of
              sea.) We just thought it was rubbish, you see! You
              don't seem to treat it very well, but if you want it
              you must have it back, we've got plenty more.
SNUGGLES      Thank you, we do need it rather badly, and I
              promise to see that it's better treated in the
              future.
```

A second episode, *The Great Disappearing Mystery*, saw the friends set off in the Doctor's 'Get Lost Machine' to a planet entirely ruled by birds – this concept would be revisited, in time. The cartoon was practically a 'Junior *Hitchhiker*', and a lot of fun, but at the time it was far from a priority for John and Douglas, as they were about to become published novelists.

I Better Warn You, I'm In A Meeeean Mood!

'A publisher came and asked me to write a book, which is a very good way of breaking into publishing,' Adams quipped. 'I thought it was an enormous opportunity because obviously most people have a horrendous amount of difficulty writing a novel on spec and then trying to get anybody interested in it. And I knew that I suddenly had a chance to pole-vault through all of that.' Like so much else in his career, though, this airiness belied the painful genesis of *Hitchhiker* on the page.

After the relief of getting the first series to the finish line, Douglas was happy to assure John that they would embark on the second series together, fifty-fifty – and the same would apply to the novel adaptation which had already been suggested to them. This offer certainly never came from the myopic BBC Enterprises, who pooh-poohed Geoffrey's polite query about *Hitchhiker* albums or books with a curt insistence that radio spin-offs did not sell. A number of other publishers had more sense, but Pan Books was to come out the winner, thanks to Adams' new friendship with the similarly sizeable publisher Nick Webb, who had been alerted to the radio show by his girlfriend's kid brother, and quickly decided that it would work at least equally well on the page. He took Lloyd and Adams for a drink that May and snapped up the rights to a prose adaptation credited equally to the pair, and – despite a slight frostiness when Webb had to justify spending £3,000 on a radio comedy that nobody at Pan had heard of to his editorial director Sonny Mehta – all was cordiality and excitement. After all their years of trying to convince people that comedy sci-fi was a winner, the two happy geeks were at last under contract to write their own book.

Then, however, Douglas had pause to reflect. *Hitchhiker* was the one extended fiction that he had created from scratch, and it was only the demands of *Who* that prevented him finishing it on his own. John might have started his own novel, but where was the sense in having him adapt Douglas' solo work in that way? Writing with his best friend had given Douglas great confidence, but his mind was made up – he could do the novel on his own, and he should, and he would. He must have known, however, that John would be less than ecstatic at the idea, so he felt the best way – certainly the less emotionally fraught way, for his English sensibility – was to explain his decision in writing, getting it totally straight. John would understand. Although he was just in the next office at the BBC, Douglas wrote the letter, and popped it in the BBC's internal mail. He was now a solo novelist. And once again, he had to take poor Arthur back to Earth, and lie him back down in the mud for his nightmare to begin afresh, in prose form.

Nobody could blame Lloyd for his heartbroken reaction – he had been the one with ambitions to write a comedy sci-fi novel, and just on a practical level, his overdraft was such that his half of the advance would have been a huge relief. But of course, it was the cold way Douglas did it which stung the most, and although John simmered in isolation for a couple of days, inevitably the pair's paths met. John made it very clear that he wasn't prepared to be treated like an 'emotional football' any more, to which Adams' defensive reply was that he should get himself an agent. This was quickly done, but when Lloyd's new agent assured him that he could manage to bag a cut of all *Hitchhiker* earnings in perpetuity, Adams was appalled, and tracked down Lloyd to emotionally insist that he meant he should get an agent to find his own book deal, not to get litigious about the existing one. However, even in his anger John had to protest that he only wanted his original share of the advance, which he was glad to receive. Ultimately, the setback was the making of Lloyd – at around this period *To The Manor Born*, a radio pilot on which he had worked hard, was also transferring to TV without him, and after so many triumphs at Radio 4 he had finally had enough, and so marched over to BBC TV demanding a chance to prove himself – which quickly led to the creation of *Not The Nine O'Clock*

News. Incidentally, although he was to receive £35 for one minute of unidentified screentime in that hugely influential sketch show's first series, Adams was to be predictably withering about his friend's success, insisting with an unusually poor eye for simile that '*Not The Nine O'Clock News* is to *Monty Python* what The Monkees were to The Beatles'. If he had seen the pilot, in which a fat tycoon surrounded by go-go dancers was referred to as 'Douglas Adams and his accountants', he would no doubt have been even more scathing. After the last series of *Not*, Lloyd and his collaborator Sean Hardie mused over a sitcom idea which Lloyd dubbed *Rich Bastard*, about a successful millionaire who nonetheless harbours jealousy for his poorer, nonentity neighbour. The target of this project would not have passed Douglas by, had it come to fruition.

If any genuine bad blood between the two friends seems short-lived, credit legendarily goes to Janet Thrift, that spreader of sweetness and light, who intervened with a disapproving 'Boys, boys, boys!', knocked their heads together and made them make up and be friendly. It's traditional to note that their friendship was 'never quite the same' after this, but then it's not unusual for two youthful male collaborators to have a bond fuelled as much by bitter competition as fondness, and no friendship in Douglas' life would be quite as full of both – no matter how successful he became, there would always be this fear that John, the blue-eyed boy, had trumped him somehow. 'It was very silly,' Adams told Gaiman. 'On the one hand I thought, "It might be a nice idea to collaborate," and on sober reflection I thought, "No, I can do it myself." It was my own project, and I had every right to say, "No, I'll do it myself." John had helped me out, and been very well rewarded for the work. I rashly talked about collaborating, and changed my mind. I was within my rights, but I should have handled it better. You see, on the one hand, Johnny and I are incredibly good friends, and have been for ages. But we are incredibly good at rubbing each other up the wrong way. We have these ridiculous fights when I'm determined to have a go at him, and he is determined to have a go at me. So ... I think it was an overreaction on his part, but on the other hand the entire history of our relationship has been one or the other overreacting to something the other has done.'

It was, however, fortunate for Adams that his Mum had soothed the troubled waters between Lloyd and himself, as his final project as a radio producer would have been a debacle without John's help. The Footlights had staged a pantomime every year for aeons, but to celebrate the club's 95th year

David Hatch detailed Douglas to put together an all-star celebration for the festive season on Radio 2, which the latter quickly decided should be called *Black Cinderella II Goes East*. The name aside, however, he had neither the time nor the inclination to actually pen the script – fairy tales stuffed with saucy puns being pretty much anathema to him – and so he popped up to his alma mater to find the writers. Out of the hard-drinking generation who followed Adams in the Footlights, the most reliable gag writers seemed to be law student and incurable quipster Clive Anderson and hirsute languages student Rory McGrath, and he gave them their first BBC commission, putting together a sort of extended *ISIRTA* 'Prune Play' to star not just the whole cast of that now defunct show (albeit Cleese refused, until Adams begged him to at least record his part as Fairy Godfather on tape at home), but also Peter Cook as Prince Disgusting, and a whole host of successful Footlighters going right back to Richard 'Stinker' Murdoch. The rookie producer's trust in the students was somewhat misplaced, however, and one of the most beautifully ironic moments in Adams' life came when the pair missed their script deadline, compelling the panicked producer to storm up to Cambridge, heading right from the train to the pub where he knew he would find them both – the Baron of Beef, just opposite St. John's whereupon he angrily berated them at length for their lax attitude to meeting deadlines, and all but sent them to their rooms until they had handed over an hour's worth of magical sauce. In the end, the pair had to pass the script on to a woman at the station to hand over to Douglas at Liverpool Street.

Adams clearly meant business with the panto, but his skills as a producer simply weren't up to the task, and with just days to go until the recording he was forced to go cap in hand to the neighbouring office and ask for Lloyd's help. To most of the cast who took part, it seemed that John was the producer, and Douglas was just there to hang out with the stars. Adams had his pride, to say the least, but by this stage he might well have mentally clocked off altogether – earlier in the year he had been offered the role of Script Editor of *Doctor Who* and, after much agonising, had accepted, with a start date of October. 'I got very mixed up about that,' he admitted. 'Various people gave me conflicting advice – some people said, "This is obviously what you must do because it's much more along the lines of what you claim as your strengths," and other people said, "You can't desert radio immediately, just like that!" David Hatch said the latter to me very strongly, because he was head of the department, and he had given me the job. But the next

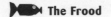

person to desert the department was David Hatch, which made me feel a little better.'

The Most Massively Useful Thing

Before getting to grips with the Doctor full-time, Adams had another urgent date with Arthur Dent, a Christmas special of *Hitchhiker* having been commissioned in August. At first, Geoffrey and Douglas intended to try a seasonal episode in which Marvin would blaze into Earth's orbit, becoming the Nativity star and crashing into a particular stable where the Infant Christ was to 'cure' the android of his depression, whereupon he was allegedly to lead everyone – including the Biblical descendants of Arthur and Ford – in a happy seasonal singalong. This undeniably cheesy idea was abandoned on the grounds of potential religious offence, in favour of a general continuation of the ongoing saga. This presaged the second series that had also been commissioned, at first as seven episodes, but ultimately whittled down to five – with the increased fee of £345 per half-hour.

The special's creation necessitated a worrying precedent when Perkins realised the only way to get Douglas to provide the script was to actually move in with him, typing up a finished version of whatever Adams could get down on paper. However, the difficulties of getting Ford and Arthur off prehistoric Earth and saving everyone else from the Bugblatter-Beast-shaped Haggunenon required further ad-hoc tinkering with the script in the studio, made possible until the last minute thanks to the first use of 'snappies' – carbon-paper rolls which rattled several copies off the typewriter at once, leading some cast members to mistakenly insist that the script was typed on lavatory paper. With Douglas now typing right up to the last minute, a new level of ultra-fast thinking was required from everyone, not least when the heavily heralded (but ultimately never quite fully realised) expert hitcher Roosta was introduced, and without anyone to play him, Wing-Davey's friend, gravel-voiced cockney actor Alan Ford, was sent for at half an hour's notice as he happened to live round the corner. Some of the rough dialogue was not just cut, but was never even included in the official script books, as the prehistoric prisoners hope to hitch their way out of trouble, despite being plastered on Arthur's 'horrible' elderflower wine:

ARTHUR	Snot 'orrible. Smerely revolting. Safine line.
FORD	Well, sherupp. Things could be worse.
ARTHUR	So you said before.
FORD	Well, eyesright wozzen eye? I mean fair's fair, they did get worse.
ARTHUR	If only I wazzen so damn zober.
FORD	Ah dingozekiness, the muzz be some way of getting off this planet other than getting high.

The duo's quandary – that nothing will ever happen if they keep drinking – had clear parallels with Adams' admission that the secret of good writing is to keep the whisky bottle locked away. There were a few plans to save our two sort-of heroes from prehistory before the neat idea of a fossilised towel leading Zaphod to the rescue was born, with one *Doctor Who*-flavoured concept quickly being abandoned:

AN IDEA THAT MIGHT BE WORTH PURSUING.
A girl from Victorian times whose grandfather is an inventor in the H.G. Wells mode. She is rather prim and unimaginative. She has, slightly unwillingly, agreed to try out her grandfather's time machine, never for a moment having the slightest inkling that it might actually work, or what it would actually mean if it did. We open the story from her point of view, describing how she gets into the machine, her grandfather twiddles the knobs and the next moment she is standing in a field where she encounters Arthur and Ford. Ford is, of course, quick to spot the significance of her story and to see the possibility of their own escape.
 I'm going off this idea.

Zaphod's re-entry into the action, suddenly headed directly to the offices of the Hitchhiker's Guide, was no less problematic. Having the Haggunenon evolve into an escape pod was an easy enough get-out, but working out the reasoning behind anything the unpredictable ex-Galactic President did resulted in more excised exposition, thanks to the handy coaxing of an Arcturan pilot (played by Scottish actor Bill Paterson, near the start of a long and rich career), demanding to know what the apparently dead two-headed egotist was up to:

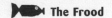

ZAPHOD   I don't know. That's what I'm here to find out. But whatever
it was meant that in the meantime I had to steal that
Infinite Improbability Drive Ship, and in order to do that
I had to become President. Now it takes a pretty weird sort
of guy to do both of those, so I was made into that guy.
You want to know what this voice of mine said to me? It
said "This is to explain to you why you're such a mindless
arrogant bum, in case it ever crossed your mind to wonder."
Yeah, I thought, I've heard of self-knowledge, but this is
ridiculous. But you know what this former self of mine
forgot to take into account? It forgot to take into account
that the new personality that's capable of stealing the
ship and everything might not be that interested in the
purpose behind it, right? Figure that one out. I've said too
much, it's time to go ...

Susan Sheridan was in such demand as a voice actor (with a major role
in the long-gestated Disney movie which would eventually be released as
The Black Cauldron) that Trillian had to be written out – though having
her 'forcibly married to the President of the Algolian Chapter of the Galactic
Rotary Club', dismissed in a couple of lines of narration, was an ignominious
end for the series' only female regular, not Douglas' finest moment. Marvin,
naturally, had to be salvaged, and starred in one of the programme's most
beloved 'sketches', in which he manages to convince a dangerous Frogstar
robot to destroy itself with frustration at the unfairness of mechanoid life.

By far the most momentous inclusion in the special when it aired that
Christmas Eve, after recording in November, was the first mention of towels.
Ken Welsh's *Guide* already stressed the many practical purposes for hitchers
keeping their towels close by, but like the number 42, *Hitchhiker*'s raising
of the humble beach towel to mythical proportions has held the imaginations of fans for decades – science fiction writer Mark W. Tiedemann even
suggested that the looped weaving of a towel resembles the shape of the
Universe itself. But, typically, it stemmed entirely from an in-joke among
Douglas' friends. Although John and Douglas were no longer co-writing the
novel, they had already booked a holiday in Corfu together to write it, along
with Mary Allen and a number of other friends. John took pleasure in writing
insouciantly while Douglas made his forehead bleed trying to capture his

sonically arresting comedy on the page – he was to leave with only twenty rough pages to show for it. One crucial outcome of the vacation was that the paucity of entertainment on offer, combined with the chilly September weather, inspired the friends to resort to parlour games after a certain measure of retsina at Taverna Manthos in the evenings. Once charades was played out, Douglas recalled an exercise favoured by an old English master Frank Halford, in which the class was required to invent new additions to the dictionary. Lloyd was particularly enraptured with the pleasure of taking well-known place names and fitting them to definitions of feelings, actions and objects which struck a chord with all the players but had never been given their own word before, and was soon making good use of the holiday by jotting down the best entries for further use.

Besides this incidental creation of a comedy classic and the fights over girls, however, the most memorable motif of the trip for the friends seemed to be towels, and Douglas' complete inability to keep track of where his had got to, on the few occasions when a trip to the beach was possible: 'Whilst I was tearing my hair out in frustration, searching the bathroom, the washing line, the bedroom, under the bed, even in the bed, everyone else in the party would sit waiting patiently, drumming their fingers on their own rolled-up towels. I realised that my difficulties with my towel were probably symptomatic of the profound disorganisation of my whole life, and that it would therefore be fair to say that anybody who was a *really* together person would be someone who would really know where their towel was ...'

At first this theory was only given a passing remark in the series, with Adams' usual fear of alienating the audience with in-jokes, but to his surprise the idea of the importance of towels was received with intense approval, and soon references were worked into every medium that *Hitchhiker* embraced: in the book, he noted from the start that veteran hitcher Ford picked up his crucial towel at Marks & Spencer (the Salisbury branch, according to the series), whereas besides the 'fossilised towel' solution to Ford and Arthur's prehistoric pickle, the Guide's opinion of towels being 'the most massively useful thing an interstellar hitchhiker can have', as written for the radio and subsequently extended for print, provided one of those monologues which many *Hitchhiker* aficionados can rattle off at will. The extract even inspired one of the most unusual formats for Douglas' work: soft furnishings. In 1979, a prototype of a *Hitchhiker* towel was turned down by none other than Marks & Spencer, but shortly after, an enterprising PR executive called

Eugen Beer saw the potential in the merchandising, and with the surprise granting of 'world towel rights', went into business marketing large beach towels with the truncated speech woven into it – only a couple of thousand were sold, making them a major collector's item today.

Douglas found he had so much to say about towels that his original entry for the Guide ended up being cut in half, with further information held over for the first episode of the second run:

Much has been written on the subject of towels, most of which stresses the many practical functions they can serve for the modern hitchhiker … However, only 'The Hitchhiker's Guide to the Galaxy' explains that the towel has a far more important psychological value, in that anyone who can hitch the length and breadth of the Galaxy, rough it, slum it, struggle against mind-boggling odds, win through, and still know where his towel is, is clearly a man to be reckoned with. Hence a phrase which has passed into hitchhiking slang, as in 'Hey, you sass that hoopy Ford Prefect? There's a frood who <u>really</u> knows where his towel is!' Sass means 'know', 'be aware of', 'meet', 'have sex with'. Hoopy means 'really together guy' and frood means 'really amazingly together guy'.

Developing his own galactic vernacular for the series was one of Adams' particular pleasures, from Zaphod's excited cry 'Freeeow' to using the Prophet Zarquon-based curse 'zark' and, later, 'Belgium' to circumvent broadcasting the word 'fuck', and of course, celebrating the hitching ideal of the hoopy frood. 'Hoopy' began as a noun, but the creator was soon using it as an adjective in the book, whereas 'frood' may have come from a simple merging of 'friend' and 'dude' – although the production team did receive a business card from a furniture manufacturer called Frood, but it was filed under 'coincidence'. It must be admitted, therefore, that Douglas Adams conceived 'the frood' as being someone almost, but not quite, entirely unlike himself.

Where Are You Going?

If Douglas thought he was stressed in late 1977, his workload a year later must have given him plenty of opportunity to regret the end of Lloyd's collaboration, even with six months' grace until the next recording. In the meantime, repeats of the first series and myriad other exciting opportunities for *Hitchhiker* spin-offs ramped up the pressure, causing him to admit to a particularly exposed feeling as the need to pen the second series arose: 'The first time, it was my little world, whereas the second time was like running down the high street naked. I find the whole business of writing appalling ...'

By far the greatest source of nail-biting at this time, though, came from his day job, steering the 17th series of *Who*. In fact, his first task was to rework the conclusion to the previous series, but that was just a taste of the headaches to come. When Adams was offered the job in the BBC bar, the idea was that he would pen the series conclusion, and he presumed that otherwise all he would be doing was finding interesting writers, fiddling with the odd spot of punctuation and pepping up the dialogue with a few zingers. However, 'I discovered that other writers assumed that getting the storyline together was the script editor's job. So all that year I was continually working out storylines with writers, helping others with scripts, doing substantial rewrites on other scripts and putting yet other scripts into production. All simultaneously. It was a nightmare year for the four months that I was in control it was terrific: having all these storylines in your head simultaneously. But as soon as you stop actually coping, then it becomes a nightmare ... The crazy thing about *Doctor Who*, one of the things that led to my feelings of frustration, was doing twenty-six episodes a year with one producer and one script editor. It's a workload unlike any other drama series; if you are doing a police series, say, you know what a police car looks like, what the streets look like, what criminals do. With *Doctor Who*, with every story you have to reinvent totally, but be entirely consistent with what's gone before ... I was going out of my tiny mind.'

He began in great spirits, hoping to give his childhood favourite a timely shake-up, and this time it was him taking writers to lunch – sci-fi author Christopher Priest, whose submissions never made it to the screen, and word maestro Tom Stoppard, who refused outright to be involved. Lloyd's *Gigax*-inspired pitch, *The Doomsday Contract* (in which the Earth was to be bought up by an intergalactic conglomerate) was pushed hard by Douglas, but despite a number of alterations to tailor it for a teatime audience (like, say, removing the sections with gun-toting child slaves) the story foundered, and John was too busy with *Not* to pursue it.

Of the six serials that made up Adams' series, three did not present notable problems – *The Creature From The Pit, Nightmare of Eden* and the Greek myth-inspired *The Horns of Nimon* – though none of them were a source of pride for Adams either. The series opener, *Destiny of the Daleks*, was quite another matter. Dalek creator Terry Nation was unflattering about Adams' skills, describing him as more of an 'ideas man' than a script editor, but this seems unfair considering the famous tale of how *Destiny* was presented to Douglas as little more than a few pages of rough scraps and 'explosions in corridors', which the rookie had to mould into a usable script. The resultant four-parter was replete with discernible Adamsian flavours, with the plot hanging on a crucial game of rock-paper-scissors, and a controversial opening sequence explaining the Time Lady Romana's regeneration (with Mary Tamm giving way to Lalla Ward, who had guest-starred in the previous adventure), in which the Doctor's companion tried on new bodies as if they were cocktail dresses – something which has caused endless head-scratching and ret-conning from *Who* fans ever since. Adams' insistence that the *Hitchhiker* and *Who* universes had no meaningful connection was also undermined by his decision to show the Doctor scoffing at a book, *Origins of the Universe*, written by *Hitchhiker*'s notorious hack, Oolon Colluphid.

Planning the remaining episodes, Douglas was still insistent that his series finale would be the Krikkit invasion plot, but Graham Williams was equally adamant that it was beyond their means: 'I had in mind a story that I wanted to do and the producer said, "No, that's over the top. I don't want to do that story. Come up with something else." I so much liked my story that I kept on and on about it, thinking that eventually he'd run out of time and have to accept the story because it would be ready to go ...' However, the second episode, David Fisher's *The Gamble With Time* – a 1920s Monte Carlo-set *Bulldog Drummond* pastiche involving a villain who had made a fortune by travelling in time and forcing Da Vinci to paint numerous copies of the *Mona Lisa* – would require a more hair-whitening display of Adams' ingenuity. As he explained, 'one of our regular stalwart writers (who we'd left alone as he was a reliable guy) turned out to have been having terrible family problems – his wife had left him, and he was in a real turmoil. He'd done his best, but he didn't have a script that was going to work, and we were in deep trouble. This was Friday, and the producer came to me and said, "We've got a director coming on Monday, we have to have a new four-episode show by Monday!" So he took me back to his place, locked me in his study and hosed me down with whisky and black coffee for a few days, and there was the script. Because of the peculiar circumstances and Writers' Guild laws, it meant that it had to go out under the departmental name of David Agnew.'

Douglas already well knew the agonies of composition, but this was the most stressful example yet of being required to churn out the stuff under supervision, on a sudden-death deadline. And yet the result was *City of Death*, probably the most-cited Fan Favourite in The Show's half-century of broadcasting, with the highest-ever audience of 16 million (albeit thanks to industrial action blacking out ITV). With Williams' help, Douglas spun a tale with the finest intertwining of the series' drama and humour, which was also the first adventure to be filmed abroad – in this case, Paris. The Doctor's foiling of the villain Count Scarlioni's plan to steal seven *Mona Lisa*s – funding a time-travelling experiment in his cellar, where a scientist is enslaved for his genius, in similar fashion to how Douglas himself felt that weekend – takes a more epic turn when the Count is revealed to be an alien, Scaroth of the Jagoroth, trying to return to primordial Earth to prevent his spaceship exploding: an event which just happened to trigger the development of all life on Earth. And only the Doctor, K9, Romana II and a detective, Duggan, can stop him:

```
DUGGAN    Where do you two come from?
DOCTOR    From? Well, I suppose the best way to find out where
          you've come from is to find out where you're going
          and then work backwards.
DUGGAN    Where are you going?
DOCTOR    I don't know.
```

Adams' episodes have been criticised for being too comedic, but *City of Death* struck just the right note, and even calling in ex-Footlighters Eleanor Bron and John Cleese for cameos did not overpower the drama. 'In the things I wrote for *Doctor Who*,' he said, 'there were absurd things that happened in it, and funny things. But I feel that it is essentially a drama show, only secondarily amusing. My aim was to create apparently bizarre situations and then pursue the logic so much that it became real.' The dialogue written for Baker and Ward, during a period in which they embarked on a whirlwind romance resulting in a brief marriage, also fizzed incessantly throughout with instantly recognisable Douglas lines:

```
ROMANA      Where are we going?
DOCTOR      Are you talking philosophically or geographically?
ROMANA      Philosophically.
DOCTOR      Oh, then we're going to lunch.
```

To this day, the official line of the *Doctor Who Magazine* is that 'for many fans *City of Death* remains the show's ultimate achievement, encapsulating in four beautifully constructed episodes everything that was brave, clever, witty, dramatic, humane and heroic about *Doctor Who* at the height of its golden age.' And there is the added beauty of the idea that, having spent so long plotting the destruction of the planet, here Adams was responsible for the actual origin of all life on Earth, within the *Who* universe.

Conversely, the nightmare that was *Shada* is one of those tales that every Whovian knows all too well. Adams remained insistent on ending the series with his cricket plot, and had the full might of Tom Baker behind him, but Williams still refused to consider it. 'Finally,' Adams recalled, 'about three days before his director was due to join, I had to sit down and write something else. So I wrote *Shada,* which was a last-minute panic thing to do. Didn't particularly like it. I thought it was rather thin – at most a mediocre four-parter stretched out over six parts ... It only acquired a notoriety because it wasn't made. It's much more alive in people's imaginations because of that.' These sour grapes belie the quality of the doomed story, which was richer with inspired ideas than many of the Doctor's adventures.

Originally titled *Sunburst*, *Shada* was inspired by Douglas' old college, St. John's, here renamed St. Cedd's. St. John's is a wooden-panelled respite for retiring scholars, and also a world of portals – heavy fire doors, opening directly onto further doors. To envisage one of these leading to a TARDIS, owned by a crumbling Time Lord, Professor Chronotis, who had seen generations of students come and go for centuries without raising any suspicions in that private, cobwebbed, respectful world, was Adams' starting point for a Cambridge yarn unlike anything else in the *Who* oeuvre. Despite Douglas' disdain, to have written such a rich stand-out episode in just a few days – stretching from the world of academia to ancient Gallifreyan mythology and even introducing an all-new monster, the lava-like Krargs – was one of the writer's greatest achievements, only to be dashed by industrial action from technicians at TV Centre that autumn, when the second batch of studio sequences required to complement the already filmed location scenes had to be cancelled. Adams' cursed plot would be resurrected in numerous ways over the years, from VHS special to web animation, but its cancellation would remain one of the most problematic smudges on The Show's escutcheon. When the programme returned with an all-new production team headed by the celebrated John Nathan-Turner (who tried and failed to remount *Shada*), Adams was long gone, having handed in his resignation in August 1979. He complained to *Penthouse*, 'I was told: "We want you, Douglas, because of the specific things you'll be able to bring to the programme," which I have systematically not been allowed to do. It's too big a thing for any one person to change. This season of *Doctor Who* will look just like any other season – and I feel very disappointed about that.'

On the other hand, being free to concentrate solely on the progress of Arthur Dent, he could see that things were going well closer to home – hence the personal interview, in which he modestly assured *Penthouse*, 'If *Hitchhiker* makes money, I shall enjoy that. But what I'll enjoy most is having proved that you don't have to underestimate people. I don't like the notion that you set yourself up as saying "This is what people like, therefore this is what we'll do." That's patronising. I just want to kill the idea that you have to be bland to appeal to your market, though I know a lot of the BBC old guard still regard *Hitchhiker* as a momentary aberration, a fluke, and not really what radio comedy ought to be about.'

Something That Sounds Good?

Hitchhiker's success did not allow it to wait meekly in the wings during Douglas' tussles with the TARDIS in 1979 – but at least one new reason for poor Arthur to return to the mud required almost no input from the writer himself. Ken Campbell – clown, character actor specialising in irritants, and experimental-theatre wizard, had been tipped off about *Hitchhiker* by fans, and was instantly not especially bothered. Although nobody was better placed to attempt *Hitchhiker* on stage – in 1976 he and Chris Langham had set up the Science Fiction Theatre of Liverpool, staging a number of outlandish plays including the 22-hour record-breaker *The Warp* – Campbell was never sure he could pull it off ... unless, perhaps, he could stage it as a *ride*. Douglas was consulted and allowed Ken's team carte blanche, equally convinced that it wouldn't work, but was as surprised as anyone else when the first *Hitchhiker* play, staged in the royal surroundings of the Institute of

Contemporary Arts on Carlton Terrace in the first week of May, became such a hot ticket even Simon Jones' cries of 'But I am the original Arthur Dent!' could not gain him entry.

Campbell's frantic adaptation, reducing three hours of radio to nincty minutes, began in the foyer when the maximum of eighty punters were served steaming blue PGGBs by two usherettes, Lithos and Terros, who shared the role of The Book, just in time for them all to be thrust into their seats and safely escorted away from the destruction of the Earth. Campbell had arranged for the seating dais to be mounted on special hovercraft-style 'airpods' which allowed the audience to be smoothly pushed from scene to scene by some of the larger ticket-holders, as the cast (Langham playing an admirably 'normal' Arthur, with his then wife Sue Jones-Davies, *Life of Brian*'s Judith Iscariot, as Trillian, and the great Roger Sloman as Prosser) kept the action moving from their positions around the wall of the performance area. The very nature of the show, and its short run, ensured that thousands of fans were disappointed never to get to see it, but a far more orthodox approach was already being taken by a team out west at Theatr Clwyd, where their own creative director, Jonathan Petherbridge, set out to present a more direct adaptation of the radio scripts over a few nights, culminating in a marathon session on the final day – over time, this production would be distilled into a single evening's performance (boasting the world's only inflatable Haggunenon/Bugblatter Beast) which would form the basis of many amateur productions in the decades to come.

Although the second series of the radio programme initially began production at roughly the same time as the first theatrical version debuted, only one episode was pieced together from three sessions (with Zaphod arriving at the Frogstar to be fed into the infamous Total Perspective Vortex and driven mad by his sense of universal perspective – that is, if he wasn't such an egotist, and/or the entire escapade didn't take place in a false universe set up by Guide Editor Zarniwoop) before Perkins was forced to call a hiatus, largely for Douglas to find time to catch up.

Their parallel audio project, on the other hand, was a less fraught experience, creatively. In those days before Listen Again and torrenting, the only way most people could hear *Hitchhiker* was when it was broadcast, and although the BBC had the sense to repeat it copiously, Douglas and Geoffrey quickly realised that a commercial release was being clamoured for. Of course, BBC Enterprises missed the bus on this just as they did with the book rights, but it was clear that a *Hitchhiker* LP would be a gift for any record label. After a period of shopping around, Perkins decided that Original Records – a brand new indie label set up solely for avant-garde jazz – should be the audio home for *Hitchhiker*.

To reverse Arthur Dent back into the mud this time required Adams' favourite part of writing – pruning – rather than adding to his mountain of composition duties. For the double album's four sides, the first couple of hours of broadcast *Hitchhiker* were recreated with minimal changes to streamline the action, except in the cast, where Cindy Oswin (Lithos in Campbell's adaptation) stood in admirably for Susan Sheridan, and extra vocal bombast came from the legendary Man In Black (and *Who*'s Black Guardian) Valentine Dyall, who took over the role of Deep Thought, at roughly the same time that he recorded the ominous tones of Gargravarr, the disembodied guardian of the TPV, on radio.

Douglas did get to voice some of the warning messages on Magrathea, but lack of an Equity card otherwise dashed his hopes of getting in on the action, which still irked him: 'I regard myself as having come from the tradition of the writer-performer and having been shunted off into just writing. I think it is desperately unfair; given that my work consists basically of making work for actors, I don't see why I shouldn't be allowed to take 5% of that work that I create … If I don't actually get to perform as well, I can see that there will be increasingly little point in carrying on.' Perkins had no such problem – besides his BBC work he had begun to write and perform with an Oxford group several years his junior, particularly Angus Deayton (who would go on to be Adams' next-door neighbour throughout the 1990s), but also Helen Atkinson-Wood, Michael Fenton-Stevens and musical maestro Phil Pope. Over the next few years this fledgling *Radio Active/KYTV* gang would tour Australia and, Geoffrey excepted, the male members (with help from fellow Oxonian Richard Curtis) would create a cult smash of their own as spoof outfit The HeeBeeGeeBees, who were to be the other comedy stars on the Original Records label, releasing Pope's pastiche compendium *439 Golden Greats* alongside *An Evening Without*, with Rhys Jones, Mulville, McGrath, Anderson and Martin Bergman performing the obvious Adams sketches, 'Paranoid Society' and 'Kamikaze Pilot'.

Copyright problems required Paddy Kingsland to offer a largely new electronic soundtrack for vinyl which would go on to define the sound of *Hitchhiker* in series two and on TV, alongside musician Tim Souster, who also recorded a new version of 'Journey of the Sorcerer' which Douglas infamously requested be made 'more concave' in sound, while providing acoustic guitar. Although legal action by Paul Neil Milne-Johnson was averted in later pressings with a pointedly basic edit of his name, jumbling Peter Jones' syllables, Perkins was glad to have more high-tech equipment and just the right amount of breathing space to add an extra layer of polish to the stereophonic sounds. With a sleeve designed by Pink Floyd cover artists Storm Thorgerson and Aubrey Powell, known as Hipgnosis – a kind of minimalist technicolor psychedelia shortly to become iconic when also used for the novel – the first *Hitchhiker* album was off to the record plant. 10,000 copies were lined up for distribution, available solely through an advert supposedly placed by the mysterious Zarniwoop at the back of the new *Hitchhiker* book – which just had to be actually completed. Thousands of orders were to eventually flood in, but thanks to a computer error on the distributors' part daily order totals were mistaken as fresh orders, resulting in a massive over-estimation of demand. Once the record hit the shops the following year, with most fans having already ordered theirs, the album's sizeable sales were so fragmented that it did not register on any chart despite selling over 120,000 copies. The album would nevertheless provide the most accessible entry into *Hitchhiker* for new fans all over the world for years to come, even if nobody ultimately made any money out of it (besides Douglas, who had a special deal thanks to Original Records' management). The writer was also to earn his money by penning sleeve notes with the usual emphasis on facetiousness:

> SOME INFORMATION WHICH MAY CONFUSE YOU: The Hitchhiker's Guide to the Galaxy itself has not been published on this planet. It is not, in the long term, a viable financial proposition. In the long term, nothing on this planet is a viable proposition for reasons which the contents of this record album should make clear. If you wish to avoid the events recorded on this album, this is what you should do: 1) Leave the Earth as quickly as possible. 2) Do not procrastinate. 3) Do not panic …

A Wholly Remarkable Book

The construction of his hit radio show's novelisation was the primary nagging factor throughout Adams' tenure on *Who*, and long-suffering flatmate Canter had to endure teenage sensation Kate Bush's 'Wuthering Heights' on repeat (Douglas insisted it was the song of the year, and needed to play it like a mantra, to replenish his spirits in between bouts of writing) as the novelist resolved to not just copy out his scripts with the occasional 'he said, she said' thrown in, but to approach his saga from scratch, perfecting every twist and reversing previous compromises to suit his vision, now directly communicated to his audience without any interference beyond Pan's fixing of the odd oddity in his variable punctuation. 'I don't want to just reproduce the scripts – that'd be rip-off time,' he said. 'And I've always wanted to write a novel because, well, everyone wants to write a novel. I just know I would never have got round to it, except that someone approached me and said, "Will you write a novel based on this?"' On the other hand, such an auspicious start would ultimately be the root of many of his future struggles with book deadlines, as he felt his instant success 'was like being helicoptered to the top of Mount Everest ... or having an orgasm without the foreplay', and so he had to work all the harder to justify his easy start as a novelist.

Adams delighted in the way that the different media he fed his story through inspired each version to contradict the other, but the plot of *The Hitchhiker's Guide to the Galaxy* would stick to the events and jokes of the first four episodes very closely indeed, with one of the few stylistic additions being the inclusion of supposed extracts from the eponymous publication complete with insane page references – a detail eventually dropped for subsequent books. Douglas happily built his reputation for (at this stage, merely) sailing close to the wind when it came to publishing deadlines by telling interviewers that he had been ordered to literally stop writing and hand his manuscript over to a courier no matter where he had got to, but his intention was always to stop just short of the juncture where Lloyd had stepped in anyway – it was only the writer's umpteenth revision which was interrupted. 'I'm pleased with the way it reads,' he was to say. 'I feel it flows nicely. It feels as if it were easy to write, and I know how difficult that was to achieve.'

Numerous passages hit the dust during the final pruning stage, one of which gave further information on the Vogon's cooks – a race which continued to fascinate Adams, without ever returning to the story beyond their crucial first involvement[2] – and similarly excised for holding up the action was a lengthy and uncharacteristically scientific musing from

Arthur, presaging the famous button-pressing moment.[3] All such 'flab' was consigned to the wastepaper basket and the manuscript went on its way to Pan for a September release – albeit not to Nick Webb himself, who was to rue his departure from the company shortly after signing Douglas up but remained a good friend. After many thousands of plays of 'Wuthering Heights', at last Douglas was free to reprogram his brain and turn to the most pressing job remaining: the last few episodes of the radio programme. In fact, the schedule for the remaining episodes was totally haywire, with Perkins' booked-in summer recordings only resulting in the one episode. With time slipping away, once again Douglas had to sit down and work out where he was and what ideas he had as stepping stones towards a conclusion:

LIST OF IDEAS AND SEMI IDEAS, NOTIONS, DETAILS ETC.

Spaceship which is a terrible old jalopy, everything falling apart.

Extremely sensitive life support systems computer – someone is rude to it and it commits suicide.

Footsteps. Something terribly dramatic happens, footsteps carry on.

Journeying into another dimension just to spend an afternoon smashing up the Taj Mahal.

River with different attitudes to time.

Visigoth. Unwinnable argument.

Extremely laid back John Peel like computer at the HHGG offices.

Besides the suicidal machinery, it need hardly be added that none of these ideas ended up in his final radio adventure, which took Arthur, Ford and Zaphod to the bird-infested and shoe-spoiled planet of Brontitall, developing the avian culture concept from *Doctor Snuggles* and combining it with the writer's venom after a particularly frustrating shopping expedition on Oxford Street, trying to find a pair of shoes to fit his gigantic feet. These ideas, along with the introduction of the 'very nice and sexy' archaeologist Lintilla and her millions of clones, were outlined in Adams' notes precisely as they appeared in the eventual programmes, with an added suggestion that their stories would lead Arthur and Co. to a 'Disinterested Ruler' of the Universe who lived on a planet governed by a character only described as 'Graham Chapman King'. As the cast reassembled once again at the Paris studios to try to make sense of the desiccated second saga, once again the stressed author faced an almighty struggle to get the words on the page, and onto the air.

It's Folly To Say You Know What Is Happening

The reason why these final radio sessions were quite so legendarily fraught was that David Hatch, that master of the airwaves, made something of an uncharacteristic blunder when he managed to secure a singular honour for *Hitchhiker* – the front cover of the *Radio Times* – on the understanding that the five episodes ran not weekly, but over a single week at the very start of 1980. Where Perkins calculated that they could just about manage to end the series in time for weekly instalments, he and Lisa returned from a well-deserved holiday in September to find that they faced the very, very improbable.

'Snappies' were needed more than ever as sessions for the final four episodes commenced recording in November, postponed from July. Perkins had decided to label each episode 'Fits' for the first time, in reference to Lewis Carroll's *Hunting of the Snark*, which was to give people the impression that Carroll's surrealism was a major influence on *Hitchhiker* (particularly the Wonderland court's Rule 42. 'All Persons More Than A Mile High Must Leave The Court'), but Douglas protested: 'Lewis Carroll, curiously enough, I read when I was a little kid, and it frightened me to bits and I couldn't bear it ever since then ... As far as children's books are concerned, a much stronger influence would be *Winnie-the-Pooh*. Milne's writing is wonderful – it's easy to read and it's beautifully written, worth having a look at again.' Janet Thrift even suggested to her son that Marvin was a direct descendant of Eeyore, which he was surprised to acknowledge. However, he always insisted that his most conscious childhood influence was the *Punch* cartoonist Paul Crum, whose depiction of two hippos wallowing in mud with the caption 'I keep thinking it's Tuesday', adored by Douglas, was a good example of his unusual angle on existence.

A number of factors made the creation of this second series particularly painful for the writer – not the least of which was the concurrent script deadline, revised on more than one occasion, for a TV pilot of *Hitchhiker*. Earlier in the year Lloyd had submitted a proposal for a small-screen adaptation, which he would produce, leading in May to a formal commission by LE boss John Howard Davies of a script due by August – which was ultimately delivered in December. The requirement to begin the story once again from scratch should have been a relatively easy one, and Adams had started out writing for TV with Chapman anyway, but he could be forgiven for a slight schizophrenic feeling, with Arthur Dent poised in so many confusing situations in so many media at once. Added to this job was the extra attention from producers looking to buy into the *Hitchhiker* magic by hiring Adams for projects, with a programme for schools, *Exploration Earth: More Machines* paying him for ideas, as well as interest from the popular surreal sci-fi kids' game show *The Adventure Game,* which would have suited Douglas' puzzle-forming talents well. But he had to turn all outside offers down.

Adams' chief inhibitor, however, was the clear knowledge that there was an avid audience out there waiting to hear what happened next. 'It's very difficult because the first series was written just before the big science fiction boom took off, and now one is going back into an area where you feel you broke new ground, and suddenly there are multi-storey car parks and office blocks.' Douglas' ambition, like that of his idol Cleese, dictated a constant moving forward, and once he had a book in shops and a TV series in the pipeline, returning to his original sound-only medium must have felt regressive.

Douglas and his friends had shared their own love of science fiction, but until 1979 he had never experienced the fan community en masse. In late August Pan sent him to 'Seacon 79' in Brighton, that year's World Science Fiction convention, where he gave a talk, 'Across the Galaxy with TARDIS and Thumb', and effectively received his first taste of the fame he had been hungering for all his life. *Hitchhiker* – which was available to hear in numerous listening posts around the venue – lost out on the Hugo Award for Best Dramatic Presentation to *Superman*, but so voluble was the booing from new lovers of tea, towels and depressive robots as superhero Christopher Reeve went up to collect the award, he had the nous to announce to the crowd 'It was fixed!' – to great cheers. These were Douglas' fans, all around him, cheering his creation, but he was to admit that he only *thought* he was a sci-fi fan until he fully explored the subculture. Groucho's attitude to club-joining began to settle in for Adams very early on, but while the novelty was new, seeing the adoration his imagination had inspired made him feel considerably taller than his usual six-foot-five.

Certainly, there was a further boon to the attention, as Adams wryly acknowledged years later when he told an interviewer, 'As far as I can see most science fiction writers go to conventions to get laid, don't they?' Seemingly every review of past biographies of Douglas Adams shared one hang-up for the critic – none of the narratives provided the right amount of salacious nitty-gritty they seemed to find compulsory in such a book: 'This Douglas Adams,' they all positively frothed, 'is he man or mouse? Does he not, to put it in a nutshell …?' and so on. This work of comedy history has even less call to indulge in the gossip-magazine side of our Frood's life than predecessors, but the bonus sexual magnetism that Adams' success brought clearly figured as a definite plus for a man already hugely desirable to many women, with his mix of wise wit, boyish enthusiasm and devastating physique. Nick Webb shared a transparently suggestive anecdote about being shoved out of the way at a convention bar, mid-conversation with Douglas, by a determined and flagrantly pouting Amazonian fan, while Jon Canter volunteered the memory that his flatmate was a 'cheerful rogerer', entirely uninhibited by his libido and practically opposite to Jon, who described himself as 'a neurotic Jewish Woody Allen', regularly on the receiving end of Douglas' romantic advice and encouragement. As periodicals began chasing the funny-sci-fi whizzkid for more of his erudite interviews to publicise his book, Canter also found it a bit awkward to arrive home while Adams was in full flow, partly philosophising, partly seducing an attractive young interviewer.

Two months after Seacon 79, however, came the real eye-opener. Douglas had been excited, in early October, to spot his book in shops for the very first time while out strolling between pubs with Christopher Priest, and turned bright red with sheepish pleasure when he was recognised by the shop owner. A few weeks later Pan sent Douglas a car to take him to a signing session set up by Forbidden Planet, the one-year-old comic store opened by the Titan group on Denmark Street in central London. A lengthy distance from the shop, however, the cab was forced to slow to a crawl because the streets were packed with young people – norms, punks, hippies, freaks of all denominations – who the driver presumed were there for some form of protest. It was only when Douglas squeezed through the door of the shop that he could accept the fact that all of this was down to him. Throughout the day books dematerialised from shelves and solid hours were spent meeting the members of the improbably long and winding queue of admirers, some coyly expressing their thanks, some offering pictures of favourite characters, some literally singing their praises, some even in costume, as Slartibartfast or Zaphod, overjoyed to be meeting their new comedy hero. The eventual press coverage of this sci-fi bun-fight was hyperbolic (not least thanks to Douglas' talent for exaggeration), but it's certainly true that the signing went on for so long beyond the allotted time that he was late arriving for dinner at Terry Jones' house that evening – with an astoundingly exciting excuse. Jones must have been terribly pleased to have been wrong in his misgivings about *Hitchhiker* – he even provided a number of unused sarcastic quotes for the cover, such as 'Every word is a gem ... it's only the order they're put in that worries me.' With a sizeable initial print run of 60,000, *The Hitchhiker's Guide to the Galaxy* would hit number one within a fortnight, sell a quarter of a million within three months, and just keep on selling. 'I think the Sunday after it came out, I'd gone out to buy the newspapers, and I came back and there was a message on my answering machine from somebody at Pan Books, saying, "You should have a look at the *Sunday Times*!"' Seeing that his book was top of the charts, Adams said, 'was one of those moments in life, when you realise, "We're not in Kansas any more!"'

So success brought fame and sex and an instantly devoted following, but still any real breakthrough with money was not quite in sight. There was a lot more of it than hitherto, undeniably, as evidenced by Canter's memory of Adams popping down to the corner shop for a Coke, and coming back with an entire crate, just because he could. Shortly after, Douglas decided to move to a larger flat in Highbury New Park and invited Jon to join him as a lodger, which the latter admitted 'did mark a change'. However, authors' royalties hang in the air for six months after their books arrive on shelves, and the advance was only helping with his previously crushing overdraft. In finding new things for Arthur and Ford to get up to on Radio 4, despite a handsome rise in fee, Douglas was now clearly seeing the immense gap between radio and television salaries at which Cleese habitually sneered, so, particularly given the time constraints, it's understandable that the final quarter of the original radio *Hitchhiker* seems quite so disconnected.

The first episode to be recorded that autumn did have the added attraction of being filmed in construction for a TV feature narrated by Perkins, capturing the cast enjoying a read-through of the Nutrimatic sequence, and the producer and Kingsland trying (and not quite managing) to create the sound of two million off-key robots singing the Sirius Cybernetic Company's

Above: Christopher and Janet Adams show their pride in a strangely unmistakable newly arrived Douglas, 1952.

Left: The diminutive Frood, circa 1954.

Top left: Young Douglas and sister Sue celebrate their Scots ancestry. **Top right:** Douglas welcomes new siblings Jane and James Thrift into the family. **Bottom left:** Playing the title role in Brentwood School play *The Tramp* gave the Frood his first real taste of fame. **Bottom right:** Despite briefly being Captain of Brentwood's Junior Second XI, Adams never particularly cared for the 'dull and pointless' game of cricket.

The guerrilla outfit, Adams-Smith-Adams. Will Adams (left): "This was a publicity picture for *Several Poor Players Strutting and Fretting*. We'd borrowed the costumes from the Arts Theatre and the pictures were taken by one Mike Cotton on Cambridge station, 15 May 1973."

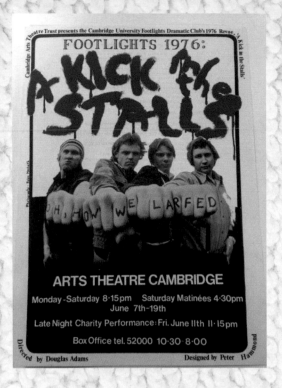

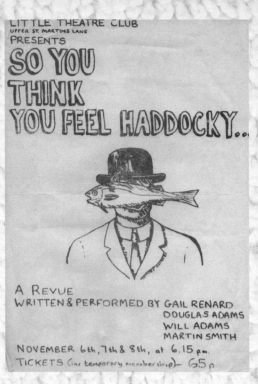

Top: Posters for Douglas' 1976 directorial effort *A Kick In The Stalls*, and the previous year's non-Footlights *So You Think You Feel Haddocky*. Will Adams: "It was the least bad of a whole string of irrelevant name suggestions, including, as I recall, 'Bunking With Grandfather' (a subtitle in a foreign film Douglas had seen). I designed the poster in a Magritte-ish way to try and give the title some 'sense'…" **Bottom:** A montage design for *The Patter of Tiny Minds'* London debut, January 1974. From top: Mary Adams (Allen), John Smith (Lloyd), Will Adams, Douglas Adams, Martin Smith. No cats were shaved in the making of this poster.

-Lady Margaret Players/J.T./Adams, Smith, Adams
Presents a Revue in the School of Pythagoras
11pm June 14th, 15th, 16th, Tickets 30p
From St. John's College Porters Lodge
and at door. Cheap day return 50p

Several Poor Players Strutting and Fretting

lady margaret/SPP/presents/
another hour upon the stage
strutting & fretting with
adams~smith~adams in the
school of pythagoras 10.30pm
nov 15.16.17 ~tickets 30p ~on sale
from st. john's college porters

THE PATTER OF TINY MINDS
a revue

adams/smith/adams
presents

the amazing three headed revue

Three further attempts
by Douglas, Martin
and Will to take
on the might of the
Footlights, and emerge
the true Cambridge
comedy kings.

CERBERUS

ADC Theatre Park Street November 6-9   11.15pm
Tickets 40p from Arts Cinema and at door. Arghh

Top & left: Adams-Smith-Adams larking around for publicity, "taken in the wilds near Madingley with someone's Land Rover on 17 October 1973…" **Above:** Young Douglas with Jon Canter in the lounge of their Holloway Road flat, circa 1979.

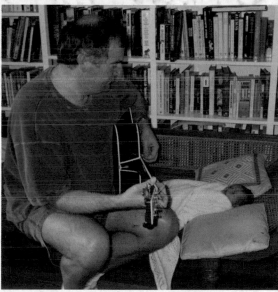

Top: Despite being the perfect host, nobody revelled in Douglas and Jane's Partially Unplugged parties more than he did. This is his reaction to the playing of David Gilmour, Margo Buchanan and Robbie McIntosh. **Bottom:** Douglas auditions the youngest member of the house band, Polly Jane Rocket Adams, aged: a few weeks.

Top: 25 November 1991: Douglas and Jane laughing through their wedding day (father of the bride Bill Belson dispensing confetti on the right), before setting off for a free reception at the Groucho Club courtesy of an incredible third Golden Pan.

Bottom left: A proud Frood backstage at Pink Floyd's Earl's Court concert after his 42nd birthday on-stage treat, with sister 'Little' Jane Thrift, October 1994.

Bottom right: Douglas' family together on the set of *Dirk Gently*, 2011. Clockwise from top left: James Thrift, Joe Thrift, Jane Thrift, Sue Adams, Max Thrift, Polly Adams and Ella Thrift.

offensive anthem 'Share and Enjoy'. The resulting episode also finally revealed the much-desired villain: Zaphod's psychiatrist Gag Halfrunt, no longer a one-line gag but a laid-back maniac determined to stamp out all trace of the Earth for fear of the Ultimate Question's discovery leading to a mass outbreak of contentment in the Galaxy – with Bill Wallis returning as the newly identified (thanks to the book) Prostetnic Vogon Jeltz, hired to do Halfrunt's dirty work. The rest of the episode largely involved the making of a decent cup of tea, and a totally unexpected pastiche of a séance. In the agnostic Douglas' Galaxy, with half an hour to fill, science and the supernatural were deemed equally viable, and death and 'the afterlife' – not to mention reincarnation, and the existence of gods, albeit rather untrustworthy ones – were all grist to the mill. He had already decided that the series' ultimate aim was to find God, the 'Disinterested Ruler', wherever and whatever he was.

The final episodes bristle with quality guest stars, including *Rock Follies* star Rula Lenska as the Lintilla clones, Ken Campbell himself playing their exterminator Poodoo (the line 'Marvin's got Poodoo' caused half an hour of hopeless corpsing against the clock), and over a year after not being able to take the job as Adams' ideal Slartibartfast, the great John Le Mesurier stepped in to portray the Wise Old Bird, which the aged gent did not enjoy, complaining, 'They made me sit in a corridor, in a draught, all afternoon.' For The Man In The Shack, the seemingly harmless solipsistic Godhead (who, like Douglas as he raced to get the scripts into the cast's hands, was compelled to create and decide the fate of people who existed only in his mind), rising star Jonathan Pryce was booked to come in for the day. But as Douglas was still hidden away trying to actually write the denouement of the series, there was no script for him to perform, besides a few vague interjections, and so Perkins asked him to step in as the ironically far more pivotal role of Zarniwoop, leaving Stephen Moore, the most avidly keen voice stand-in in the cast, to play God, receiving his dialogue with an amused 'What are you on, Douglas?' (the *Radio Times* was forced to anagrammatically credit the role to 'another', or 'Ron Hate'.) By this stage, Adams' script directions were becoming ever more desperate in their unhelpfulness:

ZAPHOD   (As he slides - we'll have to make a **very** graphic
               sound effect as I've spent the last half-hour
               trying to come up with a line which says 'I'm

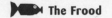

```
sliding along the ice', but haven't got one)
Weeeee hoooooo ... ahhhhh ...
(The point of that last bit of deathless writing
is that Zaphod enjoys the slide for a couple of
seconds, and then gets alarmed as he sees the
entrance coming up with nothing beyond it. Convey
that, Mark, if you will/can!)
```

And as Arthur finally became something of an action hero, fighting against the forces of the evil shoemakers, Adams added a similar challenge, that he should sound: 'Simultaneously astonished, worried about the footwarriors, and slightly disappointed. Bit of anger in there too. Come on, Simon, you can do it.'

In many ways it was a smart get-out to end the radio saga with a dithering omniscient puppeteer of the Universe, as few sci-fi properties could get away with such an improbably plotted serial, summarised with growing exhaustion every day by a quizzical Peter Jones. Discrepancies here have often been weakly explained away by Zaphod's transgression into a false universe, even though this was clearly forgotten at the time. But then, as Adams took pains to underline, any suggestion that the series had any meaningful direction was illusory: 'Writing episodically meant that when I finished one episode I had no idea about what the next one would contain. When, in the twists and turns of the plot, some event suddenly seemed to illuminate things that had gone before, I was as surprised as anyone else.'

Having written a neat ending for the first series, Adams left everything up in the air this time just in case, with the revelation that Zaphod was in cahoots to destroy the Earth, sending Arthur storming off into space on the *HoG* and stranding everyone else in that windy shack for ever. Even then, the post-production work facing Perkins and his team was horrific, with everyone working on editing and sound effects right down to the wire, night and day, until Paddy Kingsland had to beg to be allowed home because he had started hallucinating. The tape for the last five minutes of the last episode was still being sliced with razors less than an hour before its broadcast time, but Perkins had the very final task of adding wind effects and The Man In The Shack's mewing cat to the sequence, before running out into the street and handing the finished tape to a BBC employee in a fast car, who zoomed the three miles up the road to Broadcasting House and slammed the tape into the slot for broadcast with barely a minute to spare. The toughest week in the history of *Hitchhiker* was over.

'It was a big mistake,' Adams subsequently insisted. 'The first series was simply something that was there and people found. The second series had all this hoopla around it. But the speed with which we had to make it was unconscionable. It was so complicated it created nightmares.' So many of the ideas in Arthur's final audio odyssey were to be forgotten, never recycled for the books or any other *Hitchhiker* product, which could easily be blamed on their painful creation (also by the wayside lay Arthur's planned discovery of meaningful patterns in the weather, not to mention 'spider pornography'). But, Douglas added, 'A couple of years ago I was looking something up in the book of scripts and began to think, "This is like a disowned child." I've actually been unfair to it because all I remember is the hell of making it.' In years to come he was to insist that he would have been happy writing adventures on Radio 4 for his entire career, and when Peter Jones closed the twelfth half-hour:

What does the future hold for our heroes now? What does the past or present hold for that matter?

Will Arthur Dent now embark on a terrible and protracted vendetta against Zaphod Beeblebrox? Will he be all right in the Universe with only the Infinite Improbability Drive Ship, Marvin the Paranoid Android, Lintilla the archaeologist, Eddie the shipboard computer, a lot of chatty doors and a battered copy of 'THHGTTG' for company?

Who will Ford Prefect ally himself with - Arthur Dent, Zaphod Beeblebrox, or a large Pan Galactic Gargle Blaster?

Will there ever be another series of that wholly remarkable and mystifying entity 'THHGTTG'...?

Find out if you can!

… The truth is that the creator had absolutely no idea if there would be. A year or two later, it was Mark Wing-Davey who had a sneaky brainwave for a return to Radio 4, plotting with Douglas to do the first ever cross-dimension radio broadcast, airing two entirely different new Fits of *Hitchhiker* on long-wave and short-wave simultaneously, with both stories ending at the precise same point – a doomed experiment guaranteed to cause BBC bosses to crawl under their desks and moan. But, sadly, the deciding factor for Adams and radio would be one thing: money. 'While it was all very pleasant to have your own radio series,' he wrote, 'especially one that somebody had written in to say they had heard, it didn't exactly buy you lunch.'

Perfectly Natural And Nothing To Be Ashamed Of

1980 was the real turning point in Douglas' life. Three years earlier he had risen from depression to pen something which caught the imagination of a generation, but the instant result of that was heart-poundingly intense stress and snatched moments of triumph; it was only when the real money began to come in that the struggling artist was finally dead, and in his place stood the most commandingly successful millionaire epicure in British comedy and publishing – who just coincidentally still managed to struggle greatly with his art.

The alteration naturally did not escape ridicule from his old friends, some of whom were still kipping on the floor at BBC Radio LE and making sarcastic charity demands from Douglas if they saw him. Marshall and Renwick went even further, introducing irregular swipes in *The Burkiss Way* at a character called 'Mr. Different Adams' (who arrogantly drawled, 'I see comedy as a kind of isosceles triangle ...') and even convincing Peter Jones to send up his performance as The Book with a rare guest appearance, ending the 1979 Christmas special mid-sentence:

```
Somewhere, in the shady part of the Milky Way, just outside a
small, blueish star orbited by a few damp planets of dubiously
desirable reputation, there is a tiny hole in the electro-
magnetic airspace. To plug this void in the continuum, the
inscrutable monoliths of the collapsing star system of Radio 4
Light Entertainment occasionally employ a tiny, imperceptible
device known as 'The Burkiss Way'. The Hitchhiker's Guide to
the Galaxy defines this as 'A programme of infinite tedium,
which gets cheap laughs by doing pathetic parodies of other,
much more successful shows.' Its impressions are notoriously
unrecognisable. This one, for instance, sounds absolutely
nothing like me! And as if that weren't bad enough, it
invariably ends in a silly fashion, just when you least...
```

A further comedic attack one year later was sharpened by being entirely performed by the cast, with Fred Harris attempting a strangely nasal Peter Jones in a sketch so barbed as to make it a surprise that it came after Lloyd's time as producer of the show:

JO KENDALL   And there will be another edition of the television version, of the book, of the play, of the radio series, of 'THHGTTG', of the licence to print money … at the same script next week.

FRED HARRIS   We're very sorry about that. But now …

GRAMS   JOURNEY OF THE SORCERER

CHRIS EMMETT 'The Scriptwriter's Guide To The Galaxy'. By a man who would rather write 'Doctor Who'. Starring Peter Jones as this bit …

GRAMS   SCI-FI AMBIENCE

FRED HARRIS   One of the most interesting things about the Six-Headed Omniquargs of the Planet Sygosworoldon in the star system of Grudnivulgar-Actinex in the constellation of Go-And-Upset-Another-Scrabble-Board-Les-I-Really-Need-A-Name, is that they have only one word to stand for all 400 million nouns, adjectives, prepositions, verbs and adverbs. This is both a good thing and a bad thing. Bad for them, because since the word is obscene no one is actually allowed to use it anyway. But good for science fiction scriptwriters, because it enables me to go on and on and on about it for sixteen pages every week before we even start the story … (Gasps) praying I'll get to a full stop before I keel over into this synthesiser, which I'm having trouble playing anyway …

At around this time, Douglas' closest collaborators were also embarking on their own geeky comedy saga for Radio 4, concentrating on a different stable of fantasy fiction, when Geoffrey Perkins produced the star-studded series *Hordes of the Things*, written by Andrew Marshall and John Lloyd. It was an epic piece of work, sumptuously cast and filled with funny ideas, expertly trouncing Tolkien and pre-empting the BBC's own celebrated radio adaptation of *Lord of the Rings* by several months. But although this time Perkins had the perfectly honed scripts well in advance, and a schedule galaxies away from the stresses of *Hitchhiker*, the programme failed to make a lasting impression on any but the most devoted fantasy fans (with senses of humour), until its belated CD release.

All of this seemed beneath Adams to even acknowledge, as the new year revealed its own challenges, thankfully softened somewhat by the increasing figures on his bank statements. What began with a crate of Coke soon led to Balthazars of champagne with the finest, longest lunches, just as hitchhiking gave way to an obsession with flight upgrades, to reach the best hotels all over the world – and when it came to automobiles, he eventually admitted, 'I do spend a lot of money on things that I don't need, like fast cars, which is pretty silly, considering I only use them to pooter about town. I'd always promised myself that when I had some money I wouldn't do something silly like buying a flashy car, so, as soon as *Hitchhiker* went to number one in the best-seller lists, I went out and bought a Porsche 911. I hated it. Driving it around in London was like taking a Ming vase to a football match. Going for a drive was like setting out to invade Poland. I got rid of it after going into a skid coming out of Hyde Park and crashing into a wall by the Hard Rock Café … there was a huge queue of people outside, all of whom cheered loudly, so I got rid of it and got a Golf GTI.' This hubristic crash would be referenced in the second book, where a lengthy petrolhead dialogue between Ford and Zaphod transforms Hyde Park Corner into the third moon of Jaglan Beta.

Douglas had once assured John that he would be a millionaire by the time he reached 33⅓, but he was to beat that particular deadline by some years. The men of the Adams dynasty had always had a strong sense of entitlement: a love of the finer things in life seemed to be woven into his very DNA, and from the dawning of that decade of greed, the 1980s, the Bovril-sandwich-eating comedy fan evolved into rather a different creature, harder to identify with in a period of austerity – indeed, many of his friends and colleagues found him harder to identify with at the time. He could be tactless, insisting on the priciest restaurants with friends who worked to a different budget, but his nature was above all a generous one, few friends would deny – he tended to pay for all the ruinous wines.

The strangest thing of all about this transformation, however, is that Douglas had been preparing for it for so long, positively opening the whole *Hitchhiker* saga with jokes about the guilt felt by the extremely rich, and much more along those lines was to come. But although money can certainly buy you some approximation of happiness, or at least prepare the ground for happiness to grow, Douglas Adams' wealth would obviously not spell the end of his troubles. If anything, every pang of frustration he had felt at his typewriter up to this point had been only a teaser for what was to come.

FIT THE THIRD

NEMESIS

"The Guide is definitive. Reality is frequently inaccurate."

"Listen, Ford, everything's cool and froody."
"You mean everything's under control."
"No, I do not mean everything's under control.
That would not be cool and froody ..."
– Zaphod Beeblebrox and Ford Prefect

Douglas Adams was standing naked on a beach in Cornwall, staring out to sea, surrounded by wads of money he had strewn on the sand. Slightly further up the beach were a cameraman, sound man, TV director and the few other technical crew who were allowed into the 'closed set' – along with a sizeable gang of onlookers keen to see what a best-selling novelist looked like without any clothes on. He was rich, he was young, and his backside was soon to be on television – and yet he was already signalling discontent with his creation.

It was the summer of 1980, and the BBC TV adaptation of *Hitchhiker* was finally under way, but Adams had not been idle leading up to this small but slightly embarrassing cameo appearance – by the end of January that year, the second radio series and Theatr Clwyd productions had already been and gone. Chief among his active worries was the follow-up to his first book, which was already confirmed to be called *The Restaurant at the End of the Universe*, but besides knowing that his updated Milliways sequence would feature, getting the second half of his all-but-epic literary offering on the page was no less fraught than his first book had been. His chief conviction, however, was that he knew exactly how his book would end – and it would be his last word on the Hitchhiker's Guide. Even while the tide washed over his ankles as he launched his increasingly ubiquitous franchise on TV, Douglas felt ready to move on from the sci-fi saga.

Something Even More Bizarre And Inexplicable

Where the first novel had a clear narrative flow to follow, the fevered semi-synthetic events of *Hitchhiker*'s second run on radio presented the author with more of a buffet of ideas to graze on – he openly admitted to having no real direction on the wireless: 'You map out a plot, and you write the first scene, and inevitably the first scene isn't funny and you have to do something else, and you finally get the scene to be funny but it's no longer about what it was meant to be about, so you have to jack in the plot you had in mind and do a new one ... After a while, it became pointless plotting too far in advance, because it never worked, since the vast body of the material arrived serially. I'd often reach a point where I'd go, "If I knew I was going to wind up here I would have done something else there." So writing the books is an attempt to make sense of what I've already done, which usually involves rather major surgery. Especially with the second book, I was trying with hindsight to make a bit of sense out of it all. I knew how it would end, with the prehistoric Earth stuff ...'

Determined to try the well-seasoned B-Ark material in a whole new form, Douglas hoped that his new fans would be happy to see Arthur's saga reach a conclusion with him and Ford philosophically accepting their fate amongst the Golgafrinchans, making do with the knowledge that all life on Earth was to be futile, and perhaps settling down with nice girls from the less offensive minority among the B-Ark crash survivors:

> Many hours later Arthur and Mella sat and watched the moon rise over the dull red glow of the trees ...
>
> "You're very strange," she said.
>
> "No, I'm very ordinary," said Arthur, "but some very strange things have happened to me. You could say I'm more differed from than differing."
>
> "And that other world your friend talked about, the one that got pushed into a black hole."
>
> "Ah, that I don't know about. It sounds like something from the book."

"What book?"

Arthur paused. "*The Hitchhiker's Guide to the Galaxy*," he said at last.

"What's that?"

"Oh, just something I threw into the river this evening. I don't think I'll be wanting it any more," said Arthur Dent.

From there, however, 'I got very stuck because I knew how it ended but couldn't work out how to begin it. In the end I thought, "Oh well, sod it, I'll just go with the end." So I wrote the end and then wrote the chapter before that, then the one before that ... I eventually got all the way back and said, "Ah, that must be the beginning, then."' Several years later, he explained to Lloyd, 'I have a difficulty with the beginnings of books ... It's a truism that as you get older, each year goes more quickly, and the reason for that is very simple: that when you're one year old, you live through a year, and it's your whole life over again. When you're thirty, it's only a thirtieth of what you've been through so far, relatively it's a small amount. Now when you start writing a book, you think, "Well, what's the first word going to be? 'The'? I mean, is 'The' a good enough word to begin this book with? How many books have begun with the word 'The', it's got to be something more interesting than that? Maybe the first word should be 'Aardvark'...?" Because at that moment, the first word you write then is the entire book!' Clearly, Adams' brain would not let him countenance any drop in quality for his second outing in paperback.

This tortuous process was going on throughout most of 1980, and although he had a strong support network – his then-girlfriend was the blonde, attractive Pan Press Officer Jacqui Graham, while Jon Canter almost had to promote himself from housemate (or rather, lodger) to part-time secretary, fielding endless calls for Douglas from big-shot producers and other opportunists – *Restaurant* did not appear on the typewriter easily. Expectations, of course, weighed heavily on him: 'People assume by the time that you've reached a certain level of recognition and status that you must therefore have mastered something – you find that actually makes it more rather than less difficult ... I think it's partly a terribly British self-consciousness, you know, that people are actually going to read this stuff, and you're terribly embarrassed about it. So why you would then become a writer is something I really don't have a good answer for ... It's not right to say you can write what you please, and that you've earned the right to write what you please. You've earned yourself an audience, sure, but to keep that audience, you have to maintain the same standards – which is not to say you carry on doing the same thing: if you do, you're compromising in a way, because the whole point of the thing you did in the first place was that it was new and original. So you have to try and strive to be new and original, and it's a hard task.'

'Saying I write science fiction is rather like saying the Pythons do historical movies. In a way it's true but it misses the point,' he explained to the *NME* in 1982, and once again underlining the comic nature of his work over sci-fi, Adams was wont to tell interviewers, 'I particularly admire funny writers, because I know how incredibly difficult it is. Evelyn Waugh is very high up there, and Jane Austen. People have this idea that humour is in some way a sort of lesser emotion, which I don't accept at all. I think that good, funny writing is amongst the finest writing of any type.' However, one of the most mind-boggling things about Adams' second novel is that it was the first one he had written as a fan of the humorist dubbed by him 'the Mozart of the English Language', the one chap who would be most cited as a major influence on his work, not least by Adams himself: 'As a kid I read *Dan Dare* and I watched *Doctor Who*, but was never a big science fiction buff. When people are looking for influences, they always sort of look to science fiction, and never to where the real influences are, which is someone like Wodehouse, because Wodehouse, so far as I know, never wrote about robots or spaceships. But the style in many ways has its roots there ...'

'People sometimes say to me,' he added, '"Do you ever aspire to write a serious book?" And my practised glib answer to that is, "No, my aspirations are much greater than that, I aspire to write like P. G. Wodehouse."' This makes it sound, as one would expect from any humorously inclined public school boy, as if the world of the great Pelham Grenville was one which had swum into Adams' ken as a child, and in which he had delighted throughout his upbringing, but somehow he had never opened one of The Master's books until a friend presented him with a *Jeeves* novel at the turn of the 1980s, whereupon, 'I suddenly realised, with goose pimples rising all over me, that I was in the presence of a great master. Since then I have devoured his work voraciously, not merely because he is a great comic writer, but because he is arguably the greatest musician of the English language I have ever encountered. He may not have anything to say about Real Life (he would hoot at the very idea) but art practised at that level doesn't have to be *about* anything.' Wodehouse of course was the King of the comic simile, and many (famous Wodehousephile Stephen Fry among them) would pay tribute to Adams' own verve with the literary convention, albeit subverted in the famous line 'The ships hung in the sky in much the same way that bricks don't.' But while the great comic novelist was keen on the odd trans-ferred epithet (Bertie 'prongs a moody forkful' of eggs, etc.), the emotions of Adams' inanimate objects tended to be cybernetic. Douglas would be so regularly gifted with association with Wodehouse that he was asked to write a foreword for a reprinted edition of the book The Master was working on when he died, *Sunset at Blandings*:

> Master? Great genius? Oh yes. One of the most blissful joys of the English language is the fact that one of its greatest practitioners ever, one of the guys on the very top table of all, was a jokesmith. Though maybe it shouldn't be that big a surprise. Who else would be up there? Austen, of course, Dickens and Chaucer. The only one who couldn't make a joke to save his life would be Shakespeare ... Maybe it's because our greatest writing genius was incapable of being funny that we have decided that being funny doesn't count. Which is tough on Wodehouse (as if he could have cared less) because his entire genius was for being funny, and being funny in such a sublime way as to put mere poetry in the shade ... Wodehouse never burdened himself with the task of justifying the ways of God to Man, but only of making Man, for a few hours at a time, inextinguishably happy ... He doesn't need to be serious. He's better than that. He's up in the stratosphere of what the human mind can do, above tragedy and strenuous thought, where you will find Bach, Mozart, Einstein, Feynman, and Louis Armstrong, in the realms of pure, creative playfulness.

Such emphatic appreciation makes it clear that there was no writer Douglas more admired, and wished to be like – and yet, as professional writers, they could not have been further apart. Wodehouse famously lived only to write, to pour out his stories onto the typewriter seven days a week if he could, with a prodigious output tirelessly published throughout a very long life, resulting in over a hundred titles on shelves. Just as he learned Paul

Simon riffs note by painstaking note, to achieve the honour of comparison with Wodehouse Douglas Adams had to agonise over every last key press. But that was okay – Pan had set their publication date for October: they felt, surely, that would be plenty of time for any enthusiastic new author to deliver the goods ...

This Is, Of Course, Impossible

'At first, I wasn't that interested in doing a visual version of *Hitchhiker*,' Adams said in the first flush of radio success. 'But while I was working on *Doctor Who* I began to realise that we have an enormous amount of special-effects stuff which is simply not being used as it might be. If it turns out the way I'm beginning to visualise it, I think it could actually look very extraordinary ...' At first, the BBC envisaged a *Hitchhiker* cartoon, but the creator countered, 'I've never been keen on that idea, because my impulse has always been with these fantastical situations to try – I don't say I'm always successful – but to try and make them as real and solid and concrete as possible. And I think you're really stacking the odds against yourself if you go into animation, because it tends to emphasise the fantastical nature of the events. I want the events to be fantastical but to appear to be as real as possible.' When the Corporation announced the live-action series, he explained to interviewers, 'Within certain groups of people *Hitchhiker* is now very well known, but it isn't well known in England as a whole. So one of the reasons for doing it is for all those people who don't listen to the radio and can't read. To be arrogant – this is an appallingly arrogant thing to say – television may or may not be good for *Hitchhiker* but *Hitchhiker* will be good for television. Television situation comedy has got to a dire state. I say that *Hitchhiker* is actually situation comedy – sitcom does NOT have to be about newly-weds in a bedsit or whatever. I wanted to show that there is actually far more that you can do with comedy, both on radio and TV, than is being done.'

Returning his story to its sitcom roots was no regression for the comedy connoisseur, and in many ways, similar to how adapting *Hitchhiker* to prose fiction allowed him to flesh out his world (establishing that Mr. Prosser was descended from Genghis Khan, that Ford found Earthbound work as an actor while Arthur was a producer on BBC local radio and so on), the visual dimension allowed him to enrich and define his Galaxy as he saw it (with the help of an enormous team of creative people, naturally, including graphics designer Doug Burd, rookie effects designer Jim Francis and his young assistant Stuart Murdoch, who would graduate to designer for *Blackadder Goes Forth*). Just as the innovative use of glass mattes in the pilot, as supervised by designer Andrew Howe-Davis with French artist Jean Peyre, could turn an average storeroom set into a gigantic Vogon hangar (complete with salvaged Statue of Liberty just visible in the top left corner), Adams pounced on the chance to retell Arthur Dent's tale on a larger canvas, using the luxury of an extra five minutes' screen time on the usual half-hour to add extra bits of business, such as Ford's enthusiasm for Dentrassi cuisine being undermined by the muck the chefs deemed good enough for the Vogons (David Dixon would be compelled to chow down on so much blue-dyed alien food he would be struck down with a crippling case of poisoning while out Christmas shopping). Otherwise, although the first shot to be filmed was the view from a Vogon ship, taken from the top of the unopened Nat West Tower in the City of London (eventually renamed 'Tower 42'), as the initial cast and crew arrived in Balcombe, Sussex in early May to recreate the demolition of Arthur's home, plus the famous pub sequence at the Red Lion, the screenplay they worked from was essentially a direct adaptation, beginning yet again with the now legendary muddy introduction to the hero:

SEQ 5A EXT HOUSE - TK A (FILM)
ARTHUR DENT, VERY HURRIEDLY DRESSED IN WHATEVER WAS LYING
NEAREST HIS BED, IS LYING IN FRONT OF A HUGE BULLDOZER.
THE DRIVER HAS HIS FEET UP, READING THE SUN.
THE BULLDOZER IS YELLOW.
ARTHUR'S HOUSE IS JUST A SMALL COTTAGE STANDING ON ITS OWN IN
A SMALL COUNTRY LANE.

Alan J. W. Bell is a name that many comedy fans recognise as the last credit on Roy Clarke's infamously long-running Sunday teatime sitcom *Last of the Summer Wine*, a wistfully bucolic series about a gang of misbehaving pensioners. However, although a generation older than Douglas, the subsequently Emmy-winning Bell was new to the upper TV echelons in 1981, having directed two episodes of Palin & Jones' *Ripping Yarns*, and only took over the reins of Clarke's cosy classic in the same year that *Hitchhiker* was finding its way through the BBC TV system – he would also shortly bring the weirdness of Spike Milligan's *There's A Lot Of It About* to BBC2, so his pitch for the job of transplanting Douglas' radio hit to the screen as producer/director did not seem so unusual. His appointment did, however, infuriate the writer from the start, as he had hoped to have Lloyd on hand to really capture the spirit of *Hitchhiker*, preferably with Perkins in an advisory role, whereas Bell was quickly quoted as originally believing Adams' story to be unfilmable, and was somewhat dismissive of sci-fi as a genre. 'The *Hitchhiker* television series was not a happy production,' Adams was to repeatedly harrumph. 'There was a personality clash between myself and the director. And between the cast and the director. And between the tea lady and the director ...' But the truth is that anyone given the task of having the final say on how *Hitchhiker* reached TV screens throughout the UK was going to be facing a nightmare with Douglas, who obviously felt strongly on the one hand – 'It's very important that it looks as extraordinary as it sounded, and it mustn't look like *Doctor Who* or *Blake's Seven*' – but at the same time he admitted, 'All I have is a very vague visual sense about it, in the way that I started out with a vague audio sense about how *Hitchhiker* should be. We've got to work that through.' TV did not quite work that way, and somebody had to accept the poisoned chalice of bringing this nebulous striving for perfection down to budgeted reality.

Lloyd's shunting over into an 'Associate Producer' role (honorary, as the scheduling of *Not*'s third series made any active participation from him impossible) was one of many thorns in Adams' side, but his animosity towards Bell – 'I had a great deal of say in the TV series, but the producer didn't have a great deal of listen, unfortunately. I found it deeply frustrating, I must say, because it could have been something absolutely wonderful. I had a definite set of ideas about how to make it unlike anything that had been on television before. The producer wasn't interested in that ...' – belies just how much of *Hitchhiker*'s international success can be traced back to Bell's influence. It was Bell, after all, who made the momentous decision to keep Arthur in his dressing gown, cutting Adams' suggestion that his hero change into a spangly space outfit early on. Douglas and John could have worried about every shot until the dawn of the 1990s, but Bell's job was to cut Adams' invention down to size, to fit the small screen – and few would deny that he achieved that.

Douglas and Alan locked horns very early on when it came to the casting for the pilot, which Adams was determined should carry over the existing radio line-up. Although comedy boss John Howard Davies was keen for up-and-coming actor Peter Davison to take on the role of Arthur, Simon Jones' ownership of the role was considered undebatable by his friend, and eventually there was a hard-won compromise in which Geoff McGivern would lose out to yet another *Rock Follies* graduate, who had also made a startling impression as Ariel in the BBC's production of *The Tempest*, David Dixon. Hired for his unearthly appearance, Dixon was given violet contact lenses to further distinguish Ford from humanity, but this never came across on screen – the actor's decision to psych himself up to a frenzy before every cry of 'Action' did, however, help to communicate a Ford with a boundless enthusiasm (usually for being elsewhere).

The pilot was not cast-rich, but Bill Wallis was replaced as Prosser with his old Footlights contemporary Joe Melia and, losing the important link between Prosser and Jeltz, Stratford Johns and Frank Middlemass were contacted to take on the mantle of the Chief Vogon, but in the end sexagenarian veteran Martin Benson was chosen to put up with the hideous costume and make-up – designed by Dee Robson and Joan Stribling respectively, and based on Adams' direction that the race should resemble 'a Gerald Scarfe picture of Orson Welles'. Bell had even taken Sir John Gielgud to lunch, with the aged thespian complaining that nobody ever offered him sitcom roles, but the great man's agent decided that the role was beneath him.

Mike Oldfield had expressed an interest in providing a new theme for the show, to Douglas' delight, but the credits – showing a lost astronaut floating through space – were already synced to Souster's new recording. Bell also retained Paddy Kingsland on radiophonic and sound-effects duties, acknowledging to him that the show was 'a sound production with pictures', while setting out to do all he could to provide extraordinary pictures, using the best technology to achieve his aim of 'showing infinity' – the creation of matte shots is one ideal example, but besides innovative Quantel digital effects the pilot also introduced a projection-based method to place an animated Guide in Arthur's hands without the restrictions of blue-screen compositing, which caused consternation among many technical experts who were almost convinced that some kind of working hand-held computer had been developed for the series. Bell's vision, abetted by a superlative technical team, clocked up a number of impressive innovations in visual effects as they strained to make radio's imaginative suggestions seem solid.

Hitchhiker on TV would also sound the horn for a new era of computer graphics, but of course although Adams originally mused, 'What you can do with computer diagrams and computer graphics is immensely exciting,' no actual computers were used at all. It's easy to forget how embryonic the concept was in 1980, until you see the blocky hip-at-the-time gag graphics on a programme like *Three of a Kind* and realise that the real thing would have rapidly made the *Hitchhiker* TV series an eyesore. In those pioneering days of home-VCR ownership, Adams was certain that he wanted to create a dense half-hour-plus of television, with more jokes than anyone could catch in one sitting – 'I like the idea of a programme where, when you get to the end of it, you feel you didn't get it all. There are so many programmes that are half an hour long and at the end of it you're half an hour further into your life with nothing to show for it. If you didn't get it all, that's much more stimulating.' However, his script only provided the basic outline of how this would work:

THE SCENE IS REPLACED BY A COMPUTER DISPLAY WITH FLASHING
WORDS ALL OVER IT.
TRUTH SUSPICION COEFFICIENT: ZERO.
APE DESCENDED LIFE FORMS: GULLIBILITY RATING: NINE.
BETELGEUSE (prn. Bee-tle-jooce) STAR SYSTEM XY 8s. Z gamma. Life
forms carbon based.
WE THEN SEE A COMPUTER GRAPHIC OF FORD PREFECT FROM VARIOUS
ANGLES WITH SPURIOUS BIOLOGICAL READOUTS.

The credit for realising Adams' graphical ambition, providing the most lasting critical success of the project, belongs to the talented group at Pearce Studios led by South African animator (or 'graphimator') Rod Lord – and, by extension, to his teenage assistant in 1980, Kevin Davies, who would become one of *Hitchhiker*'s most envied fans, playing a creative role at junctures throughout the property's history in numerous media. Bell was editing a sequence covering a hopeful child's visit to the set of *The Empire Strikes Back* for the (subsequently tarnished) family show *Jim'll Fix It* when R2-D2's bleeping piqued the curiosity of Davies, the new assistant at Pearce Studios, which shared editing suites with the BBC. Being presented with a perfect example of his target audience for his new show, Alan was quick to canvas young Kevin on his feelings about the hallowed radio comedy being adapted for TV, and the excited lad lost no time at all in putting the director in touch with his boss, Rod. Once Bell got to see the resultant test footage of the Babel fish sequence, bringing the Guide to life with the backlit pseudo-neon presentation that would become synonymous with *Hitchhiker,* each letter of Peter Jones' narration painstakingly revealed one by one in sync with Kingsland's suitably bleepy SFX to provide the perfect illusion of what computer graphics could look like in a more sophisticated corner of the Galaxy (or on Earth, quite a few years later), the director/ producer knew that one of the trickiest elements of the adaptation was in good hands.

Adams was quick to agree, on the first of his irregular visits to Lord's studios, where he would be happy to dispense ideas for the info which flashed by each week – including, of course, further in-jokes such as naming the Guide Editor 'Web Nixo' in tribute to the man who brought him to Pan Books (although as he's described as a 'rather shifty-looking fat alien with strange beard and eyeshade ... undertakes sponsored lunch breaks for charity. Owns several charities', it was a dubious tribute). He also approved perfectly in-style blink-and-you'll-miss-it details added by the devoted animators, including the unpleasant fact that Vogons mate continually for three months every fifty years, and infamous galactic escort Eccentrica Gallumbit's entries which advertised her two-mile erogenous zones, assuring customers that she took Altairian Express and could be reached on 69-000 (with each zero representing one of her triple mammaries). 'These graphics sequences are digressions, really,' he said. 'They're commentaries on the plot, or more often on something that isn't in the plot but which is there in order to distract your attention from what's happening in the plot if it's getting boring at that point.'

The completed pilot wedded a full set of Pearce Studios' Guide sequences with the footage recorded in Sussex and at BBC TV Centre in June, utilising corridor sets recycled from *Alien* (as with *Who,* short lengths of corridor would be recycled, re-angled and reused endless times to give the illusion of not just being a few yards of painted delivery pallets – the eventual shining white *HoG* set would make good use of a spinning stage from the game show *Blankety Blank*). Young Davies was also employed for small but crucial details, such as affixing the jagged lettering of 'Don't Panic' on the Guide itself – as designed by Lord, the logo would help to set the phrase apart from its TV familiarity as Corporal Jones' catchphrase in *Dad's Army*.

Although it came in at an eye-watering £30,000 over budget, the taster generated ripples of intrigued approval throughout BBC LE once Bell had knocked it into shape, making the commission of a full series a formality. However, one further hurdle lay ahead. It was felt within the Corporation that a laugh track was needed to make the show work on screen – and as, of course, 'canned laughter' is an almost entirely imaginary phenomenon in British TV, that meant showing the first episode to a live audience of sci-fi aficionados. On 5th July the National Film Theatre was packed with fans eager to finally get to see Arthur and Ford in spectacular 2D, each issued with Vogon-illustrated guides to using the mono listening equipment provided, which was further demonstrated by Peter Jones in a specially made short film, quickly made at the BBC's Weather Centre, comprising Jones' only visual appearance in the *Hitchhiker* canon. Announcing that he was 'chosen from the many hundreds of actors who are out of work and available' to demonstrate how the programme's soundtrack had been treated by the BBC's new Babel fish modulator, and 'carefully scrambled, intensified, cross-patched, Dolby-ed, scrambled, unscrambled, scrambled again and bounced off a very large piece of toast' before it reached the headphones, the snarky elder statesman was abetted by the ever-handy Kevin as he explained the drill, read out some suitably negative listeners' letters from the *Radio Times*, subtly advertised the album and paperback, harrumphed about being taken for Simon Jones' father and the indignity of having to share a dressing room with a weather man, and got his own back by pointing out that Adams had spent so long travelling around the country signing books that an unsigned copy was worth more than a signed one. Gales of laughter followed, naturally, but in the end Douglas' insistence that a laugh track would ruin the show won out, and there would be no audience-recording sessions for the remaining five episodes, which were set to commence shooting in September – after a summer of mixed fortunes for the *Hitchhiker* brand.

Ladies And Gentlemen, Disaster Area ...

The Theatr Clwyd adaptation had been warmly received by *Hitchhiker* fans around the country, but by the time they were offered a stint at the Old Vic the company had been dramatically gazumped. In early 1980, against his better judgement, Ken Campbell had been convinced to try and outdo his success at the ICA, catering for the disappointed fans who missed out on his intimate production by turning *Hitchhiker* into a gigantic laser-filled extravaganza at celebrated rock venue the Rainbow Theatre, Finsbury Park. With the outside of the theatre transformed into a spaceport, punters discovered computerised consoles in the foyer where once again they could buy PGGBs and gigantic burgers from usherettes dressed as aliens, and then the £300,000 budget delivered an innovative revolving stage, earthquake effects, lasers courtesy of the Californian company behind the London Planetarium and even Prog King Rick Wakeman swooping down from the rafters inexplicably dressed as the Mekon, playing keyboards inside a flying saucer – all the pre-publicity made it clear that this was going to be the sci-fi event of the decade, the new *Rocky Horror*. With twenty cast members and a five-piece rock band, this was the ultimate step up from the intimate show at the ICA, an enormous undertaking ... but Campbell insisted on only being a hired director this time – an uncharacteristically shrewd decision from one of theatre's greatest risk-takers.

Thanks to the live-music element, many misconstrued the production as a musical, which was one of many direct influences from Douglas which would not allow him to eventually claim dissociation from the production. Needing a new device to replace Lloyd's Haggunenons, Adams had introduced the Universe's loudest rock band – Disaster Area – a galactically exaggerated play on his own obsession with sound systems which, along with the introduction of the Dish of the Day (an Amiglion Major Cow crafted, like much in the Rainbow production, by Kevin Davies), formed two new sequences in both the play and the second book, and subsequently the TV series. Infamously taking the name for the lead singer, an obese Elvis clone who was dead for tax reasons, from the still-thriving Islington estate agent Hotblack Desiato, Douglas even came up with some unused lyrics for the band's song about the lovers who kiss beneath an inexplicably exploding moon:

> *You know I followed you forever down the time stream,*
> *Woman like a vision from my space dreams,*
> *Forcefield time dams, star clouds, light rams,*
> *Couldn't stop me, no, couldn't stop me,*
> *Knew I would find you, knew it was written in stars of the night.*

The time is now upon us, coming real soon,
Now that I hold you 'neath this pale moon,
Hot rods, bad dreams, black holes, moonbeams,
Getting hotter! No! Burning like silver!
The moon! No! The moon! Burning like silver, explodes!
    Explodes ...!

This hyperbolic theatrical retelling of Arthur Dent's journey from Dorset mud to Prehistory quite quickly began to show signs of being a bumpy ride, with Campbell's 'anything goes' attitude translating poorly to such an ambitious production – the impressionable teen Kevin was shocked to perceive that many of the crew were out of their heads on sundry substances throughout. But then Douglas' decision on one of his visits to rehearsals, to swap around the actors playing Ford and Arthur (originally David Bett and Kim Durham, respectively) less than a week before the opening night on 16th July, was hardly helpful, adding to the show's eventual woefully unrehearsed ambience. The panicked writer flailed around to try and find someone he trusted to assist Campbell, and famously rang up the eager Geoffrey Perkins at two o'clock in the morning, only to tactlessly ask him for Sue Limb's phone number.

A few frantic days later (after an embarrassingly misjudged publicity stunt – dropping an inflatable whale off London Bridge, which only caught the attention of the unimpressed Metropolitan River Police), the whimper that was *Hitchhiker* at the Rainbow opened before the rapier-sharpening critics, with some of the costumes still being stitched together at curtain-up, and no technical rehearsal for the second half. To make matters worse, by reinserting all the fan favourites trimmed out of the ICA staging, plus the new material, the play only limped to a conclusion after midnight, to the sound of thudding chairs as the few who remained of the original two thousand punters – in a three-thousand-seater venue – ran to catch the last bus home. When the morning papers arrived, *The Guardian*'s Peter Bradshaw was only the second-most damning of the generally vitriolic critics, blasting the whole *Hitchhiker* sensation: 'I came fresh to *The Hitchhiker's Guide to the Galaxy* by Douglas Adams at the Rainbow Theatre. I emerged from it three hours later jaded and disillusioned. Either the original radio series has lost whatever wit and vitality it had by being turned into a gargantuan stage spectacular, or (could this be possible?) it was always a load of preposterous junk that happened to gain a credulous cult following ... What happens on the Rainbow stage is certainly inchoate and barely comprehensible ... What we have here is galactic whimsy.' *Time Out* was harsher, to the point of perversion: 'Campbell's attempt to turn figments of radio into refugees from pantomime lays bare as never before the awful fact that the feted Adams has no real sense of humour ...'

For all its aims to be spectacular, the production was at its heart a rather low-key ensemble piece in an alienatingly vast venue, described by Campbell as being like lighting a sparkler in the Albert Hall – and within a few weeks, although the run-time was honed and audience numbers which would have been respectable in most theatres bought tickets, those numbers dwindled so badly that the show was pulled three weeks early and the producers disappeared, owing cash. One of the few consolations from the production was that Alan Bell spotted a couple of cast members who were to end up in the TV series – albeit David Learner's Marvin would provide only the robot's body to Stephen Moore's irreplaceable voice (Moore having vetoed the discomfort of wearing a tin can), while Michael Cule would be demoted from Chief Vogon to Guard. The only other notable name in the cast was Roger Blake, soon to become a *Spitting Image* stalwart, who played the Book as a kind of space-age preacher, linking sections from a podule while exotic alien girls wrapped themselves around him.

This was *Hitchhiker*'s first real public crash-and-burn, but a lesser misstep seeded in the same month would not help very much. The success of the first album led Original Records to sign up Adams, Perkins and the team for a follow-up continuing the story along the lines of the unfinished second novel, and including the new material from the Rainbow. *The Restaurant at the End of the Universe* would be the final time that the radio cast (again, Sheridan excepted) gathered around a microphone for a quarter of a century, but although the plot gave fans a permanent record of what happened next to Arthur and Co. when the album hit the shops that November, even providing a preview of material that wouldn't debut on TV for months, Douglas and Geoffrey were dismayed when their rough recordings were pressed onto vinyl without their final crucial edit, making the finished result somewhat flabby: 'Geoffrey and I were annoyed about that. We did a rough tape but it was far too long and a bit woolly, and we decided to leave it for a few days and come back and edit it with a fresh mind. Meanwhile, unbeknownst to us, the record company had taken the rough tape and put it out. Which is why that record is A) very long on both sides, and B) full of blah.' Accompanied by a single release of Souster's theme adaptation, and despite yet another misguided publicity stunt involving live ducks which were trapped in an HMV display window (intended to echo the abstruse LP cover, depicting the B-Ark Captain's bathtime companion), the second LP equalled sales of the original – which wouldn't have been such a bad thing if Original Records' financial situation (exacerbated by modest sales of the HeeBeeGeeBees album and another dramatic over-estimation of demand which consigned many copies to bargain bins for years to come) hadn't prevented the release from delivering the healthy royalties many of the team were contracted to receive.

For all these potholes in the road to greatness, *Hitchhiker* fandom was only just building up a head of steam in the summer of 1980, and for three days at the end of September, the first-ever dedicated convention, 'Hitchercon 1', was staged in Glasgow for the benefit of a few hundred fans, who whooped at the first sight of the completed TV pilot, and their enthusiasm wasn't dinted by the airing of a recording of the Rainbow production. Adams didn't just attend, but found himself judging a Vogon poetry competition and a fancy-dress masquerade – he even spent the weekend before at a *Star Trek* convention in Leeds, just to get a feel for the occasion. The level of devotion his creation continued to inspire must have been a balm after a frustrating period, and he even intended to make good use of his enthusiastic young following for the TV show, recommending in his script that fans should be contacted to donate spaceship models for the Milliways car-park sequence. There was the added kudos of inspiring the name of a new pop-funk band, Level 42, who released their debut album in 1981.

Nonetheless, as M. J. Simpson shrewdly observed, it's telling that the definition for Glasgow in 1983's *The Meaning of Liff* was 'the feeling of infinite sadness engendered when walking through a place full of happy people fifteen years younger than yourself'. There was a time when Douglas could have found himself standing alongside that brethren of sci-fi aficionados, but now he was 'not of their element' and was beginning to feel the slightest tickle of fear, of becoming weighed down with the responsibility of keeping 'his people' happy. He had given the go-ahead for an (eventually) official fan club, ZZ9 Plural Z Alpha, and their first quarterly newsletter, *Mostly Harmless*, soon followed. That it is still running more than three decades later tells you all you need to know about the lasting devotion of the fanbase newly united in 1981, who would continue to celebrate the Galaxy of *Hitchhiker* year after year with regular 'slouch' meetings, clutching cuddly two-headed, three-armed Beeblebears – and, of course, the indispensable towels. In no time at all the ever-morphing, merging and crashing world of extended sci-fi fandom interpolated the *Hitchhiker* Universe into its strange brew, and fans around the world were even writing their own adventures for Zaphod Beeblebrox and crew, in fan-fiction publications like the Australian *Pangalia*. Douglas found it hard enough to guide his hitchhikers when he had total solo control: now that their wild misadventures seemed to be spreading like a virus, it was time to show them who was boss.

The Whooshing Sound

Although Bell was hard at work throughout the summer preparing the remaining five episodes of the TV show, Adams had too much on his plate with these other mutations of *Hitchhiker* to become a truly persistent pain in his body part – no bad thing, considering that two of his notorious suggestions were that the mice should be played by actors in suits, and that Marvin could be a man in a leotard sprayed gold. To Jim Francis' disgust, no matter what designs Douglas was shown for almost anything, he rejected, without any clear idea of what the problem was. When it came to the robot, created with slavish adherence to Marvin's description in the novel, all he could say was, 'That's not how I see him,' without any real clue about how he *should* look – the eventual 'toy robot' arrived at by Howe-Davies was never to Adams' taste, but quickly found a place in fans' hearts. Despite these concerns, it was the *Restaurant* book that surfaced as the creator's priority as August rolled around. Amid the messy divergence of *Hitchhiker* incarnations which had Douglas twisting and turning in every direction, the backwards struggle to deliver his second novel on time had not exactly been made any easier as Pan's deadline encroached rudely on the author's consciousness.

Douglas Adams is surely one of the most regularly quoted epigrammists of the 20th century, and always bobbing near the top of his most-quoted lines is the famous: 'I love deadlines. I love the whooshing sound they make as they go by.' But the real genesis of his reputation as a writer guaranteed to give publishers nervous breakdowns was the rush to get *Restaurant* ready for the printers in the autumn of 1980. 'I had put it off and put it off and got extension after extension', he admitted, until eventually Sonny Mehta, Pan's Editorial Director, contacted him and begged, 'We've given you all these extensions and we have got to have it: sudden death or else, we have to have it in four weeks. Now, how far have you got with it?' We already know that the writer's claim – 'I didn't like to tell him I hadn't started it; it seemed unfair on the poor chap's heart' – was an exaggeration, but it was still clear that the jumbled scraps he did have would require a gigantic effort to be readied for publication. Luckily, Jacqui Graham was caught in the middle, and was well placed to find a solution, renting a house for a month and imposing 'a completely monastic' existence on her boyfriend until the manuscript was up to scratch. 'It was extraordinary,' he recalled. 'One of those times you really go mad ... I can remember the moment I thought, "I can do it! I'll actually get it finished in time!" And the Paul Simon album had just come out, "One-Trick Pony", and it was the only album I had. I'd listen to it on my Walkman every second I wasn't actually sitting at the typewriter – it contributed to the sense of insanity and hypnotism that allowed me to write a book in that time.' Fittingly, the title of Simon's album was the one thing that Adams himself was striving to avoid being labelled – and eventually would fear even more with reference to *Hitchhiker*. 'Occasionally, I get a glimpse and think "This can go on for ever – it'll be terrific!"' he admitted, knowing that it would be easy on one hand to flog the adventures of Arthur Dent for all they were worth, but he had to add: 'And then I get bogged down on the very next sentence.'

Another pattern first established with the completion of *Restaurant* was the author's perfectionist distaste for his most recently completed piece of work, with the memories of the pain it caused him to write overriding any appreciation of the finished article – as he said of *Restaurant*, 'I was very unhappy with it and I had to write it under a lot of pressure, and then when it was all done I really just wanted to wash my hands of it. People wrote in and said, "It's much better than the last one"... Nonsense! But when I went back to read it again after a certain amount of time, I actually liked it a great deal more than I had when I wrote it, and I thought, "Well, maybe it was okay." Tirelessly self-critical, he insisted, 'Nobody could say anything bad about my writing that I haven't already thought ten times worse. I'm a professional at this job and do not want to have my ego massaged.' In time, his second book would become the *Hitchhiker* instalment he most begrudgingly admitted to favouring – but with his deadline just about met, and knowing that the TV series would cover the exact same plot arc, leaving Arthur and Ford with their hopeless appreciation of the unspoiled beauty of the Earth, he certainly saw *Hitchhiker* as an almost closed book, declaring, with a familiar aspiration: 'It's the last of all that, I hope … I want to try another field, now, like performing.'

If Adams had hoped that this perennial ambition would be realised by the TV series, beyond the chilly public nudism required of him on a Cornish beach that October, he must have been disappointed. He had been an extra in the Red Lion sequence, was recognisable to fans numerous times in the animated sequences, and took great pleasure in reading in all the off-screen lines to be performed by David Tate and others, triggering the flashing lights for the ticker-tape-spewing *HoG* computer (which was originally intended to resemble an old jukebox). But his largest part, so to speak, only came about because the actor hired to 'do a Stonehouse' (with reference to the Labour politician who faked his own death, leaving a pile of clothes on a Miami beach in 1974) had to drop out.

Despite an avowed intention to avoid *Who*'s reliance on quarries to stand in for alien planets, early hopes to visit Iceland or Morocco for the Magrathean sequences came to nothing, and the first post-pilot filming, a few days before Adams' nudism, had ended up based in a china-clay pit a few miles from the aforementioned beach, where Learner's first day as Marvin aided his characterisation nicely as the restrictive costume stranded him out in the miserable chalky terrain with only an umbrella while the rest of the cast and crew fled from the pelting rain.

One coincidental useful task for Douglas on location was to decorate a wall with different iterations of the number 42, as go-to guy Kevin Davies, a regular art supplier who personally illustrated the frontispiece of each week's script with in-jokes and cast portraits, was busy elsewhere. This graffiti was part of a brief introduction to the fifth episode, examining an alien religious cult that would return many years later to play a more central part in Dent's odyssey, but here they're just a passing joke about the regrettable creation of the Universe:

NARRATOR: Many races believe that it was created by some sort of god, though the Jatravartid people of Viltvodle Six …

WE NOW CUT TO A CONNECTED SEQUENCE OF CAVE DRAWINGS AND
PAINTINGS. THE CAMERA PASSES OVER THEM AS THE TEXT IS
ILLUSTRATED BY THE DRAWINGS.
CAPTION: "CAVE PAINTINGS DISCOVERED IN THE TRAVAR REGION OF
VILTVODLE VI".
THE PAINTINGS ARE AS AUTHENTIC-SEEMING AS POSSIBLE AND DONE
IN THE STYLE OF ANCIENT CAVE DRAWINGS FOUND ON EARTH: FAIRLY
DETAILED AND COMPLEX, BUT VERY PRIMITIVE WITH NO SENSE OF
PERSPECTIVE. DOTTED AROUND THE DRAWINGS ARE ALL SORTS OF (TO US)
INCOMPREHENSIBLE HIEROGLYPHICS WHICH WE MAY ASSUME TELL THE
STORY OF THE CREATION IN THE ANCIENT JATRAVARTID TONGUE.

NARRATOR: ... Firmly believe that the entire Universe was in
              fact sneezed out of the nose of a being called
              the Great Green Arkleseizure. However, the Great
              Green Arkleseizure theory was not widely accepted
              outside Viltvodle Six, and so one day ...

WE NOW CUT TO A SERIES OF WALL DRAWINGS ON A DRAB STAINED
CONCRETE WALL. THE DRAWINGS ARE IN BLACK CHARCOAL, CRUDELY DONE.
CAPTION: "DRAWINGS FOUND IN ATOMIC FALL-OUT SHELTER ON JIKTHROOM
BETA".
THE FIRST PICTURE IS A CRUDE REPRESENTATION OF DEEP THOUGHT AS
WE HAVE ALREADY SEEN IT.

NARRATOR: ... A race of hyperintelligent pan-dimensional
              beings built themselves a gigantic super computer
              called Deep Thought to calculate once and for
              all the answer to the Ultimate Question of Life,
              The Universe and Everything. For seven and a
              half million years Deep Thought computed and
              eventually announced that the answer was in
              fact 42.

PULL BACK TO REVEAL THAT THE REST OF THE CONCRETE WALL IS
COVERED WITH THE NUMBER 42 WRITTEN OVER AND OVER AGAIN IN
DIFFERENT HANDS AND IN DIFFERENT NOTATIONS. FOR INSTANCE: FORTY

TWO; 42; 101010 (WHICH IS 42 IN BINARY NOTATION) = 1120 (WHICH IS 42
IN BASE THREE). IT LOOKS AS IF IT HAS BEEN DONE DESPERATELY AND
OBSESSIVELY.

Douglas was primarily on hand to oversee Bell's handling of his baby
as the location filming continued that autumn, and as his bank balance
allowed him to develop his gourmand tendencies, he kept *The Good Food
Guide* close by and generously treated cast members to slap-up feeds
at the five-star eateries nearest to the filming locations. But the newly
minted stand-in could not have been unaware of the irony of his highest-
profile on-screen role being the illustration for his Guide monologue
about money's inability to make carbon-based life-forms happy, written
when his idea of 'good food' was tea and toast. Like his father before
him, Adams always had an ingrained taste for luxury, but at the same time
he knew that his growing fortune was changing him, in a sense making
his clinging to the free-wheeling hitcher concept less palatable: 'I can't
pretend to be the person I was ten years ago, and if I was, it would be
dishonest. At one stage, I remember thinking, "God, I'd love to go hitchhiking again!" But the whole point about hitchhiking is you do it because
it's the only method available to you. If you go out and stand on the side
of the road and think, "I'll hitchhike to Istanbul", when you know perfectly
well that you could just slap down a piece of plastic and get a first-class
ticket to Istanbul, then it's not the same experience. If you try and do it,
it'll be phoney.'

The casting of the rest of the TV series had been based on a similar
compromise as the pilot, with Moore and Tate still voicing Marvin and
Eddie, plus Valentine Dyall returning as Deep Thought and Richard
Vernon bearded and robed as Slartibartfast, but otherwise the parts were
generally newly cast by Bell. Trillian had been a particularly difficult role
to settle but, after an exhausting process, Sandra Dickinson, despite being
blonde and American rather than a British brunette, was the one actress
who really seemed to get the *Hitchhiker* humour – so much so that
although she could easily have played the part as an English rose, Adams
was so relieved to find a funny actor that he specifically told her to use her
own accent. By sheer coincidence, Dickinson had a plethora of sci-fi
credentials, featuring in *The Tomorrow People* and then being married to
the new Doctor and Bell's choice for Arthur, Peter Davison (a few years

later they would sire the actress Georgia Moffett, 'The Doctor's Daughter', who would marry the Tenth Doctor, David Tennant, in 2011). Despite having the biggest role in UK sci-fi to prepare for, Davison was such a *Hitchhiker* fan that he campaigned for any part he could get – eventually becoming unrecognisable beneath the Dish of the Day make-up, adopting a West Country accent inspired by Hotblack Desiato bodyguard Dave Prowse, the original Darth Vader, with whom he shared the impressive Milliways set.

Nobody but Mark Wing-Davey, however, was considered for Zaphod, and he had been measured up and animated for the pilot in an approximation of his completed on-screen guise long before the full series was even commissioned, so ambitious was the plan to bring the throwaway radio gag about his extra limb and cranial generosity to the screen. Adams stipulated of the heads in an early script draft, 'Obviously one of these is going to be a fake unless we can find an actor prepared to undergo some very exotic surgery. The real head and the fake head should look as far as possible absolutely identical: any shortcomings in the realism of the fake head should be matched by the make-up on the real one.' Mike Kelt was the Visual Effects expert detailed to bring Zaphod's more laid-back head to life, and as he would go on to provide visual wizardry for movies like *Prometheus* and *Les Misérables* that early space-age appendage might not be his preferred calling card – it just happens to be one of the things that almost everyone thinks of first when it comes to TV *Hitchhiker*, with a kind of affectionately patronising guffaw. So innovative was the mechanism at the time that Kelt even appeared on the BBC's science showcase *Tomorrow's World* to show it off, but with the best will in the Galaxy, the expensive effect never quite hit the spot on screen. Little wonder that the contraption, complete with burdensome upper-body shell, became Wing-Davey's nemesis – not content with swinging around looking unconvincing, regularly grinding to a halt and providing an extra physical challenge, the head famously cost considerably more than the actor himself, at £3,000. Kelt's association with the realisation of Beeblebrox on screen was particularly close – he also provided the President's third arm when it was needed, via the sophisticated technique of standing behind Wing-Davey and putting his own arm through the costume's extra sleeve. When the *HoG* crew were thrown into a heap, no attempt to obscure Kelt was even attempted, resulting in three prone actors with four sets of legs in clear sight.

Zaphod's second head was only the most prominent expense in a long itemised list which made *Hitchhiker* the most financially ambitious BBC comedy ever attempted – to the chagrin of Adams' Footlights forebears Graeme Garden, Tim Brooke-Taylor and Bill Oddie, whose madcap adventures as *The Goodies* had provided BBC2 with ten years of visually inventive satirical comedy, including Production Design from Andrew Howe-Davies. But when they turned up at TV Centre to assure the comedy department that their ninth series would be their best, they were staggered to learn that as *Hitchhiker* had burned up so much of the available licence fee money they would just have to wait until the time was right to return. Not prepared to play second fiddle to Adams' creation, the trandem-pedalling trio famously flitted to commercial rivals LWT for what turned out to be a final outing before disbanding. Writers Garden & Oddie even tried their own sci-fi sitcom for the channel, *Astronauts*, which debuted several months after *Hitchhiker*, but despite lasting for two series the adventures of a trio of bickering space explorers were soon consigned to the *Come Back Mrs Noah* sector of forgotten comedies, while Adams' TV show could not be ignored.

My Universe Is My Eyes And My Ears. Anything Else is Hearsay

When the TV series debuted on BBC2 on Monday, 5th January 1981, the final episode was still being rehearsed in the BBC's North Acton outpost (known as 'The Hilton') for studio recording on the next day. There had been just shy of two months of studio recordings, begun in November shortly after the end of location filming – taking in the freezing Peak District for Douglas to finally realise his B-Ark plot on television, and ending with a literal bang on the show's one night-time shoot, filming the face-off with Shooty and Bang-Bang on a golf course at Henley-on-Thames, with a 2 a.m. explosion so huge that it triggered calls to the constabulary and resulted in a partially melted set.

Between inevitably restrictive Union prickliness and the sheer ambition of what he was trying to capture, Alan Bell and his team had almost as much of a rough ride making the most of their studio time as Perkins and Co. had on radio – the pilot had only been completed thanks to the use of off-cut shots of Dixon and Jones taped before the lights had gone out at 10 p.m. The red tape chafed particularly on the series' grandest set piece – Milliways. The largest comedic set ever constructed at TV Centre was populated with every notable extraterrestrial featured in the previous four episodes, plus whatever else could be found in the BBC costume department to create a raucous audience of aliens, including enthusiastic fans Kevin Davies and Stuart Murdoch, and Cleo Rocos, the glamorous teenager who began her career drinking a PGGB in the pilot, and was soon finding her niche accompanying boundary-bending DJ and comic (and huge *Hitchhiker* fan) Kenny Everett in his BBC comedy shows. Bell masterminded an audacious operation to bring the Restaurant to life, with the replacement of the avuncular Hudd with Colin Jeavons in full *Cabaret* MC mode presenting a far more disturbing and threatening edge to the ceremony – but he was lucky to get it all on tape considering the time eaten up in the studio erecting a flimsy handrail to assuage the wrath of safety inspectors. The overall effect was unavoidably reminiscent of the cantina sequence in *Star Wars* (suitably, as Darth Vader himself was present), just one of a number of references to the movies, and other sci-fi properties, which belied Adams' claimed avoidance of warping known tropes with comedy – certainly, he was happy to use the George Lucas films as shorthand in the scripts, as in the infamous Vl'Hurg and G'Gugvunt face-off, which was simplified for broadcast:

VL'HURG AND A G'GUGVUNT TURN TO FACE EACH OTHER AGGRESSIVELY.
THE VL'HURG IS THE SPACE WARRIOR TYPE, DARK, EVIL AND MENACING,
ALMOST A DARTH VADER TYPE I SUPPOSE. THE G'GUGVUNT IS FAT AND
REPTILIAN AND ALSO VERY EVIL LOOKING ...
CAPTION: 'BREN BESTIAL DESIGNED BATTLE SHORTS, IN VIOLENT
COLOURS FOR VIOLENT MEN. BE VICIOUS IN STYLE. EXCLUSIVE FROM
CHIC SOLDIERY' ... 'GREEN BATTLE STEAM: MAKE THOSE HARSH MOMENTS
SWEETER. EXCLUSIVE FROM FIGHTING TOILETRIES.'

The first episode's audience of 3.5 million would make champagne corks pop today, but in TV terms at the time it was comparable to the radio show's whispered debut. This was despite a trailer specially recorded by Peter Jones, who observed, 'The full story of The Hitchhiker's Guide to the Galaxy is long, tortuous, and – to be frank – pretty obscure. Gathering information for it has caused endless problems, but quite honestly if you're the average four-headed, six-tentacled man-about-town you really wouldn't be interested. On the other hand, for any inhabitants of a measly speck of dust called Earth who happen to be listening, this might worry you … Now at this point if you do feel worried, alarmed or just plain out-and-out terrified – Don't Panic. Sit back, drink two Pan Galactic Gargle Blasters and nothing, repeat nothing, is likely to disturb your calm for quite some time …'

The critics, however, soon began to rally round TV *Hitchhiker* appreciatively, with Peter Fiddick in *The Guardian* gushing, 'What makes the *Hitchhiker* tele-version surely one of 1981's destined award-winners, and quite possibly a television classic, is the élan with which it has been brought to the screen. How they'll get all the right people in line to collect the gongs I cannot think …' In the end there were BAFTAs for Rod Lord, video editor Ian Williams and sound supervisor Mike McCarthy – plus, best of all, the Royal Television Society's award for Best Original Programme – and the influence of the animation on the evolution of computer graphics has often been celebrated. Above all, however, the TV series set in stone the general public's vision of what *Hitchhiker* was all about – to this day, most people think of Kelt's Zaphod head or Jones in his dressing gown whenever *Hitchhiker* is mentioned, and may even be unaware of any previous version. It goes to show that radio may have the best pictures, but the population at large won't even know about them until they're beamed onto a screen in their front rooms. Fiddick was right that the six episodes created in 1980 became television classics and, like the best early *Doctor Who*, they transcend or even make a virtue of the patently superseded nature of the technology powering them. Effects which would be tossed off with CG today provoke a warmer reaction when you can practically hear the cogs grinding away inside a genuine article.

Douglas Adams' real feelings at the time are hard to glean, but his description of the producer/director as a 'bone-headed wanker' and subsequent suggestion in one Australian interview that 'I'm fairly convinced that there isn't anyone working in television who couldn't do with a good smack' could not be described as gracious. One element that annoyed him was that on radio the team had been devoted to the project, but TV did not work like that, and everyone involved had other calls on their time. It was clear that there was little good blood between Alan and Douglas – Bell even gave Adams incorrect dates for dubbing sessions, to minimise interference – but the saddest thing about this is the evidently *slavish* devotion to the author's vision evident in every single sequence of the TV series, when you compare the script which left Adams' typewriter with the finished programmes. From the very first shot – recreating dawn, complete with the stipulated morning star of Venus, using only a light bulb and a model railway set – to the final image of the Guide zooming off into the abyss of space, the sci-fi-sceptic Bell used every trick in the book, with a kind of economy-minded verve, to translate Adams' imagination to television. Only the tiniest exceptions were made to this exacting approach – the cutting of a few minor sequences, like Zaphod, Ford and Trillian's experiences on a sensotape planet, or the planned episode-four preamble in which Arthur was to lose his dressing gown, for example.

And yet, despite everyone involved being keen to get back to work in late spring 1981 for another run of six episodes, Perkins being approached for a script-editor role (which he considered the worst possible job of all) and the BBC pledging that the budget would actually be doubled, Adams refused to work with Bell at all. 'I wouldn't start seriously moving on the second TV series until we'd sorted out various crucial aspects of how we were going to go about it,' he said. 'I felt very let down by the fact that though John Lloyd was meant to be producer he was rapidly moved aside, much to the detriment of the show. I'd always made it clear that I wanted Geoffrey Perkins, at the very least as a consultant. Neither of these things transpired in the first series. It was perfectly clear to myself and the cast that Alan had very little sympathy with the script. So I didn't want to go into the second series without that situation being remedied in some way, and the BBC was not prepared to come up with a remedy. That was the argument going on in the background, that was why I was not producing the scripts. I wasn't going to do the scripts until I knew we were going to do the series.'

As the year progressed, Adams *was* actually shaping the follow-up series, hoping that the BBC would give in to his demands eventually – there was talk of a need to design leopard-like costumes for Lloyd's Haggunenons, and of the *HoG* team visiting a planet where people exploded if they became too happy – the Drubbers. He laid out a whole array of directions for the show to go in next, exemplifying just how long many of his ideas – such as credulous monks, Coleridge and mission-robbed warships – would ferment inside that brain:

Ultimate truth drug. I think that this idea is nice if it's very quick. It was originally going to be a great quest, but I think it's worth about ten minutes.

Return of Slartibartfast. But in what capacity?

Astrology. How does it work if you're travelling all the time? They should meet an astrologer who wanders about.

MORE ABOUT HITCH HIKING!

Coleridge. Flying lessons. Forest toupés.

President who is paid to take the blame for everything.

Man who exists only to fulfil one specific function. His function may be needed twice in one day, and then not for another twenty or indeed twenty million years. All the time in between he is in suspended animation. We should see a bit of life from his point of view.

The submarine refuge. The sole surviving crewman who thinks he has been found and rescued when in fact he's only been found. Wonder now how good an idea this is. I think I was a bit drunk at the time.

The monks who will believe anything for a day.

The Colony warship. It was meant to be going in Hyperdrive, but it broke down and continued under normal star drive which means it's going to get to its destination in a billion years rather than five days. They have been trying to keep the spirit of battle and sense of what they are fighting for alive through countless generations ...

The man who is always busy. He's gone for lunch, he's gone to Venezuela. He's died. When's he due back? Have to find out from the reincarnation registry.

The gamble. Someone comes and offers you the opportunity of being somewhere else, but you have to take what you're given. This could be quite interesting visually in that in the middle of furious action everyone and everything else could freeze and maybe become grey and, say, Arthur, who has just wished he was somewhere else, wanders amongst these figures until he finds the man from the relocation council who offers him a new life on some really grotty asteroid, mining something awful.

Other points: get rid of Zaphod's other head, build up Trillian.

Although Adams had sworn to end the novels after just two instalments, it was a relative luxury to have Arthur and Ford in the same quandary in both prose and television – albeit getting them away from Earth's prehistory was a perennial problem, which was to take a drastic Biblical turn. The first two figures to be seen in the second TV series were not our heroes:

Opening credits. The beginning of the second series mirrors the beginning of the first. Sunrise over a hill. The hill is on earth, but it is prehistoric earth. Dramatic music.

NARRATOR: Reason notwithstanding, the Universe continues
              unabated. On millions of planets throughout the
              Galaxy new dreams are dreamt, new hopes are hoped,
              and new days continue to dawn, despite the terrible
              failure rate.

Tragic chord in the music.

NARRATOR: This particular dawn occurred over two million
              years ago on an utterly insignificant little
              blue-green planet circling an unregarded yellow
              sun … .

GRAPHIC: Planet: Gal/Sec/ ZZ9 Plural Z Alpha.
Sol 3: Earth.

HHGG Entry Eds 1-37 None
HHGG Entry Eds 38-43 "Harmless"
HHGG Entry Eds 44 "Mostly harmless"
HHGG Entry Eds 45 Entry deleted through lack of interest
HHGG Entry Eds 46 on Entry deleted through lack of planet

NARRATOR: … at the unfashionable end of the Western Spiral
              arm of the Galaxy. (Earth was) a particularly
              notorious failure and caused continual argument
              and recrimination till the planet in question

was demolished to make way for a new hyperspace
bypass some two million years later … However,
like every other event in the Universe, it was
a) Not what it seemed, b) Not finished there by a
long chalk and c) The subject of endless attempts
to make some kind of rational sense of it - again,
despite the terrible failure rate. The Hitchhiker's
Guide to the Galaxy, in a recent supplement,
describes the events in the following way, and
the account carries with it the usual Guide
guarantee, that every single fact in it might
have been checked by somebody … These, according
to some accounts, are the two people responsible
for the event …

The music swells dramatically, and we can now see two figures
silhouetted against the disc of the sun as they stand on the
brow of the hill. This will be tricky, i know, as the sunrise is
presumably a model shot, still, we're not here to enjoy ourselves,
are we? The two figures, who are adman and his assistant eev are
lightly dressed after the fashion of their planet, in very little,
other than short light beach robes. The adman, we will shortly
see, is carrying a case of curious dimensions … Around them, on the
side of the hill, everything is very beautiful. There are flowers,
fruit trees, verdant grasses. It looks a bit like the garden of
eden. The reason it looks a bit like the garden of eden, we will
eventually come to realise, is that this is the garden of eden.
Perhaps the focus should be a little softened. The whole setting
is so dreamy and idyllic it could almost be one of those wonderful
new advertisements for soft lavatory paper, it's that beautiful.

There were plans to pit these banal beauties against an advertising robot-snake, blaming the Fall of Man on commercials, but the one existing draft of this first-episode script never connects the strangers with our stranded protagonists, or explains the significance of the Eden plot, although the notes do add more flesh to the concept:

PLOT LINE. EPISODE ONE.

Ford and Arthur encounter Adman and Eve, an advertising executive and his secretary who have dropped in on the planet for an afternoon's dictation and who knows what else. They are there to have a meeting as well, with a man called "The Consultant". They are going to demonstrate to him a new device which he is particularly interested in, which is an advertising snake which slides around the grass and occasionally rears up out of it and advertises things, drinks, spaceships, apples, anything. It has the wonderful capacity of being able to advertise anything at a moment's notice. Put it in front of a pile of dogshit and it will come up with something desirable about it, and possibly a jingle as well.

Anyway, we don't see this immediately. All we see of them is that they are carrying this very long thin box, and talking about its contents in a way which excites our curiosity but doesn't of course enlighten us. They must make some point about not eating the local fruit, for some quite pragmatic reason. A company directive of some kind.

Just as we are about to see them open the box we cut to Ford and Arthur. They are waking up in some terribly badly made tents that they have made terribly badly because they're not really any good at that sort of thing ...

In addition to this alien-Eden concept was the all-pervading mysterious new figure of The Consultant, potentially another handy plot-easing tool, being a God-like figure capable of moving anything from one time and place to another. In his notes, Adams tied the character in with a figure who repeatedly came to him during the early stages of outlining a plot, but never actually made it to the page, a tragic martyr known as 'Baggy the Runch':

The Consultant: His motives, movement and history are the key to unlocking, or rather locking, this storyline. What do we know about him? God has left him in charge as he's not interested in taking any responsibility for his creation and is not up to understanding its implications. The Consultant is angry about this because he feels it is irresponsible to bring a lot of life into existence just to please yourself and then leave it to its own devices.

    This could actually be an analogy with Baggy the Runch - abandoned as a child, left helpless and purposeless having been brought into existence for no reason, he has then to justify that existence. Maybe Baggy is a galactic Messiah character, only not quite a Messiah because he hasn't come to save anyone. He has come as the son of God, as a sign to God's creation that creation has, like God's son, been abandoned to its own devices. I think Baggy the Runch is a girl. That'll get a bit of life into things at this point, it makes for a much more interesting character.

And if The Consultant didn't give him enough wriggle room to move the plot forward, he was also preoccupied with something called the Magic Moment:

It is important to understand that everything is not only possible, it has happened at least twice. This is because the Galaxy is in the grip of a Magic Moment Grade 3 (Magic Moment Grade 1 is a one-second pause every 17 million years). It is because of this Magic Moment that the Krikkitmen have chosen this time to come and get the ashes. The Magic Moment which passes through the Universe manifests itself in different ways on each world it touches ... A Magic Moment Grade 1 is that moment at which the impossible will become possible, everywhere, simultaneously. And what will that mean? Peace? Happiness? I don't know. I just don't know.

However, although numerous solutions were considered for saving our hitchers, the existing script outlines the oddest idea of all: Ford has been whittling sticks and arranging them in the ground to mark the time, complaining, 'Ford Prefect! Small, mobile, intelligent unit. Hoopiest hitcher in the Galaxy. Fastest recorded time from Betelgeuse to Altair and scored twice on the way. Measures out his miles in light years. And now what? Here I am on this miserable little planet *again*, measuring out my weeks in stick-yards.' However, he and Arthur soon detect a strange anomaly whereby the sticks mark out an invisible structure, and they follow signposts leading to an ultimate placard which brings them to their knees, swearing to spread its message far and wide. It bears the eventually infamous legend 'WE APOLOGISE FOR THE INCONVENIENCE':

ARTHUR: (WITH TREPIDATION) What do you think it is?

FORD: I don't know.

ARTHUR: Can you feel some sort of strange emanation … some sort of strange alien force beckoning us towards it?

FORD: (STARING AT ARTHUR) No. Can you?

ARTHUR: (NOT CERTAIN WHETHER HE MIGHT NOT BE MAKING A FOOL OF HIMSELF. HE IS RIGHT TO BE CONCERNED) Well, I sort of think I can.

FORD: What's it like?

ARTHUR: Well, it's a bit hard to describe. I've never been beckoned to by strange alien forces before. Except Zaphod Beeblebrox, when he wants someone to get him a drink.

FORD: Zaphod! (WE SHOULD FEEL, IF DAVID CAN CONVEY IT IN ONE WORD, THAT FORD HAS DELIBERATELY NOT EVEN THOUGHT ABOUT ZAPHOD ALL THIS TIME AND THAT HEARING HIS NAME DISTURBS HIM IN ALL SORTS OF WAYS.)

ARTHUR: Well, he's a strange alien.

FORD: Depends what you mean by alien.

ARTHUR: Depends what you mean by strange.

FORD: Shall we go and see this thing? Emanations not bothering you?

ARTHUR: (SLIGHTLY RANKLING) I can live with them.

Ford laughs. They arrive at the "thing". It turns out to be a door. Not only is it a door, but it really is just any old door. It is battered and the rather nastily applied paint is, thank goodness, beginning to peel off it. It is the sort of door which probably leads to a cellar or storeroom. It is set in its own frame, and is aligned along the line of sticks, which is why it has seemed very thin as we have approached it …

FORD: It's a door. A door! Just an ordinary nasty door!

Ford grasps the handle on his side and pulls the door open.

ARTHUR: Well, what can you see?

FORD: You. What can you see?

ARTHUR: Something totally mind-shattering.

FORD: Like what?

ARTHUR: Well, a staircase ...

FORD: Your mind shatters easily ...

Nervously Arthur goes in and follows Ford up the stairs. From Arthur's P.O.V. We look up the stairwell. It is quite a startling sight because it seems to go on up, flight after flight, storey after storey, into infinity. Arthur gasps.

ARTHUR: Are you sure this is wise?

FORD: Do you want to be wise, or just safe?

ARTHUR: Well, I think it's wise to be safe.

FORD: Wisdom comes by learning from your mistakes doesn't it?

ARTHUR: Oh yes.

FORD: We'd better make some.

Beyond the *Dirk Gently*-presaging door, the two were to find a lift which could take them up or down to any period in the planet's history, but however the time-stranded duo were destined to return to the present Adams was set on recycling his Krikkit concept just as he had the B-Ark sequence, and cricket pitches were already being scouted as far afield as Australia. Nonetheless, Douglas still refused to budge on signing anything: 'I was rather aggrieved and, to be honest, by the end of the first six episodes it became a bit of a stand-off. I didn't want to carry on doing it if we had the same producer and the BBC wouldn't change him ... It's sad. It was a perfectly good television series, but the radio series was really ground-breaking ...'

Publicising the TV show would involve plenty of pleasing exposure for Adams, including a personal interview for magazine programme *Nationwide* during studio filming. To Sue Lawley's astonished request for

Hitchhiker's secret of success, the beaming author replied, 'I can only invent reasons for that – if you actually know why something became successful, then you'd be able to do it every time. In a way, I suppose science fiction is a form of escapism, which people like at the moment ...' The following July provided a further treat for the comedy fan – first, he aided Geoffrey by making a few appearances on the Radio 4 literary panel game *Quote Unquote*, but it was a bigger treat to be given his own half-hour for the Radio 4 clip show *It Makes Me Laugh*, playing and discussing extracts from his favourite comedy records. Python was inevitably prevalent – Douglas made use of their Novel-Writing Commentary sketch to air his own agonies: 'Writer's Disease: About ninety per cent of your time is wasted on totally pointless and distracting activity, and only about ten per cent is actually spent dreaming up and composing and shaping and honing all those wonderful, exciting, soul-stirring excuses for not having got anything written. Here's a Python sketch which hardly illustrates that point at all ...' But he also took time to pay tribute to (and turn his fans on to) Woody Allen's moose routine, a Cleese monologue, a self-read extract from Vonnegut's *Slaughterhouse 5*, The Bonzo Dog Band's *The Intro & The Outro*, Pete & Dud on sex – all personably linked by Douglas, clearly enjoying the chance to flex his performance muscles, musing on computerised comedy show links, and even managing to crowbar in the biscuit story. The following year Jon Canter scripted a pilot for a similar show focusing on pop music for his ex-flatmate to present *They'll Never Play That On The Radio* – for which Douglas spoke to 'Jilted John' creator Graham Fellows, but it never became a series. By that time, Canter had amicably taken his leave as Adams' lodger, and continued to make headway as a writer and script editor, eventually working on the peerless *A Bit of Fry & Laurie*.

At the same time, *Hitchhiker* continued to have a life of its own, largely thanks to the perverse popularity of Marvin the Paranoid Android, who was almost as much in demand as Douglas himself, even bagging his own *Sunday Times* colour supplement profile in July, as dictated to Adams:

> Q: Would you like to be a human being?
> A: *If I was a human being I'd be very depressed, but then I'm very depressed already, so it hardly matters. Sometimes I think it might be quite pleasant to be a chair.*

Q: Why are you so miserable?

A: *I've been in precisely the same mood ever since I was switched on. It's just the way my circuits are connected. Very badly.*

Q: Can you repair yourself?

A: *Why should I want to do that? I'd just as soon rust.*

Q: Do you like reading?

A: *I read everything there was to read on the day I was switched on. It was all so dull I don't see any point in reading it again.*

Q: Music?

A: *Hate it.*

Q: Hobbies?

A: *Hating music.*

Q: What do you like the least?

A: *The entire multi-dimensional infinity of all creation. I don't like that at all.*

Tim Souster's TV theme single had been backed with two songs taken from the Rainbow production: one smoochy number purporting to be from the Milliways band, Reg Nullify and his Cataclysmic Combo (*Your arms, your legs, your heads, you're everything to me ...*) and a Disaster Area song, 'Only The End of the World Again', on which Douglas got to alleviate a tiny amount of frustrated-pop-star ambition by playing rhythm guitar. Stephen Moore was friends with music producer John Sinclair, and soon after the 'Journey of the Sorcerer' release disappeared into obscurity the two of them got together to have some fun with Marvin's growing celebrity (which extended to his very own 'Depreciation Society') by recording a novelty single, giving Douglas a courtesy credit allegedly just to get him out of the studio where he would otherwise burn up time vamping on his guitar. Moore and Sinclair then took charge of the depressed mechanoid's pop career on their own. Their first release on Polydor (credited to 'Depressive Discs'), the mournful synth-disco recitation 'Marvin', was backed with 'Metal Man', an unaccountably positive vignette for the Paranoid Android, saving a spaceship from a black hole, and the disc became a cult favourite, skilfully tapping into the electropop trend. However, it only reached number 52 in the charts, despite being plugged on children's show *Blue Peter* and on *Top of the Pops*, with Stuart

Murdoch donning the metallic suit to mime the non-hit. A Blockheads-referencing follow-up, 'Reasons To Be Miserable' (technically titled 'The Double B-Side', twinned with a soppy high-octane attempt at a love song called 'Marvin I Love You') fared less well and, although further releases were planned, the gloomy robot soon returned to the realms of obscure failure where he belonged. Moore did, however, land the plum job of being the first narrator of the abridged *Hitchhiker* talking books, a whole new medium to draw in the fans.

These musical sideshows aside, while refusing to deliver the series two scripts, Douglas spent most of his time travelling the world publicising his books. During the studio recordings in November, he had flown up to St. Andrews University in Scotland to give a talk and had found himself among a gaggle of authors, including the former editor of *Books and Bookmen* magazine Sally Emerson who was publicising her debut novel *Second Sight* – and just happened to eerily fit the description of Trillian. Adams had recently parted from Jacqui Graham, and seemed lost up in Scotland, so the two of them developed a comradeship – a source of frustration for Douglas, who soon discovered that Sally had only recently become married to her boyfriend since university, journalist and fellow Brentwood boy Peter Stothard, and he found himself wishing it were otherwise.

Soon after the debut of the *Hitchhiker* TV series, ABC in New York invited Adams over to discuss the creation of an American version – as ever, the idea of viewers from sea to shining sea paying the slightest attention to a man with a plummy accent complaining about the non-availability of tea was never entertained for one moment: if something was worth buying, it had to be remade from scratch. The money they were prepared to pay him to watch them pull his creation apart was too much to ignore, however, and so in January he flew to the Big Apple for the very first time. Ostensibly he was there to create a TV show and grab some publicity, but instead, he fell desperately, unwisely, dangerously in love.

I Sense Deep Needs. Got Any Leads There?

Australia and Europe were already discovering *Hitchhiker* for themselves – albeit the French version, *Le Routard Galactique*, originally took a number of liberties, renaming characters so Zaphod became 'Zappy Bibicy', while Ford was 'Ford Escort' – and, in time, France, Germany,

Finland and other countries would even record their own translations of the original radio shows, often refitting the dialogue to their own country so successfully that many fans would not even know the British roots of the comedy. Breaking America, however, was as crucial to Douglas as it had been, and remains, to almost any other commercial artist of the last century or two – Nick Webb, often his go-to guy in publishing matters, recalled Adams seething with curses for publishers who ever claimed his creation was too parochial to appeal in America. Douglas had met the fans, from every corner of the world, he knew that their nationality was irrelevant. A few minor US radio stations had broadcast the Radio 4 series, but then in March '81 National Public Radio gave it a first play across the nation, eliciting such a strong reaction that they soon repeated it. The first novel had also received a respectable readership Stateside in a hardback edition from indie publisher Crown but, in a similar situation to radio, the decision by Pocket Books to aggressively market a paperback nationwide would push things far further.

Adams' own answer to the British invasion was fuelled by the pleasing synergy which comes from a new audience discovering something a few years into its evolution – the book would launch nationwide alongside the NPR repeat, but not before an advert had appeared in *Rolling Stone* that August offering 3,000 free copies of the paperback to the first people to write to the 'Hyperspace Hitchhiking Club, Earth Div. c/o Pocket Books'. 'England, the country that gave America The Beatles and *Monty Python's Flying Circus* has just exported another zany craze – *The Hitchhiker's Guide to the Galaxy* by Doug Adams, a wild spoof available in October' ran the copy and, despite the over-familiarity, Douglas had to admit that their approach was effective – within a few years 'Doug' was explaining, 'In terms of sales these days, it is more popular in America than England (it sells twice as many books to four times as many people, so it's either twice as popular, or half as popular). I think too much is made of the difference between US and UK humour. Audiences in the US (through no fault of their own) are treated as complete idiots by the people who make programmes, and when you've been treated as an idiot for so long you tend to respond that way. But when given something with a bit more substance they tend to breathe a deep sigh of relief and say "Thank God for that!"' Adams had a further jagged pill to swallow with the introduction of a wacky anthropomorphised green planet designed for the cover by Peter Cross, usually known as the 'Cosmic Cutie', or 'Jeremy Pacman' in the UK, and known to Douglas as 'the obscene little thing'. Its use on all American *Hitchhiker* products for years to come clearly helped fans identify every new release and, despite his hopes of eradicating it, Adams was forced to admit that the 'little green blob' helped sales.

The regular use of his Python credentials in US publicity was a sharper thorn in Douglas' side, however, and he regularly had to plead to his heroes that he was not behind any attempt to cash in on their success, insisting that his time on their show was 'so inconsequential as to be hardly worth mentioning. I would certainly not lay claim to being a contributory writer for Python because Python was those six guys, and my role was quite incidental and coincidental.' Besides anything else, although at first he was happy to ask Cleese et al. to offer support and zany cover quotes, he had put his talent on the rack to get where he was, and was offended at the idea of any such leg-up – but he had his work cut out diminishing the association that he had once been so proud to achieve: 'It would get to the point where I would say to journalists, "Look, I just want to say before I say anything that I have nothing to do with Python." In fact, what made it bad was that I had written about half a dozen lines that appeared here and there. They'd say, "What, you mean MONTY Python?" "Yes, I didn't write for them." And they'd say, "What was that like?" I'd then read the account of the interview: "Douglas Adams, one of the major writers on Monty Python ..." And I kept on saying to the Pythons, "I'm sorry, I did not say this!"'

There were more losses in translation awaiting Adams at ABC. Although *Hitchhiker* always had a transatlantic flavour, with two main characters in the TV series having American accents, the need to rebuild his Universe from the ground up for US audiences was clearly offensive to the writer. 'One is told at every level of the entertainment industry that the American audience does not like or understand English humour,' he complained. 'We are told that at every level *except* that of the audience who, as far as I can see, love it. It's everybody else, the people whose job it is to tell you what the audiences like; but the people I meet here, and in the US, who are fans, are very much the same type of people. The most commonly heard plea from American audiences is "Don't let them Americanise it!" ... There are things that the British think are as English as roast beef that the Americans think are as American as apple pie. The trick is to write about people. If you write about situations that people recognise then people will respond to it.'

The executive who had snapped up *Hitchhiker*, Don Taffner, scored hits bringing Benny Hill to American audiences, and adapting *Man About The House* to become the hit *Three's Company*, but there are more disastrous tales of Americanised UK sitcoms than success stories, and Douglas' experiences were comfortably par for the course: 'It was like every horror story you've ever heard. They weren't really interested in how good it was going to be – they wanted to do a lot of special effects. They also wanted not to have to pay for them. Somehow they were managing to budget the first episode without knowing what was in it. There were terrible stories coming back after meetings with executives, remarks like, "Would an alien be green?" Eventually, everything got abandoned because the first episode's budget came to $2.2 million. It would have been the most expensive 22-minute TV show ever made. The script was terrible – I wasn't writing it ... It gives you an idea of the crazy proportion of this thing: they paid me for that week four times as much as I was originally paid to write the whole series for radio.' Perhaps the only boon from Adams' week at the production office was the Marvin design produced by the artist Ron Cobb, which finally cracked it for the robot's creator: 'It had the stooping quality which he needs. You can see on the one hand he's been designed to be dynamic and streamlined and beautiful, but he holds himself the wrong way. The design's gone to naught because he always looks just utterly pathetic.' Douglas made a mental note to consider Cobb when the inevitable movie incarnation of *Hitchhiker* came about – one tempting offer for the rights was made possible by his refusal for ABC to continue with their adaptation but, although he had to get blind drunk to ultimately say no to this unsuitable but lucrative deal, he knew that he had to get any *Hitchhiker* film right: 'I'm sometimes accused of only being in it for the money. I always knew there was a lot of money to be made out of the film, but when that was the whole thing prompting me to do it, when the only benefit was the money, I didn't want to do it. People should remember that.'

Besides book promotion, the infamous saga of the *Hitchhiker* movie would call him over the Atlantic for long periods of the rest of his life – it was the logical next step after the experience of seeing his creation visualised for BBC TV. The film rights had originally been sold almost absentmindedly to an independent producer who called up on a whim, but she would eventually be paid off in favour of the biggest guns possible. As for the TV version, eventually in November 1982 Alan Bell's show found its way onto American TV in a shorter-edit form (the series would go through many permutations, even being edited into two feature-length edits for UK VHS before the 'ultimate' cut was released on DVD), and although Simon Jones was taken aback during publicity to be applauded for the show's 'deliberately crummy' special effects, he soon joined in and laughed that yes, that had been entirely deliberate, and the programme developed a suitably cult following. Or rather, in Adams' words, 'Before the television series *Hitchhiker* was a minor minor minor cult in America, and as a result of the television series it became a minor minor cult, which is a substantial jump upwards.'

It was while suffering the ignominy of having ABC pull his baby apart, exacerbated by a painful ear infection, that Douglas' path crossed with Sally's once more, and between a self-diagnosed attack of claustrophobia in her new marriage, and the sheer heart-tugging vulnerability of the dejected six-foot-five legal alien in New York, what she described as 'the combination of his huge, masculine form and little-boy-lost manner', their friendship quickly evolved into something stronger. No greater medicine could be found for Adams than this sign that his feelings were reciprocated, and Sally quickly found that the little boy lost could turn into a passionate tornado with just the slightest encouragement. The couple flew down to Mexico when business was concluded in Manhattan, and soon after their return home, the *Evening Standard* revealed their affair to the world in the most gratifying terms for Adams: 'Strapping Douglas Adams, whose manly charms have wrought havoc in many a female breast, has made a new conquest ...' Douglas was so bowled over that he almost felt apologetic, as a sceptical intelligent man, to be so overwhelmed by pheromones and hormones. On more than one occasion he was stopped by police for failing to resist grasping Sally in a passionate embrace while doing considerable speeds on the public highway: but each time his apologies were belied by his immovable grin.

For Emerson, this was a wildly unexpected diversion from the path she had chosen, but on return to reality, with Adams using every scrap of power he had with words to assure her that she was The One for him, Sally decided that, if they were going to be together, changes would have to be made. One of the first tasks was for him to find a new home, more suited to his success than the old place shared with Canter, and Hotblack Desiato guided them to a penthouse love-nest complete with rooftop garden, down an alley only

100 yards from their office in the heart of Islington, just around the corner from the Screen On The Green cinema, in St. Alban's Place. Once it was clear that there was no chance of hiding their relationship – largely thanks to Douglas' habit of proudly telling everyone how happy he was, even taking her down to Dorset to meet his mother's family – Sally moved in a short while after, by which time Adams had already transformed the home into 'a kind of shrine' to *Hitchhiker*: he was naturally proud of his achievement, displaying posters and publicity material around the walls, but this left little room for Sally's own things.

Secondly, the more experienced literary expert convinced Adams to leave the agency run by Jill Foster, who had put up with a great deal while doing her best for her needy client but ultimately did not specialise in best-selling novelists. There was one respected figure in publishing who might have been an agent for only five years but had in that time earned a reputation for landing record-breaking deals for his authors. Ed Victor was a tall, steel-bearded New Yorker and the epitome of urbanity in person, but played the hardest ball in UK publishing when there was a deal to be struck. Evidently keen to sign up the hottest writer of the moment, Ed invited Douglas to his office and within a couple of hours of conversation not even involving lunch, hands were shaken and contracts drawn up for a close partnership which would hold for the rest of Adams' life – Ed grew to look on Douglas as more of a kid brother than a client, and lost no time in showing him what he could do for him.

Sadly, the first task was to hold Original Records upside down and shake them for all the royalties which computer malfunctions and bad business decisions had made it impossible to provide. Even the infamous Harvey Goldstein, who had represented Geoffrey Perkins for a brief period, had failed to get anywhere with them, but Victor was not a man to recognise the word 'no'. Adams had accused the Original Records management of lining their own pockets, but the truth was that they were barely making ends meet, and the new demands finally put them out of business for good. It's hard not to see this as something of a loss of innocence for Adams, for all that authors traditionally absent themselves from such business dealings. To close down a passionate indie label which had provided an indulgent home for *Hitchhiker* on vinyl – it was a crucial step towards acknowledging that he was now the fountainhead of a *Hitchhiker* industry, less Ford Prefect, more Zarniwoop. He had even set up his own production company, named Serious Productions, because 'most people I know with companies had silly names for them, so I decided I was going to have a serious name'.

The primary job for Douglas' new agent, naturally, was to land him a book deal, and although the writer had sworn that *Hitchhiker* was a closed book, Ed quickly convinced him otherwise, landing a particularly persuasive contract for a third entry in the series which maintained the arrangement with Pan but added a lot more noughts on contracts with publishing companies all over the world. Arthur might have symbolically thrown his Guide in the river, but Ford just had to fish it out again. Some aspects of the Guide would be explored in this new book, only to be thrown in the bin, with one lengthy scene explaining the pollution of time containing an aside referencing the Radio 4 show *Desert Island Discs*:

> He tossed her the book. She looked at it. She knew it perfectly
> well of course, as did everybody. There was a programme on the
> Sub-Etha radio which used every week to ask some well-known
> personality what they would take with them to a desert planet
> as well as The Hitchhiker's Guide to the Galaxy, a towel, and *The
> Songs of the Lost Land* ... She gave a sort of puzzled, interested
> shrug. It sounds very complicated but you'd recognise it if you saw
> it. People do it all the time when they're puzzled and interested
> but don't want to make too much of a thing about it yet.

Douglas' heels were still thoroughly dug in on the subject of a second TV series, though – which must have ruffled a few feathers at that August's celebratory Slartibartday in London, which he attended alongside Simon, David and Mark, who would never get the chance to appear together on the Heart of Gold set ever again. This was Douglas' penultimate convention appearance, with a contractual publicity stint at Chicago's Chicon IV in 1982 being the last gasp, but he decided that he was cripplingly uncomfortable at such events, despite his lifelong yearning to be recognised for his talent to amuse: 'I felt like such a goldfish in a bowl. I really couldn't deal with it. That may be a personality flaw, and I know I caused some resentment by not being more available, but I just feel very, very odd about it. Normally speaking, one of the things writers have is a certain amount of anonymity. I used to find that if I went to a science fiction convention I'd be so aware of people's eyes on me I'd forget how to walk. I found that very hard to deal with, which is why I stopped going to them.'

He had, however, made plans for how the series would develop, and so this time, rather than adapting dialogue and directions into prose, he would put his Krikkit story directly onto the page. The first hazard he faced, on trying to re-engineer an adventure intended for the Doctor to suit his own lackadaisical cast, was that Ford, Arthur and Co. just weren't the types to volunteer to face any danger: 'The problem is,' he reasoned, 'I have a plot which actually signifies something, and there are momentous events afoot, but I'd created such a feckless bunch of characters that before writing each scene I'd think, "Well, okay, who's involved here?" and I'd mentally go around each of the characters in my mind explaining to them what was going on, and they would all say, "Yeah? Well, so what? I don't want to get involved." Either they didn't want to get involved or they didn't understand. In the end, Slartibartfast had to become the character who had to get them all to get a move on, and that really wasn't in his nature either. You see, all the characters are essentially character parts. I had a lot of supporting roles and no main character.'

Slartibartfast's change of dynamism was thanks to his enthusiasm for CAMTIM, the Campaign For Real Time: a chronological play on the Campaign for Real Ale, CAMRA, which was supported by Douglas and fellow ale epicure Terry Jones:

"And if you are to help me ..." continued Slartibartfast.

"Ah, well, we didn't actually say that," said Ford, "I think we just want to wander off into the Galaxy and have some fun."

"If you do not help me," said Slartibartfast, "there will be no Galaxy to have any fun in."

"Well ..."

"And no fun to have in it," concluded Slartibartfast gravely.

This got home to Ford. He'd had so little fun for so long that the thought of there being no more of it to be had touched him deeply.

"What do you want us to do?" he said in a low voice.

"The first thing to do," said Slartibartfast, leaning forward and touching a button, "is to be unalarmed."

This is just one scrap of pages and pages of strong writing, under Sally's supervision, which would never be published, as the third novel began to take a shape unfamiliar to fans today. A trend was beginning, in which Adams' official summary would bear only scant resemblance to the *Life, The Universe and Everything* which was eventually released:

> The irrational adventures of Arthur Dent and Ford Prefect continue ... In this book we discover exactly why it is that the Earth has always been shunned by the rest of the Galaxy – and it's the fault of the English. Arthur and Ford begin to discover this when they are suddenly whisked from where they have been marooned on prehistoric Earth and dumped in the middle of a cricket match. Under the strangest possible circumstances they meet up again with Slartibartfast ... they set off on a task which is nothing less than that of saving the Universe from a billion-year-old plan of destruction which was first put into operation by an immortal being who was cracking up because he couldn't stand Sunday afternoons.
>
> In the course of their journey they come across a group of monks who will believe anything for a day provided that it isn't true. They visit the longest, worst and most destructive party ever held – it's into its fourth generation and still no one shows any sign of going – and they cross paths once again with Marvin the Paranoid Android who thinks he has finally found his vocation in life[4]... Having saved the Universe from pointless destruction, Arthur Dent is at the end confronted with God's final message to his creation: it is not exactly good news, but to Arthur it seems to make an awful lot of sense.

The reference to the immortal being here suggests the debut of a favourite character, Wowbagger the Infinitely Prolonged, but he was originally far more than the sharp-tongued purveyor of comic relief who appeared in *LUE* as we know it, however his actions were to tie in with the Krikkit plot.[5] The original book was also to be the first with a secondary title, as an early foreword explained:

> ...There followed a thousand years of horrifying carnage which we will skip over lightly. Anybody interested in horrifying carnage could do no better than to read P. L. Zoom's book *Krikkit: the*

Horrifying Carnage or Rad Banchelfever's *Carnage Illustrated: Vol 7, the Krikkit Wars* or Ag Bass' *Krikkit: The Statistics of Death* or Bodrim Holsenquidrim's much, much later statistical work *Krikkit: Still Counting After All These Years*. The most serious and substantial work of the hundreds of thousands of books which have been written on the Krikkit Wars is of course Professor San's monumental History Ballad entitled simply *Why, Why, Why?* and it is on account of that book that this one could well be subtitled *Because, Because, Because*.

As the two novelists shared their working days at St. Alban's Place, their wildly different approaches to their jobs must have seemed positively comical. Once again, Douglas was labouring constantly on his opening pages, and the necessity of saving Ford and Arthur before the Krikkit plot could even get under way. Despite one mention of a Golgafrinchan towel, the race were never to be referred to again – while the only joke to be recycled from the radio was Zaphod's 'Imagine I have a Kill-O-Zap blaster in my hand ...' So many beginnings were begun, one being a New York story once again concerning the 'We Apologise For The Inconvenience' message[6], one giving a quick glance around the Galaxy[7], and another being an extended examination of Arthur's nightmare[8] (featuring the first mention of 'the interconnectedness of all things'), which was reworked more than a dozen times before being ultimately condensed into the opening line: 'The regular early-morning yell of horror was the sound of Arthur Dent waking up and suddenly remembering where he was.' This also lost a particularly self-mocking paragraph:

He thought about the dream. It was a sort of science fiction nightmare, spewed up by a subconscious that must be badly disturbed. It was full of explosions, of spaceships, of mad robots. He had dreamed that the Earth had been destroyed. He had dreamed that his house had been demolished – that seemed more real. In his mind's eye he could see the end wall crashing down in the dust and rubble, it was very clear. But then it merged with something altogether more peculiar, something hideous and pestilential. He wanted to cry with frustration, or with something, at least. He saw a face laughing at him. Two faces, both the same.

He shuddered with a sudden spasm of horror as his mind's eye showed him the two faces both growing between the same pair of shoulders. The faces laughed and danced around him.

From here, with Ford and Arthur reunited despite Arthur's spoiling of a UFO rescue by planting a forest to read 'SOD OFF' from above, The Consultant[9] was going to provide the perfect excuse to move any character to wherever Adams needed them to be – a disturbing presence who stalks not just Arthur and Ford, but Trillian, and others, and whose dark eyes terrify all with the burning love that they radiate.

As for the duo's ultimate escape to the main plot as we now know it, via a ridiculously incongruous chesterfield sofa, Douglas insisted that it was not as 'random' a move as it seemed: 'Often the things that seem frivolous and whimsical are the hardest to get right ... They are stuck on prehistoric Earth, and then suddenly they find themselves on Lord's Cricket Ground, which comes about because they chased a sofa across a field. It all sounds inconsequential or illogical or whatever, but completely belies the fact that I tried over and over again, and rewrote that bit over and over, going absolutely crazy with it until I eventually found the right elements to create the air of whimsical inconsequence, if you like ... You needed all that stuff about Ford coming back and explaining ... about the flotsam and jetsam, and eddies in the space-time continuum (which was really a very silly joke, but you are allowed the odd silly joke) and the sofa, and so on. It required all that just to be able to suddenly say "Bang! Here they were somewhere else!" Because if you do just say that without getting all the rhythm right, then it doesn't work. It wouldn't have been enough for them to just be magically transported without it suddenly being a tremendous surprise coming at that moment. It's those kind of effects that take an awful lot of engineering, when you don't necessarily know what the answer is going to be, you're just thrashing around in the dark trying to find something somewhere that's going to help you get to that point. And when you're operating within a convention which says (or seems to say) "anything goes", you have to be extremely careful how you use that.'

As Emerson's novel glided off her typewriter, Adams was, as ever, honing what little he had, with every last line tested on his lover as he slowly continued work. Progress might have been faster if it hadn't been for the stream of love notes he left for her to discover around the flat – 'I already love you more than when I last saw you at quarter to three.' These would be as carefully preserved by Adams as the couple's passionate correspondence, which would be discovered by Nick Webb when writing *Wish You Were Here*, with carbon copies of Douglas' own long, fervent but joke-packed letters heartbreakingly filed away alongside Sally's replies. Although Douglas was already sharing visions of country cottages and kids, this hoarding was surely not the behaviour of a lover who feels his happiness will last for ever – but what more potent fuel for passion is there than knowing that your happiness can only be fleeting?

You're A Jerk. A Complete Kneebiter.

That the main plot of his third book had been ironed out several years earlier was more of a hindrance to Adams than a help. 'Since it was actually a plotted story, occasionally you can hear the grinding gears where I had to do something which had to establish a plot point, and at the same time had to be funny, and I'd have to overstretch to make it funny. That's the real problem: you can sort of hear the tyres screech around a few corners.' He continued, 'The struggle between substance and structure reached a pitch with the third book, as it was the one where I had a very detailed plan of the logical structure, and virtually none of that actually got into the book. I always go off at tangents, but whereas before I'd follow the tangents and go on from there, this time I was determined to go back to the plot each time. The tangents remained purely as tangents. So there was a real fight going on between the way I felt I ought to be doing things and the way things naturally end up getting done. That's why it has a slightly bitchy feeling – I keep yanking it back to where it's going even though it hasn't shown any inclination to go there ... I think I must be a very weird person.'

For all that sharing the Doctor's derring-do between Slartibartfast and Trillian (with a late flash of action from Arthur) allowed one favourite character to return and another to gain some much-needed depth of personality, the highlights of the third *Hitchhiker* book were all diversions from the plot. Many were unabashedly drawn from reality – Arthur's lost baggage on every transportation was a silly play on Adams' travelling niggles, spending eternities at airports trying to negotiate flight upgrades, while the Starship Bistromath was an almost facetiously transparent mutation of genuine bill disputes in his local Italian restaurant, right down to the obvious reference to 'Autorory' McGrath drinking himself under the table (Rory also inspired the name of the Ursa Minor Alpha Recreational Illusions Institute Award). Besides the generation-spanning flying party where Arthur meets Trillian copping off with the God Thor, a further allusion to the central role of catering in *Hitchhiker* came with a passing reference to the Holy Lunching Friars of Voondon, whose tenets were laid out in Adams' original notes:

> The Last Lunch.
> A man lives a lifetime every day. He wakes - he is born. He falls asleep - that is the death of his day's life. We feel that each day is a Holy and Sacred thing, a completeness in itself. The meaning of life must be understood by learning the meaning of a day. And the centre of life is symbolised by the centre of the day. What is at the heart of the day? What is at its centre? Lunch.

Just as there was a Biblical flavour to everything Adams was writing, this monastic theme was central to *LUE* – Arthur was to become the narrator of much of the action, thanks to his diaries[10] – confusingly written in the present tense, while also said to be drawn from interviews with an aged Dent who has found peace at the Monastery of Mon, a holy locale built atop something called 'The Perfidular Mushroom', a concept dotted throughout Adams' notes without ever being fully realised. With Simon Jones now disconnected from Arthur, the author's link with his terribly English hero certainly became more marked, and it's telling that in this period Adams started his own diary, if just to force himself into a daily habit of getting anything down on the page, even if it was just complaints about his bodily pains, and doubts about the direction of his third book (indeed, whether he should abandon the cricket business altogether), as 1981 started to go horribly wrong:

> I'm feeling extremely tired. So tired that standing up is a terrible effort, and by the time you've done it, the sheer effort of it has driven from your mind all notion of what it was you were standing up to do, and so you have to sit and think it all through once again ...
> One of the problems in my stories is that too much is simply description of states of mind in isolation, when I should have people interacting much more ...

One of the characters in the book should live in the country and have a crashed flying saucer in his garden: "Really. It happened late one night so I assumed I was dreaming it, but it was still there the following morning." He treats it as his hobby. He's been gradually sorting things out, tidying it up, putting things in neat heaps, labelling them and so on. He's not told anybody because he thinks that he's as capable of not being stupid about it as anyone else.

"Was there ... Any ...?"

"Anybody in it? Yes, it seems to be still alive but it's moving very slowly or is in a coma or something. The ship itself seems to be coping with him, but he's obviously ill, there's nothing I can do."

One day, after months, we visit him and there the creature is, groggy but managing some breakfast.

"He says he's been studying our race and culture for years - and he doesn't want to meet our leaders."

NUMBNESS.

One of _Hitchhiker_'s original inspirations was the idea of showing events of the everyday world on a macrocosmic scale, yet it seems to be more and more difficult to find anything to laugh about in the everyday world. The ability to laugh seems to depend on having some sort of concept of what, broadly speaking, is right and what is wrong, but however broadly you try to make your view of things, there are no longer any clear rights and wrongs. I think Tom Lehrer said something like that when he explained why he was giving up, or had given up, writing funny songs ...

Alright, well, here's news: We're going back to Lord's. Well, fuck it, that's what we're doing, I'm afraid. If you want the reasons - despite the fiercely adamant statement that that was precisely what we wouldn't do, then here they are. As I said to Sally in my letter, taking a silly subject and making it serious makes for better writing - or at least, for me it makes for better writing - than taking a serious subject and making it silly. Another reason: we don't have to follow the story closely. Slartibartfast, who is probably the best character you have from the point of view of your writing, can be on his own personal crusade against evil, because he sees this as a fitting occupation for a man in declining

years who therefore doesn't have to pay particular heed to what
the moral fashions are, he just wants to feel he's done something
which, according to his earliest received ideas, is worthwhile ...

The attempt to love people you don't know is dangerous, because
if you can fool yourself into thinking you can love someone you don't
know, you can fool yourself into thinking you hate them, and that
you should kill them. You build the means of their destruction,
and suddenly that becomes the means of your destruction as well.
Much better to ignore them and even the possibility of them as
well ... Here's a thought - maybe the people of Krikkit first
attempt to love the rest of the Galaxy - which simply doesn't
notice - and then decide to hate them instead.

It's not that he was utterly blocked – *LUE* was at least halfway there, over
a dozen chapters of particularly inventive antics for his beloved characters,
with a darker edge to the plot than ever before. Besides the Krikkit
business as we know it, there was The Consultant pulling strings behind
closed doors, Arthur's diaries, the Wowbagger business, Marvin finding
some kind of happiness with the Drubbers, and a brilliant courtroom
scene in which Zaphod is accused of something before he does it, and
receives a dangerous overdose of the Ultimate Truth Drug – which also
took the time to examine his relationship with Trillian in a new light.[11]
Another idea which never quite made it to the page was a planet plunged
into nuclear holocaust by a badly processed change-of-address card which
was inspired by Adams' moving woes – he would return to the concept in
another medium.

For all that the third *Hitchhiker* outing seemed set to be the strangest yet,
the two-thirds-completed manuscript was binned at the end of the year, and
rewritten absolutely from scratch. That such a dramatic move was made by
Douglas on one of the rare occasions when he looked set to meet a deadline
is made even more remarkable by his admission that he rewrote the story
'in circumstances I wouldn't want to build a bookcase under, let alone write
a book'.

These circumstances were, of course, that, as the festive season neared,
Emerson missed her husband and felt both smothered by idolisation
and overwhelmed by Adams' singular neediness: by Christmas she had
removed herself and all her belongings from the flat. Adams revelled in the

construction of good one-liners, and by any standard 'She went off with this bloke on, to me, the spurious grounds that he was her husband' is a corker, but we can be certain that it provided no comfort to the lonely Douglas, as he had to deal with his worst emotional pummelling since the dark days of 1976 all on his own. He begged Sally, insisting that no matter what she thought, she would always be The One. But finally he stood out of her way. His one telling supplication to her before she returned to new-found matrimonial bliss was that she should not, under any circumstances, please, ever go to bed with John Lloyd.

Volunteering to open himself up to such inevitable emotional pain might well have inspired the wise Adams adage 'A learning experience is something that tells you, "That thing you just did? Don't do that."' But the misery was palpable, and he called the split 'a huge domestic crisis which knocked me for six; I couldn't think of anything funny to save my life; I wanted to jump off cliffs and things like that.' Nonetheless, he had no option at that point except to stagger numbly onto another plane and head off to the West Coast of the USA for the first time, for a month-long publicity binge which must have taken enormous effort to smile through. He did, however, have the presence of mind to call Sonny Mehta and tell him that the latest draft was null and void, and needed to be reworked on his return. 'Practically every word' would be thrown out – not least the intended dedication, 'For Sally, who I love above the title' – which was cut down to the less touchingly witty 'For Sally'. As ever, suggesting direct links between Adams and his characters is a risky business, but there must be few extracts from *Hitchhiker* more telling than Trillian's abandonment of Zaphod, when seen through the prism of the author's fresh singledom, and growing creative ennui:

"Excitement and adventure and really wild things," he muttered.

"Look," she said in a sympathetic tone of voice, and sat down near him, "it's quite understandable that you're going to feel a little aimless for a bit ... You've finished the mission you've been on for years."

"I haven't been on it. I've tried to avoid being on it."

"You've still finished it."

He grunted. There seemed to be a terrific party going on in his stomach. "I think it finished me," he said. "Here I am, Zaphod Beeblebrox, I can go anywhere, do anything. I have the greatest ship in the known sky, a girl with whom things seem to be working out pretty well ..."

"Are they?"

"As far as I can tell. I'm not an expert in personal relationships ..."

Trillian raised her eyebrows.

"I am," he added, "one hell of a guy, I can do anything I want, only I just don't have the faintest idea what." He paused. "One thing," he further added, "has suddenly ceased to lead to another" – in contradiction of which he had another drink and slid gracelessly off his chair.

It is remarkable that there are so many laughs in the finished book, but at the same time you don't have to scratch many of the stand-out sequences from *LUE* too deeply to detect a more heightened air of dejection and loneliness in their design than anything before in the saga. The new, abusive version of Wowbagger provided narrative continuity from start to end (becoming such a fan favourite that eventually a website was launched offering infinite insults in his name), but the concept of a being so racked by immortality that he decides to personally offend every being in the history of the Universe in alphabetical order makes sense as the invention of an isolated and bitter man. Within Douglas' family, this period would come to be known as 'The Sally Crisis', and for a long period there was room for nothing in his head but the misery of lost love. He even outlined the plot for a story called 'The Dream Prize', about a remarkable happiness-creating gift, incessantly dreamt of by one man, who has it only briefly before the rightful owner – who has no real appreciation of its beauty and power – regains possession. The metaphor here is hardly impossible to comprehend.

As the *LUE* redraft painfully proceeded, the increase of profanity in the book seemed to speak of either a maturing or a more careless style – but then Arthur's response to his house being demolished in the first book had originally been littered with 'fucks'. It would be harder to expurgate the expletive in the Rory Award for 'The Most Gratuitous Use Of The Word "Fuck" In A Serious Screenplay', however, as it was central to the joke. Only in America, where the Cosmic Cutie had attracted a much bigger juvenile following, did the publishers insist on alternatives, substituting the inventive 'kneebiter' for Wowbagger's 'arsehole', and replacing the F-word with the tried and tested Semprini-like ultimate obscenity of 'Belgium', complete with explanation lifted from the radio.

Arthur's discovery of the secret of flying (which is, of course, to launch yourself at the ground and miss) did retain slightly more of the positivity of the original draft, and Adams admitted to being proud of its construction: 'I didn't revise any of the flying bit – it was all done first-draft. Although I cheated slightly, as, being aware I had written the entire sequence straight off, I felt slightly superstitious about it, and left things I could have revised.' Ultimately, however, Arthur's flight would come immediately after the heart of the book – indeed, the whole 'trilogy' – the meeting with the tragic Agrajag: a dark, extraordinary episode with so many conflicting tendrils of potential interpretation that it's hard to know where to begin.

Arthur mistakenly transports into his own personalised dark nightmare – a Cathedral of Hate centred on him alone – and meets the nemesis he never knew he had. With reincarnation added into the supernatural brew alongside séances and deities, Agrajag's aggravatingly regular murder at the hands of the oblivious Dent, from bowl of petunias to enraged bat monster, could easily be construed as Adams' own suffering at the typewriter in Arthur's name – and several years later he was to make the unusual move of suggesting himself for the tragic role, when the idea of a third radio series was floated. On the other hand, Dent's discomfort at his unwitting role in Agrajag's lives, while the wronged beast knows everything about him, contains echoes of Adams' experiences with fans, some of whom doted on his every sentence, exacerbating his compositional stress. (For many sci-fi fans who feel a beloved franchise has deviated from their ideal, the phrase 'it would be fair to say that he had reached a level of annoyance which now spanned the whole of time and space in its infinite umbrage' is almost putting it lightly.) When he received a letter, for instance, telling him that a fan had died happily knowing that their towel was within reach, it was intended to be heart-warming, but Douglas became horrified at the extent to which some devotees had taken his facetious creations to their hearts, and found the sense of responsibility both bewildering and burdensome.

Despite Douglas' by now traditional insistence that this would be the end, his finished draft, the best part of a year past deadline, did at least reunite the entire *HoG* crew and leave them unusually poised to spring into action should the time come again, even if Arthur did desire a quiet retirement on Krikkit. However, Adams said, 'When I got the proofs back from Pan I read through and had the niggling feeling there was something wrong. If it had been a small thing wrong I would have spotted it immediately, but it was one of those things that was so big and wrong that it takes you a while to see exactly what it is: there were two chapters missing. Those two had disappeared and actually turned up later in America, by which time the number of pages in the final bound copy had actually been determined. And that is why, in the English edition, the text of the book carries on to the very last page, there aren't any ads or anything in the back.' Although this epilogue finally settled the Ultimate Question question, by making it clear that possession of both Question and Answer would cancel out all existence, the tacked-on rendezvous with the Truth Drug-addled Prak, taking on Zaphod's original fate and being killed by his own laughter, set up further adventures even more blatantly, only teasing the quest of God's Final Message to His Creation rather than making it central to the plot – and once again bewildering Dent by making it clear that he was one of the most laughable things in existence.

This time, however, it was the critics who seemed to be saying 'when' as the book hit the shops in August 1982, with *The Times Literary Supplement* in particular sniffing, 'This third volume, though by no means lacking in enthusiastic drive, does little to suggest that the idea could or should be taken much further from here.' However, not necessarily helped by the gimmick of offering reviewers and early readers free 'cans of everything' (sealed tins containing slips of paper with the meaning of life printed on them in ink which evaporated on contact with oxygen), readers took no notice of any brickbats and, to Douglas' genuine surprise, *LUE* soon outsold both of its predecessors. Even more jaw-droppingly, that Christmas the *New York Times* best-seller list featured all three books in its top ten, making Adams the first British writer to achieve such a thing since Ian Fleming. Douglas' carefully cut-out newspaper clipping was pinned to his wall for the rest of his career, a display of pride which would of course also come to taunt him, whenever the muse was being particularly slippery.

The Meanings Of Liff And Love

The comedy and sci-fi freaks of America had so taken *Hitchhiker* to their hearts that Adams' life soon began to feel like one long luxury commute, but although his journey across the Atlantic shortly after delivery of his third book was partly recreational it was to lead to The Apparent Big One – at last, the movie was going to end up in the hands of Hollywood's hottest. For a while, Terry Jones had been keen to work with Douglas on the film, as discussed during extended sessions in Jones' local, but when the author declared that he didn't want to drag the original plot through yet another medium ('I was in danger of becoming my own word processor!'), and besides, they agreed that Arthur's adventures totally lacked the structure required for a blockbuster ninety-minute sci-fi comedy, the drinking partners, unable to settle on a fresh *Hitchhiker* idea, decided to keep their friendship non-professional. Many other movie magnates, however, were keen to hitch up to Douglas' gravy train, and his month in Malibu, in a house rented from Donna Summer, would effervesce with ruinous lunches as he mulled over offers. Best of all, though, he would not be travelling alone.

It was said above that Adams had to deal with the end of his relationship in isolation, but of course, with his network of friendships tried in the furnace of Footlights, post-grad poverty and countless parties, there were many people he could turn to. Mary Allen and he were still close, but when his daily hour-long phone calls began to reach the level of life burglary she suggested to him that the best way to avoid loneliness was to get a new lodger. After consultation, they whittled the list of potential flatmates down to just a few, including Perkins and a high-flying lawyer friend of Mary's whom Douglas had met at a party or two, Jane Belson. There had been a time when Mary and Douglas had almost drifted into an affair, but she recalled that on the close-shave evening in question they ended up performing *Macbeth* together in its entirety. She and Jane, meanwhile, had bonded over being two-timed by one Lothario, but when Mary put Jane and Douglas together in the same household there was no question of romantic match-making – in fact, numerous candidates for the flat were turned down precisely because they were likely to end up in bed with him. This seems curious in retrospect, as Douglas and Jane could not have been more uncannily matched if they had been the last remaining examples of the human species. Their differences were as complementary as their similarities, Adams recognised: 'I'm a man of obsessive enthusiasms, great bursts of energy followed by two days in bed. Jane is totally different, which is why we complement each other so well.'

A few weeks older than Douglas, Jane was born in London to Australian parents, and had been at school with Johnny Brock. After studying History & Economics at St. Hilda's College, Oxford, she worked briefly for the Treasury before being called to the Bar in 1978, eventually becoming one of the most admired and certainly the youngest barrister in the UK, specialising in divorce law. Above all, she was immensely tall, incredibly intelligent, strong-willed, and a harder chain-smoker than even Douglas at his most writer's-blocked. She also possessed a striking dark-haired, dark-eyed beauty which was inevitably instrumental in transferring Adams' longings for Sally over to her – and although Jane knew Sally better than Douglas at first, she could not help but be won over by him as well. They were so equally matched and headstrong that this was not to be the beginning of a perfect peaceful love-match but of a passionate, loud and frequently explosive relationship, which would endure largely because, at the eleventh hour, Jane would usually elect to be the one to give in to whichever of Douglas' demands had caused a particular argument. The first example of this would be accompanying him to California, taking time out of her successful matrimonial-law practice (successful despite certain gestures from her boyfriend, such as having a series of increasingly extravagant flowers delivered to her in court every hour one Valentine's Day, during particularly fraught divorce proceedings).

Incidentally, another love came into Adams' life at this juncture – he bought his first computer: 'It was a stand-alone word processor called a Nexus, which was horrendously expensive by today's standards and probably less powerful than the free calculator you'd get in a Christmas cracker.' He flirted unsuccessfully with a DEC Rainbow in America, before acquiring an Apricot on his return to Blighty – as the latter ran on MS-DOS it was the first computer which began to make any kind of sense to him.

As he left for the LA sunshine, Douglas told journalists, 'It's very important for me at the moment to do something different because I don't want to be indelibly stained with *Hitchhiker* my entire career. I probably am already, but I would like to prove to the world out there that there are other things I can do as well. I would like to write a novel which wasn't science fiction. I want to write a stage play, and the next thing I'm about to do, in fact, is in a way a slightly small thing. A friend and I are going off to write a sort of dictionary.' The third member of the Californian expedition, therefore, was John Lloyd. He and Douglas had not entirely stopped working on ideas together throughout their separate successes: one of the hit *Not* spin-offs, the brick-thick almanac *Not 1982*, being intensely material-hungry, had made good use of the 'place-name definitions' games they had played in Corfu, with the very best entries being printed as 'The

Oxtail English Dictionary'. When Douglas discovered that John planned to compile an entire book of them, however, he brought in Ed Victor and in September '81 Ed took the two friends to lunch to celebrate the landing of a deal with Pan and Faber & Faber for what would come to be published two years later as *The Meaning of Liff*. The apparent synergy with the Pythons' last movie *The Meaning of Life* was coincidental – right down to Gilliam's headstone titles, with God zapping the finishing touch to the last letter to turn 'LIFF' into 'LIFE' – but although Lloyd was keen to distance the book from the film, favouring the place-name punning of 'The Oxnard Eglish Dictionary', Adams argued for the title as one way of attracting more attention to the book, with Terry Jones' blessing. The movie seemed to owe a certain amount to Douglas anyway, featuring as it did Simon Jones in supporting roles (at Cleese's invitation, post-*Privates on Parade*), and echoing *Hitchhiker*'s astrological and philosophical silliness in Eric Idle's showstopper 'The Galaxy Song'.

At the time, there were accusations of plagiarism as the 'silly neologism' concept stemmed from a 1950s article by Paul Jennings – presumably where Douglas' teacher got the idea from – but although the approach of *Liff* was hugely different, Douglas thoughtfully sent a respectful apology to the elderly Jennings. As his dismissive reference to it above shows, *Liff* was never a major break from *Hitchhiker* for Adams but a hugely pleasurable project which he could read and reread, taking pride in it less critically than in his solo work – he even accompanied John on a special promotional stroll spotting 'Liffs' for Granada TV when the book came out, and the friends put together an update, *The Deeper Meaning of Liff*, seven years later. 'Normally I don't enjoy writing at all,' he reaffirmed at the time, 'but it was a real pleasure doing this book. But what's really nice is that my family and so on, who say, "Yes, dear, it's nice about *Hitchhiker*" – John's say the same about *Not the Nine O'Clock News* – love this book. My kid brother and sister like it. It's selling briskly, but not as well as it could do. I think that's because people have no idea what it is – it's totally enigmatic and anonymous, unless you happen to recognise our names.' In a strangely warped translation, although *Liff* definitions had no connection with the *Not* TV series, the American adaptation of the show, *Not Necessarily The News*, gave rise to cast member Rich Hall's own crazy neologisms, known as 'Sniglets'.

Although John was preoccupied with the impending stress of *Spitting Image*, there were still long days spent on the beach gazing out at the

Pacific and coming up with concepts and human quirks which demanded their own word (some failing to make the grade, such as 'Skeffington: the stray pubic hair that gets caught behind a foreskin'), but generally John masterminded the *Liff* project while Douglas was mercilessly lunched by Hollywood producers. He eventually settled on ex-*National Lampoon* art director Michael Gross and his associate Joe Medjuck, who were also new in town and were sniffing out interesting projects on behalf of *Animal House* producer Ivan Reitman. Whether it was this duo's clear appreciation of *Hitchhiker*'s humour or the apparent lack of Hollywood bullshit in the proposed production set-up which appealed to Douglas (Medjuck and Reitman being Canadian), and despite his fear that the humour of *Stripes* and *Animal House* was alien to *Hitchhiker*, it was Reitman to whom he and Ed Victor gifted the go-ahead to buy up the movie rights for £200,000, with a deal sewn up with Columbia Pictures granting Adams the first three drafts of the screenplay. The team had originally been looking for an animated follow-up to their own 1981 sci-fi comedy, *Heavy Metal* – a meathead cartoon onslaught of space clichés and Barbarella clones with gigantic mammaries – but although Adams vetoed any idea of animation, they were happy to let him try to bring his vision to life for cinema audiences.

Despite the misgivings shared with Terry, then, Douglas elected to reprocess Arthur Dent's progress from muddy Earthling to space-hiker yet again, for a whole new medium. With so much business to attend to two-thirds of the way around the planet, two questionably canonical entries in the *Hitchhiker* radio legend, giving Simon Jones and Stephen Moore their last official outings in character for over twenty years, had to go ahead with little or no input from the creator (although he did accompany Moore in character as Marvin for a guest spot on Radio 1's *Studio B15* in January 1982).

Sheila Steafel is an under-appreciated comedienne, a member of the *Week Ending* cast during Adams' brief tenure, and she presented her own Radio 4 celebration in the summer of 1982, with material written for her by the likes of Galton & Simpson, Hamilton & Jenkin and Barry Cryer – with a small spot earmarked for a *Hitchhiker* skit, which Adams dutifully delivered. It was only a squib, placed sometime before the events of *LUE* continuity-wise, but Simon was happy to show up in character for the evening's recording:

SHEILA   Hello and welcome to 'Sheila's Ear'. And I have with me
in the studio this evening a man whose travels as a
hitchhiker around the Galaxy have made him something
of a celebrity. Ladies and gentlemen - Arthur Dent ... In
your lovely, woolly dressing gown. You must be the most
well-travelled man I ever met. Can I ask you first of all-

ARTHUR   Where am I?

SHEILA   ... We're at the BBC.

ARTHUR   I thought I was in a cave.

SHEILA   Well, I know what you mean, but this is the Paris Studio,
Lower Regent Street, London ...

ARTHUR   I'm astonished. Last time I was here it was blown up ...

SHEILA   How interesting. Tell me, what are the things you
missed most about Earth?

ARTHUR   ... Well ... irreplaceable things, I suppose. Mars Bars,
primarily. Certain types of tea. And, well, I was going
to say Radio 4. But I'm a bit puzzled. Are you sure this
is really happening?

SHEILA   You missed Radio 4?

ARTHUR   Oh, certainly. 'The News Quiz', 'Just a Minute' ... it's
unique. There's nothing quite - or even faintly - like
Kenneth Williams anywhere else in the entire Galaxy ...
I've looked. Not very hard, I grant you.

SHEILA   Why don't you tell us something about your experience
of space?

ARTHUR   Well, one of the interesting things about space is really
how dull it is ... Bewilderingly so. You see, there's so
much of it and so little in it. It sometimes reminds me
of the 'Observer' ... actually, I've been living in a cave
on prehistoric Earth for the last five years. So if you
really want a lot of stuff about asteroids and ray guns,
I'm afraid you've come to the wrong chap ... I can tell you a
lot about mud and swamps and the quest for fire. Honestly,
this is the place I always dreamed of being. England now.
'The Archers'. Crumpets with Marmite. Chat shows. Funny -
now I'm here, I keep thinking I ought to pinch myself.

SHEILA   No, don't do that ...

As the 'It Was All A Dream' conclusion suggests, Adams did not labour over this final piece of radio scripting, but the sketch's eventual inclusion in the 25th anniversary edition of the *Hitchhiker* scripts qualifies it as canon. A far more difficult sketch to paste into *Hitchhiker* lore was performed for Radio 2 six weeks later, for a Roy Hudd-hosted comedy special, *The Light Entertainment Show*, for which Douglas only sent his distracted permission for his most beloved characters to drop by, with a very short, corny spot of pun-plagued patter scripted by Tony Hare and Peter Hickey:

FX	DESCENDING WHOOSH
ROY	Good heavens, it's a spaceship landing! There's no expense spared on this show, you know!
ARTHUR	Um, excuse me? I'm Arthur Dent, and I was wondering, is this the, er, the Planet Earth?
ROY	Yes!
ARTHUR	Oh, thank God for that. So you must be human?
ROY	No, I'm an Equity member.
ARTHUR	I'm so relieved to be home at last! I've been hitchhiking, halfway across the Galaxy.
ROY	What a coincidence, I'm halfway through eating one in my dressing room. Who's your friend?
ARTHUR	Oh, I'm sorry, I should have introduced you. This is Marvin, the paranoid android.
MARVIN	I think you ought to know I'm feeling very depressed ...
ROY	Well, you computerised Dusty Bin, what can I do for you?
MARVIN	Daleks!
ROY	That's nice, isn't it? Go and wash your mouth out with Brasso, go on!
ARTHUR	What we'd like to know is, could you direct us to ITV?
ROY	Certainly. Just go out through the stage door and follow the rest of the cast.
MARVIN	I've got a job as a stand-in for Metal Mickey.

Canon-wise, of course, this belongs alongside Marvin's appearance on *Blue Peter* rather than in any official script book, but it was no skin off Douglas' famous nose. He had bigger concerns than semi-official radio outings, trying to retool his creation for cinema. Before long he decided that

Islington was no place to try to write a movie, and so his return home was short-lived – once again, Jane was convinced to put her career on ice and fly back to Hollywood by her boyfriend's side at the start of 1983.

I've No Sympathy At All

The couple settled into their new home in Coldwater Canyon and Jane decided to take her Bar exams for practising US law while Douglas tried to get to grips with writing for the big screen. His first screenplay attempt was a particular fiasco – having plenty of experience writing for radio and TV, he blithely plunged in and translated his story to the screen in a similar manner to the TV series, with the result that Ivan Reitman received a 275-page screenplay treatment which would have translated into an epic evening at the multiplex since most 100-minute-movie screenplays averaged around 125 pages. In addition, this document was as packed with private jokes as his past scripts had been, but Douglas wasn't writing for his friends and colleagues any more, and his asides only conveyed his greenness to the experienced Hollywood players:

> Ford arrives. The clothes he wears are all individually OK.
> There is something about the combination of them and the way
> in which he wears them which suggests that he isn't really at
> home with Earth culture. I know this is a difficult effect to
> achieve these days as everybody seems to dress that way, but
> we can at least try to create something distinctive.

There were many carefully thought-out ways of opening up the action of the novels for a bigger canvas – the success of *Tron* even inspired Adams to hope for real computer graphics this time. But the scripts often tended to stray from strict screenplay directions into something more akin to a shooting script with added jokes, which was guaranteed to irritate any director aiming to have any creative influence on the project:

INTERIOR OF VOGON SHIP - THE BRIDGE.
It is very very ugly. It has the functional, brutal kind of ugliness
of East European cars. We can be reasonably sure that no happy or
pleasant thing has ever happened on this ship, and that any happy

or pleasant thing that attempted to happen would immediately feel very awkward and ill at ease, and would probably go and look for a dark corridor in which to happen. Luckily, the ship is full of dark corridors. Recent searches have, however, found no happy or pleasant things trying to happen in them. They have all thrown themselves off the ship. Anyway. The general spread of colours could all be found in the contents of a stomach pump.

The Vogon Captain, who looks like the offspring of a grisly one-night stand between a slug and a walrus, sits amongst an array of instruments and monitors bringing him unedifying information.

A deep and disturbing noise starts. The lights flicker and dim to suggest a massive power drain somewhere in the system.

> VOGON
> (As he stomps down the corridor) I don't know,
> apathetic bloody planet, I've no sympathy at all.

We follow him down the corridor part of the way, then stop and watch as he walks further down it. Although we never see any of them absolutely clearly, we are aware that the screens on the periphery of our vision are actually showing the Earth being demolished. Each time there is a particularly bright flare from the screen it has been preceded, by about a quarter of a second, by a louder roar than usual, and a dip in the lights. The Vogon dwindles on down the corridor. He passes an ugly Vogon child, cuffs it and makes it cry...

Gradually our POV changes and we turn to look at one of the screens clearly. Surrounding screens have now turned their attention to other matters - data readouts, security scanning of parts of the ship, commercials for Vogon toothpaste, etc. The screen on which we concentrate just shows an empty region of space with flying debris. We seem to pass through the screen and home in slowly on one of the pieces of debris. It is a tattered and charred towel flying silently through space. It flies dramatically over us, like a special effect from 'Star Wars'...

Large graphic: "TOWELS" overlaid on screen.

The screen divides into rectangles, each of which turns to reveal
a towel on the other side. Most of the towels are pretty homey,
downmarket towels, with floral patterns or cartoon characters
on them. Also one or two better ones - designer towels. (Are there
such things as designer towels? The Book of Revelation and
Nostradamus both agree that the final end will be heralded by the
advent of designer towels.)

It must have been uncommonly embarrassing for a writer as feted as
Douglas to be so out of his depth, but he knuckled down, did his research,
and worked very hard on his second draft, trying to reimagine his story
to Reitman's taste, despite the obvious challenges this presented: 'There's
a certain structural problem that I haven't quite solved,' he admitted.
'Normally, any movie has its big climax at the end. So when you have a movie
that starts with the Earth being blown up it's hard to work out exactly how
you end that movie. Of course, on the radio and television you don't need
to end it. It just carried on and on and on ...'

Reitman already had a few ideas about how he would make *Hitchhiker*
a blockbuster – Arthur Dent's Englishness was no problem, perhaps Jones
could even reprise his role, having made inroads into a film career, but
the *Saturday Night Live* stars Ivan had worked with could suit the story
well – Dan Aykroyd was a likely Ford, and a performer as magnetic as Bill
Murray could do a lot with Zaphod. Reitman was very committed to finding
a compromise that served Douglas' vision and sold plenty of popcorn,
and even tried to interest David Cronenberg in taking the reins for a 1984
release. Ultimately, though, Adams was to leave the producer's office with
sentiments which made his attitude to Alan Bell seem almost cordial – even
if the experience did gift him with numerous disingenuous anti-Hollywood
chat-show anecdotes for years to come: 'You know all the things that happen
to people in Hollywood and you think, because you know about them, they
won't happen to you. You go and you sit there and day after day goes by –
and everything that happens to people who go to Hollywood, happens to
you. I got very, very miserable there ... I eventually gave up. Myself and the
producer, we never could quite agree about how it was going to go, and
every time I rewrote it, it got worse from both our points of view.'

One particular flea ushered into Adams' ear was the impression that
Reitman was completely against having 42 as the answer to the Ultimate

Question, wanting something more audience-friendly, inspiring Douglas'
inspired grump, 'Here's a guy who's just bought two gallons of chocolate-
-chip ice cream and he's complaining about all the little black lumps in it.'
Adams had completely misconstrued Reitman's complaint, however – the
'42' joke was fine, it was just felt that such a deliberately disappointing
denouement was guaranteed to anger audiences, transforming Columbia's
sizeable investment into a turkey – he just didn't want the Deep Thought
element to provide the finale. But then, Adams was not likely to have been
listening too coolly to any of Reitman's views, having read the producer's
official notes on his second draft that July. Despite Reitman's cover-letter
request that 'I trust you will take the notes in the spirit in which they are
intended,' he hadn't even taken the time to read the whole draft before
heading off on vacation, and the writer's ego was to be kicked around with
every succeeding castigation as he turned the pages:

- Dialogue in scene 94 is bad.
- On page 116, we're introduced to yet another character·
  Slartibartfast, a funny old guy who builds fjords. I think he is
  an enjoyable character but his inclusion in this piece is totally
  arbitrary. He comes from nowhere, disappears suddenly and
  has no reason for being except to impart some third-person
  background narrative.
- Arthur joking about Slartibartfast's name in scene 104 is like a
  bad Mel Brooks sketch.
- Scene 105 – in the midst of this chasing around, we are told
  of the cleverness of dolphins as an introduction to finding out
  about how smart mice are. At about this point, I found my
  patience with the story exhausted. I should note, not because
  of the eccentricity of the ideas, but because of the utter
  randomness with which they are thrown in the stew and the
  absence of anyone to care about.

Douglas discovered many pleasures during his seven months on the West
Coast, chief among them his affinity for scuba-diving: his empathy with
dolphins was only one element of his natural penchant for the life of a sea
mammal, and diving would become one of his major pleasures in life – bathing
writ large. But although he worked his way through several more screenplay

drafts for Columbia, every rewrite only resulted in a script that pleased everyone less than the previous effort, and Adams frustratedly declared his defeat in the late summer: 'It wasn't a good period for me, nor a productive period. I had a slight case of "Farnham" – that's the feeling you get at 4.00 in the afternoon, when you haven't got enough done.' His return to Islington, bursting with tales about clueless cigar-chomping Hollywood producers, was just one clue to his greater identification with his hero: putting himself in Arthur Dent's slippers, Adams considered that a sojourn in the madness of LA would be the perfect cover story for any hitchhiker returning from mind-crushing adventures across the Galaxy. Reitman, meanwhile, had no time for adapting eccentric British novels any more: his hoped-for Ford, Aykroyd, had come up with a knock-out screenplay co-written with Harold Ramis, which also combined snarky humour with sci-fi and mysticism, to tell the story of a gang of New York paranormal investigators saving the world. *Ghostbusters* would become not just the blockbuster hit of 1984, but one of the most successful movie franchises of all time.

A return to more familiar territory was extremely desirable and so, a few months after Douglas and Jane's return home, Ed was very happy indeed to announce that his client would be writing a whole new entry for what was already incorrectly being termed his 'trilogy', for three-quarters of a million dollars – a higher sum than ever. The runaway success of the first *Hitchhiker* book had been celebrated in January with a special star-studded party at which Douglas was awarded a Golden Pan for a million sales, and so the expectations for a fourth novel were bound to be high. Adams admitted, 'Going home and having felt a bit disoriented, there was a certain amount of running for cover at that point, which is why I agreed to writing another *Hitchhiker* book – simply because it was something I knew. The problem is that you can say no to something 99 times, and you only have to say yes once and you're committed. So, to be honest, I really shouldn't have written the fourth *Hitchhiker* book, and I felt that when I was writing it. I did the best I could, but it wasn't, you know, really from the heart. It was a real trial and struggle to write it.'

Victor had wanted the fourth instalment to be known as 'God's Final Message To His Creation', as that was the main narrative reason for another episode, but Douglas was already certain that *So Long and Thanks For All The Fish* would be the title of his fourth book – aiming as far as possible to use only phrases from the first story, embellishing the impression that there was a carefully worked-out arc to his saga. What his new story would actually be, however, required more consideration – often numerous oddities or loose ends in previous books suggested his way forward, and this time the exodus of the dolphins would take precedence but, as ever, where Arthur Dent's fate would take him was far from set in stone. Another loose thread marked for development from the start was the girl in the café with the climactic revelation: he decided it was her time to step centre stage.

Although this would be his first-ever *Hitchhiker* print outing written specifically as a book rather than as an adaptation from radio or unused TV scripts, at least he wasn't actually short of ideas to pour into the stew – as the original announcement revealed, Douglas had a hankering to tell a story from the point of view of a character who had thrown themselves from a great height in order to remember something important, and although his original notes stipulated 'Can't be Arthur – he can fly', that was the first intention:

EVERYTHING YOU WANTED TO KNOW ABOUT THE FIRST
THREE BOOKS BUT NEVER THOUGHT TO ASK.

It deals with that most terrible and harrowing experience in
life – trying to remember an address which somebody told you but
you didn't write down.

At the end of *Life, the Universe and Everything* Arthur Dent was
told where to find God's Final Message to His Creation, only he
can't remember where it was. He tries everything he can to jog his
memory, meditation, mind reading, hitting himself about the head
with blunt objects – he even tries to combine them all by playing
mixed-doubles tennis – but none of it works. Still it plagues him
God's Final Message to His Creation. He can't help feeling it must
be important.

In desperation he decides to throw himself off a cliff in the
hope that his life will then flash before his eyes on the way down.
As to what will happen when he reaches the bottom – he decides
he'll meet that challenge when he gets to it. He lost all faith in
the straightforward operation of cause and effect the day he got
up intending to catch up on some reading and brush the dog and
ended up on prehistoric Earth with a man from Betelgeuse and a
spaceship-load of alien telephone sanitisers.

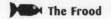

He picks a nice day, a nice cliff, and does it ... he falls ... he remembers ...

He remembers an awful lot of other things besides, which throws him into such a state of shock that he misses the ground completely and ends up in the top of a tree with scratches, bruises, and a lot to think about. All his past life on Earth takes on a completely new meaning ...

Now he really wants to find God's Final Message to His Creation, and knows where to look.

Arthur Dent is going home.

It was around this time that Adams became aware that he had attracted something in the vein of a Boswell – there were always fans who made it their business to know more about Douglas and his creation than he claimed to himself, the nonpareil being Mike 'Simo' Simpson, a luminary of the ZZ9 fan club who would eventually provide a regular service to the writer and his 'people' by acting as a hotline for facts and figures about *Hitchhiker* which were not at their fingertips. In late 1983, however, Adams was first visited by budding journalist Neil Gaiman, who interviewed his hero for *Penthouse* – particularly with a view to getting the lowdown on what was next in store for Arthur. A second press release was also to tantalise fans by giving away some of the ideas brewing in Adams' mind, most of which never got anywhere near any *Hitchhiker* product:

Along the way they meet some new people and some old, including:
Wonko the Sane and his remarkable Asylum.
Noslenda Bivenda, the Galaxy's greatest Clam opener.
An Ultra-Walrus with an embarrassing past.
A lorry driver who has the most extraordinary reason for complaining about the weather.
Marvin the Paranoid Android, for whom even the good times are bad.
Zaphod Beeblebrox, ex-Galactic President with two heads, at least one of which is saner than an emu on acid.
And introducing ... A Leg.

Ultimately only Wonko (the dolphin expert and only sane person in California, whose inside-out madhouse declaring the rest of the world insane was inspired by a genuine lawsuit-evading direction on an American packet of toothpicks), the truck-driving Rain God Rob McKenna and, of course, Marvin, put in an appearance in *SLATFATFish*, with even Zaphod staying off-stage, because, Adams admitted, 'It was like a chore – people were saying, "Let's have a Zaphod bit", and I didn't feel like doing a Zaphod bit! You see, I didn't even want to do Marvin, but then what happened was that I finally had an idea of something I wanted to do that would have to involve Marvin, which is the way it should be. I didn't have that with Zaphod.' He explained that this sentiment also soured his feelings towards the ideas he had allowed to leak out: 'I suppose one reason why a lot of that stuff never materialised was I had the feeling during that period of the whole world looking over my shoulder while I was writing. Every time someone would write to me and say, "What are you going to do with this character?" or "Why don't you do this to resolve this situation?", then you instantly shy away from it and think it's no longer yours to control. It seemed to me like there was too much to tie up and mop up in *Hitchhiker*, so that trying to write it like that would just be a continual task of knotting up the loose ends, when in fact it might be better just to think of something completely different.'

The author was, however, to indulgently explain the unused ideas to young Gaiman – the unique opener of clams which could give you 'a flicker of memory all the way back to the primeval ooze' was transparently inspired by gastronomic excesses, while the leg was at one point intended to become a silent member of the *HoG* crew for the movie, being an independently intelligent part of the Frogstar battle machine tricked into self-destruction by Marvin. Most intriguing of all, however, was the walrus which had the Beatles inspiration you would expect from Adams, unconnected to Lennon's famous psychedelic song but inspired by a memorable occasion which the schoolboy Douglas agonisingly missed: 'I got the idea after watching *Let It Be* and feeling very sorry for this obviously very embarrassed policeman having to go and make The Beatles stop playing. I mean, knowing this is actually an extraordinary moment: *The Beatles are playing live on a rooftop in London*, and this poor policeman's job was to go and tell them to stop it. I thought that somebody would be so mortified that they would do anything not to be in this embarrassing position … The thought goes through his mind, "I would do anything rather than do what I now have to do", whereupon someone appears and says to him, "Look, you have the option to either go and do this thing you don't want to do ... or I can offer you a life on a completely different planet." So he opts to go and be this strange sort of walrus creature ...' This idea was originally noted down for Arthur in the second TV series – he and Zaphod were to have a whole adventure in the grey area that appears when time is stopped (which just happens to be a never-ending cocktail party). The animal's species was decided ultimately by the UK cover design, which boasted a lenticular image alternating between a dinosaur and a walrus. These arbitrary gimmicks were bought as a job lot by Pan designer Gary Day Ellison and used on the first-edition covers – Pan's first hardback releases – without there ultimately being any relevance to the story within.

Back on home ground geographically and creatively, as 1984 rolled round Adams knew that it was time to really get to grips with honouring the breathtaking advance for his fourth book – an advance which had largely been provided by foreign publishers, including Simon & Schuster in the USA – and so, naturally, he got right to work on finding something else entirely to do. With scuba-diving an absent luxury in North London, that meant buying and playing with all the gadgets he could get his hands on – cameras, music equipment (including a synthesiser called Zaphod), and, of course, computers, with a BBC Micro and a Tandy 100 added to the TARDIS-like clutter in his top-floor lair. Discovering the capabilities of these machines was an excellent source of procrastination, but playing games on them ate up much more precious time. Douglas quickly grew tired of the basic *Space Invader*-style shoot-'em-ups then available to gamers, but he was particularly keen on the storytelling ingenuity in the text adventure games created by American coders Infocom, and mentioned his admiration for the company to a Simon & Schuster executive, remarking that unlike most games, 'There was some real wit and intelligence involved.' He was at first furious when he discovered that the executive took this as a cue to approach Infocom with an offer for a *Hitchhiker* licence, unhappy to be seen as a commercial pawn, but the idea of having his own universe meddle with the minds of thousands of gamers, doing something entirely new in the fresh field of 'Interactive Fiction', was genuinely exciting. There was the added inducement of seeing off competition from home coders – as early as 1981, Pan had absent-mindedly allowed one amateur programmer to create a text-based *Hitchhiker* title for the Commodore PET, which was a treasure-hunting yarn only loosely connected with the saga except for Eddie the Computer being your guide around a number of favourite locales, such as Milliways. When the game was sold off to UK publishers Supersoft, the legal tangles became more impenetrable, but eventually the company were forced to back down and alter every *Hitchhiker* reference in their title – with the same orders being issued to Fantasy Software, who had designed a cash-in platformer for the Spectrum entitled *The Backpacker's Guide to the Universe*.

With a clear need to flex some muscles and regain control of *Hitchhiker* for this new entertainment arena, Simon & Schuster were called off while Ed Victor dealt directly with Infocom, landing a reported seven-figure deal for Adams to collaborate on six games, beginning with an initial *Hitchhiker* adventure which, once again, would return Arthur Dent to his demolition nightmare – but this time, it would be the player's job to decide where he went from there. Infocom were based, coincidentally, at Cambridge, Massachusetts, but as Douglas and Jane took the long drive home eastwards, they called in en route at the company's New York offices to meet the technical whizz who would work with Adams on the project, Steve Meretzky. Although only a fresh fan of *Hitchhiker*, the also alarmingly tall Meretzky was the ideal man to bring it officially to the gaming audience – not least since he had added a last-minute reference to it in his first hit game *Planetfall*, with a collectible towel bearing the legend 'Escape plot #42: Don't Panic!'

The original meeting went well, and Steve and Douglas agreed on the way ahead for their game – although Adams was keen to get stuck into learning to write in Muddle code, Infocom's chosen programming language, and was always trying to create new things on his computer (he proudly showed Steve a 3D crossword puzzle designed in BASIC), they decided this posed too much of a risk, and so the work would be divided and completed separately, Adams writing text at home that would be implemented in the USA by Meretzky, once it had been sent across via the primitive electronic communication of packet-switching.

This meeting of minds was nothing, however, compared with the vision that danced into Douglas' consciousness on this visit – his very first contact with an Apple Macintosh, the 128k model not officially ushered into shops by Steve Jobs until January 1984. The neat beige machine's sheer analogue simplicity spoke to the writer, and he subsequently admitted that it had been love at first sight – henceforth every new release from Apple would find its way into his wire-webbed labyrinth of a study, offering him simultaneously the most convenient writing tool he had ever had and the most irresistible source of procrastination. After so long satirising the ticker-tape-spewing idea of what a computer was, Apple's approach to home computer use chimed perfectly with an enthusiastic amateur like Douglas: 'I adore my Macintosh, or rather my family of however many Macintoshes it is that I've recklessly accumulated over the years … The thing that has kept me enthralled and hypnotised by it in all that time is the perception that lies at the heart of its design, which is this: "There is no problem so complicated that you can't find a very simple answer to it if you look at it the right way."' Despite his upper floor's growing resemblance to a crashed spaceship, however, Douglas retained his trusty typewriter in pride of place, admitting, 'I use it when I get stuck. There's something wonderfully fundamental about hitting the keys and watching them strike the page, something a word processor will never entirely replace.'

So besotted was Douglas with the new Apple that he famously took possession of the first two models in the UK, leaving his new friend Stephen Fry to bag the third. By this point, the 1980s comedy scene had flowered so profusely that even Douglas had to admit that his hopes of being a successful comedy performer were past their best, with a new generation following in the wake of the success of *Not* who had to be embraced if he was to retain any credibility in British comedy. Pleasingly, *Hitchhiker* fandom was rife throughout the 'Alternative' generation, and not least thanks to the patronage of John Lloyd, Adams was to befriend many of the young Turks, becoming particularly chummy with *Blackadder* writers Richard Curtis (who was welcomed into Douglas and Jane's Californian pad long-term during his own first, failed attempt at making a movie) and Ben Elton, who often played host to Douglas in his Australian home. The success of the 1981 Footlights show *The Cellar Tapes* had, of course, been of particular interest to him, however. He could perhaps not be blamed for allegedly developing a crush on Emma Thompson initially, but his most lasting friendship would be with the tallest member of the cast, Stephen, who quickly established such an ubiquitous work ethic that Adams marvelled at the idea of 'a whole cupboardful of Stephen Frys all *doing things'*. One of these things involved befriending heroes like Peter Cook and Vivian Stanshall, and having been turned onto *Hitchhiker* from the first broadcast, Douglas Adams was another figure that young Fry was delighted to call a friend, particularly as the pair shared a devotion to gadgets and computers, Apple in particular, which nobody else could rival, or even fully understand: one particularly lengthy joint attempt by the friends to set up a data-sharing link, a kind of proto-Skype, was eventually abandoned when they realised they could just pick up the phone to talk to each other. Fry became like a second kid brother to Adams, the two of them testing gadgets and playing games together on the top floor while their younger sisters Jane and Jo joshed them for their geekiness. Douglas was to pay tribute to his young playmate's florid verbiage in his next book, via the odd minor character, Arthur's friend Murray Bost Henson, a polysyllabic tabloid journalist with something mysterious in his ear.

Pick Up Plotter: Your Load Is Too Heavy

The lure of the Apple Mac and the excitement of working with Meretzky on a positively pioneering project were good for Douglas, though all but guaranteed to inspire ulcers in Sonny Mehta and the team at Pan, who were holding on for the fourth instalment of Arthur Dent's adventures as 1984 progressed. Adams knew this, and made several concerted attempts to drag the words out of his imagination. He even headed down to the West Country to get away from it all, booking himself into Huntsham Court in Somerset for several weeks of uninterrupted creative genius. Sadly, his deep pockets and gregarious nature made good friends of his hosts on the very first night – he even invested in the hotel – and large swathes of his stay were subsequently spent sampling the most expensive wines in Huntsham's cellars, so he was to head back to Islington with little to show for the trip (besides, that was, a cheque for £25,000, half the payment for an American *Hitchhiker* calendar which never reached the printers, and the easiest money Adams ever made).

Creating the *Hitchhiker* game was by far the best alternative to composing *SLATFATFish* – the ultimate form of procrastination, combining experimentation with new technology with the promise of a tasty payday at the end of it. With time running short for making the Christmas market, Meretzky joined Adams at Huntsham to devise some of the craftier sections of the game, jointly coming up with the final puzzle while strolling on the beach of the Exmoor National Park. Naturally, Adams was never one to approach any project with anything less than an ultimate determination to be original, and the idea of believable interaction between program and player was to become a lifelong fascination, as he explained: 'One of the things I'd first been told about interactive fiction turned me off it, which was the idea that the audience, the reader, determines what happens. I'd been told grossly simplistic things about it ... It sounded like the writer abdicating. Once you get involved in writing these things, you discover that it's not the writer abdicating at all, it's the writer taking a completely different kind of control. It's rather like the experience of being a stand-up comic. You go and watch, for instance, Barry Humphries, one of the most brilliant guys there is at knowing how to play with an audience – what you see him do is appear to be continually inventing new material depending on what he gets from the audience ... he misleads them into thinking that when they heckle, they're actually coming up with original stuff. They're not, because he's done enough audiences to know exactly what an audience is going to say now, and he has this extraordinary sort of filing system in the back of his mind, which means that whatever the audience comes up with, he has got a response that, with a tiny bit of instant tailoring, will fit. And the audience goes away absolutely dazzled, because it looks like he's made up the whole act as he went along, and he hasn't, because he has continually provoked them to give him responses that they think they're making up ... That's exactly how you write a computer game. You're continually teasing and provoking the player.'

Adams' adventure would indeed go down in gaming history as one of the most provoking titles ever: 'The first game to move beyond being user-friendly; it's actually user-insulting – because it lies to you, it's also user-mendacious.' This wasn't just a case of Douglas coming up with a few quirky ideas – such as the Inventory containing 'No Tea', and 'The Thing Your Aunt Gave You Which You Don't Know What It Is' – and then letting the player plod through familiar text, he insisted it was based 'very, very loosely on the book, and deliberately so, because I didn't want to just do sort of a trot through the book. I've seen some games based on books, where it's just like the original text only you get to do the typing, which I think is really not a good way of doing it. So I wanted to write a game that would have the same starting point and the same kind of feel as *Hitchhiker*, the same kind of logic to it, but would go where the game wanted to go.' He defined this expansion on the original material as 'bearing as much relationship to the books as *Rosencrantz and Guildenstern are Dead* does to *Hamlet* ... It gets the player going and lulled into a false sense of security. And then all hell breaks loose and it goes through the most extraordinary number of directions. The game just glances at events which were a major part of the books, while things I used as one-line throwaways are those that I used for the game's set pieces. The reason was to keep me interested in doing it, and I wanted to make it fair for the people who haven't read the books. So readers and non-readers were, as much as possible, on an equal footing ... the game is equally difficult for both.'

In the course of the plot, as you flicked the IID switch, players would find themselves controlling not just Arthur, but Ford, Zaphod and Trillian, as they zapped around in space and time trying to work out what to do. 'The object of the game,' Douglas added, 'is to find out what the object of the game is. But I will tell you that your score is an index not just of how far you've gone along the adventure, but also of how happy you should be at that point. If you "enjoy" the beer when you drink it, you'll get more points. Believe me, you'll need all the points you can get!' Infocom went so far as to request that certain puzzles should be simplified, particularly as there was no possibility of a save option back then, and any mistake would kill you in a trice and send you right back to the start, or even worse, allow you to progress down a dead end and waste hours of lifespan. The Babel fish sequence, should you be skilled enough to get Arthur from his dark hungover beginnings to the Vogon ship in the first place, was considered the toughest challenge in any Infocom title at the time. But although the company wanted changes, Douglas blithely insisted that Steve tell his bosses to 'fuck off' – besides, an accompanying 'Invisiclues' tips guide would be available, to get players past anything too facetious and vague. The puzzles should rely on lateral thinking, but every stage of the Babel fish puzzle seemed so arbitrary, it's remarkable that anyone worked out the sequence without Douglas' facetious hints, and more remarkable still that the game was somehow marked as 'Standard' difficulty:

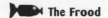

VOGON HOLD

> This is a squalid room filled with grubby mattresses, unwashed
> cups, and unidentifiable bits of smelly alien underwear. A door
> lies to port, and an airlock lies to starboard.
> Ford Prefect is here.
> Along one wall is a tall dispensing machine. In the corner is a
> glass case with a switch and a keyboard. It looks like the glass
> case contains: an atomic vector plotter.

> TAKE OFF GOWN

> Okay, you're no longer wearing the gown.

> HANG GOWN ON HOOK

> The gown is now hanging from the hook, covering a tiny hole.
> Ford yawns. "Matter transference always tires me out. I'm
> going to take a nap." He places something on top of his satchel.
> "If you have any questions, here's The Hitchhiker's Guide to the
> Galaxy." Ford lowers his voice to a whisper. "I'm not supposed
> to tell you this, but you'll never be able to finish the game without
> consulting the Guide about lots of stuff." As he curls up in the
> corner and begins snoring, you pick up The Hitchhiker's Guide.

>TAKE SATCHEL

> Taken.

> PUT SATCHEL IN FRONT OF PANEL

> Okay, the satchel is lying on its side in front of the tiny door
> panel.

> PUT JUNK MAIL ON SATCHEL

> Okay, the loose pile of junk mail is now sitting on the satchel.

> PUT TOWEL OVER DRAIN

> The towel completely covers the drain.

> PRESS DISPENSER BUTTON

> A single Babel fish shoots out of the slot. It sails across the room
> and hits the dressing gown. The fish slides down the sleeve of the
> gown and falls to the floor, landing on the towel. A split second
> later, a tiny cleaning robot whizzes across the floor, grabs the
> fish, and continues its breakneck pace toward a tiny robot panel
> at the base of the wall. The robot plows into the satchel, sending
> the Babel fish flying through the air in a graceful arc surrounded
> by a cloud of junk mail. Another robot flies in and begins madly

collecting the cluttered plume of mail. The Babel fish continues
its flight, landing with a loud "squish" in your ear.

Adams was happy to admit that he could not tell whether certain
sections were written by Steve or himself, but there was plenty of new
material, expansions on familiar asides, just when he should have been
filling his floppy disk with *SLATFATFish*'s manuscript. For instance, if you
fed a cheese sandwich to a small dog, he would fail to gobble up the
Vl'Hurg and G'Gugvunt warships when you were in their presence – your
first typed mistake would be the phrase that led them to war:

```
> LISTEN TO VL'HURG LEADER
     "Hated planet!" snarls the Vl'Hurg.
     "Home of he that dared to say 'PUT SATCHEL BY DISPENSER'" rasps
     the G'Gugvunt.
     "Detested words! Even now it sticks in my soul to hear them
     uttered," barks the Vl'Hurg, "even though ten thousand years
     have passed ..."
     "And as many senseless megadeaths! Worlds destroyed! My race and
     yours laid to waste! All because of he that dared shape the words
     'PUT SATCHEL BY DISPENSER'."
     "Torture to the Vl'Hurgish warrior heart to hear it spoken! Yet,
     even now, the hot breath of our vengeance blows hard upon this
     little world ..."
     "Vengeance on him who said 'PUT SATCHEL BY DISPENSER'."
     "Yes, there's no need to keep repeating it," growls the
     Vl'Hurg.
     "One happy thought," adds the G'Gugvunt. "After millennia of
     bloody and perpetual conflict, our races have been brought
     together by this Quest for the Source of the Offending Remark.
     Perhaps, after our vengeance has been exacted on him who said
     'PUT SATCHEL BY DISPENSER'..."
     "Will you stop saying it?"
     "...perhaps we will continue to live in peace and harmony and ..."
     "We will talk about that AFTER we ... who's this?"
     The two creatures turn and stare at you. The fleet continues to
     hurtle sunwards ...
```

Soon the patient people of Pan had to corner the author and find out just how on track the fourth book was, and the guilty shrug they received sparked pandemonium. Sonny explained to Ed that no matter what Douglas had begged him to suggest, there was absolutely no possibility of an extension – the publicity drive was planned to perfection, the cover was ready, the printers were warm, they just needed the manuscript and failure to deliver was in no way an option. Realising with mere weeks to go that Douglas only had a meagre twenty-five pages to show for his headline-generating advance, Sonny and Ed visited the flat in St. Alban's Place for an extraordinary meeting, where it was decided that in the morning Douglas would present himself at the Berkeley Hotel, where a suite had been booked (handy for running in Hyde Park), taking with him spare clothes, a typewriter (preventing the loss of whole days to Mac jiggery-pokery) and, as a special luxury, one guitar. Mehta, meanwhile, had a tower of manuscripts brought over from Pan, and a Betamax VHS set up to keep him entertained with a stack of classic movies (inspiring Ford's preoccupation with Earth cinema), while his errant author spent proper working days at the keyboard, getting Arthur's latest experiences down on paper under constant supervision. At the end of each day, Sonny would read the results, usually offering qualified encouragement as there was no time for rethinking, they would have dinner together, and then the millionaire best-selling author would be sent to bed, to prepare for another long day's on-the-spot composition in the morning. Douglas hunched over his old typewriter under Sonny's gaze, trying to create under duress, his fingers clattering over the keyboard, not always storytelling but often typing 'Who the fuck does he think he is?' and similar pages of choice abuse, before removing the paper from the typewriter, giving his captor a resigned smile and hurling the screwed-up pages in the bin (where Sonny would eventually find them, proudly displaying some of the finest invective on the Pan noticeboard for everyone to enjoy).

This frustrating and humiliating experience has gone down in publishing history, the legend of the procrastinating author – but with three decades' hindsight, the very idea of any top novelist being expected to deliver a massively anticipated new work in less than a year, while creating a computer game from scratch, seems a foolhardy arrangement from the start. Of course, the plan worked – after two weeks, the pair emerged from the Berkeley with a manuscript containing a beginning, a middle and an end, of sorts, and proceeded to get so rip-roaringly drunk together that they all but wiped their memories of that fraught fortnight. Mehta would never go through anything like this again, though: the next time a deadline had Adams' name on it his newly appointed Literary Editor, Sue Freestone – an incisive and, crucially, eminently patient American publishing expert – would have the job of coaxing the final full stop out of him.

The book which resulted from Douglas' fortnight of imprisonment, although the slimmest *Hitchhiker* volume for obvious reasons, went on to be another best-seller – but, in a short time, fans and author seemed largely in accord that it was the weakest entry, and Adams got a perverse kick out of his usual post-publication game of apologising and explaining what he saw as the book's shortfalls: 'The reason you get to be good in the first place is that you work very, very hard at getting it right, and as a result you think, "Well, therefore the world will have to listen to whatever I write." You fall into a trap, and that's when you have to work doubly hard to make sure you don't let stuff by that isn't good enough. And I'm afraid, I think, that was the fault with *SLATFATFish* – I just completely lost my way.' He complained further, 'One problem with the book, and there are many, is that up to that point I had been writing pure fantasy, which I'd had to do as I'd destroyed the Earth in the first reel, so to speak. So my job was to make the fantastical and dreamlike appear to be as real and solid as possible, that was always the crux of *Hitchhiker*. Whereas in *SLATFATFish* a curious kind of thing happened. I got back to the everyday and somehow for the first time it seemed to be unreal and dreamlike. It was rather in reverse. I think it's largely because I thought I'd get rid of this problem of not having the Earth there to relate to by just bringing it back, and I suppose a part of me knew, a part of me said that you can't really do that. So therefore it wasn't the real Earth, and therefore it was bound to become unreal and dreamlike, and that was really a problem with the book.'

The logic of the *Hitchhiker* Universe was always drastically elastic, and although it was preferable to find a real scientific solution to any plot problem, as we have seen, mystical, or at least preternatural, elements were not off the menu for Adams when he needed to make a leap. Arthur's sudden ability to attune himself to emotions and sensations telepathically, the ease with which he uses Mac software to find the woman he loves (living in Adams' actual flat in Islington, where Arthur's prehistoric cave had been) and the continued mastery of flight, all required hefty leaps of imagination to grease the gears of the plot, although in some ways, like the sheer joy of requited love that the hero experiences, these abilities could be seen as compensation for all of the horrible things that Adams kept doing to Dent every time he wrote a *Hitchhiker* instalment. It is said of the spruced-up Arthur that 'Only the eyes still said that whatever it was the Universe thought it was doing to him, he would still like it please to stop' – but it was not the Universe, it was Adams. As he told Gaiman, 'Arthur has undergone a fundamental change by then, because up to that point he has been our representative in a fantastical world, he has been Everyman, the person we can relate to, and through whose eyes we have seen the strange things that have happened. Now suddenly it's been turned around, and we have a real everyday Earth, and this character who, far from being our representative, has just spent the last eight years of his life alternately living in a cave on prehistoric Earth or being flung around the Galaxy. So he is no longer someone through whose eyes we can see things. The whole thing has turned upside down, and I don't think I had got to grips with that until I was too far committed.'

Whether this analysis was deliberate misdirection or not, with Simon no longer wearing the dressing gown there was an undeniable further stride towards the self-referential in *SLATFATFish*, with Dent's computer wizardry and Californian travels the least of his links to the author's recent experiences – he was even given the infamous biscuit story to relate, as a spot of decisive rights-assertion from the man who really experienced the etiquette disaster which had ballooned into an urban myth in the intervening years, claimed by people all over the world as their own tale, no matter how many times Douglas repeated the anecdote on publicity drives and on the other side of David Letterman's desk. 'Arthur, I think, is the one I guess is closest to me,' he admitted. 'I mean, I usually say, "No, it has nothing to do with me; he's just my idea of an ordinary person." But it's hardly a coincidence my idea of an ordinary person is someone rather tall and dark-haired, and slightly sort of vague and bewildered by the world, um, and works for the BBC. And if Arthur's the one who's most regularly bewildered, Ford is usually the one bewildering him. So that's the relationship there, quite a fertile one. Ford is definitely not me, he's the vehicle for all the stuff that comes at Arthur that he finds so hard to deal with or understand.'

But of course, the romance of Arthur and Fenchurch was the most hotly insinuated piece of disguised memoir in the novel, and Adams was forced to fudge: 'It's always difficult bringing the biographical element in, because the connections are never that obvious. I suppose my life was a bit more stable by that point, but on the other hand it was rendered unstable by trying to write that book.' Fenchurch, he insisted, was 'not based on any particular person, she's based on a number of different thoughts or observations of people or incidents. The idea of Arthur falling in love with her was really going very much into adolescent memories.' Sally Emerson, however, has said that Douglas told her that she was the inspiration, and certain details were directly inspired by their affair, such as the raffle-ticket-selling old woman who disturbs Arthur and Fenchurch's first tête-à-tête, suggested by a busybody in a New York diner who told Sally and Douglas that she had never seen two people so in love. All this must have been quite tough for Jane Belson to swallow, but in actuality Jane was surely the *real* Fenchurch – in hindsight, Sally was Trillian, the unreachable fantasy girl, whereas Jane was the ideal match; she stayed, she understood, she was Douglas' ideal travelling companion.

Adams' first and last sex scene was to prove a particularly contentious insertion for many fans, with young Neil Gaiman apparently speaking for them all when he told Douglas that he considered the undeniably contemptuous preamble which closes with 'Those who wish to know should read on. Others may wish to skip on to the last chapter which is a good bit and has Marvin in it', to be 'patronising and unfair'. But although it gives quite a clear view of the direct approach Adams was forced to make, jammed so desperately up against the clock, it's also surely one of the biggest laughs in a book which is only sprinkled with jokes, rather than constructed out of them. The chapter could have been considerably more hardcore at one point, with Douglas experimenting with erotic writing (involving an aside about the difference between an ice lolly, which shrinks as it is licked and sucked, and a specific part of the male anatomy), although this was abandoned with a note to himself: 'Jittery with sex – Erotic writing. It's no good just saying "Put this in there, lick that." You have to entice the reader until the reader feels … jittery with sex …'

The infamous preamble remained, however, one of a list of gripes from fans that has always marked *SLATFATFish* down overwhelmingly as the least loved in the original five-part trilogy. Gaiman was ungainsayable when he suggested that the normal writing and editing process would have ironed out a number of shortfalls and many elements, such as the Rain God trucker, are underdeveloped and fail to pay off fully. The cataclysmic silliness of the space robot's trip to Bournemouth was only documented cursorily, and as for the return of Earth – in Arthur's own words, the reason quite simply boiled down to 'Just life.' It's well claimed that the secret of Douglas Adams' comic prose is the perfectionist scrupulousness of his editing and re-editing methods, but from *SLATFATFish* onwards, *Hitchhiker* in particular was to be far less meticulously compact – getting any words down at all was the major hurdle in the first place. On the other hand, the lack of editing time for the fourth book did allow the first expletive in the US editions, as there was no time to find a way around Adams' emphatic 'fuck', and 'Belgium' would not have worked in that context.

Fan-baiting or not, though, no re-edit would have talked Douglas out of the contentious decision to have the lights go out in Marvin's eyes for 'absolutely the very last time ever' on the planet of Sevorbeupstry, after Arthur and Fenchurch follow Prak's directions to God's Last Message ('We apologise for the inconvenience' finally finding its place in the saga). Admittedly, Marvin's patient existence laps around the Universe's lifespan more than once, so any 'death' could only be symbolic of the author's sincerity about ending the *Hitchhiker* series for good, but Adams continued, 'It's very strange, that walking-across-the-desert scene, when they find the message. I felt very haunted by that when I wrote it – it's not particularly funny or anything, but curiously enough I was very proud of it. I actually felt very sorry for, and sympathetic with Marvin in that I felt close to the character in a way that sometimes I hadn't because I was just doing it out of duty. But yes, the book is lighter-weight than the others. In a sense I came close to owning up to that on the last page.' This last page was part of one of the oddest passages Adams ever wrote, an epilogue seemingly obscure but, considering the pressure under which it was written, clearly self-pityingly autobiographical. Never mind Arthur or Marvin, if Douglas had any one avatar it was 'one of the greatest benefactors of all lifekind', a genetic engineer who fails his planet due to his inability to knuckle down and design a race of superwarriors, being interested in so many other things like looking out of windows – but everything works out for the best in the end, *because* of his procrastination.

'There was a point to this story, but it has temporarily escaped the chronicler's mind', then, was to be the full stop in the saga of The Hitchhiker's Guide to the Galaxy. Adams' bungling star-skipping anti-hero was happy at last, and he could leave him be. Yes, cinema remained unconquered, but when Reitman was done with his ghosts the project would roll on without any sweating into the QWERTY from him – as he told Kevin Davies in 1985, 'Apparently there are a lot of lunches going on about it, but I haven't been invited to any of the recent ones – it's a long way to Los Angeles, for lunch.' This time, it really was 'quite definitely definite': time to move on.

FIT THE FOURTH

ESCAPE

"This Time There Would Be No Witnesses."

He picked up his towel and ran cheerfully for the door. Life had been a little dull of late. It showed every sign now of becoming extremely froody.
– Mostly Harmless

Despite the author's familiar *mea culpa*, *So Long and Thanks For All The Fish* was another massive seller, showing that the pedantic rewriting and compacting of every paragraph was not an entirely indispensable secret of *Hitchhiker*'s success. The computer game also shifted the best part of half a million copies, flying off shelves complete with marketing gimmicks, 'Feelies', in every disk box – including your own fluff, demolition orders in English and Vogon and even a tiny space fleet which were notable by their absence in a small plastic bag. Douglas set off on his travels around the world to promote both products, buoyed further by a new US airing for the radio show, arranged by Infocom. 1984 ended with the discovery of a new use for his towel, inching across a frozen Lake Michigan on it for a photo opportunity, but on his return home he pledged to stick to the UK for as long as possible, exploring the new creative freedom he had claimed. Nevertheless, exciting *Hitchhiker* royalties poured in from surprising quarters of the globe, letting him know that Dent's capers were becoming as popular in Japan as they were throughout Europe and the USA.

There Is Nothing They Will Not Do

Hitchhiker business was to remain thrillingly marginal to Adams as 1985 progressed, and he could savour the sensation of being free of deadlines and generally have a froody time of it. 'I had to leave *Hitchhiker*,' he said, 'because I felt I was continually in danger of only being able to sustain it by imitating myself. I had to get out and start something new.' This was a familiar claim, but this time it was true: 'At last! I'd actually got to the stage where I'd completely forgotten what it was I was intending to do in the first place, I only knew what I was doing sort of at everybody else's demand ... I had mental and emotional indigestion for a longish stage. The process of writing books is actually very miserable, you sit in a room all by yourself day after day trying to be funny onto a piece of paper or a computer screen or whatever it is ... and you think, "Why am I stuck up here trying to think of something funny and I can't, this is actually a miserable way of earning a living, why am I doing it?" "Well, because there's a lot of money to be made out of it." "Well, the original reason was something else ..."'

Douglas delegated the editing of the first *Hitchhiker* radio-script book to Geoffrey Perkins, and had reached the stage, seven years on, when he could look back at his first success almost as the work of another man. 1985 was a year of talking about *Hitchhiker* a lot, of course – he even enjoyed his very first online chat, courtesy of the Micronet Celebrity Chatline – and he found himself relishing the use of the past tense. Neil Gaiman had also inherited from his colleague Richard Hollis the task of writing for Titan Publishing the first book on Douglas' career – *Don't Panic* – a project which had been mooted since before the turn of the decade, and Adams gave all the guarded exposition that he could. However, he decided to draw the line at that summer's first *Hitchhiker* convention arranged by the fan club ZZ9 Plural Alpha Z, who had enjoyed a modest meet (or rather, 'slouch') two years earlier, but the charity weekend in Birmingham was planned as a spectacular, with Eddie the Computer greeting fans from their hotel room TVs, and guests including Mark Wing-Davey and Alan Bell. To fans' disgruntlement, the Great Creator only participated via a bemused boozy interview, videoed by Kevin Davies.

Besides Beer's luxury towels to add to the relatively modest range of merchandise (Ed Victor's assistant Maggie Phillips took great pleasure in telling eager product-pitchers to come up with their own franchise ideas and leave Douglas alone), Adams did have another Infocom game in the works, of course – but not *Hitchhiker*. The company had hoped to continue the book adaptations, picking up the narrative on the surface of Magrathea, but Douglas insisted that he was suffering from acute 'sequelitis' and they agreed to defer the next instalment until his preferred idea could be brought to life. *Bureaucracy* was another text adventure, which took the overriding theme of so much of Adams' comedy and brought it blatantly centre-stage. There would be no links to *Hitchhiker* whatsoever, and no science fiction element. This worried those at Infocom who had cut cheques for their star signing, but to keep him happy they went with his idea, based on a frenetic pitch over lunch that had everyone choking on their nouvelle cuisine. Douglas had any number of stories of insane red tape to refer to, but it was the Kafkaesque challenge of making his bank understand that he had moved to Islington which really triggered the project – an *Indiana Jones*-style epic quest to have your change of address card recognised by the Powers That Be. 'There are some things in there which aren't really bureaucracy,' he conceded, 'but are just sort of tedious, annoying things – like when you go to a hamburger restaurant, and you just want a hamburger, and the waitress keeps on asking you questions, you know, about how you want it done, what sort of potatoes you want, do you want them this, do you want them that – and you say, "Just bring me a fucking hamburger!" So I built that into the program. It was a chance to do all the things that annoy you.' The game was announced in May 1985, without Meretzky on board, and, in truth, Douglas drifted away from direct involvement early in development. Infocom threw hosts of programmers at the project but, by the time it appeared in shops two years later, text adventures were already old news. Douglas had helped to underline this by working on the LucasArts/Activision game tie-in to Jim Henson and Terry Jones' fantasy movie *Labyrinth*, which brought impressive (for the time) visuals to the text format, and featured a very telling sequence where a romantic cinema rendezvous is spoiled by the intrusion of a pesky nerd. Although the *Restaurant* Infocom game, intended to be called *Milliways*, was started by coder Stu Galley and went through a number of conceptual stages (with ideas involving puzzles in Slartibartfast's laboratory, and the challenge of being cool enough to get into Milliways), any promise of a further *Hitchhiker* text adventure sank with Infocom at the end of the decade.

Adams had any number of further game ideas which never got beyond the wildly theoretical stage – such as programming Ronald Reagan to deal with political debates, fudging issues and answering questions based on no inherent intelligence. The idea was that, once emulated, the computerised World Leader could link up with similar games for Thatcher and others, creating a kind of 120k United Nations of computers all talking nonsense to each other. 'After that,' he recalled, 'we were going to do a program called

God, and program all God's attributes into it, and you'd have all the different denominations of God on it ... you know, a Methodist God, a Jewish God, and so on ... I wanted to be the first person to have computer software burned in the Bible Belt, which I felt was a rite of passage that any young medium had to pass through. However, with the recession in the American computer industry, all that came to nothing, largely because the people who wanted to do it with me discovered they didn't have cars or money or jobs.'

When *Bureaucracy* hit one of its numerous brick walls, Douglas passed on the salvaging duty to his old Cambridge love rival and outrageous polymath Michael Bywater – pilot, organist, Procol Harum fan and caustic humorist, who shared Adams' technological obsessions as the resident computer expert at *Punch* magazine. Although Michael hadn't had a hit in the vein of *Hitchhiker* to catapult him to fame, the two friends were equally matched in wit, intellect and tech-geekiness, and the more time they spent together, the more the mercurial, bespectacled and impecunious Bywater's unique brand of brilliance, belligerence and lackadaisical charm impressed Adams, and he knew that Bywater could be trusted to bring *Bureaucracy* to life (as well as doing much of the writing for the doomed *Milliways,* for which he posited such suitably facetious tricks as penalising players for gaining top scores, and generally controlled Arthur and Co. with an effortlessly Adamsian style).

The jungle antics of *Bureaucracy*, however, were to come from Adams' real experiences, thanks to an unexpected phone call. In truth, Douglas had for a while been dropping unsubtle hints in the right quarters that he was interested in creating something to do with conservation, but when the *Observer* colour supplement asked him to fly out to Madagascar to track down one of the precious surviving members of the lemur family, the aye-aye, it was still a pleasant surprise, even if his subsequent claim that he thought they had the wrong guy was somewhat disingenuous.

Zoological non-fiction and jungle exploration seemed quite a departure, but perhaps the time was auspicious for a new start. Between the return from the US and the Madagascar offer, Douglas' stepmother called him and his sister Sue down to the Droitwich Spa Hospital, where their father was in a critical condition. Having progressed from teacher to parole officer to management consultant and lecturer ('I expect there is some rationale behind my father's life', Douglas shrugged), the middle-aged Mr. Adams made a point of keeping fit and exercising as he dealt with high blood pressure. Despite this, Christopher passed away that June at the age of 58, very shortly after the dutiful Douglas had been excused his long bedside vigil for a quick sleep (which he described as 'bloody typical Dad'). We can only nosily conjecture the extent to which Douglas was harmed by his father's distance, or perhaps even Adams senior's envy of his son's self-made success but, though there might have been a coolness of affection between them, there was no rancour. 'My father was a fantasist, full of ideas that never quite worked,' Douglas said. 'We didn't have a good relationship but it's been an interesting journey discovering just how much I'm like him. I have an ounce more grip on the real world, and in the end I was given approbation and he wasn't.' He confided that he felt a definite chill when he saw Christopher laid out before him, so very like himself, and his psychological promotion to the male head of his bloodline went hand in hand with his planned new direction in life.

Whether emotional turmoil played its part or not, Douglas proposed to Jane in 1985, but within a short while of her positive answer both found themselves backing off in a game of 'altar chicken'. There were to be numerous false alarms, epic, loud and dazzlingly erudite confrontations, and passionate reunions over the coming years – Jane estimated that three of the nine years of their combustible courtship were spent apart – but Douglas and Jane remained a golden couple among a wide and glittering network of the decade's bright young things, media darlings and powerful players.

Both had always had their own particular flair for hosting parties and, as a couple, their social events could famously rival any shindig thrown by David Frost. Besides the ubiquity of champagne by the jeroboam, their parties were most legendary for the musical entertainment on offer, with annual carol services (inviting only the very best singers) and much-anticipated 'Partially Unplugged' sessions from members of Douglas' favourite bands who happened to accept invitations – Gary Brooker, David Gilmour, and particularly his close friend Robbie McIntosh, the guitarist who joined Paul 'Wix' Wickens in Paul McCartney's touring band.

On such occasions the Adams/Belson home would be rammed on every level with not just the couple's closest friends but Adams' new pals from the upper echelons of Alternative comedy, Hollywood producers, leading scientists, authors and academics – Sir Clive Sinclair arguing about Intelligent Design with an exasperated computer programmer here, Salman Rushdie and Hugh Laurie sitting cross-legged with a Monkee over by the band, Jim

Henson standing by the door with a huge salmon just so he could provoke Douglas into namechecking his latest novel and, in one particular corner, some kind of libidinous entanglement involving one famous actress so debauched that the details are legally best left undefined even three decades on. The food could never be anything but the best, glasses were kept sparklingly topped up and a fug of tobacco hung in the air – the smoke was said to have a surprisingly high legality quotient considering the number of musicians at the party, though there was inevitably the odd white crumb speckling the bathroom, for all the hosts' shared distaste for the illegal side of entertaining. But it was always all about the music, and though Douglas no doubt burned to join in, and did, there was no greater pleasure for him than being squeezed in among his family and friends, inches away from his favourite performers filling his home with reverberating rock and roll. Despite all the tempestuousness of their relationship, Douglas and Jane provided the nucleus of a social maelstrom, and there never seemed any doubt that they belonged together, married or not.

The briefly engaged couple flew off together for the Madagascar assignment, and there met the twenty-six-year-old zoologist Mark Carwardine for the first time. After so long living the high life with first-class travel and hotel room service, a gulf existed between Mark and Douglas – the former was outraged when Adams abandoned a brand new state-of-the-art Nikon camera because it was too heavy to include in his luggage – but Adams' sheer enthusiasm and sincerity for their shared challenge soon began to diminish the gulf, particularly when they were lucky enough to find and photograph an aye-aye on their second night of trying: the first time the tiny vampirish mammal had been photographed in the wild. This brief face-off with a creature so many millions of years divorced from our own mammalian clan was to prove one of the great revelations in Adams' life – a life of star-gazing brought back down to Earth with a realisation of the precious treasures of evolution on this one uncannily living planet. The rediscovery of zoological fascination would also be a signpost on his journey from 'serious agnostic' to passionate atheist.

'The whole expedition was the most tremendous experience,' he enthused. 'I'd just done a promotional tour of the USA before this and was convinced I was turning into a room-service bore. This really sorted me out.' Mark apologised for the hard concrete sleeping options and insanitary transport, but Douglas earnestly assured him that it was precisely what he needed. Maybe the rich man slumming it on a brief trip to the jungle could be seen as an easy route to redemption from mindless luxury, but the urgent message of conservation which Carwardine wanted to drum into the world was one which Douglas now equally passionately wished to help deliver, and he made a pact with Mark that they would extend the aye-aye expedition severalfold when time allowed, to highlight a whole host of fellow endangered Earth-dwellers, raising the alarm with humour, in a project he came to describe as 'a cross between *Life on Earth* and *Three Men In a Boat*'. He had the name – *Last Chance To See* – now he just needed to find the space in his diary. 'I'd been given a thread to pull,' he said, 'and following that lead began to open up issues to me that became the object of the greatest fascination.'

With so many offers for him to sift through daily, Douglas' diary – or rather, this being the 1980s, his bulging Filofax – was far from empty, and taking on one new writing job was going to fill it further. In the summer of '85 Richard Curtis and his friends had all marvelled at the *Live Aid* broadcast, and the idea quickly evolved to extend the charitable theme to comedy, supporting the Charity Arts organisation with a live show, at first just as Cleese had initiated the *Secret Policeman's Ball*s for Amnesty. Before long, though, the newly forged Comic Relief had bigger ideas: a telethon, a Cliff Richard cover in the charts, red noses – and, of course, an obligatory tie-in book. No name could sell more copies of such a thing than Adams', and the defeated comic relished his chance to work with his hip funny friends and be a central part of the greatest collaborative pursuit in British comedy history. Naturally, Richard and the extremely organised ex-Footlighter Peter Fincham would be the ones making sure that *The Utterly Utterly Merry Comic Relief Christmas Book* was kept on the rails, but Douglas took his overseer role seriously. Having written bumph for *Hitchhiker* theatre programmes and the computer game he was bursting with ideas, and certainly shared Curtis' charitable spur: his sense of logical conservation was not confined to those who had not evolved to use fire – he was a humanist as well as a budding zoologist. Douglas was never a champagne socialist but he was certainly a champagne Green Party supporter and, as the preoccupation with wealth-related guilt in his books shows, he might have been an accidental capitalist but he was far to the left of your average millionaire. So committed was he to this new cause, in fact, that – yes, for Comic Relief he would extract some brand new *Hitchhiker* material out of his exhausted imagination, bumping up potential sales even further than the involvement of the likes of Rowan Atkinson, The Young Ones, Sue Townsend's Adrian Mole and Palin & Jones would guarantee. (Not to mention a cameo from an actual Beatle, thanks to Palin roping in George Harrison to introduce his *Biggles* pastiche.)

His old school chum Griff also did his bit with one very poor joke, he being otherwise preoccupied with his and Mel Smith's own *Lavishly Tooled Instant Coffee Table Book*, co-written with McGrath and Anderson, which featured a poison lampoon of *Hitchhiker*, 'So Long, and Thanks For All The Advance', which was so startlingly scathing it could only have come from comedians who really knew Douglas better than anyone – 'additional material' for the book came courtesy of Canter and Lloyd. Alongside an image of a fat wallet floating in space, the cod advert continued:

'Far out in the uncharted backwaters of the unfashionable end of the western spiral arm of the Galaxy lies a small unregarded yellow sun.'

This opening paragraph – yes, PARAGRAPH – made publishing history! So fantastic were the sales of the book that the ape-descended life-form that wrote it was persuaded to do it again. Yes, Douglas Adams wrote out exactly the same paragraph to begin his next book. And, incredibly, it worked! The people of Earth gave him enough little pieces of green paper to buy as many digital watches as he could possibly want. But still the life-descended ape-form publishers were not happy. Which was odd. Because Douglas was delirious ...

And now, two thousand years after they nailed a man to his typewriter for thinking those pieces of paper were a pretty neat idea, here it is again! ... So DON'T PANIC – here it is. Nearly twenty pages of positively the last *Hitchhiker's* book. For a while ...

ABOUT THE AUTHOR: Douglas Adams is not married, has no children, and still doesn't live in Surrey. He does, however, have a Porsche, and a Golf GTi Cabriolet, both of which are equipped with car-phones. He has a dozen computers, an enormous hi-fi, a flat in Islington, a house in Islington, an apartment in New York, and a top literary agent ...

THIS BOOK IS MADE ENTIRELY FROM RECYCLED IDEAS

In a way, this swipe had been compounded by the duo's 1985 movie outing, *Morons From Outer Space*, which blatantly made good use of the idea of interstellar hitching when Smith's lonely alien tries to thumb his way back to his friends, who have crash-landed on Earth – but the film's box-office drubbing was punishment enough. Besides, Douglas was to get slight revenge in his next novel by mentioning an 'Alternative comedian' who spent his money from lager commercials on yuppie warehouse conversions.

As an ex-sketch writer devoted to Wodehouse, it's positively mysterious that short stories never played a larger part in Adams' career – he often had more distinct complex ideas than any novel's plot could accommodate, each could find their own place in a neater format and honed to perfection without the kind of long-term dedication that inspired the vintage writers' adage 'Writing comes easy – all you have to do is stare at a blank piece of paper until your forehead bleeds.' And yet Douglas' only real flirtation with the format came at Comic Relief's bequest. Rather than rustle up something too obvious involving Marvin, Adams' eventual use of his brand was to take a deliberately less obviously crowd-pleasing route, visiting the youth of the character he had most shied away from of late, Zaphod – albeit the young hero doesn't actually do very much within the plot.

In a tale reminiscent of *Alien*, the sole employee of The Beeblebrox Salvage and Really Wild Stuff Corporation is on hand to discover that a hideously dangerous life form has escaped to Earth – this humanoid Sirius Cybernetics creation seems harmless, but as 'there is nothing they will not do if allowed, and nothing they will not be allowed to do' there is a strong suggestion that the eventual demolition of the Earth may have something to do with stopping them. Another concerted effort to pillory Reagan, the clown with his finger on the button throughout the decade, the plan backfired somewhat when readers missed the clues and wondered whether the creatures were supposed to be Jesus. Although the book contains a healthy measure of blasphemy, for a stocking-filler uniting two joyful themes – comedy and Christmas – there is an overriding gloom to much of the *Utterly Merry* book, a sense of mid-1980s nuclear paranoia which should have made Adams' intentions clear. The 'Save The Earth' sentiment returns in 'A Christmas Fairly Story', an even shorter gag-packed squib written by Terry Jones, illustrated by regular collaborator Michael Foreman and partially reworked by the editor, while Douglas took the chance to put his name next to another Python once again with 'The Private Life of Genghis

Khan'. The obscurity of their *Out of the Trees* sketch gave Adams the licence to rework his and Chapman's ideas in prose, and as there wasn't anything in the vein of a punchline in the original sketch, he decided to fold it back into *Hitchhiker* canon with a late appearance from Wowbagger the Infinitely Prolonged, safe in the knowledge that most readers would have read *LUE*.

These early years for the charity were incidentally to inspire the first novel from *Bridget Jones* creator Helen Fielding, an old Oxford friend of Curtis who directed some of the earliest films from Africa. At the time she was also John Lloyd's girlfriend, and her subsequent lightly fictionalised debut, *Cause Celeb*, gives a unique insight into the private lives of the 1980s comedy elite. Lloyd's fear that he was the inspiration for the heroine's dashing, brilliant TV presenter boyfriend was allayed by the author's reassurance that the only character she considered to be taken directly from real life was the immensely tall and clumsy superstar comedian Julian Alman – a gadget-obsessed millionaire who, despite having the gall to request an upgrade on a shaky plane to a refugee camp, is essentially decent and loveable – but 'never had a man been more debilitated by wealth than Julian'. He, she could not deny, was Douglas.

The *Utterly Merry* book was eventually released in the autumn of 1986 – claimed by Adams in a letter to contributors to be 'the first comedy book ever to be finished less than three months late', although, in an ironic shift of roles, one spread covered Lenny Henry's inability to give Douglas material on time. But despite the aforementioned religion-baiting being relatively mild, the book's successful first print run of half a million copies was overshadowed by a deeply uncharitable campaign from Christian pressure groups to ban the book, due to items such as The Young Ones' Nativity, and 'The Gospel According To A Sheep', a charming squib written by Curtis with input from Adams. There was to be no reprint as a result, giving the 'Christian' groups the satisfaction of knowing that they had ensured a higher level of suffering in the world than there would otherwise have been.

Douglas' Comic Relief work was all in a good cause, which of course lightened his conscience greatly about the lack of any other writing he managed to do at this time – but there was, once again, a crucial deadline lurking in the shadows. 'There's an awful lot of things I want to do, and the major thing, the core, is going to have to be writing books,' he admitted reluctantly. 'I feel written out with *Hitchhiker* and I don't feel I have anything more to say in that particular medium, there are other things I want to do. I've been thinking of writing in the horror/mystery/occult area. Really the whole thing is to find a whole new set of characters and a new environment – it isn't just that it's new, but that it's an environment and a set of characters that I, now at age 33, thought up, rather than what I came up with when I was 25.' The new deadline came courtesy of one of the biggest deals in publishing – on 10th January 1986, Ed Victor presided magisterially over the telephonic auction of publishing rights to the next two Douglas Adams books, and hung up two hours later with a Simon & Schuster deal to the tune of $2.2 million, while the UK rights moved Douglas from Pan to Heinemann for a more sedate £575k. Douglas had everything in place for creating his much-mooted horror mystery, his first concerted attempt to do something new since Arthur Dent first faced those bulldozers. He bravely decided to attempt to honour both book deals in one year, delivering the first novel by Christmas '86 for a spring release, and then moving on to the follow-up.

Another reason to shun his most famous creation came in 1986, with a new draft of the *Hitchhiker* movie credited to Douglas and Reitman hireling Abbie Bernstein, which the mortified author called 'the worst script I've ever read. Unfortunately, it has my name on it, whereas I did not contribute a single comma to it ... I'm appalled to think how much harm that script has done my reputation over the years.' Palpably retuned for an American fratboy audience (Ford seems positively to be written for John Belushi, despite the actor's death in 1982), the new draft was packed with all-new twists and events, largely based on action-packed attempts to thwart the Vogons and save the world – and the romance between Arthur and Trillian which would remain predictably central to all movie concepts henceforth.

Having so profoundly rejected any continuation of *Hitchhiker*, Adams was keen to try something very different, but eventually he had to come to terms with his own imagination, and in lieu of writing anything he sat at his typewriter and explained to himself: 'The fantastical and extraordinary is my forte. That is for sure. That is what I can do. I think that I'm probably not very good at doing everyday kind of stuff. Hate to think what that says about me, but there it is. I think my everyday stuff is good for being a counterpoint to the things I do best – the fantastical.'

This admission was just a way of warming up his typing fingers. By the end of the year, he boasted one sentence of his new creation: 'High on a rocky promontory sat an Electric Monk on a bored horse ...'

The Fundamental Interconnectedness Of All Things

Sue Freestone was of course perturbed to only have one sentence to work with as the first deadline arrived, but Douglas had his reasons – not just the Comic Relief book and the plans for travelling with Carwardine, but obviously there was all that money to spend. He had already bought an apartment in New York, in the same block as Simon Jones and his new wife Nancy Lewis, Monty Python's American manager, whom he had met on the set of *The Meaning of Life*. Douglas and Jane's property nightmares back home in London, however, could fill a book of their own. A vast wreck of a Georgian house on Duncan Terrace was envisaged as the ideal modern millionaire's home, a party venue par excellence, with the guidance of Adams' inspirational architect neighbours. There would be positively infinite power points for Douglas' gadgets on the top floor, a sound system costing as much as a reasonably sized family home and, in the basement, a swimming pool – though this last plan was stymied thanks to the proximity of the Royal Bank of Scotland's vaults, and the basement eventually became home to Douglas' sister Jane (now known as 'Little Jane') as she started medical training in the metropolis. Through nobody's fault, due to a farcical catalogue of problems involving dry rot, astronomical ambition and the need to gut the entire four storey edifice, however, Duncan Terrace became a stereotypical money pit as the project expanded and mutated.

The bottom line would have been enough to make any millionaire flinch, but it just so happened that the building's development clashed with one of the darker misfortunes in Adams' life, when it emerged that the accountant he had trusted from his first major pay cheque – and who had personally okayed the Duncan Terrace venture – had desperately used a six-figure sum of Adams' money to shore up an unrecoverable investment, and suddenly there was a black hole in Douglas' finances. 'The shock was indescribable,' he admitted. 'I thought I was rich and the next moment I thought I was bankrupt. I don't understand money at all, I just understand shopping.' The financially naive writer had split his income three ways when it started rolling in – one third for pleasure, one for retirement, and a final third to the accountant to cover tax; though as the allusion to Hotblack Desiato spending a year dead for tax reasons suggests, Adams would have no truck with tricksy tax avoidance at first. The nightmare of finding his tax savings up in smoke deepened when attempts to take legal action against the man responsible were stopped in their tracks by the accountant's suicide. At once, the perceived largesse of the rich man slumming it in the jungle or giving up his time for charity was replaced by a genuine need to recoup his losses, with some hard forehead-bleeding: 'It means I'm actually working for my living again, as opposed to, you know, earning money I don't need. I've always known that I was going to have to earn a lot of money one way or another simply because I have no idea how money works, and therefore I just don't keep hold of it very well – and I can never quite work out why.'

Freestone helpfully pointed out that his one existing sentence wasn't quite enough to constitute a publishing sensation, but Adams responded with a self-imposed stretch of concerted composition: 'I spent a year thinking about it, worrying that I couldn't do it and getting into a bit of a panic. And then finally I'd got enough ideas assembled, and from the moment I passed the deadline, I sat down, wrote it, and finished it in a matter of two or three weeks. It's certainly the book I've enjoyed writing the most for ages, and I feel that I've now got a new lease of life, because I was getting so bloody bored with *Hitchhiker*. It had been ruling my life for the best part of ten years.' When asked by eager fans what to expect from the new books, he replied, 'They will be recognisably me but radically different – at least from my point of view. The story is based on here and now but the explanation turns out to be science fiction.' This is really the nub of Dirk Gently's universe – the fact that the first inkling of his Holistic Detective Agency concerned an alien robot on a distant planet showed that this was no huge departure for Adams in terms of content (not least since *Hitchhiker* was already packed with the supernatural), but a crucial sidestep in terms of mood and form. Within a few chapters of *Hitchhiker*, we are in outer space and almost anything can happen, but what would be a silly joke to Arthur Dent could be the basis of a truly sinister mystery to Dirk Gently.

Above all, it was the freedom to be only as amusing as the story demanded which drew a line in the sand for this new project: 'One of my objectives with this book is, although it is going to be a comedy, it is not, as *Hitchhiker* was, going to be primarily a comedy, because with *Hitchhiker* everything would have to bow and bend to the jokes, and often you would have to abandon bits of plot or turn them on their heads, or do real violence to a plot in order to get the joke to be funny. What I want to do with this is a tightly organised plot with a lot of ideas packed in it, and then *allow* it to be funny when it wants to be, but not force it to be funny. Once that's straight, then all sorts of things become naturally funny ... *Hitchhiker* was always, first, foremost, primarily, at every level, a comedy. I think that in the past I've too often been facetious – just because I haven't been able to think of something quite funny enough, but there's got to be something funny here because this is meant to be a funny book, etc. And so I think – I hope – I will have become less facetious. I find facetiousness very irritating.'

Michael Bywater shrewdly observed that Adams' humour at its best came from bathos – undermining the epic with the everyday – and this largely came about via his characters' reactions to the fantastical nature of Life, the Universe and Everything. As ever, Adams had a great many ideas to explore within his plot, which he described as 'a ghost-horror-detective-whodunnit-time-travel-romantic-musical-comedy-epic. My original intention was to have a cookery supplement as well, but I dropped that.' The humour still came largely from the characters who were trying to deal with what the Universe was doing to them, and in Bywater, he found his new hero all but fully formed. When it was confirmed that the rotund and bespectacled chain-smoking, huckstering, eccentrically brilliant but equally arrogant eponymous detective was directly drawn from aspects of his own character, Bywater confessed that he was not sure whether to be disgusted or flattered. However, the pseudo-genius formerly known as Svlad Cjelli, 'more like a succession of extraordinary events than a person', does not even appear in the narrative until Chapter 13, introduced with Wodehousian subtlety as 'a pair of binoculars', and that left room for Adams to invent his own versions of the traditional stock characters of any great detective story – the suspects (albeit this was more of a 'who done what and why' than a 'whodunnit'), the cynical police rival, Sergeant Gilks, and of course, Dirk's Watson, or Hastings. Having fielded so many inquiries about the autobiographical nature of Arthur Dent's latest mishaps, there can be no doubt that Richard MacDuff, the notably tall, wealthy Cambridge graduate, Islington resident, computer programmer, music obsessive and abominable boyfriend, was explicitly created as an example of how Adams really saw himself – he even credited an essay he had been working on, 'Music and Fractal Landscapes', to his idealised avatar.

The other key new character was, of course, not new at all, but the aged Gallifreyan from *Shada*, Professor Urban Chronotis, here known as 'Reg', short for Regius Professor of Chronology. The mysterious atmosphere of St. John's, that world of doors within doors, proved too tempting to leave as an abandoned TV script and, once again, Douglas was doing his bit for recycling. But as with all the best science fiction, the beauty of *Who*, and indeed *Hitchhiker*, is that every event, from the grandest epoch to the tiniest oddity, can be explained one way or another without recourse to 'magic', albeit with a joyfully perverse attitude to science as we know it. This is why ideas which took root in Adams' mind via the freedom of The Show's format could be so irresistibly intricate and imaginative, ideal for translating into a fresh universe with its own explanations for every outlandish knot in the plot. Besides, the fact that Reg is obviously never identified as a Time Lord added a whole new layer of mystery about what he really was – and if anything, the ultimate peril in the plot was drawn from *City of Death* rather than *Shada*. *Dirk* also featured its own plot-greasing equivalent of the IID – Gently's much-repressed clairvoyance, rationalised as a belief in the 'fundamental interconnectedness of things', wherein any great coincidence must on some quantum level be the result of a logical process. Allied to this was his refutation of Sherlock Holmes' famous quote that 'Once you have discounted the impossible, then whatever remains, however improbable, must be the truth', with Dirk insistent that 'The impossible often has a kind of integrity to it which the merely improbable lacks.'

In his self-imposed frenzy of storytelling, Adams also had an over-abundance of other fresh ideas to add to the mix – a believable model for life after death, many musings on the nature of quantum physics, an idea of who it really was who prevented Coleridge from getting on with *Kubla Khan*, an irresistible ecological dimension, and – as Bach's *Chorale Number 5* echoed repeatedly around his writing station – the true inspiration for Johann Sebastian's heavenly message. Critics lauded the remarkable neatness with which so many disparate concepts were married, and Adams rightly glowed: 'I'm terribly pleased with it, I must say. I think one of the things that'll catch people by surprise a bit is that because my books so far tended to be very episodic – it's one thing after another for about 180 pages, whereupon it stops – this book, for a long way, appears as if it's a lot of apparently wildly unconnected events, which gradually all turn out to be part of the same thing going on.'

Perhaps the greatest success, however, was the creation of Dirk, and the seemingly effortless comedy arising from his Ukridge-like foibles, and despicable rapport with clients. Having not just completed Dirk's first case for publication, but even saved time by typesetting it himself on his Mac, the wind seemed fair for Douglas' stated intent to breeze straight through into Gently's second credulity-stretching adventure, which he had tentatively entitled either 'The Fridges of Despond', 'The TV Dinners of Doom', 'Where Are They Now?', 'Darkness, Doubt & Dirk Gently' or 'Dirk Gently and the Agony of Doubt' before settling on a title taken directly from the franchise from which he was still consciously fleeing, *The Long Dark Tea-Time of the Soul*.

For Gods' Sake Help Me

The triumph of completing the first *Dirk* book, however – albeit post-deadline – was not to be repeated second time around. The dream schedule had slipped, and this was to be Adams' first book ever to slip past not just the manuscript deadline but the print one.

Douglas' starting point this time was guilt, with plans for a character literally frozen with guilt until reassured by a witch that they were actually a perfectly decent person. Ultimately, though, the time travel and ghostly goings-on of the first book were to be replaced by a phenomenon familiar from *Hitchhiker* – the existence of Gods, and specifically, Nordic deities. That the reader is supposed to take the Thunder God Thor as depicted in *Tea-Time* as entirely distinct from the lunk who makes a move on Trillian in *LUE* – or any of the Gods enjoying the Milliways floor show – can be safely assumed. But then, the simplistic idea that the main distinction between *Hitchhiker* and *Dirk* is the level of humour is complicated by the fact that *SLATFATFish* had already shown a dramatically more mature style than Douglas' previous books, and had depicted a Rain God among us. Unlike the Gods who popped into existence shortly after the creation of *Hitchhiker*'s Universe, however, these Asgardians (who travel between plains of existence via King's Cross station, very like *Harry Potter*'s Platform 9¾) are literally created from human faith, and then are left to wander the planet long after belief in them has dwindled. There were far fewer threads to intertwine in the follow-up – just side orders of satire of the music industry and the transmogrification of inanimate objects – and also almost no continuity from the first story. Although he volunteered a particular kinship with the oversized, frustrated Thor (which perhaps throws a different light on the Thunder God's bedside confrontation with his frail father), Adams' previous alter ego MacDuff was forgotten, and Dirk had a new co-protagonist in the shape of New Yorker Kate Schechter, a great step forward for Adams in terms of believable female characterisation, albeit another alpha female.

With a fresh deadline wearily moved back to October 1988, this comparably straightforward case still refused to slide off Douglas' fingers and onto his floppy disk. An extra layer of peril was added to the stress by the ticking clock of his exit from the country. He and Mark Carwardine, having agreed on a number of pins to stick into the atlas on their tour of the endangered, had slowly pieced together an itinerary over the years since the run-in with the aye-aye, and it was finally time to set off around the world for the bulk of the research – luckily also coinciding with Douglas' reluctant agreement with his financial advisers to disappear from home soil for a year for, regrettably, tax purposes, a decade after his observation 'Tax exile is the usual fate reserved for those who are determined to make a fool of themselves in public.'

An Australian publicity tour was set in stone as the kick-off for this exile but, as the day of departure neared, Gently's latest adventure remained a mess of hot potatoes, severed heads, goblins, Gods and fridges (not to mention something to do with novelist Harold Robbins having live chickens delivered to his hotel rooms, a curious aside requiring a legal switch of the name to 'Howard Bell'). In the end, he insisted that the book was only finished thanks to his not sleeping for three days, interspersing intense writing stints with bursts of sweating over his exercise bike, to the eight-minutes-twenty-three-seconds of Mozart's *Piano Concerto in A Major* – although he was still trying to ensure all loose ends were tied up in the taxi on the way to his flight to Perth. Even on arrival on the other side of the planet, he phoned Sue Freestone to tell her that another 500 words were necessary, which he ended up writing longhand, hungover from a night on the town with Ben Elton, and dictating long-distance to his editor, before correcting the final manuscript via that decade's defining communication mode: fax. 'It's different from Tolstoy, isn't it?' he was to chatter to Terry Wogan on one of his infamously verbose visits to the *Wogan* couch. 'But the strange thing is, under those circumstances you actually come up with all the best stuff. Stuff you couldn't have written any other way.'

Every Adams book was released with an explosion of publicity silliness, but perhaps *Tea-Time*'s gimmick was the oddest. By a circuitous route, Pan's team had overheard Janet Thrift joking that she could write a book more quickly than her son, and this prompted them to ask her to advertise his new book, selling badges decorated with Thrift-flower-decorated teacups as part of 'T-Day' – and ultimately finding herself as a cardboard cut-out in bookshops all over the country. Whether this helped or not, ultimately *Tea-Time* was well received, to which Douglas mused, 'It goes up and down, every author has a cyclical thing which doesn't actually bear any relation to which was the good book and which was the bad book, and critics love you for a bit until they decide it's time to hate you. And actually the reviews in England were largely by people who had hated me for a bit, and were extremely irritated to discover they thought this was a good book, and had to say so with words like "infuriatingly" all over the place.' Asked about his next novel, he added, 'This is gonna be a kind of a thriller, very different, set in Brazil, on the Ivory Coast and Easter Island. But put it this way, when I used to write History essays at school, my History master used to say, "Fewer jokes, more facts, please, Adams!" So basically I always write comedy of one kind or another, but this will be more of a thriller.' This story never surfaced, but then his first priority was the move into non-fiction.

Besides a dangling bushel of the very hottest high-tech cameras and gadgets and half the works of Dickens, as Douglas embarked on his own personal Last Chance To See wild life forms such as the Komodo Dragon in Indonesia, his beloved dopy flightless parrot, the Kakapo, in New Zealand, and the ultimately elusive, now entirely vanished Yangtze River Dolphin, the adventurer also took along the anguish of another split from Jane, which this time seemed somewhat final (although, in an unfortunate repetition of the *LUE* dedication, *Tea-Time* had gone off to the printers inscribed 'For Jane'). 'We've spent eight years wondering if it's a good idea to marry,' he over-shared with one broadsheet journalist at the time. 'We're trapped because it's so nearly right, but when you're in your thirties you ask too many interesting questions. The idea of going out and having to fancy people again terrifies me, though.' Douglas' foibles were enough to generate any number of passionate battles of will between the two, as was joshingly alluded to by John Lloyd in his introduction to his old friend for an on-stage Q&A in 1987, publicising the first *Dirk* book: 'Douglas Adams is enormously fat, and his proudest boast is that he is taller, younger and has better eyesight than I do … He lives in Islington with a lady barrister and an Apple Macintosh, but we both know which one he really wants to marry.' Newly added to the relationship's baggage, however, was an explosive broodiness in Douglas, which the brilliant barrister Jane did not feel ready to share. Much has always been made of the female body clock, but the male desire to procreate can burn just as ferociously, and Adams felt that there was no time like the present. He was even heard to complain, when Lloyd first became a father at the turn of the 1990s, that 'that bastard has beaten me again'. Adams only hoped that their time apart would do them good, as well as get him away from the building site of Duncan Terrace.

For the details of Douglas and Mark's voyages, of course, you should accept no substitute to reading *LCTS* in its erudite entirety. Their travels were also to form the basis of a Radio 4 series of the same name, broadcast in October 1989. Hence the infamous scrabble to find condoms in Beijing – to waterproof a microphone – and an impressive display of subsequent thespianism from Douglas when the recording of his near-bilious reaction to the sight of a Komodo Dragon swallowing a goat was accidentally wiped and had to be recreated at the BBC. In many ways all of Adams' past successes had been the perfect training for this form of ecological travelogue as he, Mark, producer Gaynor Shutte and their crew travelled this Wonderful World getting just a glimpse of how the supposed most intelligent life form was coping with the balance of nature which affects all life – and dealing, on the way, with galloping international bureaucracy beyond even Adams' imagination. *Dirk* had already brought the author's focus back down to Earth, but as *Hitchhiker* was essentially a spoof travel guide, packed with quizzical observations of both our species and numerous entirely alien evolutionary specimens, there was little need for a shift in approach to give the reader a startlingly fresh perspective on Life on Earth.

Sadly, despite the collaborative nature of the *LCTS* book, the more experienced procrastinator Adams was not the best influence on Carwardine, and there were far more dazzling wildly gesticulatory discussions in restaurants in the south of France than there were full working days of prose construction. The text was therefore eventually delivered to Heinemann for its 1990 publication lacking a few of their exploits, including a brush with the Amazonian manatee which strengthened Douglas' eerie feeling of connection to such vastly divergent members of lifekind – the theory that humans had a crucial stage of evolutionary development in an aquatic or semi-aquatic environment several million years ago was one of his most cherished hypotheses of anthropological archaeology. Perhaps Adams' experiences in Zaire provided the strongest sense of connection to the so-called Animal Kingdom, though – and try as he might not to anthropomorphise the individuals they encountered, his admiration for the Silverback Gorilla he had the honour to meet, albeit only briefly, shone out of the page. In the unnatural world, Douglas could be more tribal than was healthy, and he recalled being introduced at a party to a six-foot-five big-nosed man called Douglas, and storming out with confusion at the affront to his uniqueness – but he found it hard to resist identifying with the slouching, maturing head of the band of gorillas. However, rather than depicting him, or any other individual subjects, with typical observational reference to human behaviour, he strove to 'bridge the imaginative gap' between Us and Them by considering the world from their sensory perceptions – after all, we didn't just see the whale fall in *Hitchhiker*, we fell with him: 'When I was doing *Hitchhiker* I was always trying to find different perspectives on everyday things so that we would see them afresh. And I suddenly realised that the animals in the world, because they all have completely different perceptual systems, the world we see is only specific to us, and from every other animal's point of view it's a completely different place. I also discovered that because I had an external and important subject to deal with I didn't feel any kind of compulsion to be funny the whole time – and oddly enough a lot of people have said it's the funniest book I've written.' This perceptual imaginative technique was further complicated by making contact with the tragic Northern White Rhino, whose powerful nasal apparatus made scent by far their most crucial perception when making sense of the poacher-riddled world around them. Douglas particularly bound himself to the causes of these last two species, becoming a high-profile supporter of Save The Rhino and managing to talk Bill Gates into slipping a six-figure sum into the coffers of a Silverback Gorilla charity.

Albeit not released until two years after the book, *LCTS* became truly multimedia when it also spawned a CD-ROM for Mac and PC packed with the team's photographs, recordings, extra details and even out-takes, and as with every other part of the project, critics lauded Adams and Co. for such excellent work, heralding it as funny, stirring, and incisively intelligent. But, he complained, '*LCTS* was a book I really wanted to promote as much as I could, because the Earth's endangered species is a huge topic to talk about. The thing I don't like about doing promotion usually is that you have to sit there and whinge on about yourself. But here was a big issue I really wanted to talk about and I was expecting to do the normal round of press, TV and radio. But nobody was interested. They just said, "It isn't what he normally does so we'll pass on this, thank you very much." As a result the book didn't do very well. I had spent two years and £150,000 of my own money doing it. I thought it was the most important thing I'd ever done and I could not get anyone to pay attention.'

Adams simply could not escape the elephant in the room whenever he tried to interest others in his new passions: 'There is a sort of diehard *Hitchhiker* audience that wants *Hitchhiker*, more *Hitchhiker*, and nothing but *Hitchhiker*. So they sort of read *Dirk Gently* and said, "Very nice, like that … when are you going to do more *Hitchhiker*?" and I'd say, "I'm not going to, ever again!"'

You Live And Learn. At Any Rate, You Live …

Many personal ups and downs greeted Douglas at the end of his financial exile. He sorrowfully joined the crowd at the funeral of his stepfather Ron Thrift, who was so popular that the entire village of Stalbridge came out in mourning, and his next book was dedicated to him. At around this time, though, at least Duncan Terrace was finally ready for him to move in his treasure trove of gadgetry – and it was more welcome still that Jane and he crossed the threshold together, inevitably magnetised as they always were. On 25th November 1991, when Pan threw a special party for Douglas at the Groucho Club to mark the publication of *LCTS* and to celebrate his third Golden Pan, in the company of an exhaustively sparkling list of his closest friends and all his family Adams tapped his glass for attention and announced that, 'after a whirlwind ten-year romance', Jane and he had been and gone and made things official in front of witnesses at Finsbury Town Hall that very afternoon. The nation's number one celebrity hang-out exploded with cheers for the indivisible newlyweds, as their friends marvelled at the secrecy of the happy event and pondered about the patter of small feet. Only an uncharitable minority mused that the whole thing was staged to justify Adams' epigram: 'Well, we'd tried everything else, so we thought we'd try marriage.'

But there was another unseen presence on Douglas' wedding day, somewhere in the shadows of that exquisitely wrought mind. At the same time as the beleaguered Frood had been exhaustedly shaking off one contract three years earlier, he had signed another one with Heinemann, promising two books with only a loose idea of a deadline, the first release eventually tentatively set for the autumn of 1991. Ed Victor had long campaigned for Adams to turn the brief aside on the Starship *Titanic* from *LUE* into a full narrative, with or without the *Hitchhiker* regulars – indeed, Adams had been mulling it over as a TV series or a movie for many years – and so the title was tentatively applied to one half of the contract. When the publishers had pressurised the author to come up with the other title ten months before the wedding, he had bowed to the inevitable, and decided to Give Them What They Wanted. Despite the usage of the title by the ZZ9 fan club for over a decade, his chosen recycled phrase from his first *Hitchhiker* outing this time was *Mostly Harmless* – so, yes, he told the world, Arthur Dent's journey was not yet complete.

Douglas and Jane's wedding had already taken place one month *after* the original deadline for this new instalment; but that was just warming-up for Adams, who had a few ideas but had never felt so detached from Arthur's odyssey. On the other hand, he sighed, 'Quite often people have said to me, particularly when I was doing the *Dirk Gently* books, "Aren't you essentially still doing the same stuff?" I remember one interview I did on breakfast television for the first *Dirk* novel, and the interviewer said in a rather peremptory way, "This book is like all your other books, isn't it? It's just a lot of ideas." I was stumped by that.' So much had happened since he left his alter ego happily coupled with Fenchurch, and his distance from the Universe he had created guaranteed a whole new level of deadline-dodging. Not that he could claim total alienation from *Hitchhiker* – in 1988 the radio series had been one of the first BBC programmes to be released on CD and, from 1990, Dove Audiobooks had been paying Douglas to read the full unabridged versions of all the novels, providing perhaps the ultimate iteration of the stories. This was one more way of flexing his performing muscles, and although he could be rather wooden off-script, and generally avoided outright characterisations and accents, Adams' renditions of the books brought the action and interaction marvellously to life, conveying Marvin's sombre monotone, Zaphod's drawl and so on, never betraying any hint of angst about being tied to *Hitchhiker* for ever. He explained to audiences at his readings, 'I'm not very good at accents. There are lots of different characters and I basically divide them into: "Posh Quiet", "Posh Loud", "Less Posh Quiet", "Less Posh Loud", and "Australian". But there aren't any Australians in *Hitchhiker* ...'

Hugely increased opportunities for avoiding writing had come Adams' way in the intervening years, and public speaking in particular was becoming the source of more income than ever before. Douglas had first found the knack of communicating his angle on the Universe to audiences after his first novel's publication, and the exhausting round of literary events demanding his presence all over the world in the dozen or so years since then had honed his flair for working an audience. As he was happy to admit, 'What remains of the urge to perform I use up by occasionally going and doing dramatic readings from the books around American colleges and that kind of thing.' However, the respect and indeed adoration for him within the scientific community saw him being asked more and more to give talks about anything above and beyond his writing, which opened whole new doors for him as a respected *thinker*, not just a writer – his manifold entertaining philosophies need not be simplified again here, lectures can be found all over the Internet, transcribed and recorded.

A key character within this scientific fan base was of course Professor Richard Dawkins, who had first contacted Adams with praise for Gently's original outing, just as the author was marvelling at the ideas in Dawkins' works of evolutionary biology and in 1991 Dawkins invited his new friend to read the 'Dish of the Day' extract at his Royal Society Christmas Lecture for Young People. Douglas also introduced Richard to his wife-to-be, former Romana II Lalla Ward, and they bonded in the shelter of Adams and Stephen Fry at one of the famous Adams-Belson parties. Committed atheist Jane had argued with Douglas for years about his agnosticism, but it took Richard to remove the last vestiges of doubt in Adams' mind, or at least for him to admit, 'If it turned out that there was a God, I would feel I'd been the victim of a monumental confidence trick. I'd feel that the Universe was playing silly buggers. I'll wait and see, but I won't lose any sleep over it.' One of Dawkins' most cherished Adams lines was coined long before the writer totally relinquished any faith, Ford's musing on the apparent myth of Magrathea: 'Isn't it enough to see that a garden is beautiful without having to believe that there are fairies at the bottom of it too?'

Douglas was also in demand to share his musings on technology with the computer industry, and had been involved with a plethora of projects to further understanding of what the future might hold. Several years earlier, his and Meretzky's mutual friend Christopher Cerf had recommended Adams as consultant for a Jim Henson TV feature to be called *The Muppet Institute of Technology*, with Fozzie Bear working at the 'Department of Artificial Stupidity', but the special failed to appear. In the mid-1990s he was also invited to be part of an exclusive group known as the Apple Masters who met to indulge in blue-sky thinking about what lay ahead, and he even starred in an extended ad for the company. The existing *Hitchhiker* novels were among the first to be released as e-books on Apple's first reading gadget, but Douglas was peeved to be pipped to the distinction of being the first major author to release a book online by Stephen King.

His most concerted tech-promoting project, however, was 1990's *Hyperland*, a TV special originally intended to be part of a series master-minded by producer Max Whitby (who also headed up the *LCTS* CD-ROM) and co-produced by Apple and the BBC. Of course Whitby had to pigeonhole Adams and type up a dictated script to get it done, but the writer could have found no better way of turning his face from his publisher's demands than by expounding on the hugely urgent issue of how the Internet would change our lives, at the very start of the decade which would see millions getting online, considerably later to the party than Douglas himself. The icing on the cake was the reunion with Tom Baker, who was cast to play the role of 'software agent', explaining to the confused everyman Adams how the Internet would, or could, work – with Douglas' singular preoccupation, interactive entertainment, central to the programme. Viewed now (so very easily, thanks to YouTube), this comic documentary may not have been perfectly prescient, but therein lies the drawback of being so very ahead of the curve – for every ten correct predictions, those you educate can always find at least one clunky howler. But when you consider that the programme was aired at the same time as Tim Berners-Lee was only just completing his proposal for the World Wide Web, it was a remarkable primer for what was to come.

Ed Victor and the Heinemann top rank soon, however, began to breathe more heavily down Douglas' neck about the first half of the contract, and it was becoming harder than ever for him to find reasonable excuses for waiting until after the next deadline had passed, no matter how blasé his basking in his reputation seemed to be on his numerous chat-show appearances. He got big laughs on old friend Clive Anderson's Channel 4 show when he confided, 'I have this strange relationship with publishers, whereby they give me a lot of money to write a book and I … don't. And I can't understand it! As far as I'm concerned, once they've paid me that seems to be the deal.' One year later, he mused further on his by now infamous approach: 'I'm the absolute archetype of the sort of writer who does the last 90% of the work in the last 10% of the time … It becomes a sort of Zen problem, because there has to be a deadline that everybody believes, including myself, and having broken so many previous ones, you never quite believe in whatever the current one is … I spend about a year in a state of panic. I do all sorts of outlines that instantly get abandoned because they don't work. But I'm determined to crack the schematics problem because I know that if I could work to a detailed plot I'd write better books.'

One possible source for added agonisation over settling down to work on a fresh *Hitchhiker* outing was the realisation that his creation was no longer the only internationally successful British sci-fi comedy, with Rob Grant and Doug Naylor's spaceship sitcom *Red Dwarf* a few years into its run on BBC2, and the writers were going from strength to strength with their own novelisations, comics and other merchandise. Grant & Naylor's painful journey to getting the go-ahead for the series in the first place bears a striking similarity to Adams' frustrations in the late 1970s, which would be nonsensical were it not for the fact that the *Hitchhiker* TV series was not considered a promising example of the genre to the TV bigwigs they were courting. The extent to which Douglas' creation influenced *Red Dwarf* has always been oddly unexplored in the past, with Naylor dismissive of any suggestion of comparison, while Adams only offered a terse and unconvincing 'I have of course heard of *Red Dwarf*, but I've never seen it.' Rob Grant, however, happily admits to being a big fan of the radio series and the books, while being certain that his and Doug's creation owed little to *Hitchhiker* – even notwithstanding subconscious parallels, such as a whole episode extrapolated from Ford's anecdote about playing billiards with planets. Above all, their universe, which follows the antics not of a modern-day everyman but of futuristic menial workers plunged three million years further into the empty expanse of deep space (which, crucially, is devoid of aliens), was always designed as a play on the traditional studio-based suburban sitcom with a live audience, very much at odds with how Adams always saw *Hitchhiker*.

When asked by Anderson about the return of the creation which made his name, however, there seemed to be no trouble brewing when he announced, 'I'd had such a long rest from *Hitchhiker* … what was good about it, as far as I was concerned, was that it was a sort of perfect vehicle for me to explore the ideas that I'm interested in. I'm no longer bored with it, because I haven't done it for seven years, so … "Let's pull it out of the cupboard: yes, it seems rather fun! Yes, there's no reason why I can't, I'm *allowed* to do it!" I realised I'd had a mental block about doing *Hitchhiker*, only because I had to allow myself to get free from it. Now that I'm free from it, it's actually quite fun to do it again.' But as he mentally took his *Hitchhiker* dolls down from the attic, and tried to recall what each of the characters were up to and what could be done with them, the only star that he knew would definitely feature in the new outing was, he said: 'Arthur.' After several years of leaving his hapless hero happily in love, poor Dent was going to have to be plucked from his bliss and once again plunged into a plot guaranteed to strengthen his extreme distrust of the Universe in general. Not to disappoint fans, Adams hastily continued, 'I suspect Marvin will probably make a brief appearance. Ford is a sort of off-stage presence. I haven't made my mind up about Zaphod because I see Zaphod now as being an irredeemably seventies character, a guy who's perpetually stuck in flares …' He was already toying with a number of ways to bring Marvin back, including an episode in which the itinerant hitcher Dent is embarrassed to bump into the android again, shortly after seeing him 'die'[12], but that strand was to end up condensed into one paragraph starring Ford, without any reference to *Hitchhiker*'s gloomy break-out star. Adams unapologetically explained, 'Of course I'm extremely grateful to the fans, but it's a question of expectations, and you tend to bridle a lot at some of them. I mean, people always ask for more Marvin, and I can't do him as an obligation. Marvin doesn't appear at all in *MH*. I had a few scenes in the back of my mind I could have done, but they never turned out to be relevant. It would have been shoehorning them in. Not that I haven't done quite a bit of shoehorning in my time, but I didn't want Marvin to be a chore … I do find the whole thing quite tricky, the idea that there's a bit of the inside of your head that has somehow gone public and people can wander around in. It's like sitting here in the house and having a stranger walk in and say, "I don't think much of that sofa."'

There were two overriding concepts which Douglas felt would drive *MH*: first, the fun that could be had with multi-dimensionality, the butterfly-wing flaps which can fundamentally influence who we actually are – indeed, the eventual book would be singularly obsessed with what makes us who we are, with numerous solipsistic reflections on individual perception, shared between characters. Also, as there was no sign of him achieving fatherhood himself, Adams was sold on the idea of Dent suddenly finding himself an ill-prepared father, trying to come to terms with an adolescent daughter he never knew he had – Random Dent. As happened so often, this primary motivation for the story was not to actually pop up in the narrative until past the halfway mark, but in theory, Adams said, 'It's the story of Arthur Dent's daughter. She is the daughter of an immigrant, living in a world where nobody's ever heard of the Earth, and Arthur's banging on about it all the time because it's so important to him. And she knows nothing whatsoever about this, but nevertheless, Earth as a home is the environment which made her what she is, so in the end she gets driven to go back to Earth, and find where she came from, and why.'

The major loose thread he had to pull, however, was Agrajag's reveal, that Arthur Dent could not die until he had visited Stavromula Beta – and perhaps it was time. However, at this stage, the twist that the fateful region was much closer to home than Arthur suspected had yet to be devised, as his creator fiddled with scraps of potential chapters:

> Springtime is the best time on Stavromula Beta. The rains are less torrential, acid levels are low, and for a period of about two weeks very few of the plants actually attack people. Stavromula Beta is Eden before the fall. Everything is lovely, but there is something they are supposed not to do ...

Adams had a whole mess of half-started story ideas and nebulous concepts to try and recycle this time round, including pages of biography for Baggy The Runch[13] (now a forgotten 'founding editor' of the Guide) and his time with the boghogs on a planet called NowWhat, which ultimately became one of many alternative Earths in a minor passage in the book. None of this was gelling together as any kind of cogent narrative, however, and with 1992 carved in stone as the immovable endgame, the time for booking hotel rooms and bundling the giant procrastinator in the back of a van was drawing near.

... You Also PANIC!

Arthur's fate could have been harsher – Adams' first intention was to kill off Fenchurch in the ship crash which stranded Dent as the sandwich maker on the primitive planet of Lamuella, but ultimately her plural-zone-related disappearance gave him an all-new hopeless quest which could fuel Adams' idea for his troubled hero to return to his galactic hobo ways, exploring the Universe in search of his lost love and some meaning to his life. Arthur's story was not the one that most exercised Douglas this time, however. At first, his handwritten notebooks reveal that he began sketching out a way for Beeblebrox to return, as well as Marvin:

> Zaphod has fallen on hard times and had to take to life as a pirate. Well, maybe not a pirate, but a ... (He comes up with another definition.) When this is challenged his cool snaps and he shouts "How do ya think I feel about it?" ... He insists on having Marvin hold them up with the gun while he has a good cry and complain about his lot. Marvin does his job (un)complainingly ...

But this doodling came to nothing – both characters would remain off-stage throughout, albeit Zaphod was still part of the tapestry of the others' lives, which would be disturbed by the dabbling with dimensions. Above all, so long after limiting her as a perfect object of adoration, Trillian would take centre stage this time – or rather, to make up for past short-comings, there would be two of her – the one we know, who had a lift in the *HoG*, and ... who?

> Tricia is an agony aunt? She keeps mice. Arthur gets her pregnant at the end of <u>LUE</u>. Trillian abandoned Random - which is her crime - she actually committed it. But even if it hadn't happened - if Random hadn't been born - the crime was still a latent one ... Tricia is exactly the same as Trillian, except that she hasn't done the things Trillian has done, simply because circumstances have been different. How about the business of when Zaphod picks her up at a party? There has to be something else that happened. Did Arthur see him off? Did she not respond to him? Did he not come? ... When she asks if Random is the daughter of her and Zaphod, Random says no - you and Arthur. Tricia can't believe it. With Zaphod - of course - she couldn't breed. Maybe that's one of the reasons why she slept with Arthur at that moment ... Tricia is appalled at the idea that she would have gone with Arthur ... How old is she now? 42.

Trillian's pregnancy would ultimately be triggered by a semen donation made by Arthur to pay his way around the Galaxy.

Once again, Douglas had so many apparently disparate ideas to accommodate – the *LCTS*-inspired fictional zoology of the perfectly normal beasts and the boghogs, a race of aliens who lived on a diet of Earth TV[14] who would evolve into the dangerously amnesiac Grebulons, and somehow connected to all this was the idea of Rupert, the newly discovered tenth planet in our solar system, and how that would affect the laughable horoscope industry, as promoted by the likes of astrologer Russell Grant:

> Astrology, says the Guide, is a very curious kind of thing. There is not a planet in the Galaxy where something of the sort has not developed. Astrology, the belief that whirling lumps of rock at light years' distance know something about your day that you don't. That's one small step of faith for a man. Then there's the belief which goes with it that some overweight jerk with blow-dried hair knows something about what the whirling lumps of rock at light years' distance know about your day that you don't. That's a giant leap for mankind ...
>
> Astrology, according to one of the tersest entries in that most wholly remarkable and indispensable of all works of reference and philosophy, The Hitchhiker's Guide to the Galaxy, sucks.
>
> But, the entry continues, it is pointless to argue about it because the plain truth is that people <u>like</u> to believe things. The more absurd a proposition, the greater satisfaction there is to be derived from believing it. Astrology is simply the commercial application of this principle.
>
> The editor of the Guide at that time was one Lajawag Rankbat, the most egregiously skunk-like of all the Guide's editors, and he was so impressed with the force of this argument that he deleted the passage and substituted a horoscope section in future editions and, sure enough, it was a great popular success and contributed greatly to the commercial prosperity of the Guide ...

And what of the Guide itself? The preponderance of drafted pages describing past editors such as Lajawag[15] and Baggy showed that Douglas knew his other central 'character' had to have a large part to play, but what? It was all such a tangled web that he decided to quickly think about something else entirely.

Luckily, a dream opportunity for delaying progress came along – Melvyn Bragg, editor of the ITV arts strand *The South Bank Show*, contacted Douglas with a request to cover the writing of the new *Hitchhiker* book on his programme, to which the author replied that, with the best will in the galaxy, he wasn't actually writing it, but what about a documentary about the very act of not writing something? The agonies, the procrastination, the whooshing sound of deadlines speeding by – he could write it, star in it, make it something really special … and get his mind off his current inability to deliver the goods.

The resultant programme would be so ambitious that it would have at least one foot in the official *Hitchhiker* canon. Adams penned a gloriously self-indulgent script, opening with the Electric Monk (Fry & Laurie's Footlights compadre Paul Shearer), as narrated by Peter Jones after over a decade away from Book duty: 'The Monk currently believed that the valley and everything in the valley and around it, including the Monk itself and the Monk's horse, was a uniform shade of pale pink. Even more surprisingly, the Monk believed Douglas Adams was working feverishly on a new book … But curiously enough, despite having sold 198 squigwizillion books, Douglas Adams still found it very hard to believe that he could actually write them. He needed other people – or things – to believe it for him.'

Since Vonnegut first began messing around with the laws keeping characters safely locked into a narrative in *Slaughterhouse 5*, if not before, one familiar sci-fi trope has been the hero's realisation that they are fictional, and that their creator has a lot of explaining to do. When it comes to the relationship between Douglas and Arthur, nothing could be more awkward – finally, poor Arthur could find out exactly who it was who had been doing such terrible things to him for so many years.

Adams' friends Jones, Dixon and Moore were happy to come back for the sentimental reprise, and Bywater made a predictably superb Dirk, with Shearer doubling as MacDuff. Simon might have had to rely on not-quite-authentic hair to match his appearance of a decade previously (he had worn a hairpiece even then, but that was because of a severe haircut due to another role, rather than the ravages of time) and the only bit of Marvin which could be tracked down was the head, requiring a stand-in to wear a heavy coat while Moore provided the voice, but the general theme certainly

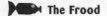

fitted in with the heavily solipsistic, multidimensional, perception-skewing theme of the next book. Plus, as Adams and the crew revisited his past lives, restaging his experiences at Cambridge and as a bodyguard, plus indulging in lengthy anti-theistic debates with Dawkins, nobody was better placed to undermine any hint of self-absorption in the project than the author's own creations:

INT. KITCHEN. DAY.
THE ELECTRIC MONK sits reading the 'National Enquirer', but puts it away sheepishly when he realises the camera is on him.

MONK   (SPEAKS WITH A HIGH-PITCHED METALLIC WELSH ACCENT)
I think the most difficult thing about being a character in a Douglas Adams novel is not so much wondering what's going to happen next, as wondering if anything's going to happen next. You never really know if your character's going to develop into something really rather complex and interesting, stop dead and never be mentioned again, or just unexpectedly turn into a Coca-Cola vending machine. Plays havoc with your sense of motivation.

Pan left to reveal MARVIN sat in a large coat at the kitchen table.

MARVIN   How do you think I feel? One minute I'm there being pushed around all the time - "Open entry bay number three, Marvin!", "Marvin, can you stay and fight off this gigantic battle machine?" - and then they run off and abandon me. Everything abandons me in the end. Even my body abandoned me, you know. Why d'you think I'm sitting here in a mouldy old raincoat? Every single bit of me fell off - rather enthusiastically, I thought...

THE ELECTRIC MONK looks incredibly irritated. Gazes upwards.

MONK   What do you think they're talking about up there?

MARVIN   Oh, the usual thing - "I went to Cambridge, that was very interesting, I joined Footlights, that was very interesting, I left Cambridge, that was very interesting." They all lead exactly the same lives and say exactly the same things about them, and then claim, against all the available evidence, that it's very interesting...

Arthur and Ford materialise in modern-day Islington and find their way to Duncan Terrace, where the Monk, Dirk, Marvin and an eagle have amassed to will their creator on to meeting his current deadline, but any attempt to intervene directly is foiled by the paradox of Creator meeting Creation, so Arthur can only hear the unforgivable things said about him by Douglas from the next room, as he tries to get to the bottom of the current insanity surrounding him:

ARTHUR stands on steps by DOUGLAS' bookcase, reading from 'The Restaurant at the End of the Universe' while THE ELECTRIC MONK sits at the piano playing and singing 'I Believe'.

ARTHUR   "...You could say I'm more differed from than differing..." Arthur Dent! It is me! (CLOSES BOOK) Douglas Adams? He must be a biographer!

INT. ISLINGTON. DAY.

As DOUGLAS expounds his theories, ARTHUR explores the house, determined to find a way into the lounge.

DOUGLAS   I think it's important to understand where our perception came from, and what illusions it might create. If you imagine Man first waking up in his world and looking around, early Man, it's rather like a puddle waking up and thinking, "Hm! This is a rather interesting world I find myself in. It fits me rather precisely, doesn't it? In fact, it fits me staggeringly precisely! It can hardly be coincidence. I think this hole was made precisely to fit me into it..." That I think is the illusion we suffer from, and the only way you get away from that illusion, is to see things from other perspectives. And there are two areas in which we can do that, one is to try and understand the perceptual world of other animals, and the other is the perceptual world that computers now open up to us, which give us the ability to re-manipulate the data that we actually manipulate in our heads, to create the world we live in.

MELVYN   And is this coming into your new book, 'Mostly Harmless'?

DOUGLAS   Yes... it comes into the story, but I think it's very much at the heart of what the book is about...

INT. DOUGLAS' STUDY. DAY.

FORD is exploring Douglas' Apple Mac as ARTHUR excitedly bustles in with copies of the 'Hitchhiker' books.

ARTHUR   Ford! Look at this! Look at these!

FORD   I know.

ARTHUR   These books are about me! This is my biography!

FORD   Your biography?

ARTHUR   Yes, well, you get a mention in it here and there, background fill. Otherwise, this is the story of my life!

FORD   Arthur, this is fiction.

ARTHUR   What do you mean?

FORD   It's as though you, we, us, real, living people have somehow been dragged into a parallel universe in which we are fictional entities...

ARTHUR   What does it all mean?

FORD   ...Does the term 'ZZ9 Plural Z Alpha' mean anything to you?

ARTHUR   Should it?

FORD   The Galactic sector coordinates of Earth. Try and remember it. 'Plural' means it's on a kinda quantum faultline. All the possible Earths continually interfere with each other... But why a writer in one possible Earth would actually be imagining events in another..?

Armed with this knowledge, the two hitchhikers take charge, and begin to write their own lives – culminating in Arthur dictating dialogue between Trillian and himself discussing Fenchurch, perhaps thrown together by Adams just for the documentary, but otherwise seeming to underline his feeling that *SLATFATFish* was a misstep, and should be discounted – luckily, the 'it was all a dream' cop-out never actually made it into the finished novel:

"I know, it was odd. I can't really account for it. It didn't seem real somehow, either. The whole place had a kind of dreamlike quality to it," said Arthur.

"I think everything has a dreamlike quality to you, Arthur," said Trillian.

"Um ... what did you say?"

"Never mind."

"She didn't have her feet on the ground."

"Must have been a good relationship, the two of you."

"No, I mean quite literally they didn't quite touch the ground. There was about a two-millimetre gap. Two millimetres may not sound a lot but when it's between you and the ground I think it's magnificent."

"You sure you didn't dream the whole thing, Arthur?"

"Oh, far from sure. Very far ... I mean, every dream that I have involves sitting at the kitchen table going through my accounts, and then watching a bit of television. Then I wake up and discover that I'm living on an alien planet. Makes you wonder, doesn't it? I mean, how does your life strike you?"

Within this fantasy, as part of an improvised scene mocking Adams' pursuit of a 'Y-shaped plot', Sue Freestone is shown explaining to her errant charge that they had four weeks until all hell broke loose, with the book's cover design finalised, the printers ready to roll, and all publicity in place. However, this bit was not wholly fantastical. Nonetheless, another deadline disappeared over the horizon, the *South Bank Show* episode was broadcast without an accompanying book release, and still *MH* remained a tangle of disjointed ideas.

By now Heinemann, newly bought up by Random House, had given up on the second half of their contract and sold any second-book rights back to Pan while retaining the omnibus rights to all the books – but that only affirmed the company's resolve to get their *Hitchhiker* book out of Douglas. In March, the inevitable occurred: Sue once again had to book an expensive hotel suite, and Adams was back in stir until a coherent novel materialised – with one day's freedom allowed, for his 40th birthday. With his usual bursts of sustained concentration, the disparate strands began to weave together – albeit with a familiarly episodic feel, as Dent travelled from spaceport to spaceport looking for some kind of meaning to his predicament, before eventually settling down and finding his place among the simple folk of Lamuella:

> Arthur has become part of this primitive life. His contribution to their way of life is the 'invention' of sandwiches. Amazingly difficult to think of anything else he can pass on, really. I mean, what would you do? Microwave oven? I don't even know how they work when I've got a manual, let alone how to build one. And they need electricity. I eventually discovered that when I found the manual ...

In a kind of magnified recurrence of the tussle which brought the IID into existence, Douglas finally realised that he would have to pull something pretty remarkable from his sleeve to bring all his ideas together, resulting in perhaps the most audacious level of plot lubrication in fiction – almost from the very first page of *MH*, the reader would be explicitly instructed not to think too hard about the coincidence-riddled, overlapping, endlessly confusing tangle of events which unfolded, because such things are beyond human comprehension. All we need to know is that everything makes some sense within the WSOGMM, or 'Whole Sort of General Mish Mash' which is all existence as we know it – or rather, it doesn't exist but 'is just the sum total of all the different ways there would be of looking at it if it did.' And who, ultimately, is the one to understand and control all of this, the Scientia Ex Machina to blame for anything which occurs between the (already printed) book covers? The Hitchhiker's Guide to the Galaxy, and its all-new feature 'Temporal Reverse Engineering', which has the stated benefit of allowing the Guide to summon any transport its owner desires seemingly at will, but with the ultimate result that literally any imaginable event in any dimension can be brought to pass in the same way – and, of course, this power is in the worst hands possible.

What could be more perfect, as Adams painfully struggled to make sense of his narrative, than to have the very subject which had made him and plagued him since his mid-twenties turn out to be not just the perfect narrative device but the final, unvanquishable villain? Or at least, this was the Guide Mark II – 'the single most astounding thing of any kind ever. Coming soon to a dimension near you!' – a sinister redesign bearing the legend 'PANIC!' which unfolds into a pan-dimensional bird-shaped model so powerful that even Ford, the ultimate slacker, realises the danger of having it fall into the wrong hands – such as, for instance, a confused and dejected adolescent like Random Frequent Flyer Dent:

"What the hell are you?" demanded Random.

"I am The Guide. In your universe I am your Guide. In fact I inhabit what is technically known as the Whole Sort of General Mish Mash … Your universe is vast to you. Vast in time, vast in space. That's because of the filters through which you perceive it. But I was built with no filters at all, which means I perceive the mishmash which contains all possible universes but which has, itself, no size at all. For me, anything is possible. I am omniscient and omnipotent, extremely vain, and, what is more, I come in a handy self-carrying package. You have to work out how much of the above is true."

A slow smile spread over Random's face. "You bloody little thing. You've been winding me up!"

"As I said, anything is possible."

As the pressure grew increasingly unbearable, at least Adams could bow out with some kind of return to the freewheeling spirit that inspired *Hitchhiker* in the first place. For all that he himself was a massively powerful trademark in his own right, he made the malevolent power behind this new Guide the Vogon-controlled InfiDim Enterprises, a bland but deadly corporation that has destroyed the groovy spirit of Megadodo Publications in a manner not dissimilar to John Birt's business-like rule at the BBC. As the oleaginous new editor Van Harl tells Ford, "What we do is we sell one Guide billions and billions of times. We exploit the multidimensional nature of the Universe to cut down on manufacturing costs. And we don't sell to penniless hitchhikers. What a stupid notion that was! Find the one section of the market that, more or less by definition, doesn't have any money, and try and sell to it. No. We sell to the affluent business traveller and his vacationing wife in a billion, billion different futures … This is the most radical, dynamic and thrusting business venture in the entire multidimensional infinity of space/time/probability ever." From one angle, the story of the Guide update could be seen as a warning against the ever-upgrading march of new technology, but of course, this being Douglas, that was never the case – it was the idea of our futures being in the hands of greedy faceless corporations which exercised him.

Still, progress remained tortuous and soon Bywater was sent for, to move in and offer support – even writing pages of material which Adams was invited to rewrite, just to keep up momentum, as nobody appreciated Douglas' need for collaboration as well as he did. But in the presence of Michael and Sue, halfway through this final concerted push, Douglas Adams eventually buckled, fell to the floor, and openly wept with the sheer frustration of trying to provide yet another instalment of the saga which he could never escape. Bereft of all dignity, he wailed to them, that he just *could not do it any more.*

This is worth dwelling on for a moment. Adams, as his old friends continually brayed, was a blithely rich, successful man. What right could this well-born, physically imposing, world-famous, influential, prideful millionaire epicure have to command our sympathy, just because he could not type up the adventures of a gang of intergalactic losers? But the task at hand should be immaterial – if you knew a postman or a dinner lady who broke down and wept bitter tears because of the frustrations that their job made them feel, it would simply be a human reaction to feel sorry for them, and, if possible, to offer support and solutions to their problems. The very best support offered to Adams during this emotional crisis by his friends, however – even Sue, whose whole job revolved around forcing him to meet deadlines – was to tell him, in short, not to bother. Bywater recalled the madness of Douglas' final compositional crisis as being akin to a Victorian asylum, his huge distraught friend crashing around the suite blinded with tears, as Michael tried to make the desperate 'schmuck' understand that the Earth could carry on spinning perfectly well without another bloody outing for Arthur Dent. Bitterly, Douglas poured out his fears to Jane, apologetically agonising that if he failed to meet the next deadline he could be taken to court, they would have to pay back the whopping advance, and would probably have to downsize their whole way of life ... To which his pragmatic wife replied, in short, 'So what?' She was more than strong enough to support the both of them, and it was not, she assured him without a hint of irony, the end of the world. Adams had spent so long living the high life as the world-famous author that the idea of failure being ultimately harmless, that he was loved and protected whether he provided the goods or not, had simply never occurred to him.

From that point onwards, assured beyond all doubt that the only people likely to really care whether *MH* reached bookshops or not – certainly, at the expense of his own sanity – were Heinemann's board of directors and the voracious fans awaiting their long-delayed slab of space sass, Adams' progression towards completion of the fifth entry in the *Hitchhiker* trilogy clicked onto the right track. There was just one thing left, he assured Michael and Sue, and that was to absolutely inextricably finish and seal off the world of *Hitchhiker* once and for all – no happy endings, no loose threads or cheeky ellipses, just Armageddon, and a full stop. His supporters offered up seven different ways in which the novel could reach such a cataclysmic conclusion and, as we all know, he opted to bring poor Arthur to a dead end on the planet where it all began – or certainly, one very much like it – in the fateful venue of London club Stavro Mueller Beta (street number 42), as somewhere, just out of orbit, Prostetnic Vogon Jeltz awaited the irrevocable demolition of all possible Planet Earths within the notoriously tricky sector of ZZ9 Plural Z Alpha:

> (Arthur) wondered what he should do, but he only wondered it idly. Around him people were beginning to rush and shout a lot, but it was suddenly very clear to him that there was nothing to be done, not now or ever. Through the new strangeness of noise and light he could just make out the shape of Ford Prefect sitting back and laughing wildly. A tremendous feeling of peace came over him. He knew that at last, for once and for ever, it was now all, finally, over.

MH was released in October 1992 and, of course, it rapidly became a best-seller, beguiling fans who had felt short-changed by the previous novel. As Douglas himself complained, his 'methods', excruciating though they were, did tend to work.

It's Time For You To Take Responsibility ...

It would make dramatic sense at this juncture to say that Douglas Adams' association with *Hitchhiker* ended on that hideously final note – but, of course, it didn't, and 1993 continued the renaissance of interest and industry for what was already considered a comedy classic.

First of all there was the matter of the DC Comics adaptation, which Adams had signed off on two years previously, consigning another iteration of Arthur to lie down in the mud in a whole new format. With the first three novels bought up for the comic-strip treatment by the company – plus a series of trading cards based on the strips – some of the best writing and inking talent was attached, but Douglas was to be so blasé about the project that he wasn't even sure which books were adapted. His only involvement, besides ordering numerous redesigns of Marvin to make him as utterly featureless as possible, was to insist stringently that the (largely British) team Americanised as little as possible of his work bar the spelling, ruling out a switch to 'cellphones' from 'digital watches', and sticking slavishly to the book, even though every version of *Hitchhiker* had benefited from differing wildly from the others. As a result, the first periodical releases of the comics were a disappointment to many fans and, although it was a shame that only the first three books of the trilogy emerged in strip format, it's moot whether many comics fans were turned on to *Hitchhiker* by what they read.

Meanwhile, Jones and Dixon were not out of costume for very long, thanks to that nonpareil of *Hitchhiker* fans, Kevin Davies, who in the years since his youthful enthusiasm for the show had continued to carve out a career in animation, including work on *Who Framed Roger Rabbit?*. Over a decade earlier, young Kevin had been a familiar figure throughout every stage of the TV series' creation, turning up with the heavy video equipment of the day to capture as much of the programme's production as possible, and he suggested to Douglas and the BBC that he had the makings of a superlative 'Making Of'. The series had been released on video in 1992, but BBC Worldwide took the unusual move of including an invitation for fans to get in touch if they were interested in Kevin's special feature, and obviously enough consumers did so to give the project the green light. Besides all-new interviews and, of course, the priceless period footage, Davies decided to frame the documentary with further dramatised appearances from Arthur and Ford, this time bringing back veteran Vogon Michael Cule to accompany them, plus a mute but miraculously reupholstered Marvin (Jim Francis knew where to find the body – Kevin had even stored it in his lounge during conventions).

The conceit was simpler than *The South Bank Show* – Arthur hitches his way home (in a ship from *Blake's 7*, pursued by the TARDIS), pushing his way past a mountain of post à la *SLATFATFish*, and settles down on his bed to read what his own Guide has to say about his TV adventures (with particular consternation at the input from some actor called Simon Jones).

Kevin's experience stood him and his team in good stead for mixing live action and animation, as Arthur's cartoon Babel fish educated him about the show's animation techniques, and the denouement featured particularly pleasing computer graphics for the time when Ford arrived to save his old friend from the pursuing Vogon by explaining that the whole place was just a computer simulation, which gradually powered down as the Universe blinked out of existence around them.

Numerous continuations of *Hitchhiker* off the page were under consideration at this time, with Davies finding Adams open to all sorts of suggestions, about another TV series, or maybe, despite previous misgivings, an animation. The idea which got furthest, however, was the original plan to record a third radio series, referred to as 'The Tertiary Phase' by Douglas, which would adapt *LUE* to *Hitchhiker*'s indigenous format. The project was instigated by BBC Worldwide, based on the phenomenal CD sales of the original two phases, but although he was eventually to opine that it 'was a case of letting the marketing people tell me what to do, which is never really a good idea', he seemed amenable at the time: 'It would be great and I'd love to do it but only if I was doing it myself and as heavily involved as in the previous one. And I don't see when I'm going to have time for that ... Then I turned forty and I began to realise that I wasn't going to have time to do all the things I wanted to do, and everyone wanted a third radio series so I actually thought I should give it to them.'

Douglas was already working on one radio-based scheme with Lloyd and Eugen Beer, hoping to win the licence for an independent speech station, Radio Barking, with a 'God slot' on Wodehouse presented by himself, but as that bid was doomed to failure he gave a new Radio 4 series serious consideration. He had long admired the bombastic audio presentations of Dirk Maggs, who had started out in radio comedy but soon made a big impression with impressive 'audio movies' for Radio 1, featuring Superman and Batman, and having approved Dirk's hiring as producer (Perkins being immersed in his rise to the very top of the TV comedy tree), the two found a shared obsession with the latest audio technology. However, the hiring of experienced radio writer Alick Rowe appalled Douglas when he found the first episode featured a talking dinosaur, which may have given the prehistoric Arthur someone with whom he could exposit but made no palaeontological sense, and also had worrying echoes of *Dimension of Miracles*. After what Adams was to euphemise as 'argy-bargy and shenanigans and so on', he reluctantly took to the keyboard to do it himself, even though he had originally insisted that writing *LUE* twice already felt like enough. When the issue of the huge plot disparities between the books and the last radio 'Fits' was put to him, suggesting that fans might smell a rat, he cordially replied that such fans could take a running jump. He was nonetheless bursting with fresh ideas and had found an ideal collaborator in Maggs, a sparky drummer and producer – plus the original cast had been sounded out, with cricket commentators Brian Johnstone and Fred Trueman hired to play themselves. But, after a period of experimentation, Adams reluctantly pulled the plug. One reason for this reluctance was that he had hoped to finally perform in his own series: one day Dirk arrived at Duncan Terrace to find Douglas cueing up a particular extract from his *LUE* audiobook, and he asked his producer which role he felt might suit him best, as Agrajag's agony echoed around the study. Maggs feigned ignorance, but it was clear that this was the one character with whom the writer most identified. Once Dirk had tackled the unpleasant job of letting down all the talent who had been primed to take part, he agreed with Adams that the Tertiary Phase was just on ice for a while, but they would get round to it eventually.

Adding to this activity, as a result of Davies' splendid work on the 'Making Of', when Adams was approached by publishers Weidenfeld & Nicolson with the idea of using the latest digital-art software to bring his first novel to life in a big deluxe illustrated edition, he suggested Davies to mastermind the project without delay. After a successful test shot, it was agreed that the book would be approached as a 'print movie', opening with credits for the cast and crew including photographer Michael Joseph, and going on to unfold as a kind of blueprint for the *Hitchhiker* film which continued to rumble on in development, having briefly been under the supervision of fellow Ed Victor client David Puttnam, in a slow process that Adams would come to describe as 'like trying to grill a steak by having a succession of people coming into the room and breathing on it.'

In fact, despite the nadir of *MH*, Douglas' attitude to *Hitchhiker* had never been more buoyantly philosophical, thanks to the intervention of two musical heroes. First of all, another famous client of Victor's had given Adams a stern talking-to after a bout of authorial moaning, as he was to recall: 'There was a period where I got heartily sick of it, and I really never wanted to hear anything more about it again, and I would almost scream at anybody who used the words to me … *Hitchhiker* now is something from the past that I feel very fond of; it was great, it was terrific, and it's been very good to me. I had a conversation a little while ago with Pete Townshend of The Who, and I think at that point I was saying, "Oh God, I hope I'm not just remembered as the person who wrote *Hitchhiker*!" And he kind of reprimanded me a little bit, he said, "Look, I have the same thing with *Tommy*, and for a while I thought like that. The thing is, when you've got something like that in your history, it opens an awful lot of doors. It allows you to do a lot of other things. People remember that. It's something one should be grateful for." And I thought that was quite right.' Then there was Adams' friendship with bobble-hatted Monkee Mike 'Nez' Nesmith, which dated back to his first trip to LA, where the two bonded over a shared love of Paul Crum's cartoons, particularly the jaundiced hippos. With Nez's help, it was in 1993 that Adams finally decided to scrape together $350,000 to buy back the movie rights to his baby, and retake command of the project. It was claimed that this required a remortgage and wiping out his pension fund, but as Sony reportedly offered £100,000 just for the game rights it could not have been too much of a risk. The first mooted director for the film was John Lloyd, who had moved into directing commercials with great success, but as he had yet to move into features (avoiding poisonous offers such as lacklustre *Naked Gun* sequels), everything remained up in the air. Nonetheless, Adams was glad to be quoted in October that the film was 'off the back burner, and being singed on the front burner'.

Sadly, despite sterling work from all involved (including Douglas and Ed, who cameoed as Shooty and Bang-Bang for a shoot within Stringfellow's nightclub, in which Adams is seen struggling with his latest unpublished novel, which appears to be *Goldilocks & the Three Bears*), the *iH2G2* book was perhaps the least fortunate iteration of the story of all when it hit the shops in September 1994. Many of the images were wonderfully playful, with Adams requesting untypical illustrations such as the legless Arcturan MegaDonkey dragging itself through the sand, but the cast of models was so unusual that a whole new footnote had to be added for Zaphod, adding an unusually topical note, with reference to the BSE crisis:

Subjective impressions may vary according to local reality miscalibrations and the perceptual systems of the observer. For instance, any entity suffering from HSSE, or Mad Human Disease, will probably perceive the President's hair as being short and dark, and should consult a qualified Peripsychosemiolothanatician immediately.

The book struggled partly due to the easily shop-soiled silver dust jacket and the painful £25 RRP, but to a modern reader, although the scenes are still enjoyable, it's the wacky use of fonts and skewed design, betraying the primitive nature of the software being used, which gives *iH2G2* an unmis-takably early-1990s look that makes the book one of the most dated artefacts in the entire *Hitchhiker* Universe. What most annoyed Douglas, however, was the resounding shrug which greeted his own carefully-designed '42' puzzle – a grid of orbs, seven by six, which he claimed harboured ten different ways of finding the celebrated number (blue-tinted orbs roughly made out the shape of the digits, yellow-tinted ones presented the Roman numerals XLII, the Earth was in the 42nd position, the barcode translated as 42, all the lines made 42 in binary, and so on). 'The point of the puzzle,' he said, 'was this: everybody was looking for hidden meanings and puzzles and significances in what I had written. So I thought that just for a change I would actually construct a puzzle and see how many people solved it. Of course, nobody paid it any attention. I think that's terribly significant.'

The unwieldy glittery collector's items presented a novel experience for Adams when they were massively remaindered, and he ultimately bought up all the stock he could to sell online, which he admitted was 'as a way of making money, probably up there with selling pencils from a cup.' But by this time, such things really didn't have any power to bother Douglas – three months before the new book hit the shops, Polly Jane Rocket (as in the salad leaf craved by Jane in pregnancy, rather than the space vehicle) Adams had been born, and her ecstatic 42-year-old father had little interest in *Hitchhiker*, or indeed anything else, for the foreseeable future: 'I had always thought babies would limit me, get in the way of me achieving certain things, but having Polly has filled all sorts of holes in my life I never knew were there. It's good to have something around which is manifestly much more important than anything else in your life.'

By The Galactic Laws Of Salvage ...

Admittedly, he made one definite exception to his new-found obsession with fatherhood: on his inevitably significance-steeped 42nd birthday back in March, Adams' friend David Gilmour had presented him with an exclusive voucher to join Pink Floyd for two of the songs in their set at Earl's Court in October – this was also a partial repayment for Adams' suggestion that the band's latest album should be called *The Division Bell*, for which he made Gilmour donate £5,000 to environmental causes. There are very few authors who didn't set out to be something else, or who did not continue to harbour other artistic ambitions, and Douglas had formed an occasional duo with Ken Follett, called The Hard Covers, who supported Stephen King's Rock Bottom Remainders on at least one occasion. But sharing a stage with his heroes (without having to dress up as Mr. Gumby this time) was a different magnitude of excitement, and as ever, he rehearsed every single note of 'Brain Damage' and 'Eclipse' with scientific exactitude, only being out of sync with the rest of the band by half a beat. Of course, the crowd, instantly recognising the guest performer who dwarfed everyone else on stage, gave him a riotous ovation. Incidentally, Adams received further musical tribute three years later, when the career-defining album from Radiohead reached the top of the charts with a title inspired by Zaphod's dialogue, *OK Computer*, and featuring the song 'Paranoid Android', inspired by Marvin (though he missed similar tributes from Coldplay, the tracks '42' and 'Don't Panic'). Adams never stopped experimenting with his own music, and admitted on *Desert Island Discs* in 1994 that 'I have one album in me, which I'm determined to make.' Despite disdaining concept albums, he modestly mused that his record would be 'something along the lines of *Sgt Pepper*, I should think'.

Otherwise, as his friends all noted, Douglas had little time for anything but Polly: 'Apart from being a source of enormous joy and pleasure,' he beamed, 'it's just fascinating watching somebody beginning to make sense of the world, and seeing those models beginning to erect themselves in her head.' For someone who had so obsessively concerned himself with perspectives on life, becoming a father after such a long time of hoping had the added bonus of providing the ultimate test subject for his observations on human nature. Nick Webb shared an exemplary story of seeing baby Polly beached on her father's sizeable tummy, and his delight in observing her tiny face, taking in all the stimuli around her, as he announced, 'Look, she's rebooting!' There was no doubt that Douglas was to be one of those proud parents with one major topic of conversation for quite some time, albeit his doting on Polly was leavened by Jane's creation of a handy warning acronym for when guests began to tire of the subject – 'DODAG' stood for 'Darling, Our Daughter's A Genius'.

A year after Polly's birth – and one year before she was given her own Apple Mac – Douglas and Jane's house was filled with their closest friends and family for a form of Humanist Christening, in which Jane's friend Sue Lloyd-Roberts, Mary Allen, Johnny Brock and 'Michael Caligula Bywater', rather than pledging to turn away from sin for their god-daughter, each signed an expertly drawn-up contract promising to educate and care for their charge in their own inimitable ways – Bywater's oath was 'To tutor the Child in the ways of boozing, whoring, falling down drunk, shooting up down and every which way and playing the piano like unto an angel.' The ceremony was both very funny, naturally, but also touching, as Douglas unabashedly shared his awed pride with a reading of Keats' *On First Looking Into Chapman's Homer*, much quoted by Wodehouse: 'Then felt I like some watcher of the skies / When a new planet swims into his ken ...' Nobody could have known with what senseless rapidity the comic ceremony would turn out to provide crucial support for the oblivious tot, but few babies could have been surrounded with a richer network of love and protection, thanks to Douglas and Jane's wealth of friendship.

A number of pursuits popped up over the ensuing years – Douglas continued to support his conservation charities, heading Kilimanjaro-wards in 1995 (he never expected to actually get to the top) with his sister Jane and a few friends dressed up in a rhino suit designed by Gerald Scarfe, to raise money for the White Rhino appeal, and he also began writing various regular articles for *The Guardian*, *Independent* and technology magazines. However, with being a Dad paramount (and although another book deal was hanging in the air almost precisely in the way bricks don't), for the rest of the decade Adams decided to take a far more relaxed, workaday attitude to life, as part of The Digital Village – one of a plethora of hot new multi-media (or rather, 'multiple media', the distinction being that they would recreate specific projects across separate formats) dot.com start-ups, but with the undeniable USP of having Douglas as 'Chief Fantasist'. He still had his own company, which he had recently renamed Completely Unexpected

Productions, but with this new organisation he felt he could achieve far more, and best of all, not do it alone: 'When I started out I worked on radio, I worked on TV, I worked on stage. I enjoyed and experimented with different media, working with people and, wherever possible, fiddling with bits of equipment. Then I accidentally wrote a best-selling novel and the consequence was that I had to write another and then another. After a decade or so of this I became a little crazed at the thought of spending my entire working life sitting in a room by myself typing. Hence The Digital Village.'

TDV arose from Douglas' association with TV producer Robbie Stamp and his boss at Central TV, Richard Creasey. Adams had always been up for the odd TV appearance, eloquently eulogising Graham Chapman on *The Late Show* in 1989 – although some bookings had proven too odd for his tastes, such as a *Tomorrow's World* Christmas special two months after that, which saw him inveigled into playing a gadget-based game of *Call My Bluff* with Eartha Kitt. That shambles earned one cry of 'Never again!' for his PA to note, but a firmer one was to follow his appearance on *Have I Got News For You*, timed to coincide with *MH* publicity. The Hat Trick panel game (originally to have been called *John Lloyd's Newsround* and presented by the man himself), was only in its fourth series of nearly fifty and counting, with Adams' neighbour Angus Deayton still in the chair, but they arranged a line-up which could never be surpassed when Douglas accompanied Paul Merton, versus Ian Hislop and Peter Cook. Expectations from such a legendary clash could only be too high, however, and though Douglas sported himself well, gagster Merton managed to effortlessly top any laugh his Oxbridge cohorts could come up with, leaving his teammate feeling somewhat thwarted. 'I'm not a wit,' he insisted. 'A wit says something funny on the spot. A comedy writer says something very funny two minutes later … Or in my case, two weeks later.'

He swore off all ad-libbed TV after that, but was passionate about the idea of presenting something scripted and meaningful, created with Stamp and Creasey. Although their planned documentary series *Life, The Universe and Evolution* never came to pass (the closest Adams came to presenting any more TV was the recording of special inserts for the BBC's 25th anniversary repackaging of Jacob Bronowski's groundbreaking series *The Ascent of Man* in 1998), it did lead to the trio forming the nucleus of an all-new company designed largely to make the kind of programmes and multimedia products which gave the Chief Fantasist's fascinations free rein. Ed Victor was at first reluctant to get involved, but Douglas talked him round into joining the team, even offering office space while the organisation found its feet. After so long trapped in solo composition, being part of a creative team was balm to Adams, who enthused, 'It's rather liked being in the film industry in about 1905, when the whole industry is actually being invented around you, and every idea you have is a new one.'

The company had a whole roster of dream enterprises which would never see the light of day, not all of them purely Douglas' pet projects. He would have been Executive Producer of drama series *Avatar Forest* had all gone to plan, while he had even bigger plans to act as Gene Roddenberry on his own epic (and totally tongue-out-of-cheek) sci-fi drama *The Secret Empire*, 'an alternative history of technology and space travel' which would have featured a small group of characters who find themselves reborn, *Blackadder*-style, at the cutting edge of different technologies at century-long junctures – but in this universe, space travel became widespread after Apollo 13. Whether this idea would have incorporated his further TV concept, a kind of modern *Canterbury Tales* strand called *The Oracle at Delphixus,* packed with space travellers telling tales, we will never know. TDV projects which did see the light of day included an album by Douglas' friend Robbie McIntosh, and a recording of Adams' superlative – and infamously perspiration-drenched – performance of *Hitchhiker* highlights in front of an invited audience at Islington's Almeida Theatre in August 1995. Despite his regrettable decision to wear a grey shirt under punishing lights, this selection, with the Agrajag confrontation given pride of place, showed Douglas at his absolute best as a comedian, the closest thing we have to a stand-up set from him. All of these products were dwarfed, however, by the attention given to Douglas' return to game development.

Starship Titanic has its place in the longish history of videogames that have suffered on the rack of overlong development, but it is far from the most disastrous. In the time since Infocom's closure, the bug-eyed monsters which turned Adams off gaming had reigned supreme, but he felt that the time was finally right to marry the latest graphics to a more cerebral challenge, and once again the emphasis was firmly placed on pushing the boundaries of player interaction – making the core hurdle of the game's creation the development of a speech parser unlike any other. 'It seemed to me,' he wrote, 'that what the computer enabled us to do was to reach back to the days before printing and recreate the old art of interactive storytelling. They didn't call it interactive in those days, of course. They didn't know of anything that wasn't interactive, so they didn't need a special name for it.' TDV had a superlative team of experts, and hired the brightest young things to work alongside them at their Camden Town offices, many working through the night to achieve Douglas' quite realistic aim, not to actually give life to an infallible chatty robot but to create the *illusion* of conversive intelligence via an engine which evolved into 'Spookitalk'. Money was always tight, even though the company was significantly supported by Adams' old friend Alex Catto, who had provided the venue for the original '42' debate, with investment from Apple (who provided all technology) and others. But an early bid from one bunch of venture capitalists for one-third of the company was turned down due to the common dot.com malady of overestimating the company's worth, and this one decision was to prove a fatal handicap in the long run. *ST* was also co-funded by Simon & Schuster Interactive, in a deal which included a tie-in novel and audiobook.

This is not the story of the brave sleepless coders, however; all their hard work was in service to a new Douglas Adams adventure. That it was fundamentally connected to the *Hitchhiker* Universe by dint of its basic premise – a famous luxury space liner undergoes a Spontaneous Massive Existence Failure on its maiden voyage – was inescapable, but beyond that, not one hint was given anywhere in the story, in any format, or all its reams of supporting material, that this is the same universe in any dimension. (In fact, any attempt to reference *Hitchhiker* by the player is specifically rebuffed as 'mixing up universes'.) However, to understand the plot that Adams wanted to unfold requires comparison of the game (fundamentally a first-person point-and-click adventure, inspired by *Myst*) with the novel, and the history of the latter was even more painful than the technical development, which was originally slated to see CD-ROMs hitting the shops for Christmas 1997 but ultimately had to be overhauled and salvaged by S&S to get it out four months later than planned – with extra grief added for an even later appearance on Mac.

Firstly, Douglas could not work on satisfying the game's punishing demands for dialogue and background material alone. Writer Neil Richards was hired by TDV and, alongside him, Bywater was brought in to expertly channel Adams' humour just as he did at Infocom (with additional material from respected comedy scribe Debbie Barham). The team worked together seamlessly and genially to bring to life the defective ship as designed with art-deco elegance by architect Isabel Molina and illustrator Oscar Chichoni, with all its half-mad service robots and pseudo-Edwardian literature, safe in the knowledge that Adams' esoteric forebear Robert Sheckley had agreed to turn the plot outline into the accompanying novel, and although the sci-fi pioneer had a shakier reputation than Adams he delivered his manuscript well on time. The problem was, for reasons that will never now be known to us thanks to the development of paper-shredding technology, the novel in question was quickly labelled *unpublishable* by everyone who tried to make sense of it. At first Douglas insisted that he would drive himself mad by sitting down and writing the thing himself if need be, rather than have such a book go out with his name on it (the name 'Douglas Adams' was too commercial not to put it up front on the cover, no matter who did all the hard work). 'Writing novels is what I normally do, and here was a peach because, in an amazing departure from my normal practice, I had developed a story which not only had a beginning but also a middle and (phenomenally enough) a recognisable end. However, the publishers insisted that the novel would have to come out at the same time as the game to enable them to sell it. (This struck me as odd since they had managed previously to sell books of mine without any attendant CD-ROM game at all, but this is publisher logic, and publishers are, as we all know, from the planet Zog.) I couldn't do both simultaneously.'

He realised he had made an obviously preposterous bid, and there was little surprise when Michael Bywater volunteered to steal away and put all his in-depth knowledge of the ship and its fate (gleaned not just from writing the game, but the spoof on-board magazine and website bumph) to good use by spending the three available weeks before deadline obsessively typing up a more readable novelisation, providing a handy extra income for himself into the bargain. Sadly, despite their close collaboration, this solution didn't fill Douglas with much more confidence that it would get done than his own volunteering, and he agonised as much to Jane – on whose advice, it seems (Belson being very much on the side of Michael's ex-wife since their divorce), he decided to plump for a third option.

Part of the task of bringing the ship to life with all its hilarious personalities had of course required extensive recording sessions for every possible permutation of dialogue, besides the music provided by 'Wix' Wickens. Phil Pope was one of the central cast, but the guests of honour were John

Cleese, who agreed to voice an eccentric bomb only under the pointless pseudonym of 'Kim Bread' (a nom de plume that he first requested for his *City of Death* cameo), and Terry Jones, who Douglas knew was born to play the screeching ship's parrot. If the parrot flapped into your presence while you were talking to the bomb, you effectively had one-third of Monty Python entertaining you as you solved puzzles, which would surely guarantee high sales. But having been highly tickled by the sketches and test animations he was shown at TDV, Jones let it be known that he was keen to be involved in any way that was useful – and so Adams called him up with the invitation to divorce himself from humanity for the time it took to pad out his treatment into a full, funny narrative. By sheer luck, Terry thought it would be an amusing challenge, his only stipulation being that he wanted to write it entirely in the nude, to which Douglas readily assented. But in an unpleasant echo of the bust-up with Lloyd eighteen years earlier, Bywater was incandescent with mortified anger at being so disenfranchised after all his hard work, and once again Douglas' decision to explain his move via letter, to the man he saw most days, his daughter's godfather, was not the way to return everything to sweetness and light. Lawyers were teased with a potential earner, and though they were not to be needed, the pair's long friendship only begrudgingly limped on from that point. Jones' paperback reached the shops in time – unlike the game – and sold a respectable 80,000 copies, being certainly professional, cogent, and occasionally very funny – it was only in comparison with real *Hitchhiker* that it suffered.

The thesis, antithesis and synthesis of *ST* in its two formats remain the same – and even where they differ, Terry was furnished with a general overview of the main protagonists and their story arcs – but for all that he himself had been an influence on Douglas' humour since adolescence, and that he packed the novel with suitably Adamsian ideas and jokes, Jones' book had a very different, earthier tone throughout. Both iterations tell another tale of corporate skulduggery: the Starship *Titanic* is designed by the superior masters of the planet Blerontin, the masterstroke of the greatest genius in the Galaxy, the vain Leovinus, though actually constructed by the under-appreciated craftsmen of neighbouring Yassacca. However, the ship – including the goddess-like figure who powers her, Titania, Leovinus' creation and one true love – has been jerry-built as an insurance scam by the great genius' partners, and after its disastrous SMEF the *Titanic* crashes dramatically into a house on Earth. In the game, this is your cue (egged on by a short clip of Douglas yelling at you from your TV to get on with it) to board the mighty vessel and begin putting things right on board, but the novel personifies this role with a trio of Earthlings – Lisa, a hard-nosed LA lawyer, her boyfriend Dan, and Netty, who appears to be a shallow beauty at first but ultimately becomes the real heroine. The game presents the player with a series of interlinked challenges, beginning (of course) with the task of securing an upgrade from the bureaucratic Deskbot, before recording a melody (actually composed by Adams) in the music section, finding the ingredients of a galactic cocktail, and so on, usually leading to the reclamation of different parts of Titania's missing anatomy, whereas the progress made by the novel's trio takes a number of unique turns. It's easily forgotten, leaving aside his medieval scholarship and magical children's stories, that Terry Jones is probably the naughtiest Python alive, and his work has regularly featured themes that go beyond the bawdy to the downright filthy. Where Adams spent pages prefacing his one vaguely erotic passage with awkward disclaimers, Jones' characters – whether as a result of naked composition or not – rip each others' clothes off at the earliest possible opportunity (albeit that opportunity is presumed imminent death), and once Lisa seduces the one alien protagonist, The Journalist (known as 'The' for short), the aroused Blerontinian spends much of the rest of the book panting for further fornication, Earth-style.

As suggested by their Comic Relief collaboration, Jones' jokes tended to be far more freewheeling and therefore numerous than Adams fans were used to, while the traditional sci-fi problem of alien interaction, elegantly solved by Douglas with the Babel fish, was simply slapped aside by Jones with a Blerontinian's explanation that their native language is all but identical to English, which is 'pretty convenient for writers of science fiction' – a spot of fantastically facetious fourth-wall-breaking that no deadline would have compelled Adams to include. However, perhaps aided by the danger-ously compacted composition time, this facetiousness is at least entirely consistent – the book is openly silly from the very first page:

> "Where is Leovinus?" demanded the Gat of Blerontis, Chief
> Quantity Surveyor of the entire North Eastern Gas District of the
> planet of Blerontin. "No! I do not want another bloody fish-paste
> sandwich!"

He did not exactly use the word 'bloody' because it did not exist in the Blerontin language. The word he used could be more literally translated as 'similar in size to the left earlobe', but the meaning was much closer to 'bloody'. Nor did he actually use the phrase 'fish-paste', since fish do not exist on Blerontin in the form in which we would understand them to be fish. But when one is translating from a language used by a civilisation of which we know nothing, located as far away as the centre of the Galaxy, one has to approximate. Similarly the Gat of Blerontis was not exactly a 'Quantity Surveyor' and certainly the term 'North Eastern Gas District' gives no idea at all about the magnificence and grandeur of his position. Look, perhaps I'd better start again ...

In the introduction (which, in astonishing testament to the rushed production, was mis-formatted with vast swathes of tabs, breaking the text up over a dozen pages), the man with his name at the top of the book assured the reader that Terry 'has written an altogether sillier, naughtier and more wonderful novel than I would have done and in doing so has earned himself an altogether unique credit – "Parrot and Novel by Terry Jones"'. Although few *Hitchhiker* fans agreed with Douglas' verdict, it was an incredible achievement for a man who had never even written sci-fi before.

Both narratives conclude with a return to Earth (in a 3D mini-game, on CD-ROM), and a meeting with Leovinus (another 'greatest genius in the Galaxy' not unlike Adams' imprisoned avatar in the *SLATFATFish* epilogue) who is played in the game, of course, by the Frood himself, with unashamed reference to his reputation for cerebral dominance, and the outstanding topography of his face was also scanned in for one section of the game, alongside Stamp and original producer Ted Barnes. As Leovinus, Adams gave the victorious player a short valedictory speech which seemed to belie the millions of pounds spent on the project by touchingly having all the hallmarks of a home video filmed in the park and featuring a large and not terribly gifted actor wrapped in a curtain. And yet, though relatively innocuous on its first viewing in 1998, in hindsight Douglas' cameo has attained a strangely haunting quality:

Good afternoon, my name is Leovinus. You probably know that.
I'm sorry about what's happened to you, I'm even more sorry

about what's happened to me. You have lost a house, I have lost a life and a dream. You may not care about my life and my dream. Well, I don't really care about your house. Building this ship was my dream and now that dream is over. All I want is the love of a good woman and also a fishing rod. Thank you for restoring Titania. I know she isn't real, well, she's real but she's not really real if you see what I mean. So to be honest I'm more inclined to place long-term faith in the fishing rod. By the galactic laws of salvage, this ship is now yours. There is nothing like her in the Universe. I wish you joy of her. I hope you managed to sort out the bomb. As for me, don't try to look for me, you won't find me. My life's work is done, and I've gone fishing. Goodbye.

Despite the game's sore-thumb resemblance in any gaming environment, it garnered reasonable reviews in the spring of 1998 and won a 'Codie' award, without halting the march of console titles that favour bloodlust over lateral thinking – and, with thirty talented staff members working over two years, without profit. 'What we decided to do in this game,' Douglas sighed, 'was go for the non-psychopath sector of the market. And that was a little hubristic because there really isn't a non-psychopath sector of the market.'

If *ST* made any great impression, it was as one of the leading examples of cross-platform media, packed with extra content in a way that is now almost expected in modern gaming: a secret Yassaccan intranet proved so popular with gamers who found their way there that a secret forum community thrived online for years. There was even the option of downloading the entire novel online for free – the only hitch being that every word was listed in alphabetical order.

The Hitchhiker's Guide To Earth

Alongside *ST*'s eventful development, a team had been working continually on TDV's other primary project, which would eventually, slowly and painfully mutate into the current h2g2.com – a concept envisaged from nothing by Adams and its other instigators, but which in modern parlance would fundamentally boil down to 'Wikipedia with snark'. Apple had actually looked into the possibility of some form of 'real' Hitchhiker's Guide in the 1980s, but finally, technology was beginning to catch up with the model of online reference which Douglas had described all those years earlier (Ford's updating of his Guide entries on the Sub-Etha Net in *SLATFATFish* no longer has the slightest hint of technological exoticism) and, in tribute to the techie seer, the code driving the site would become known as 'DNA'.

So many of the features of this intended 'Hitchhiker's Guide to Earth' are now taken for granted thanks to a wide array of sites, apps and online options, but Douglas would not be the man to make his clear vision of the future a popular reality. 'When I invented *Hitchhiker*,' he said, 'I didn't think of myself as being a predictive science fiction writer, but I kept returning to the Guide as a good idea – something that, instead of being compiled by an editor, everyone could work on together. But there were two things that needed to be in place. One is the web, which lets people share everything. But there's a limitation on the web in terms of creating a real-time, on-the-fly collaborative guide – people log in at their desks. The real change takes place when the second shoe falls, which is mobile computing, and that is beginning to arrive now. We're beginning to get Internet access on mobile phones and PDAs. That creates a sea change, because suddenly people will be able to get information that is appropriate to where they are and who they are – standing outside the cinema or a restaurant or waiting for a bus or plane. Or sitting having a cup of coffee at a café. With h2g2, you can look up where you are at that moment to see what it says, and if the information you need is not there you add it in yourself. For example, a remark about the coffee you're drinking or a comment that the waiter is very rude.'

The idea, of course, was that this network of reference and review would be totally user-led, corralled by a small editorial team – which TDV could ill afford. There had been more convoluted plans, as masterminded by one short-lived project overseer, to fill the site with cartoon 'Hitcher' avatars for all members, but these were quickly abandoned in favour of the more straightforward model of website which Adams helped launch live on *Tomorrow's World* from the British Library in April 1999 – triggering, inevitably, a horrific server crash when thousands of potential contributors all logged on at once, many to offer such scintillating copy as "teh anser is 42!!!1!" *(sic)*.

The all-important mobile aspect of h2g2 outlined by Adams above was supposedly to come into play with the WAP launch eight months later, made possible by the intervention of Vodaphone, but this deal had the crippling problem that they retained any proceeds. In fact, so many money-making schemes were wildly bandied around at the company meetings, to try and make h2g2's wonderful plans pay off, not just for the creators but for their employees and the survival of TDV itself, that Douglas' new-found equanimity with *Hitchhiker*'s popularity stretched further, into a desire to use any part of the lore to raise revenue. A trading post was immaculately prepared, linked to a scheme, in those pre-Bitcoin days, to pay Researchers with 'Altairian Dollars', until it was pointed out that they didn't actually have so much as a towel to *sell* online. A scheme to set up a chain of restaurants called 'Milliways', where diners could lunch via webcam with friends all over the world, was whispered to be on the verge of being funded by an Arabian princess, but that was just one more massively improbable notion to add to the markers on the company's bumpy ride.

Douglas earned ovations for his inventive lectures on science and technology, including a barnstorming ad hoc address in front of the brightest scientists in the UK at the Cambridge Digital Biota 2 in 1998, titled *Is There An Artificial God?* (in which he attempted to explain about 'the four ages of sand' and never quite got there, but nobody minded). He felt at home in such cerebral company, and often reflected, 'Certainly, in my field, I've frequently been struck by correspondences between the way that a physicist goes about trying to get new ideas, new perceptions about the way things work, and the way that, as a comedy writer, it is the sudden unexpected correspondences and corellations between hitherto disconnected things which suddenly lead you onto a new principle, a new insight ...'

However, his own submissions for h2g2 (besides his initial call to all potential Researchers: 'We have the first snowflake, now let's build a blizzard') tended to be more modest, comprising the pernickety English rules of tea-making, and post-Christmas hangover cures. Under the moniker of 'DNA', Douglas of course had the user number 42, but was equally likely to be found on his own forum on douglasadams.com, launched in late '98. Of course, he had been savvy with life online for longer than almost anyone, mixing with his fans, and regularly popped up on newsgroups and fan communities (often connected to Pink Floyd or gadgetry), similar to the way in which his flirting with desktop publishing in the mid-1980s inspired him to send fans a short-lived round robin called 'The Ring Pull', letting them know what he had been up to. The WWW made all such communication easier, of course: 'Cyberspace is – or can be – a good, friendly and egalitarian place to meet. I enjoy corresponding with people in completely different areas of the net that have nothing to do with who I am, but are just about things I'm interested in. I get the occasional "Excuse me for asking, but are you the Adams who wrote ...?" etc., which is fine, but I really like to leave it behind if I can. What I don't enjoy is being picked on by smartasses. I guess it comes with the territory, but I still don't like it, and this is me saying so. If you have some involved reason for thinking that I am not me, then please sort it out for yourself and don't bother me with it. I know who I am, and if you have a problem with that, then it stays your problem.'

It's hard to deny that much of the tone of Adams' contributions to his own forum tended to give the impression of a really rather grumpy old one-time-comedy-sci-fi writer as the 1990s progressed. When that famous face would pop up in the media, Douglas' voluminous body seemed in some ways to be ageing at a faster rate than those of his contemporaries, with his close-cropped thinning white hair aesthetically adding a decade or two onto his forty-plus years, particularly given his adoption of spectacles (a particular wrench, as he used to revel in taking unnecessary eye tests just for the pleasure of being told by opticians that he had the best eyesight they had ever encountered). With ageing in mind, he continued to be wary of his health as his rich appetites pushed him up towards the nineteen-stone mark and he was diagnosed with high blood pressure and Type 2 diabetes, and so his exercise regime remained as vigorous as his size could cope with. As if to complement his more professorial appearance, his online demeanour also often seemed increasingly irascible, his perspectives on life's short-falls sometimes plain crabby, where once he could laugh at anything. But then, being an online celebrity obviously has many pitfalls, and this was Web pre-2.0, the careful PR-conscious etiquette of Twitter was many years off, he could be grumpy if he wanted to. Just as Douglas volubly regretted favouring the Arts over Science, he was candid about admitting to the phenomenon that eventually befalls the majority of comedians – the middle-aged loss of love for Comedy itself. Peter Cook once ominously foretold that Britain was in danger of 'sinking giggling into the sea', and by the turn of the millennium Adams wrote a piece which showed he was in accord, inspired by what seems to have been a famous stand-up set by George Carlin:

> I'm often asked if I'm not a bit of a turncoat. Twenty years
> (help!) ago in *Hitchhiker,* I made my reputation making fun of

science and technology: depressed robots, uncooperative lifts, doors with ludicrously over-designed user interfaces (what's wrong with just pushing them?), and so on. Now I seem to have become one of technology's chief advocates … Nowadays everybody's a comedian, even the weather girls and continuity announcers. We laugh at everything. Not intelligently any more, not with sudden shock, astonishment, or revelation, just relentlessly and meaninglessly … There's always a moment when you start to fall out of love, whether it's with a person or an idea or a cause, even if it's one you only narrate to yourself years after the event: a tiny thing, a wrong word, a false note, which means that things can never be quite the same again. For me it was hearing a stand-up comedian make the following observation: "These scientists, eh? They're so stupid! You know those black-box flight recorders they put on aeroplanes? And you know they're meant to be indestructible? It's always the thing that doesn't get smashed? So *why don't they make the planes out of the same stuff?*" The audience roared with laughter at how stupid scientists were, couldn't think their way out of a paper bag, but I sat feeling uncomfortable. Was I just being pedantic to feel that the joke didn't really work because flight recorders are made out of titanium and that if you made planes out of titanium rather than aluminium, they'd be far too heavy to get off the ground in the first place? I began to pick away at the joke. Supposing Eric Morecambe had said it? Would it be funny then? Well, not quite, because that would have relied on the audience seeing that Eric was being dumb – in other words, they would have had to know as a matter of common knowledge about the relative weights of titanium and aluminium. There was no way of deconstructing the joke (if you think this is obsessive behaviour, you should try living with it) that didn't rely on the teller and the audience complacently conspiring together to jeer at someone *who knew more than they did.* It sent a chill down my spine, and still does. I felt betrayed by comedy in the same way that gangsta rap now makes me feel betrayed by rock music. I also began to wonder how many of the jokes I was making were just, well, ignorant.

Adams' natural wit was not in danger of dimming, but he was to insist, 'We're at a very, very interesting point in our history, at all sorts of cross-roads for the human race. If we're going to understand and respond to them properly, we need to make some perspective shifts, and it would be inter-esting to work out ways of telling stories which illustrate that. They might well be ironic in all kinds of ways, and funny where appropriate, but if I'm no longer saying, "My first job is to be funny", then I might end up doing something that satisfies me slightly more.'

Perhaps he had good reason not to resemble a sunbeam too closely at this time, however – in the wake of the legendary 'dot.com crash' of 2000, with all of TDV's problems coming to a head, he was soon quoted as lamenting, 'I just lost my brilliant dot.com company, which, like everybody else's brilliant dot.com company, was based on the idea that if you multiply zero by a suffi-ciently large number it will suddenly turn into something.' In early 2001 the BBC would quite fittingly overtake the hosting of h2g2 for the next decade, making 'DNA' a crucial part of its online technology – which seemed to be some small consolation.

I've Been All Over The Future. Spend Half My Time There.

Although the company originally intended above all to make superior television, the only other TDV productions of note were broadcast on Radio 4, right where Adams' career began. Douglas' was a familiar voice on the world's greatest spoken-word station, although in the spring of 2000 his task was a heavy one – to pay tribute to the great Peter Jones, who had only become funnier with every passing year as the star of *Just a Minute* but became the first core member of the *Hitchhiker* team to pass away, at the age of 79, assumedly putting the kibosh on any further wireless adventures for Arthur and Co.

In TDV's death throes, Adams presented two radio projects – *The Internet: The Last Battleground of the Twentieth Century*, and a short series broadcast at the end of 2000, which he tried to prevent being called *The Hitchhiker's Guide to the Future* but soon settled for the inevitable. In a way they were attempts to save a lot of time by sharing his views of modern technology with the world – he had become such a guru, he was repeatedly approached after his lectures by terrified people from the fields of publishing, broadcasting and so on, wondering how their media could survive in the brave new world – with *H2GF*, he could outline their very real need to fear once and for all. The documentaries were of course wittily presented, mingling expert opinion – the fascinating sound of tech experts riding the wave of a new era – with Adams' personal take on the Internet: 'I only wish it had been around when I was growing up. I was at boarding school in Essex, and when I was about fourteen my family moved down to Dorset, where it was beautiful, but I didn't know anybody. And since I was away at school for two-thirds of the year, I never really got the chance to, and was pretty lonely. Being able to reach people via the Internet would have transformed my life – I wouldn't have just sat at home reading science fiction and listening to the radio and ... actually, maybe it was just as well, come to think of it.'

Adams' reputation for epigrams of solid gold has always made his name one of those likely to be credited with punchy but misattributed modern adages – the one about bleeding from the forehead was one he specifically denied, and he was equally not the originator of Danny Hillis' wise claim that 'technology is the word we use for things that don't work yet'. Of the pages and pages of Adams quotes we can now summon up at will, however, one of the most pleasing takes a similar approach:

> I've come up with a set of rules that describe our reactions to technologies:
> 1. Anything that is in the world when you're born is normal and ordinary and is just a natural part of the way the world works.
> 2. Anything that's invented between when you're fifteen and thirty-five is new and exciting and revolutionary and you can probably get a career in it.
> 3. Anything invented after you're thirty-five is against the natural order of things.

Admittedly, some of Adams' technological musings now seem so understandably green that it's hard to resist an urge to hug him when, for instance, he aired his frustrations with early mobile technology: 'You can't win. If the machine's small enough to go in your pocket it's too small to type on. Well, I've found the answer. Forgive me if you knew this already, perhaps I'm the last person in the world to find this out. Anyway, the answer is this: you grip the palmtop between both hands and you type with your thumbs. Seriously. It works. It feels a bit awkward to begin with, and your hands ache a little from using unaccustomed muscles, but you get used to it surprisingly quickly. I've clocked up 1,000 words now ...' To any modern teenager with thumb muscles like walnuts, this charming discovery must seem like a caveman realising that mammoth hides are warm in the winter.

The new radio series opened many eyes to what was just around the corner in the new millennium, and launched with a whole host of accompanying videos and extra material on the website – a credit to TDV, but obviously never a financial one. However, perhaps the most exciting announcement made by TDV towards the end came in late '98 – although, in a familiar pattern, it would come to nothing. In a different universe, however, the summer of 2000 was to have seen the launch of 'a brand new *Hitchhiker* game for home computers and consoles, which is currently being described as "an action-adventure game involving cricket, tea, petunias and very long lunches"'. As the press release went on to establish, the reason this 3D adventure was mooted was the surely absolutely final, long-cherished appearance of the ultimate pea under Adams' mattress – this time, the *Hitchhiker* movie was going to happen. Honestly.

It was with great regret that Adams and Nesmith's deal had fallen through a few years earlier, but they pledged to work together some day, maybe on a *Dirk* movie which seemed equally improbable, but a way of bringing Gently's first adventure to the screen had occurred to Adams when he saw a celebrated Oxford Playhouse adaptation, and enjoyed it enough to revisit for a second staging, made possible by the financial patronage of Rowan Atkinson. Whatever his and Nez's joint venture would be, Douglas said, 'I just hope that there will be other projects in the future that he and I will work on together, because I like him enormously and we get on very well. And also, the more time I get to spend in Santa Fe, the better.' James Cameron was briefly dangled as a potential helmer after he and Douglas hit it off on a white-water-rafting expedition – by this time, Cameron's own *Titanic* project had become an immeasurably bigger hit than Adams'. Before long, though, a great consolation was to come along in the form of Jay Roach, a director and producer with a deft comic touch who was just about to enjoy his first major hit when he met Douglas – *Austin Powers* being one of the surprise blockbusters of the late 1990s, a left-field spy spoof which

had itself been through development hell before proving everybody wrong.
Not only was Roach a huge *Hitchhiker* fan, his star Mike Myers was also
keen to add his name to the long list of possible Zaphods. Obviously, by this
stage Douglas approached any movie announcement with a similar tremu-
lousness to The Boy Who Cried Wolf's latter expostulations, but he was
certain he had found the right collaborator this time: 'The key to the whole
thing, in many ways, was when I met Jay Roach, because I hit it off very
well with him, and thought, "Here's a very bright, intelligent guy. Not only
is he a bright, intelligent guy, but here's a measure of how bright and intelligent he is: he wants me to work very closely on his movie." Which is always
something that endears a writer to a director. In fact, when I was making
the original radio series, it was unheard of to do what I did, because I'd just
written it, but I kind of inserted myself in the whole production process.
The producer/director was a little surprised by this, but in the end took it in
very good grace. So I had a huge amount to do with the way the programme
developed, and that's exactly what Jay wants me to do on this movie. So I
felt, "Great, here's somebody I can do business with!" Obviously I'm saying
that at the beginning of a process that's going to take two years. So who
knows what's going to happen? All I can say is that at this point in the game,
things are set as fair as they possibly could be. I feel very optimistic and
excited about that.'

With the two of them working together, before the end of the year 'twenty
years of constipation' seemed to be over when a solid deal was hammered
out with Caravan, subsequently renamed Spyglass Entertainment, an indie
company who were nonetheless 'joined at the hip' with the ultimate media
juggernaut (and infamous warper of English Literature properties) Disney.
Some fans were already climbing the walls at the idea of the House of Mouse
Disneyfying their beloved *Hitchhiker*, but Douglas fired back, 'There's a lot
of misunderstanding about the fact that this is going to be a Disney movie.
Disney is a huge media empire and it doesn't just make Walt Disney pictures.
Yes, it made *Bambi* (first movie I ever saw), but it also made *Pulp Fiction*.'
(The film whose 'adrenaline shot' sequence caused Douglas to faint on a
plane.)

There was briefly a plan to adapt the books for Imax cinemas in forty-
minute episodes: 'I'm tremendously excited about Imax, because I don't
feel it's been used properly ... What I realised was that you don't have to
use the whole of the screen all the time, or you can use different parts of

it. So I can imagine the movie opening with Arthur Dent's bedroom in the bottom corner and there's Arthur waking up and so on. The rest of the screen is black, but then gradually you can see that there are stars, and a Vogon Constructor Fleet moving through the darkness. I think this has tremendous potential.' This format would also circumvent the seemingly impossible task of fitting the narrative to a ninety-minute slot, but it soon became apparent that an Imax exclusive would be commercial death.

Hitchhiker was one of a group of fantasy properties – *Good Omens* and *Watchmen* being prevalent examples – which were stuck in development hell for so long that crazy rumours were a mainstay of every movie magazine and site. It's true that Adams was content to envisage either Hugh Laurie or Hugh Grant – in his first burst of Richard Curtis-fuelled popularity – as Arthur (the only character that he insisted had to be British), with Jim Carrey exercising his box-office gold facial muscles as Zaphod, but it always seemed too early for any rumour to mean anything, and he teased, 'Anything else is hearsay and Chinese whispers. Especially the stuff from an unnamed "reliable source". I'd like to try an experiment, and here it is : I hereby categorically deny that the part of Arthur Dent is going to be played by Oprah Winfrey.'

Adams gloomily suggested that the new interest was largely down to the success of another sci-fi comedy, based on a comic book, *Men in Black*, which certainly brought the alien community down to Earth, and featured a miniaturised Galaxy and an everyman who discovers a very silly extraterrestrial world on his doorstep. But otherwise the hit had so little in common with *Hitchhiker* that there was more than a hint of paranoia in Douglas' insinuations when he said, '*Men in Black* came out this past year, so suddenly somebody has done it already. And *MiB* is .... How can I put this delicately? There were elements of it I found quite familiar, shall we say? And suddenly a comedy science fiction movie that was very much in the same vein as *Hitchhiker* became one of the most successful movies ever made. So that kind of changed the landscape a little bit ... It's been very frustrating not to have made it in the last fifteen years,' he added, unnecessarily, 'nevertheless, I feel extremely buoyed by the fact that one can make a much, much, much better movie out of it now than one could have fifteen years ago ... If I said I wasn't highly delighted about this, I would, of course, be a lying bastard. Although it's been a long, long wait since the idea was first mooted, now is a better time to make it than then. However, I do want to be cautious. Announcing an agreement to do a deal is a very different thing from announcing the release of a movie.' *MiB* comparisons may seem spurious, but 1999 saw the release of a film with a clearer debt to *Hitchhiker* – *Galaxy Quest* told the tale of a gang of Grebulon-like aliens who beg the cast of a thinly veiled *Star Trek* TV show to fight for them, notable among this useless crew being Alan Rickman as a morose Spock cypher, and Sam Rockwell as the biggest loser on board.

After a couple of years of working with the new set-up, facing a minimum of ten return trips a year (despite his love of gadgetry, Douglas hated satellite-linked virtual meetings), and still harbouring a feeling of exclusion from discussions (triggering his infamous open letter to Disney executive David Vogel, exhaustively including every possible way to contact him, so 'If you manage not to reach me, I shall know you're trying not to very, very hard indeed'), Adams was confident enough with the movie's progress to make a truly enormous decision. After much no doubt vociferous conference with Jane, who was always reluctant to Americanise, the Adams family were officially to decamp to the USA, permanently. Jane had qualified to practise law there (even if she never did) while Polly would grow up with great teeth and lots of solar Vitamin E, and not one element of the film's production would escape her father (it also did no harm that the Pacific coast offered a far more convenient base for scuba-diving, his greatest pleasure). 'I love the sense of space and the "can do" attitude of Americans,' he insisted. 'It's a good place to bring up children, and even the state schools are considered of excellent quality. Living in Islington, we would probably have to move to get Polly in a good school anyway. That or send her across town.' Adams' hatred of LA was more than cancelled out by his devotion to quieter idyllic locales along the coast, particularly Santa Barbara, which just happened to be a rather cosy distance from John Cleese's ranch. Douglas even managed to persuade his old mentor to make a fleeting cameo as an interviewer in a special pop video for his friend Margo Buchanan's track *Rockstar*, featuring six-year-old Polly in the title role, which was made to test the capabilities of Apple's new iMovie software – Adams proudly showed off Polly's first starring role to anyone in sight.

He made sure to leave the move until after attending Paul McCartney's legendary return to The Cavern Club, backed up by old mate David Gilmour, and prior to decamping to the sunshine full-time Douglas explained, 'People may say the grass is always greener on the other side, but it is, and there's a reason for it – we call it crop rotation.' Our Frood always tended to be modest about his reputation as a prophet, but it would ultimately be to everyone's dismay that his worst predictions were the conclusion to his assurance to Dawkins: 'The world is a thing of utter inordinate complexity and richness and strangeness … the opportunity to spend seventy or eighty years of your life in such a universe is time well spent, as far as I am concerned.' Then there was his valedictory recommendation that it was a good idea, 'in the depths of middle age, just upping sticks and going somewhere else. You reinvent your life and start again. It is invigorating.'

So, This Is It …

As the family settled into their new glamorous gated community in the village of Montecito, work continued apace on the movie – even though it had already been badly derailed once by Disney's offer of a green light for a $45m budget, whereas Adams was holding out for nearly double that amount to really bring his vision to screens. Ed Victor was beside himself at his client and friend's obstruction to finally getting the project over and done with, but Adams insisted that he couldn't bear for the film to be dismissed as 'cheesy'. '*Hitchhiker* is cheesy!' Ed countered. 'That's its charm. It's not *Star Wars*. You keep on wanting to make *Star Wars* with jokes. But it's not!' But after nearly two decades of frustrated gestation, Douglas needed to see his creation reach the world's multiplexes in the grandest form possible, and he wasn't about to compromise after so much struggle. It was as if, having triumphed in pretty much every medium in which he reworked the story – albeit with reservations in visual formats – *Hitchhiker* positively *demanded* this last tribute from the creator, this one final piece of the puzzle which had escaped his grasp, a sleek reimagining in the biggest entertainment arena of all, for the Frood to gain that most American of concepts, 'closure'.

Victor was as keen as anyone for the film simply to *get made*, and with a very good reason, of course – there was still a further Douglas Adams novel under contract, but this time the Pan-Macmillan deal was particularly extraordinary, representing a whole new world of hopeful, silent, fervid dreaming that they would get the book they paid for. It had been the best part of a decade since *MH*, but deadlines were no longer a phenomenon Adams would enjoy hearing whoosh by, they were merely dispensed with, in the hope that the great man would *eventually* come through with his next adventure – although, it was felt, the longer the gaps between novels, the weaker the selling power that the author's name radiated from bookshelves.

Going under a whole host of titles, like previous books, Adams' eighth novel was originally teased at the start of the 1990s as a third Dirk adventure, 'A Spoon Too Short', before the knowing replacement *Salmon of Doubt* became public knowledge. The title was an inversion of the Celtic legend of the Salmon of Knowledge (a mystical fish caught by Finn McCool after seven hard years, but then harvested of its precious drops of wisdom when his back is turned – fundamentally, a warning against procrastination) but not one scrap of material has surfaced to explain any specific relevance to the book Adams was trying, from time to time, to write.

As usual, he had a number of plot strands to juggle with, and no clear idea of how to weave them together, though the chapters continuing Gently's saga – still featuring Kate and the frustrated Thor – contained some of the very funniest material written for the detective, which belied any claimed desire to move away from comedy. This time Dirk was alerted to the problem of a cat with its hindquarters stuck in another dimension, and the novelty of a mysterious figure paying money into his usually negative bank account, and this would somehow incorporate one of Adams' most brilliant passages, trying to envisage the world from the point of view of a rampaging white rhino in LA. One press release – Pan going so far as to mindlessly optimistically release a planned cover image – of course cleared nothing up:

Dirk Gently, hired by someone he never meets, to do a
job that is never specified, starts following people at random.
His investigations lead him to Los Angeles, through the nasal
membranes of a rhinoceros, to a distant future dominated by estate
agents and heavily armed kangaroos. Jokes, lightly poached fish, and
the emergent properties of complex systems form the background
to Dirk Gently's most baffling and incomprehensible case.

Some extracts would perhaps have been deleted if Adams had ever reached a polishing phase, including the awkward directness of his narrative voice when he admitted, on introducing a well-dressed character, 'I'm very bad at clothes and if I started telling you that it was an Armani this or a What's-her-name Farhi that, you would know instinctively that I was faking it, and since you are taking the trouble to read what I have written, I intend to treat you with respect even if I do, occasionally and in a friendly and well-meaning kind of way, lie to you.' Nevertheless, the plot had been written up to at least a handful of perfectly pitched chapters, and boasted some brilliant new Gently philosophy, such as 'Solutions nearly always come from the direction you least expect, which means there's no point trying to look in that direction because it won't be coming from there ... Logic comes afterwards. It's how we retrace our steps. It's being wise after the event. Before the event you have to be very silly.' But despite all this, Adams simply dropped the idea halfway through the decade, feeling Dirk simply didn't fit the story which remained hidden somewhere within that mighty brain, resulting in a most unexpected planned switch: 'For some reason I couldn't get it going, so I had put it aside. I didn't know what to do with it. I looked at the material again about a year later, and suddenly thought, "Actually, the reason is that the ideas and the character don't match. I've tried to go for the wrong kind of ideas, and these ideas would actually fit much better in a *Hitchhiker* book, but I don't want to write another *Hitchhiker* book at the moment." So I sort of put them on one side. And maybe one day I will write another *Hitchhiker* book, because there's an awful lot of material sitting around waiting to go in it.'

Much to his own surprise, the time away from Arthur and cohorts had allowed many ideas involving them to take root in Douglas' mind, and he was happy to let fans be assured that, contrary to all evidence, *Hitchhiker* was not dead, and his angry conclusion to the 'last' *Hitchhiker* book did not in any way preclude a further entry in the 'increasingly inaccurately named trilogy': 'Someone said to me the other day, "Are they all really dead?" And I had to say, "Well, this is A) fiction, it's B) *science* fiction, and it's C) *comedy* science fiction ... what do you mean by 'really'?" As far as I was concerned, killing them all off at the end was just a question of being sort of neat and tidy about it.' That ending provided another bonus this time round, he reflected, to *Doctor Who Magazine*'s eager query about further hitching adventures: 'I hesitate to say "never again" because look what happened to Sean Connery! So I can't say "never again" because then I'll immediately go off and do another one. Actually, it would be much easier to do another one now than previously, because I took the precaution of killing off all the characters at the end of the last one. It's much easier to start it off because I know where all the characters are – they're dead! In a science fiction novel death is not a hindrance to anything. A lot of people got very upset about that as if one's actually killed real people in some way. These are characters in a science fiction novel, for God's sake! In the past they would all end up scattered everywhere at the end of a novel, so in the next novel you write you spend the first third of it acting less like an author and more like a sheepdog, trying to round all the characters up. That's one of the reasons Zaphod didn't appear in the last book, because I just couldn't work out how to gather him in.'

With all past nightmares forgotten, Douglas was adamant, 'There will come a point where I will write a sixth *Hitchhiker* book. I kind of want to do that because people have said, quite rightly, that *MH* is a very bleak book. And it *was* a bleak book. The reason for that is very simple – I was having a lousy year, for all sorts of personal reasons that I don't want to go into, I just had a thoroughly miserable year, and I was trying to write a book against that background. And, guess what? It was a rather bleak book! I would love to finish *Hitchhiker* on a slightly more upbeat note, so five seems to be a wrong kind of number, six is a better kind of number. I think a lot of the stuff which was originally in *Salmon* really wasn't working, and could be yanked out and put together with some new thoughts.'

One strand which survives to tantalise fans for ever documented a character called Dave who lives in his own self-made environment, millions of years after the extinction of humanity, and that could feasibly have led to some further source of irritation for Dent. And then, of course, he also had those radio-based events on the Planet of the Birds involving the cloned archaelogist Lintilla borne in mind, for folding back into the novel canon. Douglas' last documented views on the best of his *Hitchhiker* work showed that when it came to favourites, 'In different moods I will feel either the radio or the book … it's got to be one of those, hasn't it? I feel differently about each of them. The radio series was where it originated; that's where the seed grew … On the other hand, the appeal of the books to me is that it's just me. The great appeal of a book to any writer is that it is just them. That's it. There's nobody else involved. That's not quite true, of course, because the thing developed out of a radio series in the first place, and there is a sense in there of all the people who have contributed, in one way or another, to the radio show that it grew out of. But, nevertheless, there is a "this-is-all-my-own-work" feel about a book.'

But then, two years after this positivity, Douglas told interviewers that whatever book he was working on, it would be neither *Dirk* nor *Hitchhiker*.

In truth, he was suffering from his usual lack of inclination to put in the hours and honour contracts, but in theory he had at least four separate titles evolving in his imagination. One completely stand-alone idea was pencilled in as *The Difference Engineer*, which seemed to hark back to his very first plot outline for *Hitchhiker*, in which an Earthling finds himself caught up in a galaxy split by war, with one side headed by a Goddess-like 'She' figure, originally to be called Mrs Rogers. In this story, the everyman hero was to be a mechanic who fixes a crashed spaceship and joins its owners without realising that they are actually the bad guys. He also had a *LCTS* follow-up in mind for the future, for when Polly reached a certain stage: 'I think I'll wait for her hormones to kick in, then I'll be off.'

With no publisher threatening to imprison him in a luxury hotel suite, however, none of Adams' literary exploits could take precedence over the film. Despite the slow evolution of his screenplay, Douglas' celebrated nose was put somewhat out of joint by the reaction to his impassioned open letter to Vogel being the hiring of a new writer, Josh Friedman, who had scripted *Chain Reaction*. Douglas was hurt by his appointment, but was assured by the producers that it was normal practice, that Friedman was a craftsman who could make the story work how Hollywood needed it to. Although he was already a *Hitchhiker* fan, the screenplay that Friedman produced was leaked online and, in a repeat of the unpleasantness with Abbie Bernstein, the revolted reactions from fans dragged Douglas' name into the mud. The entertainment website IGN uploaded an excoriating script review, saving particular disgust for the new concept of Zaphod's extra arm and head being able to shoot out at will, thanks to CG effects, which Douglas and Jay had worked out together.

The apparent addition of new characters (Jeltz's equally horrible colleague Kwaltz and Galactic Vice President Questular Rontok, there to guide the Vogon villains' bureaucratic antagonism) also wrinkled brows. But they were furrowed further by the whole second act, which introduced another hitherto unknown figure, Humma Kavula, a shady nightclub owner – somewhere between Sallah in *Indiana Jones* and James Bond's Q – who points them towards the final act, on Magrathea:

INT. HUMMA KAVULA'S SPACE STATION. STRIP ROOM.
Smoky, noisy. On a small stage, an alien CREATURE is stripping. It has many legs and tentacles, some arbitrarily covered with small

tasselly garments which it waves around. An AUDIENCE of mixed
species watches. Most are bored, but a few creatures of the same
species as the stripper watch with excitement. The last piece of
cloth comes off with a flourish to reveal a patch of skin which
pulsates with a green light. The creatures watching go crazy.
They pulsate green all over and shout "Hubba hubba hubba!"
Creatures of other species look blankly into their drinks. Zaphod,
Ford, Trillian and Arthur move along the back wall, through a
small door and into …
INT. HUMMA KAVULA'S SPACE STATION. COMEDY ROOM.
A large LIZARD is on stage, completely still. After a few seconds it
moves slightly. An audience of lizards falls about laughing. Ford
confides to Arthur.

FORD

It's all in the timing.

Arthur watches in blank incomprehension as fresh screeches of
laughter go round the audience.

FORD (cont'd)

Plus you gotta be a lizard.

Humma Kavula, a big disreputable guy, quietly hugs Zaphod.

HUMMA KAVULA

My man! Through here.

He ushers them into a back room.

The Questular character went through a number of changes, from being
the good guy who has to deal with Zaphod's messes (spending huge swathes
of screen time spouting exposition with 'nerdy engineer' Eldred Varsimon,
the *HoG* designer detailed to track the ship down), to the film's main villain,
the malign hand guiding the Vogons – such dramatic shifts show how loosely
the character was drawn, right up to Adams' last draft.

The episodic nature of the source material demanded some kind of
completely unique middle section, and Douglas was always clear when he
said, 'The best thing I can say about the movie is that it will be specifically
contradicting the first book.' But he shared fans' dismay at the leaked script,
and indeed sat down right away and rattled off a whole new draft from
scratch, for free, taking on board Friedman's useful additions but bringing
it more in line with his own plans. Completing the new features was the

idea that the Vogons' home planet guided their small-minded adhesion to red tape by having a natural defence against original thought – rocks which rain down to crush anyone with a good idea – a Magrathean brainwave, part of their plan to create a race of drones which went so badly wrong that the planet-makers disappeared into hibernation. Adams was so proud of this blend of evolutionary philosophy and broad slapstick that he handed around copies to everyone at TDV, fresh off the plane from LA on one of his last visits home.

Despite over twenty years of being a target for fans, he had become something of a literary fanboy himself, thanks to discovering the wonders of J. K. Rowling's *Harry Potter* series – at first with Polly in mind, but ultimately with even more child-like passion than she could muster. Douglas had been keen to write something for children himself since before Polly was born (only managing to pen a few scraps of comical non-fiction) and his work was on a long list of inspirations for *Harry Potter* – Rowling told Adams that half her ideas tended to be dropped because *Hitchhiker* had got there first. But the success of the boy-wizard series, by then the biggest publishing phenomenon since *Hitchhiker* over twenty years earlier, soon overtook his achievements, to become an unassailable international mania. The very last time Simon Brett, *Hitchhiker*'s co-midwife, saw his old friend was at a special event for authors at Buckingham Palace, where he noted that Douglas was like a giddy schoolboy at the prospect of meeting Jo Rowling, while assuring Simon that he had made a positive decision, from that point on, to concentrate solely on what he knew he was good at: writing books. Incidentally, this event was also the very closest that Adams ever came to meeting his one equal in the world of witty fantasy, Terry Pratchett. Never 'rivals', these two great pillars of fantastical humour had simply never had any cause to meet before, but recognised each other immediately, and managed to say 'Hello!', 'Pardon?' and 'I'm sorry?' to each other, before being divided by a flood of partygoers. This would be Douglas' last short visit to his homeland.

Adams' promise to Brett to get stuck into some serious novel-writing seemed sincere, and there was a rather good reason for it. Yet again, as that red-letter year for sci-fi fans, 2001, rolled round, the film seemed to have hit another rock, which this time saw the trusty Jay Roach forced to jump ship and work on films with smoother runways to existence – another *Austin Powers* sequel, and further entries in his *Meet The Parents* series.

311

Once again feeling defeated, Adams could not blame Roach, and told him sadly, 'Hollywood is filled with Vogons who think they're poets.' Between this new body blow and his absolute consternation at the election of what he saw as the stupidest President in World History, worse than Beeblebrox and Reagan combined, Douglas was finally beginning to come round to Jane's view that this American adventure could only be a short-term move, no matter how Polly had bloomed in the new world, and if things weren't moving satisfactorily with Disney by the summer of 2002 they would all return home.

Until then, the Frood just had to keep things together, weather the latest Hollywood storm, toy with his numerous novel plot strands, enjoy a lot of the best lunches that LA could throw at him – and, of course, keep on exercising, successfully beating his diabetes and making sure that the enormous machinery which powered his six-foot-five frame was in the best condition. He had already had one slight scare: he was in the habit, after completing his workout at Platinum Fitness, one of Santa Barbara's most exclusive gyms, to visit the Adams' new friends, the Ogles, an Australian family who lived just over the road. One week, round about the time of the broadcast of the final visionary episode of *H2GF* back in the UK, he had arrived looking grey and exhausted, and had slept like a log on his hosts' bed, waking up refreshed but with a tingling sensation in one arm. He was concerned, but doctors tested him in every possible way and found nothing wrong with him that wouldn't be expected in a preposterously tall nearly-fifty-year-old regular cigarette-quitter and gourmand.

And so it was with no great concern that Douglas checked into the gym that Friday morning one week later, 11th May 2001, prepared to be put through his paces on the aerobic stair machine – with music, naturally, his constant companion in his earphones as he pounded the contraption. The sun was (inevitably) shining in Santa Barbara, the BBC had saved h2g2 from destruction, the weekend lay ahead and his mother was somewhere in the air ready for a welcome visit from Stalbridge. There might have been an extra spring in his step, as just two days earlier the Minor Planet Center had announced that the asteroid 18610, not long identified as hanging around somewhere between Mars and Jupiter, had been given the official name of 'Arthurdent' – an asteroid newly discovered at this time would also, in a couple of years, receive the name 25924 'Douglasadams', while biology had already paid tribute with the 1995 naming of a species of New

Above: The boys of the Paris Theatre studios thumbing a lift, January 1980. From left: The Frood, Geoffrey Perkins, David Tate, Geoff McGivern, Mark Wing-Davey, Simon Jones and, for one afternoon only, Alan Ford as expert hitcher Roosta.

Right: The Voice of the Book for the 2014 Radio 4 live broadcast, John Lloyd, with his old friend and collaborator/sparring partner looking on approvingly.

Below: The 21st-century generation at the BBC Radio Theatre, March 2014. From top, left to right: Marvin the Paranoid Android, Stephen Moore, Geoff McGivern, Toby Longworth, Simon Jones, Mark Wing-Davey, Neil Sleat, Ken Humphrey, Susan Sheridan, Samantha Béart, Andrew Secombe, Philip Pope and Dirk Maggs.

Top: "Wretched, isn't it?" – Marvin the Paranoid Android and Arthur Dent contemplate the crushing inevitability of ending up in a quarry, 1981.

Bottom left: 'I'm with stupid' – Mark Wing-Davey's animatronic nemesis is one of the most enduring memories people have of the 1981 BBC TV series, although the fact that Mike Kelt's fake head cost more than the actor himself rather added insult to injury.

Bottom right: David Hatch landed *Hitchhiker* the singular honour of a *Radio Times* front cover in 1980… on the nightmarish condition that the first radio series went out over one week.

Top: Kevin J. Davies, the *Hitchhiker* fan nonpareil, just a teenager when he chanced to land the job of providing the TV series' animations alongside Rod Lord, designer of numerous props, and still a crucial part of nearly every *Hitchhiker* event to this day.

Bottom: Mark, Simon and Douglas at Slartibartday 1981, debating the possibility of a third *Hitchhiker* radio outing following alternate plots across medium- and long-wave Radio 4. The possibility ultimately turned out to be 0.0.

The Hitchhiker's Guide to the Galaxy

Volume Five in
TCHHIKER'S GUIDE TO THE GALAXY

DOUGLAS ADAMS

KER'S

MASTERWORK

the

chhiker's Guide
to the Galaxy

PANIC

THE HITCHHIKER'S GUIDE TO THE GALAXY
ORIGINAL RADIO SCRIPTS

MOSTLY
HARMLESS

Edited and
prod

Douglas Adams

two in
HIKER'S GUIDE TO THE GALAXY

DON'T
PANIC

UGLAS
AMS

the Hitchhiker
GUIDE
to the galaxy
คู่มือท่องกาแล็กซี
ฉบับนักโบก

THE HITCHHIKER'S GUIDE TO THE GALAXY

Douglas Adams
แกนไท ประเสริฐกุล แปล

STAURANT AT
F THE UNIVERSE

UGLAS ADAMS

Foreword by Terry Jones

Top: The cast of 1994's *The Illustrated Hitchhiker's Guide to the Galaxy* relax between shots with 'Director' Kevin J. Davies. From left: Trillian (Tali), Arthur Dent (Jonathan Lermit), Zaphod Beeblebrox (Francis Johnson) and Ford Prefect (Tom Finnis).

Above: Poster for a touring production of Jonathan Petherbridge's faithful stage adaptation; Pan Galactic Gargle Blaster advert from the programme for the disastrous 1980 production at the Rainbow Theatre; and artwork from DC Comics' 1993 adaptation.

Top: Zooey Deschanel's Trillian on the Heart of Gold with Warwick Davis' Marvin (voiced by Alan Rickman). Both are still popular cosplay punts to this day.

Centre: Ford (Mos Def), Arthur (Martin Freeman) and Zaphod (Sam Rockwell) arrive to save Trillian from the Bugblatter Beast of Traal – or, certainly, from Vogon bureaucracy.

Below: The results of pressing the IID button are always entirely unpredictable – knitted by-products now fetch high prices on eBay.

Douglas Noël Adams: Writer,
11 March 1952–11 May 2001.

There's a frood who really knew
where his towel was.

Zealand fish, *Bidenichthys beeblebroxi*. Douglas could content himself that he, and his characters, had left a permanent mark on both our planet and the Galaxy itself.

It was a workout that Douglas was well used to. After the requisite twenty sweaty minutes of invisible stair climbing, and although stomach crunches were to be the next ordeal, the exhausted Frood accepted his towel from his trainer, laid his monolithic frame down on a bench and, as the next exercise was prepared, noisily rolled off the bench and onto the floor, unconscious. When his personal trainer, Peter, was certain that this wasn't a wonderful joke or a ploy to knock off early, an ambulance was called, rushing a heavy stretcher all the way to hospital, but Adams never regained any sign of consciousness, no last words, not a sound. The sudden cardiac arrest would have been so immediate and powerful as to be entirely painless – the hardware which powered Douglas Adams simply stopped working, irreparably.

It would be temptingly pat to observe, as so many have, the poetry of Douglas having his towel within reach in his final moments, or to make reference to how 'the lights went out in his eyes for absolutely the last time ever', or any number of observations of improbably interconnected glibness. But the truth is that there was nothing poetic about the death of Douglas Adams at the age of 49. Dramatically it doesn't work at all; it was just wrong, and has felt wrong every day since. His end was not a 'pleasing punctuation point' or an ironic fate, it was a sudden and totally unwelcome random event in a Universe which, by its very nature, only exists because it makes no sense at all.

FIT THE FIFTH

APRÈS-VIE

"The Standard Repository of all Knowledge and Wisdom"

He hoped and prayed that there wasn't an afterlife. Then he realised there was a contradiction involved here and merely hoped that there wasn't an afterlife. He would feel very, very embarrassed meeting everybody.

– So Long, And Thanks For All The Fish

Janet Thrift is beloved for her affectionate and matronly indispensability in any emotional crisis, hence her son's cheeky depiction of her as a kind-hearted back-up personality for Eddie, and she always had a mysterious sense for when her eldest child was in need. Sue Freestone recalled a time when Douglas' lawn became embarrassingly overgrown, but despite his love of gadgetry he had no lawnmower and exhausted everyone around him by complaining about the chore day after day – until his Mum appeared in Islington, having driven all the way from Stalbridge with a hover-mower, with which she proceeded to immaculately tidy Douglas' lawn before packing the machine up and driving all the way home, without a word. Adams insisted that nobody had said a thing to her about the state of the garden. But even Janet could not be expected to straighten out the scene which awaited her in California that spring day – the ravenous paparazzi camping outside the Santa Barbara home, the fiercely tough Jane overwhelmed by sudden widowhood, and, of course, a confused and devastated six-year-old grand-daughter, robbed of the father who had made her the centre of his universe for his last years on Earth.

How the three most important females in Douglas Adams' life coped on that day can hardly be imagined, but as this is a celebration of comedy and not an exploitative 'real-life tragedy' story, we do have the luxury of being able to draw a veil, leave such pain behind and move forward in time thirteen years, to what currently passes for the present day.

The Girl In The Café

My journey to lunch with a Philosophy fresher whom I had never previously met was liberally littered with details most of us take in our stride, but which would surely be a source of excitement and even amusement to Douglas Adams if he could just see them.

One glance at the high street would tell him that Apple, thanks to the efforts of Steve Jobs and the creative wizards he championed, are no longer the underdog for computing connoisseurs, but have triumphed again and again over all competitors, becoming the Empire where once they were the Rebel Elite. iPods, launched in the same year as Adams' death, seamlessly proliferate on the bus to my lunch meeting. One metal-speckled teenager in a 'GEEK' T-shirt (in the last decade, the word 'geek' has been widely reclaimed by many to mean 'somebody who likes some things'. Actual geeks remain infuriated by this) is obliviously immersed in the 50th-anniversary special of *Doctor Who* on their iPad, while others use their i- or otherwise smartphones to tweet or answer emails on the go, and I use my meagre phone coverage to look up the latest news on the Monty Python reunion at the O2. Another passenger is enjoying one of the many publications spun off from John Lloyd's multimedia juggernaut of comical intellectual curiosity, *QI*, which could surely have conquered Adams' fear of panel games. The division between Science and the Arts so often bemoaned by Douglas has never been slimmer, with Professor Brian Cox the poster boy for a new-found popular approach to astrology and physics which has helped to further the march of the 'geeks are cool' school. I look up the agreed lunch venue on my iPhone's GoogleMaps app and note that one customer has left a comment warning against the quiche, before pocketing the gadget again.

Nick Webb stated that 'Douglas Adams' returned 941,000 references on Google in February 2003 – in February 2014 it had crept up to 1,420,000. The march of technology does not slacken, and though we may still be ensnared in mazes of wires and far from Douglas' expectation of 'computers as disposable and numerous as grains of sand' it can so easily seem like we are living in the world that Adams spent so long preparing us for – and he is not here to appreciate it. His memes and epigrams permeate the Internet, and every social network. We are overwhelmingly now all equipped with our very own Hitchhiker's Guides, mobiles, tablets and iPads, used almost unthinkingly, gazing into our glowing screens with glazed eyes as we amble down the street like lamp-post fodder, looking for wi-fi to check our messages or watch a video featuring an eccentric feline. Once I reach my stop, I use my own Guide to follow a convenient flashing dot to the café chosen by my lunching partner for our rendezvous.

Buoyantly greeting me from our table in the café is a young woman – notably tall, dark hair, brown eyes, unmistakable signs of Adams physiognomy softened by Belson genes: Polly Adams at twenty looks as much like one of Douglas' heroines as his daughter, and almost every syllable she speaks seems modulated by a stifled laugh: 'Being genetically fifty per cent my father, logically every other word I say should be brilliant! You just have to work out where to start ...' And so our lunch begins.

'When the 50th anniversary of *Doctor Who* was going on,' she continues, 'a bunch of people tweeted me saying, "Your Dad's on the telly!" so I tuned in to BBC3, and it was him talking about how he wrote *City of Death*: "I was given a weekend to write this, I just drank a lot of whisky and wrote it!" And I'm going, "Genetically, that might work for me too ... I've got an essay due in Monday, I wonder!"' Our meeting has been made possible by the completion of her first wave of exams, but meeting a twenty-year-old woman for the first time and inquiring about tragic family history is such a curious situation to find oneself in, that my first real question is quite far along the obvious scale: given the famously philosophical nature of her father's work, why follow in the footsteps of Vroomfondel and Majikthise?

Polly understandably registers the corny opener, but enthusiastically responds, 'I get really excited by Science and History and lots of other things which aren't necessarily Philosophy. But I never actually enjoyed being taught any of those things, whereas I can use what I learn in Philosophy to go and teach myself more exciting things. People always ask why I'm not doing a Science degree when I get really excited about Science, but someone who specialises in Physics – I can learn as much as they do, and they spent three years doing it ... In my second lecture, the lecturer quoted the "God disappears in a puff of logic" extract, and at the end I went down and said, "It was really funny that you chose that quote, because ..." and so on, and he said that it was listening to *Hitchhiker* that got him into Philosophy, and now he's teaching me because of that. That's brilliant!'

With less expansive but equally enthusiastic gestures as those of the father who seemed to disappear thirteen years previously, we discuss many of her interests – travelling, often with close friends such as Neil Gaiman and his wife, comedy and student entertainment, what scientists may be sniffing out at CERN, but of course the biggest questions concerning The Frood are beyond her to recall so long after the event, being a shy child only just brought out of her shell by Californian sun at the time it all ended so abruptly – she measures her childhood in *Harry Potter* editions, British and American.

The most important thing I learn is, of course, that she has not lived her entire life in the shadow of Douglas Adams and *The Hitchhiker's Guide To The Galaxy* – she has read the first two or three books, but naturally proselytises about *Last Chance To See* with greater fervour. Nevertheless, the extended *Hitchhiker* clan forms a strong part of the network of families that have grounded and sustained Polly, helping to make her the friendly, genuine person I meet, when cliché and stereotype would suggest either an egregious rebel or a pampered princess. Although her whole career lies ahead of her (not including a summer job working alongside the *QI* elves), and she is adamant that it will unfold by her own merit, not because of her famous name, she is now the lynchpin of any and every decision made in Adams' name. Robbie Stamp is the man with all the plans to develop and operate, but nothing could ever go ahead within the *Hitchhiker* Universe without the say-so of the creator's daughter.

This is, however, a very new inheritance for Polly to come to terms with, and the Douglas Adams name has been extremely busy throughout the century.

That *Hitchhiker* would outlive its creator was never in doubt.

I May Not Have Gone Where I Intended To Go …

'Douglas, you left the party far too soon. All your friends, even those who never met you, will miss you.' Maybe it's fitting that this post by Stephen Fry on his old friend's personal website was the very first inkling the wider world received that something absolutely appalling had happened. We're now well used to seeing 'RIP' messages surfacing on Twitter and online news

317

services, but by sharing his immediate grief with the world in that way, Fry was at least keeping Adams in the vanguard of Internet development – the message was received dumbfoundedly by thousands of Douglas' fans at once and, as the man himself noted in only the second paragraph of his final novel, bad news travels so fast that the Hingefreel people of Arkintoofle Minor tried to harness it as spaceship fuel. The incomprehension was total: when a beloved figure dies too soon, of course fans find it hard to process, but this was an entirely new level of seemingly nonsensical deprivation. How could the man who was always so far ahead of the curve, the Earth's most popular guide to the future, Fry's 'Poet of New Stuff', have left us all at such an insanely early and crucial juncture in our journey?

The practicalities nonetheless had to be gone through, and after five days Douglas Adams was cremated in Santa Barbara, with his closest West Coast friends in attendance, and copious Beatles songs playing. It was only four months later that the terrible information really began to be processed, when Jane and Polly had returned to Islington and Douglas' army of relatives, friends and collaborators (including some with whom he would never be properly reconciled, and those, like Lloyd, who had for ever lost their counterparts) were brought together in the exalted surroundings of St. Martin-in-the-Fields, Trafalgar Square, for a suitably grand and eclectic memorial service. In another move guaranteed to be greatly to Adams' theoretical approval, the service was streamed live online, and videoclips were posted on the BBC website for fans all over the world to share the mourning and life celebration no matter where they were. Although slightly overshadowed by the events of 9/11 one week earlier, it was the cathartic event that the still-stunned congregation required – the obligatory religious element was more than balanced out by the participation of Dawkins, there were speeches from Douglas' sisters Sue and Jane and brother James, and friends including Johnny Brock and Robbie Stamp, sharing just a tiny percentage of the millions of anecdotes about the ungainly, generous genius that they knew, there was Bach, 'Rockstar' and Procol Harum, plus David Gilmour generating thousands of shivers with an acoustic rendition of 'Wish You Were Here'.

Almost finally, Simon Jones took to the lectern to say goodbye to Arthur Dent's puppeteer: 'He said he'd written the part with me in mind … So for years I've tried to get to grips with the problem of how I always saw myself, and how Douglas apparently perceived me: a befuddled Englishman abroad, forever in search of a decent cup of tea. Only in the last few months, though, have I realised that the truth may be somewhat different … Arthur may in fact be Douglas himself: the man who perhaps could never quite get the hang of Thursdays … The more I think about it, perhaps it's my vanity that made me think he had indeed written the part for me; I was in fact performing Douglas. All I really know is that he was an immensely loyal and giving friend, to whom I owe more than I can say.'

In time, Adams' ashes would find permanent rest in Highgate Cemetery, where before long grateful fans began a tradition of leaving on his grave pens, pencils, and all manner of writing paraphernalia – slightly ironic tributes for a man who favoured gadgets, but in death Douglas Adams was immediately transformed into a kind of secular patron saint of procrastinating writers everywhere. If he struggled so badly, the thought runs, and achieved so much, there must be hope for all of us with the slightest yen to weave words together.

And so that was that. By the end of 2001, with the tributes over and special programmes broadcast on BBC2 and Radio 4 – *Omnibus: The Man Who Blew Up The World* and *So Long* … – the truth had to be faced: the greatest sci-fi humorist of all time, indeed one of the finest humorists in the history of English Literature, was no longer with us, we had no backup, and there would be no more missed deadlines, no more books, and no fresh angles on the Universe to change the way we think.

Except – Adams had left so many loose threads, spread across so many universes. During the memorial service itself, Ed Victor announced that a collection of unpublished material edited by Adams' American editor, Peter Guzzardi, was already in the works, with the title *So Long* favoured by Jane – this would surface several months later as *The Salmon of Doubt*. The author's friend Chris Ogle had carefully retrieved everything from the numerous Macs stationed around Douglas' study, and Ed had passed a precious disk on to Peter, who then had the enviable but taxing task of trying to piece together the closest thing possible to a coherent version of what would have been Adams' next novel. Guzzardi's *Salmon* would have made for a very slim volume on its own (even though reams of unpublished *Dirk* remained, including a whole narrative involving a mafioso, Gently's exploding Jaguar and Satan), so the editor then joined forces with Sue Freestone and Jane to agree on their personal choices of other pieces to accompany the unfinished narrative, including, eerily, Adams' own introduction to P. G. Wodehouse's final unfinished book, which also 'suddenly, heartbreakingly, stopped in mid-flow' with all plot threads waving in the air. Including Douglas' *Sunset at Blandings* essay was a positive and incontrovertible answer to anyone who argued against the publication of any author's raw material, even that of true perfectionists like Douglas and Plum. In hindsight, there is some weight in the criticism that the book which finally cancelled out Douglas' outstanding contract was too much of a lucky dip. We now know that there was such a wealth of great material direct from Adams' keyboard which could have been used, and the inclusion of, for instance, interviews from magazines and websites might have been a mistake (one highlighted by the audiobook, which required poor Simon to incongruously read out the whole thing verbatim). Still, presumed to be the last word from a Master as it was, hordes of fans gratefully devoured the book – but it was to prove just a taster for a continuing industry.

If any cult is to become a religion, the first requirement is the permanent absence of the figurehead. From 2001 onwards, 'Douglas Adams' was to become a phenomenon in the way he could not have been when he was a funny author with the longest pipelines in the business. Just as Perkins sometimes had to fix things to keep the writer from being around to complicate and prolong editing sessions, the absence of Adams – although personally crushing for every creative individual involved, friend or fan – has not hampered the development and release of more creations bearing his hallowed name than at any period of his career. The obvious problem with the situation is that it becomes a crucial requirement for everyone who accepts the task of keeping 'The Douglas Adams Universe' alive to decide and announce 'What Douglas Would Have Wanted'. This triggers an equal and instant reaction from millions of fans, drawing up battle lines for or against every tribute and adaptation as soon as they are so much as mooted. To try and predict the thought processes of such a unique mind must be a near-impossibility even to his closest friends. 'Near-impossibility is right,' Ed Victor admits, 'but there are occasions when we feel absolutely clear about what Douglas would *not* have wanted.' Jane was, naturally, the ultimate arbiter for many years, and creatively Robbie has been the collaborator to carry that flame. Adams' creative partnerships had a history of imploding, which could make Stamp's position akin to winning a game of 'pass the parcel', but the crucial difference with Robbie is that he never sought to lock horns with Douglas creatively in the way that Lloyd or Bywater did – he was always primarily the facilitator for Douglas' ideas, and that remains largely the case now that those ideas are in stasis.

Two of the less controversial releases followed *Salmon* by a year or so – the authorised biography *Wish You Were Here*, a blithely intellectual journey through Adams' psyche which benefited from being written by his friend and original commissioning editor Nick Webb (who also left the party too soon in 2012) and made the reader feel they knew the writer better, despite only glancing at whole swathes of his career. On the other hand there was the weightier approach of *Hitchhiker*, by the man acknowledged by Adams himself to be the world expert, M. J. Simpson, which was as densely detailed as could be expected from a dedicated devotee. Subsequently, a number of unofficial books hit the shops, numerous essay collections, two studies of 'The Science of Hitchhiker' in English and German, and one on the series' philosophy, all full of wild surmises such as Marvin, Eddie and The Guide Mark II being Christ, God and the Holy Spirit respectively. (Think about it for a bit. But only a bit.)

In one case, 'WDWHW' was specifically ignored, with the release of new *Hitchhiker* editions with abstract cover designs once again from the legendary Storm Thorgerson which had specifically disappointed Adams in his life, and been vetoed (nobody can presume what he would have made of subsequent editions, featuring cartoon stickers to create your own design). Similarly, he always vetoed novelisations of his *Who* stories (because he didn't want anyone else to do them, and could not be paid enough to do them himself), but subsequent novels based on *Shada* and *City of Death*, by Gareth Roberts, have both headed to the shops without triggering the Apocalypse.

In any case, by the time the two biographies were in the shops, they were made less definitive by parallel developments with Douglas' two greatest unfinished projects.

... But I Think I Have Ended Up Where I Needed To Be

There was actually one almost forgotten *Hitchhiker* adaptation which slotted in before our two primary projects got off the ground, airing in the spring of 2003: *The Big Read* was the BBC's attempt to find the nation's favourite book, with the ten strongest contenders given a half-hour of celebration and vote-urging on BBC1. The first *Hitchhiker* novel would ultimately come in fourth (beating *Harry Potter* but just kept off the dais by *His Dark Materials, Pride and Prejudice* and *The Lord of the Rings*), with the championing of Sanjeev Bhaskar, who took viewers on an emotional journey through his life as an Adams fan, from catching the radio show as a child right up to his own comedy career. Of course, he bagged the role of Arthur for himself in the dramatised sections, with Spencer Brown as Ford, Roger Lloyd Pack as Slartibartfast, and a host of celebrity cameos, including Nigel Planer voicing Marvin, comedy duo Adam & Joe facing off with Stephen Hawking's Deep Thought, and Patrick Moore as The Guide. This unique cast, however, was not as newsworthy as the impending reunion of the original one.

Dirk Maggs was as good as his word, and work recommenced on the long-hoped-for Tertiary Phase after the fillip of the cast reunions at Douglas' memorial service. Not since The Beatles' work on 'Free As A Bird' a decade earlier had such a heatedly anticipated posthumous project gone into operation and, like the band, Maggs and his team had to proceed with the supposition that the absent team-member was just on holiday, or otherwise unavailable, lest the weight of respect for the dead hold up the creative flow. Since the 1993 false start, a second attempt to return *Hitchhiker* to radio via TDV had been scuppered in '97 by movie developments, but a conversation between Maggs and Above The Title producer Bruce Hyman at St. Martin-in-the-Fields led to a deal, bringing in Hyman's colleague Helen Chatwell and script editor John Langford, which was officially announced in November 2003 – *LUE* was finally coming to life in glorious cinematic audio. Simon says, 'Peter Jones and I used to have lunch every five years or so and he'd complain, "Why can't we do some more?" And I'd reply, "Well, Douglas just wants to do other media. He always has a bee in his bonnet about doing the movie …" We just fancied the employment, but it would also draw a line under it – *Hitchhiker* started on radio, and it should finish on radio, that's what we kept saying.'

As this was no longer a production directly from Maggs' old home at BBC Radio LE, the defunct Paris Theatre was replaced by The Soundhouse Studios in Acton as the location for the long-awaited recall of the original Arthur, Ford, Trillian, Zaphod and Marvin after nearly a quarter of a century (albeit once again Stephen Moore was in a cupboard, but at least, he reflected, this time they allowed him a window), not to mention the return of the original Announcer, John Marsh. The careers of the primary cast had shot them off in all directions, with Susan Sheridan's voice in constant demand particularly for animation, Simon Jones applauded in the New York theatre, and Mark Wing-Davey a New York-based director and academic who had to fly the furthest, from Australia, to take part. Like Stephen Moore, whose enviable comedic successes made him father to both Adrian Mole and Harry Enfield's Kevin, Geoffrey McGivern's career may have been as a character actor rather than the megastar he was proclaimed to be at Cambridge, but he can content himself that no other actor in the history of TV comedy has displayed such range, supporting so many disparate stars in so many programmes – from Smith & Jones to Fry & Laurie to Reeves & Mortimer to *This Is Jinsy*, Geoff has made himself *the* go-to man for generations of comedians. Naturally, the central role in the cast was vacant without Peter Jones, the third actor to take permanent leave after David Tate in 1996 and Richard Vernon a year later. There was, however, something pleasing about the hiring of Jones' friend William Franklyn to fill that crucial vacuum, the avuncular audio raised eyebrow, and it crowned a long career for Franklyn before he himself passed away in 2006. The final recasting surprise came courtesy of the extraordinary – and now, sadly, also late – Richard Griffiths, leaving Vernon Dursley behind to inherit Slartibartfast's role from Richard Vernon.

It was really Simon's job to help fill the Douglas-shaped chasm at the heart of the project, but he recalled the experience as 'Unalloyed pleasure. I was relieved to find that the years had been kind to those of us who remained. Susan, whom I hadn't seen in an age, looked exactly the same – younger, perhaps. Geoff and Mark I'd seen frequently over the years, so if they've deteriorated I've not noticed. I would, and I'm sure they would, prefer to say they'd matured, like fine old bottles of port. I have to admit, having lost most of my hair, and seen the remnant turn grey, that I felt more battle-scarred than the rest. But regardless of how we look, we *sounded* exactly the same, and thanks to the miracle of radio we were, and are, the same people we ever were … It really was striking, the ease with which we assumed our old characters. Perhaps we never shed them.' Hyman reflected, 'How Geoffrey and his team managed to make *Hitchhiker* with just quarter-inch tape and a razor blade I cannot think. Our studio looked like the flight deck on the *Heart of Gold*.' But despite Maggs' experimental usage of all the latest sound technology it was the actors who came first, and the daily process at the Soundhouse was a genuine love-in for all.

Besides guest stars like Joanna Lumley, Leslie Phillips lending his charming drawl to Hactar, and Chris Langham swapping Dent for Prak, Maggs' revived

Hitchhiker relied on a core group of comedy stalwarts including regular collaborator Toby Longworth as Jeltz (sadly the original Vogon, Bill Wallis, was unavailable and died in 2013) and Harry Secombe's son Andrew, plus the Oxford alumni who had starred alongside Perkins in *Radio Active*, Michael Fenton Stevens and the maestro Phil Pope – who surrendered general epic soundtrack composition to Adams' childhood friend and McCartney augmenter Wix Wickens, while using his flair for pastiche to record the Krikkit people's McCartney-esque ballad, 'Everything's So Lovely'.

Maggs' cinematic audio stylings never precisely aped the ambience achieved by Perkins (though it was closer than Adams had envisaged in '93, as he'd planned to dump the theme music for something higher-octane, Frankie Goes To Hollywood's 'Two Tribes'). But when *LUE* finally made it to Radio 4 in the autumn of 2004, there were few fans who were not overjoyed to go along with this all-new 'upgrade' of a BBC Radio legend:

```
Int. The book ambience


FX            A steady and untroubling musical drone unfolds,
              layered with the sounds of the book's animations.
THE VOICE     [PETER] This is the story of The Hitchhiker's Guide
              to the Galaxy, [WILLIAM] - BZT! - perhaps the most
              remarkable, certainly the [PETER] most successful
              book - BZT! - [WILLIAM] ever to come out of the
              great publishing corporations of [PETER] - BZT!
              - Ursa Minor. [WILLIAM] - BZT! - Now in its seven
              to the power of sixteenth edition, it has been
              continuously revised and upgraded, including being
              fitted with a highly experimental jo-jo-jog-proof,
              splash-resistant heat-shield, - BZT! - (Raspy voice)
              and a sophisticated new voice circuit - not always
              with complete - BZT! - success.
```

In fact, the closest any of the subsequent Phases ever came to sticking out a tongue at purist *Hitchhiker* fans was in overcoming the tricky hurdle of how to explain away the non sequitur of the Secondary Phase – but at least the solution went beyond Adams' idea of ignoring any plot holes entirely:

ZAPHOD	… What did happen, by the way?
TRILLIAN	(Who is not alone in looking for a way to explain this unavoidable anomaly) You had a double psychotic episode, ran off to Ursa Minor to prove some conspiracy theory, only to be found days later wandering the corridors of the Hitchhiker's Guide looking for Zarniwoop, a free lunch and a stiff drink. But not in that order.
ZAPHOD	Which proves I <u>was</u> there, right?
TRILLIAN	Well, I wasn't.
ZAPHOD	Wow - totally too much excitement, adventure and really wild things …
TRILLIAN	They're all hallucinations!
ZAPHOD	Hey, the Total Perspective Vortex was not a hallucination!
TRILLIAN	Or you had one Pan Galactic Gargle Blaster too many.
ZAPHOD	(Stung) (Reflex) That's not technically possible.

No matter how starry the cast might have been, however, there was one performance, at the series' halfway point, which caught the listener off guard, when a very familiar voice cut in to snarl, 'Bet you weren't expecting to see me again!' It was Douglas, making his long desired appearance in his own radio saga over a decade since he had requested the role of Agrajag, and three years since he had been prevented from ever joining his friends at the microphone in the usual way. However, thanks to his audiobook recording, plus a certain measure of added hissing, and flapping wings courtesy of an old umbrella, the wronged Agrajag was to reincarnate one more time:

FX	Agrajag and Arthur breathing for a moment. Then:
AGRAJAG	… Born in darkness, raised in darkness. One morning I poked my head out for the first time into the bright new world and got it split open by what felt like some primitive instrument made of flint.
ARTHUR	What?
AGRAJAG	Made by you, Arthur Dent, and wielded by you. You turned my skin into a bag for keeping interesting

> stones in. I happen to know that because in my next
> life I came back as a fly again and you swatted me.
> Again ... The interesting thing about reincarnation
> is that most people, most spirits, are not aware
> that it is happening to them.

ARTHUR   Er, look, I really ... (Reacts through following)

AGRAJAG   I was aware. That is, I became aware. Gradually.
          I could hardly help it, could I, when the same
          thing kept happening, over and over and over
          again! Every life I ever lived, I got killed by
          Arthur Dent. Any world, any body, any time, I'm just
          getting settled down, along comes Arthur Dent
          - pow, he kills me ... Hard not to notice! Bit of a
          memory-jogger! Bit of a bloody giveaway! ... Dent, you
          multiple-me-murderer!!!

Jones described the experience of playing opposite his late friend as 'distinctly surreal', which can safely be deemed a dramatic understatement. Of course, it wasn't just the posthumous performance which raised neck hairs throughout the listening audience when this sixteenth Fit was broadcast, but the horrific and complex context – a dead man was playing a reincarnated habitual murder victim, and swearing to kill his murderer, who was created by himself, and played by his surviving friend. By 'default' – if such a mind-mangling matrix of coincidence and tragedy could be summed up as 'default' – the Tertiary Phase had resulted in one of the most extraordinary pieces of radio ever broadcast, more so than anything in the original Phases – and another much-needed element of closure was achieved in Douglas' afterlife.

For this and many other reasons the new series was very warmly received, but if the fresh instalments were to receive an easy ride thanks to a combination of quality production and sentiment, the parallel universe being developed miles away on the northern fringes of the capital presented as big a gamble as ever. Although the two projects were dimensions apart, Maggs and Co. were invited to visit the set of the *Hitchhiker* movie and must have thanked their stars that they had the listening audience's imagination doing all the hard work for them.

An Important And Popular Fact

The absolutely incontrovertible confirmation that production was finally going to roll on one of the most troubled movies of all time came at around the same time as the Tertiary Phase announcement. But, of course, even subsequent to Douglas' quarter-century quest, many perils had to be overleapt before the world could know, at last, that an all-new Arthur Dent was preparing to lie down in the mud before the bulldozers on big screens around the world.

Robbie Stamp had been heartlessly pressed for details of the movie's future by journalists within a few days of Adams' passing, but it wasn't until Jane insisted that Douglas' hard work should be made to pay off that he went into action to guide the continually washed-up project back into full sail. A new broom at Disney – or rather, Disney's subsidiary Touchstone Pictures – had swept away all the film's foundations, but between Stamp, Adams' estate, Spyglass and Jay Roach, who deeply regretted having to let Douglas down, a devoted team was formed to stop the Disney do-si-do. 'I never met a more inspirational person than Douglas,' Roach told *Variety*. 'He was 6'5" and built like a tackle, with a booming laugh and great storytelling abilities, and the most refreshing take on life. He'd take me to these exotic restaurants, order everything on the menu and we'd spend hours talking. He was an authority on everything from technology to evolutionary theory, but his message was all about getting people to look outside themselves and not be so narcissistic. I wanted to spread that spirit with the film.'

Roach's ace was to bring in Karey Kirkpatrick, a Southern gentleman and Disney freelancer who had nonetheless managed to sell Nick Park and Peter Lord's tale of poultry heroism on a Yorkshire farm, *Chicken Run*, to cinema audiences all around the world. Kirkpatrick was to become a *Hitchhiker* obsessive in the course of his work, but had he known the target he was painting on his forehead he might have demurred. As it was, the writer's fresh approach to the endlessly redrafted screenplay did the trick. It's true that his input was downplayed to allay fans' fears – he could not have qualified for his co-writing credit unless a significant amount of the screenplay was his own work – but if anyone could provide a bridge between the eccentric raw material and the merchandising dreams of the financiers, he was the man.

At a crunch meeting with the biggest guns, Karey read the assembled executives the opening passage from *Restaurant*, summarising the whole first misadventure, and assured them, 'There's your movie! The Story So Far! And it *has* to be about Arthur Dent. You discover the Galaxy through Arthur's eyes, so it has to be his movie.' This final observation may seem gobsmackingly obvious, but Douglas had been so buffeted by notes and criticisms over the years that every angle had been considered, from making it Zaphod's story to 'The Vogon Movie'. But for all his controversial additions, Kirkpatrick worked hard to return *Hitchhiker* to its roots, if anything, reintroducing jokes, ideas and remnants of *Hitchhiker* lore into the script which Adams had long jettisoned to please producers (even including, at one point, the entire Vogon ship section).

Perhaps chief among these changes, due to the emphasis on the Jatravartid religion in *Restaurant*'s plot summary, was the transformation of Zaphod's black market pal Humma Kavula into the head of the Temple of the Great Green Arkleseizure, having allegedly changed his piratical ways after defeat in the Presidential elections by Zaphod (despite his strong campaign 'Don't Vote For Stupid'). As a result, the creation of the POV Gun, now desired by Humma, became credited to Deep Thought – a beautifully rendered Buddha figure, just as imagined by Adams, except with the voice of Helen Mirren and a cheeky Apple logo hidden away.

With this new villain in place, the ever-fluctuating Vice President Rontok was retooled as a female Vogon companion, chasing her boss across the Galaxy for love, providing a new romantic angle to Zaphod's story which freed up Trillian and Arthur for a happy ending. The romantic element was always going to be one of the most horrifically jagged pills for old-school fans to swallow, but although Adams had been keen to avoid anything so straight-forward as boy-meets-girl, it is the most glaring example of how Hollywood, and particularly Disney, needed by very definition to sand off the edges of Adams' wild creation and squeeze it into something akin to a familiar mould. From the very start, the *Hitchhiker* movie was never intended to translate faithfully the bumbling complexity of the radio programme or the novels onto the screen, it was meant to turn the basic story into a big, bright, popcorn-peddling blockbuster – and besides, it wasn't as if Douglas hadn't extracted huge amounts of material out of Arthur and Trillian's will-they-won't-they relationship in every other incarnation. Fans know they were never destined to be together, but for Hollywood? It just had to be. Kirkpatrick worked hard to find a balance between Dent's declaration of love and *Hitchhiker*'s rejection of soppiness, and although the eventual 'The only question I've ever wanted an answer to is "Is she the one?"' speech still turned many a stalwart fan's stomach (despite being instantly undermined by a revolted mouse) the love story could have been far more heretical. With the new emphasis on Dent, somewhere the idea arose to make Trillian half-alien, making Arthur literally the last human alive:

```
                    BENJY MOUSE
    It looks like we won't be needing the new Earth after all,
    now that we've found the only living native of the planet.
                    SLARTIBARTFAST
    But … they've nearly finished the oceans!
                    FRANKY MOUSE
    That will be all, Slartibartfast. (Slarty, slightly hurt,
    backs away and leaves.)
                    ARTHUR
    I'm sorry, when you say "the only living native" - do you
    mean me? What about …
                    BENJY MOUSE
    We performed some rudimentary DNA tests on the ship.
    She's half-native. Her real father was a Blahardid, the
    hyper-intelligent yet hopelessly nomadic race native
    to the planet Bastablon, who apparently popped in to
    Earth for a one-nighter with one Ms. Francis McMillan.
                    TRILLIAN
    Which explains a lot.
```

Much of the film was created with this concept in place before it was blessedly dropped, as the franchise-breaking transgression that it was. Any change designed to make *Hitchhiker* more palatable to multiplex punters could only move it further from the source that fans adored. But Stamp insists, 'Douglas wanted a *Hollywood* movie. It just so happens that this is a Hollywood movie in which a whale falls to the ground while musing on the nature of the relationship between language and existence.' This unique moment in cinematic history was further elevated by the performance of loveable musical comedian Bill Bailey – one of a number of comedy stars keen to take any role going, with The League of Gentlemen also providing many voices, as well as Steve Pemberton taking on the role of Prosser. In a wonderfully strange development, bagging the voice of Jeltz provided Richard Griffiths with the chance to play major *Hitchhiker* characters in two different media at once.

Karey's new honing of the screenplay was the final dusting of sugar required to trigger a genuine green light from Disney – although Spyglass bosses had to stump up their own money to pay the writer's fee, so determined were they to see the movie go ahead. Roach, unable to avoid the latest *Fockers* sequel, recommended eccentric director Spike Jonze to mastermind the shooting, but Jonze wisely saw that it was the ideal first feature for two fellow music-video helmers Hammer & Tongs, otherwise known as director Garth Jennings and producer Nick Goldsmith, who just happened to operate from a canal boat in Islington, about ten minutes away from Adams' own home. Both being lifelong fans, they instantly decided that they could not bear to be the men to ruin *Hitchhiker*, and so the screenplay sat unread for a long time before Garth cracked, picked it up, and realised that Karey had pulled off the Improbable. When pitching their approach to Disney via conference call, Jennings rigged up a red velvet curtain attached to his chair by strings, which opened up to reveal the legend 'Don't Panic!' on the Californian monitor as he pulled back the chair, which won over the money men at once and also gave a clue about the tirelessly creative and crafty approach the duo would take to Douglas' movie. Jennings briefly considered repaying their debt to Jonze by casting him as Ford, alongside Adam Buxton's Arthur, during the earliest experimental stages of production.

It had always been the casting of the core *Hitchhiker* gang that had most obsessed film-news portals since the rights were first sold. Perhaps most importantly, it was the Hollywood-friendly equivalent of Peter Jones that proved the biggest challenge. For a while, *Bagpuss* creator Oliver Postgate was brought in to lend his cosy tones to The Book, just as he had narrated his own sci-fi silliness in *The Clangers*. But he counted himself out of the job after a few attempts, and Hammer & Tongs were compelled to bring in one of the most ubiquitous, beloved and authoritative voices in the business – coincidentally dearly associated with Adams himself – Stephen Fry. That the material was familiar and well suited to Fry was obvious, and his velvety voice in many ways set the tone for the entire production, particularly when synced up with the all-new cartoon Guide animations designed by art collective Shynola to be as far removed from the famous designs of Rod Lord and Co. as possible.

The hero himself was the second key part of the puzzle, and although any number of posh Simon Jones ciphers had been mooted in the past Martin Freeman was a decidedly different Arthur Dent from any who had gone before. A star of the then prevalent naturalistic school of sitcom, Freeman had been busy with low-key comedy appearances for many years before *The Office* propelled him to fame as the series' everyman figure, Tim. Arthur's cut-glass accent was softened into a slightly adenoidal, glottal-stop-flecked delivery, but as the actor's subsequent success as Bilbo in *The Hobbit* and Watson in *Sherlock* suggests, he was the ideal man to make any audience root for him. Although he had read half the 'trilogy', Freeman shared a lukewarm knowledge of *Hitchhiker* with his on-screen hitching partner, New York hip-hop artist Mos Def, though both ingested the works hungrily on set, as Mos' laconic take on Ford began to take shape. The rest of the core cast were diehard devotees, particularly Slartibartfast Bill Nighy, and Zooey Deschanel, on the cusp of being crowned the Queen of Kook in sitcom *New Girl* – her casting as another American Trillian was no more controversial than Mos Def being the first black Ford Prefect. *Galaxy Quest* alumni completed the *HoG* crew, with Sam Rockwell winning the hotly mooted role of Zaphod despite originally auditioning for Ford, combining suspicions of Clinton and Bush with extreme rock-star posturing, while Alan Rickman made a return to nasal whining by providing the voice for Marvin. The deceptively cute robot himself was personified by seasoned pro Warwick Davis, who suffered uncomplainingly many of the same indignities as David Learner, albeit with the luxury of a stand-in where necessary.

There were numerous eerie echoes of TV *Hitchhiker* and indeed of Douglas' life and career in general as Hammer, Tongs and their massed family of creatives spanned the summer of 2004 bringing Hollywood *Hitchhiker* to life at Elstree Studios and on location, from the time the very first shot was celebrated (the Islington party scene) on 19th April. Once again, exotic location scouting eventually landed the cast and crew – soaked by rain – in a Welsh quarry, and the first day on the exquisite *HoG* deck coincided with the third anniversary of Douglas' death, marked with a minute's silence and a mass photograph of everyone working on the film, thumbs aloft, celebrating the near-realisation of Adams' main ambition. The man himself was of course worked into the film numerous times, largely thanks to the facial mapping carried out for *Starship Titanic*, with the Jatravartid Temple decorated with enormous moulds of the author's nose, Douglas and Jane in pride of place on the teacup design skirting the *HoG* itself, and subtle but heart-stopping cameos as a large-nosed planet in Slartibartfast's construction area, and as part of the IID effects in the very last shot. Nobody could escape the metaphorical ghost haunting the movie, which was either comforting and tributary, or in rather dodgy taste, depending on your point of view. For those who went with the movie, however, the moment when that unmistakable visage soars across the Magrathean backdrop, as Slartibartfast reveals the truth about life on Earth to an overwhelmed Arthur, was no less electrifying a sequence than the late author's reincarnation as Agrajag on radio. For a dead man, Douglas certainly knew how to make an impression.

Resistance Is Useless!

No matter where you stand on the *Hitchhiker* movie, it was such a divisive project that it tends to be one of the first things people mention when the name arises these days, with one schism of fandom judging another depending on their pro- or anti-stance. Even Robbie Stamp now admits: 'A lot of people did love it, a lot of people didn't. I'm not precious about the movie, there were things that didn't work …' However, only the most churlish misanthrope would gainsay his passionate contention: 'The one thing that I can say absolutely categorically is that everybody – and I mean *everybody*, cast, crew, studios, Disney, Spyglass, *everybody* working on that movie cared passionately to try and do their best for Douglas. It really was an immensely respectful labour of love.' So many measures were taken to try and communicate this crucial sense of Adams' nearest and dearest being on-side, from featuring the author's family in the early shots of Earth (Janet Thrift unflappably reading the paper while bedlam breaks out around her), to creating a new recording of 'Journey of the Sorcerer' to prickle veterans' necks, to cameos from the TV Marvin queuing up on Vogsphere (slightly marred by Freeman's double take), plus, of course, Simon Jones putting in an indispensable appearance as the Magrathean security system (complete with ersatz 3D and the added line 'Your death may be recorded for training purposes'), that it's fair to say that the core creative team felt well protected from the ire of hidebound *Hitchhiker* fans. 'I maintain that it was only because I said to Robbie at one of Jane's parties,' Jones laughs, 'that if he didn't put one of us in, that the fans would probably, er … well, I would tell the fans where he lived. So they squeezed me in. They said that I was going to be the only part of the film in 3D – I watched it with 3D glasses, and it bloody well doesn't look 3D to me!' Having taken such conciliatory measures, the cast even went so far as to film fake scenes just for fun, spoofing the precarious situation by featuring a badass Dent kicking Vogon butt Rambo-style, safely assuming that fans would know it was a joke.

With post-production near completion, however, the truly perfidious element had to come in to play – promotion, merchandising, and all aspects of finally flogging this lovingly crafted, quirky British film to popcorn punters the world over. There was, inevitably, a bigger flood of *Hitchhiker* memorabilia coming onto the market in 2005 than ever before, with a new tie-in edition of the novel and a 'Making Of' book, a Fry-narrated audiobook (with the rest of the 'trilogy' picked up by Freeman), ill-advised toy-gun replicas, desk tidies, mugs, a set of cuddly knitted characters (inspired by the IID's rearrangement of the *HoG* crew into woollen dolls), and an oddly limited range of action figures in two sizes, leaving out Ford and Trillian but including two Vogons. Only Marvin flew off the shelves, and the little white android now fetches insane prices on eBay.

The first palpable crack in this shining new model appeared when journalists and *Hitchhiker* experts who had been carefully courted throughout production with set visits and insider status were shown a rough-cut of the film. It would be preferable at this stage not to risk any bond of solidarity with past Adams biographers were it not for the fact that, chief among this experimental audience, M. J. Simpson then made himself very much part of the story by rapidly writing a 10,000-word online review which began in a disappointed tone and only grew more outraged from that point on. Some time was spent picking apart the junctures where the plot did not so much creak as choke, but the observation that 'the film also suffers by having an entirely nonsensical plot … driven by convenience and unexplained happenings' is an odd observation for anyone familiar with *Hitchhiker,* with its wild get-out clauses and fudged cliffhangers. (How did Marvin really escape that sun? Why did Deodat have the same forenames as Dent? Why were 'cavemen' on Earth thousands of years before the earliest fossil records? How did Eddie know all the words to 'You'll Never Walk Alone'? As we all know, there are always simple, or silly, answers to any question that *Hitchhiker* throws up in any medium.) But for all the expletive-packed hyperbole of Simpson's demolition, it has to be said that the review did not waste too much time taking the easily dismissible sci-fi fan route of laboriously over-thinking the canonicity of the adaptation but correctly aimed squarely at *Hitchhiker*'s true *raison d'être*: the jokes, which Simpson noted were regularly blunted, skewed or dropped entirely in favour of what he saw as unworthy invention – even if, he was clear to point out, such decisions were made by Adams himself when he was alive. The review made no martyr of Douglas, but blamed him as much as anyone for any perceived shortfall.

No official embargo had been put in place, so when LA heavies began setting phones ablaze with demands to know who was getting fired over this debacle, with the review going so far as to be splashed across the *New York Post*, there was no answer but to reassure the suits that there was always going to be some degree of warfare within a fanbase as passionate as *Hitchhiker*'s but that its impact on the movie's box-office performance would be minimal. And it was true: by that point lines were already drawn up between those desperate to see any supposed 'Disneyfication' of Douglas' work fail, and the diehards, buoyed by the glowing early verdicts from Ain'tItCoolNews.com, who saw it as their hero's final triumph – with Simpson caught in the cross-fire, subject to the worst excesses of online abuse. No more ignoble accusation could be cast in either direction than that ultimate put-down 'FANBOY!' – the pro- camp deeming the 'fanboys' to be viciously decrying any perversion of their beloved *Hitchhiker* (or rather, the *Hitchhiker* which exists only in their own heads), the anti- bunch accusing 'fanboys' of blinding themselves to the film's disrespectful flaws, and both sides, of course, believing themselves fervently to be speaking on behalf of the absent creator. The issue even arose during press junkets, Bill Nighy leading with his celebrated snort and a deliberately unpublishable slur on the reviewer, followed by the admission, 'I read the first 500 words, I couldn't do the next 10,000 ...'

Whatever dent this spat caused in the tsunami of goodwill which accompanied the film's release on 28th March 2005, the UK opening weekend chalked up a pleasingly apt £4.2 million, resulting in delighted messages from Touchstone to everyone involved – it was officially a hit, and performed with no less verve in the USA ... but only briefly, with cinema attendance very quickly tailing off, the biggest fans having bought their tickets early. Ever since, the movie has occupied a strange hinterland between success and failure – more than doubling its budget in takings, but not stacking up enough profit for a sequel to be dreamt of – neither a turkey nor a blockbuster. This equivocation only fuels the continuing feuds, a decade later.

To many long-standing *Hitchhiker* fans, there isn't even any real argument about the film's flaws, since they are evident. The plot objectively fails to add up, partly due to last-minute edits removing lots of exposition and background colour, such as Slartibartfast's apology to Arthur, echoing the Golgafrincham problem:

> SLARTIBARTFAST
>
> The Galaxy was in a shambles, you see. Everyone enjoying themselves being singers and comedians and really creative things like that. No one doing the boring jobs.
>
> ARTHUR
>
> Oh, you had that problem, too?
>
> SLARTIBARTFAST
>
> In spades. So a species was genetically engineered to do those jobs: tax inspectors, traffic wardens, government officials. We built a special planet for them. Problem was, some clever clogs made it so any time one of the creatures had an interesting idea it would get a hefty smack around the face.
>
> ARTHUR
>
> What? You did that? I've been there!
>
> SLARTIBARTFAST
>
> Then I gather you've met some of the inhabitants.
>
> ARTHUR
>
> The Vogons?
>
> SLARTIBARTFAST
>
> Relentless blighters.

If there had been a sequel, it could also have tied up other inconsistencies and dropped threads, such as the entire Humma Kavula strand, but, as it stands, the story arc is unquestionably haphazard. There are also few fans who would prefer the way Zaphod's heads were handled, with a CG pop-up second head, to the dozy animatronic model of 1981. In addition, Simpson was right to observe that reinserting many of the best lines could easily have upped the laugh quota, rather than replacing classic dialogue with sub-par gags – particularly the pun-ishing material meted out for Marvin, worsened by redubs with Rickman forced to add even weaker cutesy grumbles.

However, the real division between the movie 'lovers' and 'haters' lies in *whether any of that really matters or not.*

Because there is one certain area in which the film's detractors have been proven wrong: the crucial issue of whether neophytes would be repelled and confused by the film, or sucked into Douglas Adams' Universe, making the movie a springboard to growing the international ranks of *Hitchhiker* fans. What it was apparently impossible for many existing fans of the franchise to see was that Garth Jennings had created one of the most uniquely silly sci-fi comedies of all time, an arrestingly philosophical odyssey – not in comparison with the rest of *Hitchhiker*, but compared with *Men in Black* and its ilk. It's a Disney romp with John Malkovich laying bare the silliness of all organised religion with a single 'Bless you', a science fiction film in which the enemy is bureaucracy, heroes turn into sofas and dolphins presage their final dive into the infinity of space by singing 'So Long And Thanks For All The Fish', a show-stopping musical number about life on Earth composed, alongside the soundtrack, by Joby Talbot. (Douglas would have been overjoyed to know that Paul McCartney dropped by Abbey Road for one orchestral recording, although sadly the rousing campaign theme 'Zaphod Beeblebrox For President', recorded by Talbot's Divine Comedy colleague Neil Hannon, never made the cut.) Also, although of course a certain crucial measure of CG was provided by *Harry Potter* effects company Cinesite, it was the puppetry of the Jim Henson Creature Workshop, bringing the cobwebbed excrescence of the Vogons to life, which gave the film a comfortingly corporeal, traditional feel, far from the dead-eyed design of the *Star Wars* prequels. Above all, this flawed concoction beguiled and intrigued many thousands of movie fans unfamiliar with the mishaps of Arthur Dent, and fulfilled the ultimate purpose of any reboot, spin-off or adaptation – to capture virgin imaginations off guard, and send the audience right back to the source material.

Thanks to the movie, the *Hitchhiker* fanbase has multiplied, beyond question. All you have to do is search for any of the comedy's central memes on Google Image Search – 'Arthur Dent', 'Marvin Paranoid Android' – and top among the searches will be the iconography not of the TV series or any other iterations, but that of the 2005 film, not just regurgitated, but embraced and celebrated by fans, painted in portraits on DeviantArt. com by *Hitchhiker* lovers all over the world, some young enough never to have even shared a planet with Douglas. Every iteration of *Hitchhiker* famously contradicted or otherwise differed from every other, and there would have been a strange aptness in Hollywood condensing the other four books in the 'trilogy' into an *actual* trilogy, presenting the most simplified, multiplex-friendly remoulding of the entire *Hitchhiker* saga imaginable. Nonetheless, for the fresh froods who were introduced to Adams' work by the movie, when they read the books many still see Martin, Zooey and Co. in those roles, defining that Galaxy for a generation, just as surely as Simon Jones' gang had managed to do over twenty years earlier.

Jennings went on to direct the lauded *Son of Rambow*, and when asked whether he would do things differently, replies, 'It was amazing, a beautiful time, but good God, yes, I can't imagine anyone making their first film – let alone *Hitchhiker* – and not thinking afterwards, "Maybe I could have done that a bit better ..." I say that not wanting to take anything away from any of us who worked on the film, because everyone did throw themselves into it – literally in many cases, I sent Mos and Martin through a fifteen-foot drop, and they were *shitting* themselves! "Can't we do this with CG?" "No, you have to fall through the floor for this to be funny!" So maybe I'd do things differently, but it's not as bad as some of the haircuts I've had; I'd rather go back and fix those.'

How Are We For Time?

Little did they know that it was therefore win-win for Maggs and the Soundhouse family as they returned to work – the attempted blockbuster would either lure in new listeners, or simply make them look better in comparison, being the real, original cast, finally ending the cycle of stories that Douglas wrote, in the medium which gave them life. 'People have asked if the release of the film and the broadcast of the last two radio series so close together was a problem,' Dirk said, 'but we were always creating different but complementary realities for *Hitchhiker*, and the simple fact is that Douglas wanted both these projects to happen. It's dreadful that he isn't here to enjoy the coincidence, but wherever he is on the Probability Curve he will be happy about it. It is, in fact, a very Douglassy sort of coincidence.'

Adams' only recorded thought about the last two books was that neither deserved more than four episodes each, and so the Quandary and Quintessential Phases would be recorded back to back. Despite the

more pure goodwill surrounding the project, Maggs believed, 'There
was a hard core who were not going to be happy with anything we did,
which was tough for them, as *LUE* was the series as Douglas wanted it,
for better or worse ... He asked for utter fidelity and the promise had
to be honoured. The last two novels would be a different bowl of Babel
fish altogether ... from here on I was Off The Map.' Dirk decided to take
inventive steps to give the final eight episodes more of a strident story
arc, creating all-new action aboard Jeltz's ship, which was 'a conscious
decision to reverse expectations and by doing so warn those familiar with
the sequencing of the novels that the gloves, if not off, were going to be
loaded with the odd horseshoe ... The next two series I thought, "I've
done my homage to Simon Brett and Geoffrey and their production style."
So it was great to go to Ford in Han Dold City, with the cop wars going
on and everything. Because *SLATFATFish* was such a relatively quiet book,
there was a challenge to keep the emotional content, but also give it some
forward propulsion, with the whole idea that the Vogons are plotting all
the way through ... the fun of writing the Vogon Court of Inquiry scene
was that I was trying to write an Adams/Smith/Adams sketch, very much
a sort of "Kamikaze Pilot" homage. I never added anything I couldn't find
a precedent for somewhere in Douglas' work, much as I love to go off on
one myself, I had no right to do that – that was as far as I dared push it.'
Indeed, only slight changes were really made, such as combining Vann Harl
and Zarniwoop into one major villain, and Maggs was lucky that the Guide
Mk II provided every excuse possible for tying up all 26 Fits, including that
pesky second Phase, as the conclusion rumbled ever onwards:

ZAPHOD	Gargravarr, my psychiatrist, the Presidency, the Krikkit robots - it was all a front! The Vogons set it all up. And this guy's been controlling it all from here, at the Hitchhiker's Guide.
FORD	Which guy?
ZAPHOD	Zarniwoop. Vann Harl! He's a Vogon! A plastic-surgery'd, liposucked, fake-tanned, business-suited Vogon Boss! The Big Cheese with a Side Order of Jewelled Crab!
FORD	But why would the Vogons want to take over the Guide?

ZAPHOD	Their paperwork was backing up. Every time they thought they had destroyed a planet in a Plural Zone, it reappeared. They need to stop the whole bureaucracy imploding so they develop a way to bridge the zones, so they can impose the system on all available realities. Some aquatic mammals from Earth gave them the idea. Dent's an aquatic mammal, isn't he?
FORD	He likes taking baths, but I don't think he's much of a physicist.

Better use than ever was made of the new recording technology, particularly Ford's dealings with the orgasmic robot Colin, inspiring a powerful mental image of the melon-sized drone whizzing around in Dolby Digital 5.1, via a special speaker physically moved around the recording space by Paul Weir, which was to prove one of the funniest sequences in the latter Phases – largely, of course, due to the sublime performance from Secombe. 'The sound stage is the entire 360-degree area,' Dirk explained. 'You are literally at the centre of the action ... Although stereo is ideal for a casual listen, a playback in 5.1 surround is to experience *Hitchhiker* in a more intense and involving way than ever before. Douglas would have loved it.'

While the big-screen version premiered alongside these final radio programmes, the Soundhouse could also boast a few film stars among the fresh faces around the microphone, with Jane Horrocks bringing Lancashire charm to the role of Fenchurch and Christian Slater, in town for the stage version of *One Flew Over The Cuckoo's Nest*, a shoo-in for Wonko the Sane. Although McGivern and Moore regretted the lack of opportunities for them to double up roles, the auspiciousness of the project brought in the best vocal performers that Dirk and the team could have wished for, with Miriam Margolyes, Jackie Mason, June Whitfield and Douglas' old schoolfriend Griff Rhys Jones (as Old Thrashbarg) joined by another *Hitchhiker* media-straddler, Stephen Fry, who took the role all but written for him, Murray Bost Henson. Pope and Fenton-Stevens' old mucker Geoffrey Perkins also took the time to finally make his own cameo appearance, in the perfect role of Arthur's laid-back boss at BBC LE.

One major addition to the cast was young actress Samantha Béart as Random, a huge fan of the books who greatly lowered the cast's average

age. But the remaining remarkable thing about the final episodes was the return of so many *Hitchhiker* alumni from myriad universes, all keen to get in on the fun before the pips were sounded after the final-ever episode. Roy Hudd and Jonathan Pryce reprised their roles from the original series and Bill Paterson was ideal for the larger role of Rain God Rob McKenna, while *Hitchhiker* luminaries including Michael Cule and Kevin Davies (once again, filming everything for posterity) made vocal cameos. Most pleasing of all, Sandra Dickinson finally joined the radio team as the alternative Trillian, and David Dixon likewise gracefully rescinded his role of Ford, to intimidate Arthur as a familiar-sounding charity worker:

ECOLOGICAL MAN	Hi, can I help you?
ARTHUR	Is this Friends of the Planet?
ECOMAN	That's what it says over the window.
ARTHUR	Yes, right, I'm here in Islington doing a bit of, um - research into its prehistory, and I was passing your shop and it occurred to me that I'd like to give you some money to help save the dolphins.
	(A pause)
ECOMAN	Very funny.
ARTHUR	To free them from captivity ... So I was passing and saw your shop and - are you all right?
ECOMAN	Actually, you're rather annoying me ...
ARTHUR	Do we know each other?
ECOMAN	Do I look like the sort of person who'd spend time with you?
ARTHUR	Sorry. Must be having déja vu ...

The final returning actor was Rula Lenska, the third radio Voice of the Book, this time providing the misleadingly seductive voice of the Guide Mark II but also reprising her role as Lintilla, for the latter-day Phases' grand conclusion, the culmination of all Maggs and company's careful reworking of the 'trilogy'. Douglas always openly bemoaned the juddering full stop of *Mostly Harmless*, and this was a chance to right that wrong. Maggs wrote: 'This is an Infinite Universe created by Douglas Adams, full of Multiple Realities, existing on

Parallel Layers. If, as Douglas constantly suggests, absolutely *anything* is possible – be it achieved through reverse-temporal engineering by the Guide Mark II, or through the unknown, unknowable knowledge of the Dolphins, or through sheer blind coincidence – which has ever stalked Arthur Dent and revealed itself to be his friend, no matter how Improbably – then the inescapable truth is that The End of *Mostly Harmless* is, at best, *An* End.' The growing darkness of the final episodes certainly required plenty of engineering to regain any semblance of the situation comedy that the programme was planned to be over a quarter of a century previously, particularly given the chilling, flat sound of Douglas himself, breathing his last as another terminal Agrajag reincarnation. So it's surely forgivable that they decided to take the kitchen-sink-included route, throwing in half a dozen possible endings – be it the full-on *Dallas* option, with Arthur and numerous Lintillas in the shower on the *HoG*, Fenchurch and Arthur taking on the bulldozers together, or the ultimate extended hitchhike down memory lane, taking in every character's happy ending, and even necessitating a final appearance from Peter Jones, thanks to the hidden talent of only the second alien species with whom Arthur ever made contact:

THE VOICE (PJ) The Babel fish is small, yellow and leech-like, and probably the oddest thing in the Universe ...

THE VOICE (WF) Another ability evolved by the Babel fish is its tactic for self-preservation. Only one other aquatic creature in the Universe has developed the Babel fish's capacity for Continuous Probability Transference in the picosecond before unavoidable destruction. Thus, as Earth's Plural Zone folds itself away like a card table after a particularly energetic hand of snap, the Babel fishes, their hosts and any cetaceans in the vicinity simultaneously flick into existence in any alternative layers of reality they can inhabit along the Probability Curve. In the case of Arthur Dent, this leads to several probable realities ... But perhaps the alternative that best suits the Babel fishes - and their hosts - is the convivial safety of a location and a time far, far removed from uncertainty, improbability, or sobriety ...

an infinite loop of bistromathics where dinner guests
wait patiently for each other to turn up.

Int. Milliways

FX	The Restaurant at the End of the Universe in full swing.
MAX	(Through PA, In background) Welcome one and all to Milliways, the Restaurant at the End of the Universe! I'm Max Quordlepleen, and tonight and every night I'll be with you right through to the End of History itself!
FX	Applause and laughter, continues under with Max...
ARTHUR	Ford... last question, I promise, but... if the Babel fish is so versatile, how come it's never saved my life - our lives - before?
FORD	You didn't die before.
ARTHUR	So what happened to us? How were we saved?
FORD	Ah, well, our scrape with death took place in a Plural Zone, where organic life forms in the vicinity of a Babel fish share its kinetic bridge to all available dimensions and are transported too. The only other life forms who can make the jump are dolphins. Have you noticed what's outside the restaurant, for miles and miles in every direction?
TRILLIAN	Who could miss them? Thousands of interlinked blue lagoons, glowing under the stars...
ARTHUR	...Filled with dolphins.
FORD	The dolphins learned how to jump dimensions from the Babel fish. In return, the Babel fish learnt a thing or two about where to have a good time from the dolphins. Quid pro quo. Pass that Ol' Janx Spirit, Zaphod
ZAPHOD	(Pouring) One for you, Ford, baby - two for me... Come on, monkey man, hurry up with that menu, I'm hungrier than a Bugblatter Beast in a weight-loss clinic.

ARTHUR	You'll have to wait. Random's having a problem with the Dish of the Day.
RANDOM	I want the veggie option.
FORD	Waitress! Can you bring over a talking cauliflower?
FENCHURCH	(Approaching) Yes, sir, I will - oh - is there a Zaphod Beeblebrox on this table?
ZAPHOD	That's my name, dollface. Don't wear it out.
ARTHUR	Good grief-!

With Arthur finally reunited with the love of his life, a brazenly senti-mental chorus of 'Auld Lang Syne' gave way to a coda of that jangling banjo for an absolutely last time, and the entire radio saga, bookending nearly three decades of Galaxy-skipping madness, came to a close. With only a few canonical exceptions, such as the full Dish of the Day meeting, the 'Young Zaphod' story or, arguably, ideas such as the POV Gun, the programmes broadcast on Radio 4 between 1978 and 2005 probably represent the most authoritative iteration of *Hitchhiker* there will ever be, particularly in the extended CD cuts. Although commercially available in many audio editions – not to mention the supporting material in releases like the *Douglas Adams at the BBC* triple CD set – the series' occasional repeats on digital station Radio 4 Extra still help to lure in *Hitchhiker* virgins to this day.

The experience had been so pleasurable for all that within two years many of the team re-formed to bring Dirk Gently's adventures to the airwaves, with Harry Enfield excelling in the title role, supported not just by the familiar voices of Longworth, Pope, Fenton-Stevens et al., but by Olivia Coleman as a more sidekick-oriented Janice, Jim Carter as Gilks and guests including Susan Sheridan and, in the role of Odin, Stephen Moore. Naturally, making the first dizzyingly threaded narrative work in audio took more audacious adaptation and exposition than anything in *Hitchhiker*, and many changes were made to link the action of the two existing books, such as making MacDuff a kind of Professor Brian Cox figure, ex-keyboardist for the band who recorded 'Hot Potato' – but Maggs took a bigger risk by working in refer-ences to the other universe, such as having MacDuff work for a company called Sirius Cybernetics, with a highly familiar catchy company jingle and mobile ringtone. To make Marvin's manufacturers an Earthling outfit made no sense whatsoever, in this dimension at least, but such references were never expected to be taken as anything more than a bit of fun. The links would have gone further – the two series were well received, and were to tie up into a more holistic trilogy, with a naturally dramatically padded outing for *Salmon of Doubt* in which Enfield's Dirk was to end up at a party in Islington with some guy called Phil who had a parrot cage on his shoulder … but this plan was nixed when Maggs left Above The Title to create his own company, named Perfectly Normal Productions in tribute.

When the radio programme that started it all reached its rambling but pleasing conclusion, most people surely felt that, at last, *Hitchhiker* had come to the very end of its life. These people, however, quite drastically underestimated the power of that Galaxy, and those characters, to survive against all probability – the book was not closed yet.

Diddle-ee-aye Irishness

Though the developments of 2005 had of course inspired any number of ructions within the *Hitchhiker* fan community, merrymakers with towels, fake heads and mountains of merchandise for Simon, Geoff or whoever had made the journey to sign were still a prerequisite for every sci-fi convention going, in any country. In addition, the annual tradition of Towel Day had been celebrated from Innsbruck to Santa Barbara in Douglas' name every 25th May, since two weeks after his death. It had, however, been a long time since there had been a specific *Hitchhiker* event, when Hitchcon 2009 came around in October of that year at London's South Bank Centre. There was a chat-show event hosted by Clive Anderson, a new recipe for PGGBs, and a special announcement by Ed Victor with the news that Dirk Gently would be finding a circuitous route to TV screens in the near future.

Although already naturally celebrated for his own work in a plethora of fields, Stephen Fry has had to act as his old friend's understudy numerous times since 2001 and, in a busy year for the estate, Fry was also appearing on TV (and in a glossy coffee-table book) with Mark Carwardine in a timely follow-up to *Last Chance To See*, twenty years on, catching up with the species that Douglas and Mark had documented for radio. Sadly the Yangtze River Dolphin was no more, with the Northern White Rhino faring little better; but (despite getting his arm viciously broken on camera) Stephen found more welcome news of many of the other species flagged up by his friend and predecessor: the aye-aye, mountain gorilla, manatee and, infamously, one very passionate little green kakapo.

Hitchcon also provided a reunion of the original cast on stage, but this was not their first live performance – Simon had observed that everyone was having so much fun recording the programmes that they could have sold tickets, and when the fifth annual Douglas Adams Memorial Lecture came round at the Royal Geographical Society in 2008 (another regular tribute to the great man, held in aid of Save The Rhino) a special rendition of selections from the show was enjoyed by all, with *Simpsons* star Harry Shearer as Slartibartfast and Geoffrey Perkins making his one appearance as The Voice of the Book. Tragically, this was a final performance from *Hitchhiker*'s co-architect, as shortly afterwards British Comedy was robbed of his talents by a heart defect that suddenly and randomly struck the great man down at 55, as he was crossing the road.

The primary reason Hitchcon was arranged, however, would have been un-dreamt of by the *Hitchhiker* faithful even one year earlier. One year and one month before the fans came together, 42 days before the 30th anniversary of the original publication of Douglas' first book, Penguin and Pan Macmillan announced that they had joined forces to honour the author's hopes of following *Mostly Harmless* with something less painful: the sixth entry in the *Hitchhiker* series, *And Another Thing* … . The title was taken this time from *SLATFATFish*, as Arthur trudged home in the rain: 'The storm had now definitely abated, and what thunder there was now grumbled over more distant hills, like a man saying "And another thing …" twenty minutes after admitting he's lost the argument.'

With Adams still undeniably not among the living, this should have been the fanbase equivalent of an H-bomb. But, perhaps in the wake of the movie's divisive splash, there was a surprising level of acceptance that Jane had permitted another author to dust off Douglas' toys and play around with them. He was also an Ed Victor client, but the selection of Irish fantasy author Eoin Colfer as the chalice-receiver in question seemed to make a surprising amount of sense to the majority anyway – he certainly did not need the money or exposure, as it was the massive success of his own boundary-stretching children's series *Artemis Fowl*, following the gadget- and mythology-festooned machinations of the eponymous evil child genius, which put him forward for the dangerous honour, Jane and Polly having enjoyed the series together. Home life for Douglas' widow and daughter had long stabilised as the century progressed, and Jane married George Lloyd-Roberts, a tower of strength in the wake of Douglas' loss, with a job in the City and two grown children of his own. The two had known each other longer than Jane ever knew Douglas, as he was the brother of her best friend and one of Polly's 'Godparents', the Emmy-winning broadcaster Sue Lloyd-Roberts. None of this, however, moved Jane to fulfil her role as Douglas' creative executor one iota less fiercely, and so the licence to continue Arthur Dent's aggravation-filled existence in print was not one given lightly.

Nor, if Colfer's carefully phrased disclaimers are to be believed, was his acceptance arrived at without much careful thought, he having been a genuine fan since he was a geeky teenager in Wexford. When the news broke, Simon Jones was even interviewed in character for Radio 4's *Today* programme, with Arthur complaining bitterly that his peace had been disturbed once again. It's traditional for anyone taking on the Adams mantle to insist on an instinctive repulsion from the idea, knowing that nobody can replace the man himself, only for them to eventually relent, in the knowledge that someone less scrupulous could be next in line, and if the job has to be done … and so on. Colfer knew for sure that he was putting his head between the jaws of *Hitchhiker*'s more rabid devotees, and at first tried his best to prevent any panic – even joining one of many 'Stop Eoin Colfer Writing *Hitchhiker*' Facebook groups and being met with a barrage of crap-slinging from all around the world. But after a while, although of course the book would be released amid a pervasive cloud of disclaimers, he realised that all he could do was log off, and write the book as he saw fit. With one notable dispensation for good taste (Marvin's death, he felt, was sacrosanct), Colfer wrote a book with as much of himself in it as any of Douglas' instalments had been infused with his own personality. Not only was one of the main characters, Hillman Hunter (you see what he did there), a deliberately clichéd, indeed, fake, Irishman – 'a stereotype Paddy from a bygone era, as imagined by an ex-patriot Celt with emerald-tinted spectacles and a head full of whiskey and nostalgia … With regards to diddle-ee-aye Irishness, Hillman Hunter was the whole bag of potatoes' – but *AAT*'s plot was wholly concerned with the subject of religious faith and mythology, taking Adams' Norse God preoccupation and exploring it more than ever before. It is in fact Zaphod's story, decades after his creator dismissed the Galactic President as 'irredeemably seventies': Beeblebrox's action-hero antics in Asgard take up a huge expanse of a novel which is more than twice the length of the first book, and by far the longest *Hitchhiker* entry to date – if, indeed, you choose to accept it as such a thing. Therein lies the key

– when it comes to drawing a line in the sand, death is pretty much the ultimate marker. Anything else carrying the *Hitchhiker* name post-2001 simply comes with an extra pinch of salt: you buy into it or you don't – you can't stop it, no matter how many Facebook groups you set up.

Having presaged this epic gambit with a quote from Jack Black's comedy 'rawk' outfit Tenacious D ('We have travelled through space and time, my friends, to rock this house again!'), the tricky issue of saving the core cast from Club Beta is accomplished by Zaphod himself, although the ease of turning the tables in Adams' Universe is celebrated by having any number of solutions to *MH*'s cliffhanger outlined in each character's 'dream construct' escape, including Maggs' Babel fish idea. Arthur and Ford, however – the latter medicated by the spliff equivalent of a PGGB, the awesomely mellowing 'joystick' – are largely sidelined as bystanders to what unfolds, as a hitherto unknown colony of other humans (who admittedly rather spoil the loneliness of Dent's survival, and make no sense in the context of 1970s Earth as we know it) are pursued to their new Magrathean-built planet Nano by the relentless Vogons. Arthur spends most of his time dressed in his school uniform trying not to fall in love with a ship's computer who has taken the form of Fenchurch, occasionally stepping in to try and be a better father to Random – by the end of the narrative, happy ending ripped from his grasp, he remains alone, and threatened by Vogons.

In terms of fan-baiting, the only major development made by *AAT* – besides the survival of the human race, and an inkling of positive evolution in Vogon society thanks to Jeltz's perversely compassionate son Constant Mown – is the strange love affair between Trillian and, of all people, Wowbagger (now given the forename 'Bowerick'), which sees them zoom off together for a mortal happy-ever-after. However, all developments are at least tastefully put in context from the very start by the author's decision to couch his story as precisely what it was, an adjunct to the five-part trilogy set in stone by Adams' death:

> Let us say, for example, that you are on an eight-hour layover
> in Port Brasta without enough credit for a Gargle Blaster on your
> implant, and if upon realising that you know almost nothing
> about this supposedly wonderful book you hold in your hands,
> you decide out of sheer brain-fogging boredom to type the words
> 'the hitchhiker's guide to the galaxy' into the search bar on The

Hitchhiker's Guide to the Galaxy, what results will this flippant tappery yield?

Firstly, an animated icon appears in a flash of pixels and informs you that there are three results, which is confusing as there are obviously five listed below, numbered in the usual order ... Each of these five results is a lengthy article, accompanied by many hours of video and audio files and some dramatic reconstructions featuring quite well known actors. This is not the story of those articles.

But if you scroll down past article five, ignoring the offers to remortgage your kidneys and lengthen your pormwrangler, you will come to a line in tiny font that reads 'If you liked this, then you might also like to read ...' Have your icon rub itself along this link and you will be led to a text-only appendix with absolutely no audio and not so much as a frame of video shot by a student director who made the whole thing in his bedroom and paid his drama soc. mates with sandwiches.

This is the story of that appendix.

The novel also has a very different format, featuring regular 'Guide Notes' with ridiculous suggestions for further reading, one of which was a specific tribute to the original DNA, which could only have been picked up on by the most savvy fans:

Guide Note: Technically speaking, Doxy Ribonu-Clegg did not invent the SubEtha, rather he discovered its existence. The SubEtha waves had been around for at least as long as the gods, just waiting for someone to pump some data into them. The legend goes that Ribonu-Clegg had been lying on his back in a field on his home planet. As he gazed blearily up through the wedge of space suspended above him it occurred to the renowned professor that all this space was loaded with information and that perhaps it would be possible to transport some information of his own through the cosmic conduits if only he could make it small enough. So Ribonu-Clegg hurried back to his rudimentary lab and constructed the first ever set of SubEtha transmitters using pepper grinders, several live pinky rats, various cannibalised lab machines and some professional-standard hairdressing scissors. Once these components were connected, Ribonu-Clegg fed in the photopix from his wedding album and prayed they would be reassembled on the other side of the room. They were not, but the national lottery numbers for the following evening did show up, which encouraged the professor to patent his invention. Ribonu-Clegg used his winnings to hire a team of shark lawyers who successfully sued eighty-nine companies that invented actual working SubEtha transmitters, making the professor the richest man on the planet until he fell into his lawyers' tank and they followed their instincts and ate him ...

Although he could be notably cutting about critics, Adams could quite comfortably afford to ignore any verdict on his books for most of his career, thanks to such a devoted following. This, however, was never going to be the case with the first *Hitchhiker* novel since his death, and numerous breaths were bated in expectation of a punishing hail of invective headed Colfer's way. By and large, however, quite the opposite happened. The practice of extending literary creations beyond their authors' lives has become increasingly accepted in recent years, with zombies plaguing half of Jane Austen's output and Sebastian Faulks becoming the literary equiv- alent of Rory Bremner, puppeteering not just James Bond but the truly inimitable Jeeves. Adams has, however, been at rest for a considerably briefer period than other authors and so, even with the family's support, sensitivities were surely heightened as each reviewer received their early copies. By the time Hitchcon came round, with comedy geek supremo Dara O'Briain testing Eoin's *Hitchhiker* knowledge in front of a rowdy crowd and queues stretching out to the crack of doom to get copies of the new story signed, the critics had delivered generally glowing reviews for 'the best post-mortem impersonation' that many had encountered, the *Observer* observing 'Colfer has pulled off the near-impossible. It's faithful to Adams' humour, it's also got his rhythm and the footfall that made his style so often (badly) imitated.' Few of those who would never have given the project their time of day had their minds changed, and continued to mumble into their towels, but that Colfer had managed to get away with it was otherwise never in doubt, setting a precedent which is unlikely not to be followed: the *Hitchhiker* Universe was now safely immortal, beyond the non-canonical obscurity of fan-fiction. Jane, characteristically, provided the answer to the deadly question of 'WDWHW' when Ed phoned her up after publication wondering whether they had done the wrong thing: 'Douglas hated every book he ever published when it was published,' she replied. 'So why should this one be any different?'

The biggest question of all for Colfer's story, however, remains: is it funny? Tiresome though it is to recycle the truism, the question is of course inevitably subjective, but in terms of intent, *AAT* was certainly a far more comedic offering than Adams had attempted since *LUE*, with gags studded through every page. Admittedly, being freed from the arguable strictures of children's writing had ironically inspired Colfer to take a more infantile approach than his forebear, with smatterings of innuendo (usually involving 'pormwranglers') which would probably have revolted Adams, but the gag rate was so high that any dropped clangers were usually followed by a more cerebral laugh before the page was even turned. Dirk Maggs was so impressed that he tried and failed to interest Radio 4 in an adaptation on two separate occasions – 'I enjoyed *AAT*,' Dirk adds, 'and I thought, *why not?* I actually think it's got more gags than latter *Hitchhiker*, so I pitched it because I thought it would be a funny radio series.' He was unsuccessful, but BBC Radio has an infamous horror of sci-fi comedy, despite numerous programmes following in *Hitchhiker*'s wake, from *Paradise Lost In Space* to Radio 2 sitcom *Welcome To Our Village, Please Invade Carefully*. Sci-fi comedy hasn't fared much better on UK TV, post-*Red Dwarf*, with already forgotten shows like *Hyperdrive* making the sub-genre as taboo as it was when Douglas was fighting to get his own made in the 1970s.

AAT did however feature on radio, in a highly abridged reading performed by Peter Serafinowicz as the Book, with Steven Mangan as everyone else – though at the time this ultimate celebrity *Hitchhiker* fan was already in the frame for a more significant Adams-inspired role. The eventual *Dirk Gently* TV show, consciously circumnavigating the problems presented by the books, was ultimately homeopathic Adams. No ghosts, primordial aliens or wormholes to Valhalla here – *Dirk Gently* rather took the *X-Files* approach (a show Douglas personally decried for its conspiracy-theory-feeding philosophy), with original plots verging on the convincing side of near-future science: preternatural concepts conceivably smiled upon by Adams (a coma patient reanimated with a computer-generated consciousness, a time-travelling cat) but steering well clear of the supernatural element which the novels took in their stride. Also, although Darren Boyd, Helen Baxendale and Jason Watkins could have been fine casting for Richard, Susan and Gilks in a tighter adaptation, it was self-confessed Adams obsessive and *Celebrity Mastermind* (specialist subject: *Hitchhiker*) champion Steven Mangan in the title role who most emphatically belied the Svlad of the books. Just as each episode took a smattering of references and jokes from *Dirk* lore and dropped them into totally new fabrications, Mangan crafted his own egregious hero with the Gently name: likeably despicable, with some of the detective's qualities of cowardice, greed and arrogance, but without one of Dirk's visual signifiers or, indeed, his nicotine addiction. Not that the show wasn't a great deal of fun, from its thumping mystery-theme-tune opening to the final reveal of the interconnectedness of all things in each plot, and if BBC4 hadn't made its period of drama production so very brief, preferring to buy in Scandinavian cop shows, *Dirk Gently* could have gone on to rival *Sherlock*. But of all the productions detailed in this book, that series does objectively remain the one 'adaptation' most divorced from the material actually generated by our Frood as he hunched, brows furiously knitted, over his keyboard. In 2014 director Max Landis announced a new TV and comic series, directly inspired by the Oxford play, which could signal a new lease of life for Dirk.

On The Road Again

Similarly mixed fortunes ultimately awaited the most recent project to carry the *Hitchhiker* name, but as with *Dirk*, none of the problems could fairly be laid at the late author's door. Yet another cast reunion had raised the roof at the Hammersmith Apollo as part of a special show marking Douglas' 60th birthday in 2012 – the celebration filled the gigantic venue to the rafters and featured a bill chock-full of Adamsian acts, from John Lloyd sharing Liffs new and old (presaging the publication of a third collection, *Afterliff*, created with Jon Canter and with input from fans all over the world) to dancing rhinos, a Will Adams & Martin Smith reunion, and David Gilmour and many of Adams' musician friends playing his favourite music (plus the HeeBeeGeeBees). But of course, the centrepiece was always going to be live *Hitchhiker*.

The triple stage success of the original radio cast inspired Maggs to get the gang together for a live tour of the UK in the autumn, with the *ISIHAC* teams having proven that live 'radio recording' shows could become a big hit, and the fledgling Perfectly Normal Productions was advised and supported by theatrical professionals. Like any *Hitchhiker* project, a dizzying maze of rights issues required Dirk to forge an all-new show, 'based on the books' rather than on the BBC series. This required a careful selection of scenes, returning many of *Hitchhiker*'s set pieces to their sketch roots, culminating in Longworth's Slartibartfast raising the struggles of CAMTIM to find some kind of order in the proceedings:

SLARTY   Earthman, have you noticed anything strange lately?

ARTHUR   Where do you want me to start?!

SLARTY   Sudden temporal shifts? Finding yourself suddenly in new, strange environments?

ARTHUR   Yes, yes, exactly.

SLARTY   Dry throat, depression, lank, lifeless hair?

ARTHUR   Not so much … hang on, where's this going?

SLARTY   The time streams have become very polluted, yours in particular. Eddies in the space-time continuum, you see.

ARTHUR   Is he? (Waits for groans - and applause - to die down.) I'm suddenly getting an awful sense of déja vu.

SLARTY   Precisely. You shouldn't be here, Dentarthurdent.

ARTHUR   Well, I'm glad someone agrees with me.

SLARTY   Or rather, you shouldn't be here yet. Have you heard of the shoe event horizon? The B-Ark? Old Thrashbarg and the perfectly normal beasts?

ARTHUR   No. No, I haven't.

SLARTY   All of these events should be in your past, but they have not occurred. According to our records you have missed out whole chapters of your life … You must start again!

ARTHUR   WHAT? I've been blown up, asphyxiated, blown up, chased by a loony fruit bat and blown up twice! Which part of that little lot would I precisely want to repeat?

Simon, Geoff, Susan and Mark were supported by Pope, Béart, Secombe and others, plus Moore's Marvin was personified by a much-applauded robot puppet constructed out of tape recorders and microphones, with a radio for a head, controlled by Dirk's son Tom. The evening's entertainment was also augmented by a live band playing the theme, a Beatles-ish rendition of Pope's 'Everything Is Lovely', and generally adding bombast, while Dirk split his time between percussion and performing exuberant live sound effects alongside Ken Humphrey – though it was as visual as any radio show could be, with Vogon masks, an inflatable Earth, fights with Algolian Suntigers, and numerous references to the passing of time in the main cast (particularly Random's concern that her crusty dressing-gowned father had escaped from hospital). The evening took punters on a tour through Dent's mishaps at breakneck speed, occasionally pausing for a very silly mix of pantomime and music hall: a singalong version of 'Share & Enjoy', or having the audience provide the correct cheers for the Norse Gods in Milliways. But the centrepiece was the star guest appearance … from Agrajag. The unavoidable eeriness of reviving Douglas for the role disappeared with a live audience, as the sheer silliness of this one poor soul choosing just the wrong time to face his nemesis was brought out by the laughter – over a decade after his death, at last, Douglas Adams was performing, and filling theatres with voluble mirth once again. Having extended its scope from Python-inspired radio silliness to the multi-layered intellectual comic drama of the novels, with the live show, *Hitchhiker* somehow returned home. 'Because we did the recordings quite separately, we never quite got to know each other,' Sheridan says. 'They'd all been at Cambridge, of course – but it took us thirty years to get to know each other, so there's much more of a friendship between us now, plus we're all a lot older, so there's a kind of understanding between us that maybe we didn't have when we were in our twenties.'

The evening's mix of comedy and music earned warm plaudits and filled the houses with mirth on its inaugural tour up and down the country – with a few exceptions, Maggs noted: 'Occasionally you'd see one or two fans, they'd order front-row seats, right in front of Geoff and Simon, and sit with their towels draped over their lap, arms folded, and an expression of pure fury on their faces, because *this was not meant to be funny!* You weren't meant to get two thousand people falling about laughing at it, it was too sacred for that! It's a very sad thing, to see people who haven't "got it".' Everyone in the cast and crew commented on the wide array of the fans sent out into the night happily grinning and humming 'Marvin', be they old-school fans or Beeblebear-clutching newbies. But there was one audience member who mattered the most to Maggs. Early on in the first tour, Jane Thrift brought her mother to see the show on its Southampton date, and as Dirk fussed over the VIPs, Janet admitted, 'All these people dressed up in dressing gowns and carrying towels, it's a bit like a cult, isn't it? I'm not sure I like it.' She admitted that she and Ron often nodded off during the show's original broadcasts, and had never really grasped what made people love *Hitchhiker* so much. However, in the interval, the powerful octogenarian approached Dirk and, intending to give him a playful pat, slapped him hard in front of everyone. Before he could stammer his apologies, however, she protested loudly, 'I loved it! I didn't know it was so funny!' 'We had some great nights on both tours,' Dirk says, 'but that summed it all up for me – Douglas' Mum realised how funny her son was that night. That was the culmination of everything for me, because that was why we were there, the laughter in the room – for all his genius, cleverness, prescience and predictions, it made his Mum laugh.'

With such a hit night out and everyone in the team, veteran and fan, all having such a ball, a further follow-up tour seemed a must. It was just a shame that the second outing came up against all-too-foreseeable hazards. From the start, one of the show's selling points was the Voice of the Book, which was performed by a number of famous figures, including friends Miriam Margolyes, Rula Lenska, Anita Dobson, Clive Anderson, Billy Boyd and Neil Gaiman, sci-fi luminaries Anthony Daniels, Colin Baker and Danny John-Jules, and comedians Hugh Dennis, Phill Jupitus, Graeme Garden, Jon Culshaw and Barry Cryer – and so it was no major problem when Mark Wing-Davey had to cry off a second lap of honour in Zaphod's kilt (the Presidency being assumed by musical comic Mitch Benn), it all added to the eclectic range of talent on offer for every date on the tour. However, a drop-off in attendance worried the cast and Maggs' team alike, and it seemed clear that the itinerary worked out by the promoters simply wasn't helping, opting as it did for more out-of-the-way venues. It's natural to complain about tours which only stop off at the biggest cities, but the fact is that it's easier for big venues to draw in crowds from all round the provinces, whereas actually playing the provinces makes it harder to appeal to everyone. This problem could have been overcome if it hadn't been for the fact that the visual spectacle added to the proceedings made it such an expensive show to stage that eventually a halt had to be called to the tour before finances shifted into the red, with many ticket-holding fans bitterly disappointed not to get to see their heroes in action at the micro- phone. Because that was, of course, what anybody bought a ticket for – to see the original cast performing Douglas Adams' words live on stage: no further spectacle was needed.

But it's hard to keep *Hitchhiker* down for long and the following year another welcome repeat of the original programme on Radio 4 Extra was accompanied by a new HD iteration of the Infocom adventure on the BBC website. Thanks to the vanilla Radio 4's 'Character Invasion Day' on Saturday, 29th March 2014, however, the real gilt on the deal (pre-empted by a grumpiness face-off between *Today* presenter John Humphries and Marvin, which Marvin lost) was a positively unheard-of phenomenon – a live radio comedy performance broadcast from the BBC Radio Theatre in front of an audience whose hooting excitement belied the 10 a.m. scheduling.

Besides the 35th anniversary of the first book's publication, there was no major anniversary in 2014, and so the improbability of all this celebration coinciding exactly with the deadline for this very book must run into considerable figures. But how fortunate it was to be there at the BBC, mere yards from the gym where it all began, having chronicled the four decades of mutation that *Hitchhiker* has undergone since Peter Jones first sat down at the microphone and said those six or seven words. I could even have captured the entire thing on my iPhone had the battery lasted the morning (to repeat, we are still far off Douglas' technological utopia).

From John Lloyd, the morning's Voice of the Book, sitting in his leather armchair next to Douglas' photo stage left, to spot effects supremo Ken Humphrey brewing up an audio PGGB stage right, the entire cast, Moore included, arm round his puppet counterpart, were all there for the probably final hurrah, Kevin Davies capturing it all on camera for Dirk, as the ringmaster himself conducted the proceedings like a maestro to fit the strict live timings. Several thousand fans applied for the three hundred tickets, but in the happy crowds were Douglas' family up from Stalbridge, towelled luminaries from the ZZ9 club, and even the man perhaps most responsible for everyone being there: Douglas' teacher, Frank Halford. As Maggs observed at the end of the triumphant one hour fifteen minutes, it felt like a pretty good place to end.

What further celebrations may still materialise from the Perfectly Normal organisation is anyone's guess, but fans do generally appreciate that anything done in Douglas' name is done out of love, and is passed through a vehemently exacting vetting process before any green light is given. But as for this vexing question of whether anything can be canonical without Adams' input, it is often forgotten just what a team player Douglas was when *Hitchhiker* was created, both on radio and in print, from the guidance of Brett and Perkins and collaboration with Lloyd to Freestone and Bywater's roles in getting *MH* onto the page. So it's no wonder that a collaborative process, headed by those who knew and loved Douglas, should yield joyful results. Maggs reasons, 'He was under immense pressure to deliver superlative stuff, he was surrounded by people who were creative in their own right and would offer ideas, he had a brain full of information, all the books he read, and – no man is an island, he is going to synthesise material. John Lloyd we know contributed an awful lot into the early series, so it really boils down to "Would *Hitchhiker* be what it is, unless those people had in their own way helped Douglas, because they loved him?" It would maybe not have survived beyond the first radio series or become a book, it might have only been a wonderful flash in the pan, but it's because Douglas was surrounded by people who were intensely creative and liked him intensely, that it became much bigger than the sum of its parts. And the fact that it's lived beyond Douglas is kind of the same synthesis going on, even in absentia.'

Let's See You Get Out Of This One, Dent!

As time flashes by, the way the *Hitchhiker* Galaxy develops is bound to mutate further, and the sad truth is that any decision made since September 2011 lacks one tenacious source of approval, after Jane Belson lost a long fight against lung cancer. Just as the vacuum left by Douglas had to be compensated for by his surviving friends creatively, this double loss necessarily strengthened the network of devoted friends and family that had supported Polly as she grew up. When the 60th Birthday Bash came round, everyone taking part even recorded special messages for Douglas' daughter, although on a personal level the most significant support in her life has come from Neil Gaiman and now, of course, from her stepfather George.

'We do well together,' Polly tells me, as our long lunch eventually nears its conclusion. 'My Mum's best friend is his sister, and my godmother. So until they got married, in 2005, I hadn't put two and two together, he was just "My Godmother's Brother Who Lives With Us"… When they got married, I just thought, "Great! He's my stepdad," which is a less lengthy title. Then Neil turned up, and he's very good at doing the Dad bits, although obviously he's usually in America, but the two of them sort of complement each other really well ... It works well for me. I'm very lucky to have such people around. It means now I have all these brilliant relationships with my parents' friends, aunts, uncles, teachers, whatever, much closer than we would otherwise have been.'

It's human nature to feel some kind of pity for anyone deprived of their parents at such an unfairly young age, but there's a great deal about Polly Adams which seems to make such a reaction ridiculous – she is in no way a victim, or a sob-story; she is, if she would forgive the term, quite unmistakably froody. She now also has a lot of unlooked-for responsibility when it comes to helping to please the towel-carrying hitchers of this world while protecting the legacy of the father she knew all too briefly. For a first-year student, she has many extra-curricular calls on her time, and behind the scenes Ed, Robbie and Co. are always keen to find new ways both to introduce the existing canon of Douglas Adams' work to new fans and to develop more of the incredible unfinished creations he left behind.

Rifling through those precious hard-drive contents, arriving at a folder marked 'DNA MASTERWORKS', Stamp reels off the titles of currently inexplicable pitches in addition to those mentioned earlier, some of which may be just the vaguest nuggets, while some cannot be discussed because they are boldly marked 'for development' – 'Hal Silver', 'Heavenly Fire', 'Stanley's Machines', 'The High Jump', 'Ancient Seas' (an epic exploration of the aquatic ape theory), 'The Tramp Lord', screenplay drafts for *Starship Titanic* and *Dirk Gently* ... These are all potential posthumous hits which may well make Adams fans reappraise their hero yet again. For Robbie, though, there is one clear priority: 'We got h2g2.com back from the BBC, and we've been able to create a structure where a third of the company's shares are set aside in trust on behalf of the community, because it's a user-generated site – the company with the trust is Field Researchers Ltd., and the company that owns it all is Not Panicking Ltd. It's entirely volunteer-run at the moment, we have a team of getting on for forty-two people all round the world, and the dream Douglas and the original TDV team had of creating a real Earth Guide is still very much alive.' There is one glaring issue here, but he is quick to head it off: 'Wikipedia is an encyclopaedia, and I have massive respect for it, but we can position ourselves almost in exactly the same way that the Hitchhiker's Guide is positioned against The Encyclopaedia Galactica, our job is to be a Guide, with some of the patchiness and irreverence you can do with a Guide.'

This alternative Guide is already there for you to join up to, become an H2G2 Researcher, and begin sharing your take on the world with the community, but the real turning point will come when the app is available. The paucity of official Adams apps has been somewhat odd considering his keen adoption of every new techie concept, but this should change soon and see off the few unofficial cash-ins found in any app store. Similarly, the official online homes for Adams and his work need to evolve – there is 6of3.com, launched, as the name suggests, to promote Colfer's book, which is replete with fascinating material largely from Davies, but Adams' own website and even the TDV company site have been left to float adrift like virtual Mary Celestes, so a fresh online home should also be just around the corner.

There is a dimension to these activities that goes beyond the furthering of a brand. Having become a millionaire so early in life, of course Douglas wanted to do as much good in this world as he could. So not only is his legacy the continued promotion of Save The Rhino and other animal charities but, Stamp continues: 'We've also set up the Hitchhiker's Guide to the Galaxy Foundation, which has already started to use the h2g2 community to find small charities where a relatively small sum can have really big significance in literacy – one example, an orphanage in India which takes girls from very poor backgrounds, and has just got its first five students into university; we made sure that all books and teaching materials for an entire year were paid for. We define literacy very broadly – what did Douglas love? He loved the world of ideas. And that's one of the things I miss most about him to this day – his endless hunger and curiosity. He was just an immensely curious man. So the broad thrust of the Foundation is helping to support things which allow us to communicate with each other and share ideas.'

What of the *Hitchhiker* Universe itself? An all-new videogame adventure has been on the cards for decades now. In current-gen console terms, reliving Arthur's lives would translate into something akin to *Fable* crossed with *Mass Effect*, and numerous companies have made grand announcements about forthcoming *Hitchhiker* titles – to no avail, but the excitement that each announcement generates suggests that it is an area very likely to be explored, learning from the mistakes of *Starship Titanic*. There is even some talk of a fresh TV adaptation, introducing a new aesthetic to the Galaxy, and another generation of young actors to guide the Heart of Gold. 'If they get the right people involved,' Robbie concludes, 'I think that TV is a much better format for it than a feature film – it will allow that discursive, slightly episodic quality that's there in the books, to breathe. And there's a lot more material to mine. It's going to be interesting.' Of course, you can be assured that any new iteration will be certain to specifically contradict everything that has gone before.

However these ideas develop, be in no doubt that *Hitchhiker* is still out there, and the evolution of the Galaxy that Douglas Adams created is an ongoing process – all it requires at the moment is for a bureaucrat to rubber-stamp a few legal documents, and creative teams can be brought together to manipulate Arthur Dent into the muddy paths of bulldozers yet again. For many, a metaphorical line in the sand will never be enough, and the entire intellectual property should be placed in stasis for ever. But regrettably for those of that belief they are in the wrong universe: humanity has enjoyed recycling and extending its most cherished stories for millennia, and *Hitchhiker* entered the cultural soup to stay over thirty-five years ago. Having warped our view of this and an infinite number of other universes from before the Big Bang to coffee and cigars at Milliways, the richness of the Galaxy that Adams has left behind will prove irresistible to fans, academics and extraordinarily wealthy media corporations for as long as our culture sustains, just as other creations, from *Pride and Prejudice* to *Batman*, are rebooted, bowdlerised and otherwise engorged with new films, games, books and apps from decade to decade. For now, there is a small devoted coterie of those whom Douglas loved, and whose job it is to ensure that every subsequent twist in the *Hitchhiker* story is designed entirely in line with the unavoidably nebulous concept of 'WDWHW'.

The Hitchhiker's Guide to the Galaxy remains the most widely beloved creation of Douglas Adams, one of our most adored humorists. However, no fan can ever forget that it was never the work which gave him the most pleasure, and in which he had the most pride. Although the antics of Arthur, Ford and their cohorts made him a very rich man and brought him the fame he always desired (albeit not as John Cleese), in Adams' own estimation the work he wanted to be remembered for was *Last Chance To See* – that touching, passionate love letter to Life On Earth which has inspired so many people to devote their lives to preserving it in all its manifold and bizarre forms.

But then, *LCTS* would not be the creation of which Adams was most proud, were he still on this planet. Potentially sentimental though it may be, anyone who knew Douglas, and witnessed the happiness he found in his last few years, would agree that his greatest source of pride, were he here now, is sitting opposite me in a café discussing her own developing philosophies of life, the universe, and everything.

Polly Adams has now become central to every decision made within the Adams estate, a familiar situation faced in the past by the likes of Christophers Milne and Tolkien, but she has no immediate intentions of following Martin Amis or Rhianna Pratchett in taking on the family trade – she has her own life to lead: 'I try not to do too many things where I'm there exclusively as "Polly-daughter-of-Douglas", because that's not a role that I want to get stuck in. There are some things that I say yes to because they're cool, but mostly I do things where I can just be Polly, who's here in her own right ...' As we take our leave (noting the pleasing coincidence that the café happens to be in the exact neighbourhood which stood in for Islington for the *Dirk Gently* series) there can be no mistaking Polly's adoration for her missing father, and her sincerity when it comes to taking care of his Universe, but the undergraduate is only just beginning her own journey, and has plenty of time to find her own place in life: 'I'm in a useful position where being "Douglas' daughter" is something I can avoid, and be independent from, but it can also come in handy when I need it, and the possibility of creating things with it as a springboard is a great thing, because I love creating things. I do improv here at university, we have a society ...' And with a stated intent to catch a show one of these days, we go our separate ways in the darkness, faces lit with the glow of our own personal guides.

Perfectly Normal Paranoia

Douglas Adams' total book sales internationally are at around the 20 million mark, and have been translated into more than thirty languages, including Korean and Hebrew but not, as yet, Klingon. Why is it, then, that *Hitchhiker* seems incapable of passing into obscurity, planetary destruction aside? Admittedly, its most basic inspirations also both flourish in the 21st century – the Python team sold out the O2 in seconds, and *Doctor Who* has never been bigger. Despite Douglas' strong insistence that his creation was entirely separate, the fictional universes of *Hitchhiker* and *Who* have converged regularly since Russell T. Davies' triumphant reboot (both Davies and Steven Moffat cite *City of Death* as The New Show's inspiration, and the former penned an introduction for a re-release of the first book), with the Tenth Doctor saving the world in pyjamas and claiming the look to be 'Very Arthur Dent – now there was a nice man', as well as identifying an intelligent shade of blue as a Hooloovoo at the Pyramid of the Rings of Akhaten. The sheer time spent by fans debating the canonicity of such things should buy any sci-fi franchise a century or two of lifespan (crossovers already proliferate in fan – and, doubtless, slash – fiction).

But there's more to *Hitchhiker* than sci-fi, and there's more to it than comedy. The blend is significant, of course – sci-fi obsessiveness can be such a terribly serious trap to fall into, so it's natural that a deliberate decision not to take any of it seriously (adopted very early on by Adams with his oft-stated 'Belgium the fans' approach) provides an irresistible safety valve for genre fans who can retain a sense of humour. When it comes to mixing the genres, *Hitchhiker* has always been the paragon – through *Red Dwarf, Men in Black, Futurama, Galaxy Quest, Bravest Warriors, Rick & Morty* and many more, no sci-fi comedy would dare deny its debt to Douglas. The final part of Pegg, Wright & Frost's 'Cornetto' movie trilogy, *The World's End*, was positively an homage, not least due to the reunion of Martin Freeman and Bill Nighy for the brilliantly Adamsian conclusion.

Above and beyond the star-skipping action and the silly jokes, though, it is the Adams philosophy, and how *Hitchhiker* makes us both think and feel, as residents of Planet Earth, of any creed or colour, which continues to appeal – a feeling which goes right back to the drunken stargazing of a hitch-hiking gap-year student in a field in Innsbruck over forty years ago. Okay, so humanity may be a blip on an insignificant little blue-green planet on the Western Spiral Arm of the Galaxy, we may be stuck thinking iPhones are a pretty neat idea and have no idea what the real meaning of Life, the Universe and Everything is – but, give or take the odd bureaucratic nightmare, that's just froody. This is, after all, a Wonderful World, and we should appreciate what we've got (looking after it is not Somebody Else's Problem). The garden *is* beautiful without the need for fairies at the bottom of it.

If, however, we should find a way to hitch into the stars and make contact with any other form of life, *Hitchhiker* tells us that they will no doubt be much the same as us – they will be 'normal', inasmuch as anyone has ever worked out what normal is anyway. They may have an extra head here, a breast there, but they will be subject to all the same insecurities and face the same Vogon-like frustrations as we all do in our puny human lives, they will feel that same sense of paranoia and probably have just as hazy an idea of why the Universe exists as we do – the chances of finding out what really is going on being so absurdly remote that the only thing to do is to say hang the sense of it, hitch a ride, pour yourself a drink that feels like having your brains smashed out by a slice of lemon wrapped round a large gold brick, and keep yourself occupied. Science may have achieved wonderful things, and will continue to do so, but perhaps it is better to be happy than right any day.

We laugh at Marvin's relentless misery because we recognise his personality flaws as genuinely our own, but if the Paranoid Android's designer had any Final Message to those he left behind, it must surely be the life-affirmingly positive outlook which concluded *The Hitchhiker's Guide to the Future*, broadcast in Douglas' final months:

> There is an argument that says we have stopped, or at least pressed the pause button, on human evolution. Evolutionary change usually occurs as the result of continual abrasion between organisms and their environment. However, Man, the tool-maker, has created a buffer zone around himself. To begin with, this was just shelter and clothes, but then as our tool-making skills developed, the buffer zone became more sophisticated, with agriculture, or medicine – if our crops fail, we don't die, if we injure ourselves, we don't die, if it's too hot or too cold, we don't die, if we're stupid, we're elected to high office … Now, I don't want to make any rash statements about what Life is – any class of objects which includes both a bath sponge and Beethoven is going to be hard to define with any great precision. But it's fair to say that anything lifelike is going to exhibit certain things, like complexity, self-organisation and the ability to process and respond to information in some way. Computers themselves are not really good examples of lifelike things, but when you consider the vast tangled *network* of computers which now inhabits this buffer zone, the way in which information now flows through it and generates organisation within the channels through which it flows, and the way it manages the passage of information between ourselves and our environment, then the buffer zone begins to look less like the walls of a house keeping out the cold, and more

like a virtual epidermis, responding to it … Before long, computers will be as trivial and plentiful as chairs, paper, grains of sand. Instead of calculating with streams of electrons moving around silicon chips, we will be calculating with beams of light, with organic molecules, and then, as quantum computers arrive, with other universes. It is as if we are part of a huge multi-billion-year project to turn dumb matter into smart matter.

Should we be excited, or alarmed? … The future is invented by those who are excited about it, and it has never been as inventable as it is now.

'Our generation of scientists and technologists now are the people who were brought up on a diet of science fiction many years ago,' he reflected. 'Their ideas are predicated on what they read about in their youth. So it's very important that we give ourselves optimistic views of the future. If we allow ourselves to be hypnotised by the view of the future where the whole world will look like a sort of rusty version of LA, then that's what we'll get. But on the other hand, if we see the technologies coming along at the moment, things we are actively involved in creating and using and thinking creatively and constructively about in the best possible way, then we're more likely to get something great coming out of it. The models we have in our mind are very important.'

Positive Thinking, Douglas Adams concluded, was the key – if you envisage a dystopia, it's all too likely to come true, and we will lose hope. But thanks to The Frood, when we now look up at the stars, we can nurse an inkling that we are all part of something potentially remarkable, that one day we will be up there, and if we travel hopefully, we can expect to find excitement, adventure and really wild things.

DO NOT READ THESE ACKNOWLEDGEMENTS EITHER

> The last ever dolphin message was misinterpreted as a surprisingly sophisticated attempt to do a double-backwards-somersault through a hoop whilst whistling the 'Star Spangled Banner', but in fact the message was this…
>
> – The Book, *The Hitchhiker's Guide To The Galaxy*

… Or at least, don't read this unless disclaimers, exposition and heartfelt grovelling are your kind of thing – otherwise, you should proceed directly to the appendices, which are a good bit, and do actually have Marvin in them. But having enjoyed the sensation of walking on comparatively virgin snow with my first books, on *I'm Sorry I Haven't a Clue* and *Blackadder*, the decision to add to the Douglas Adams library was obviously not taken lightly. 'What, another one?' was the reasonable wail from some quarters, not least my own, as I just had to walk to my own bookcase to find previous *Hitchhiker* histories courtesy of Neil Gaiman, Nick Webb and M. J. Simpson, alongside my dog-eared copies of *Hitchhiker* and the rest of the Adams oeuvre. The official fan club ZZ9 Plural Z Alpha have been publishing their own quarterly newsletter, *Mostly Harmless*, for over three decades: what more could there be to say?

The problem with writing non-fiction is that unless you have an unquenchable passion for your subject matter, you're liable either to write a lacklustre book or have a breakdown. Adams himself presented the dangers characteristically adroitly in a draft of *The Salmon of Doubt*:

> Biographers often name their pets after their subjects … It's so they've got someone to shout at when they get fed up. You spend hours wading through someone banging on about the teleological suspension of the ethical or whatever and sometimes you just need

to be able to shout "Oh, shut up, Kierkegaard, for Christ's sake!"
Some biographers use a small wooden ornament or a potted plant,
but most prefer something you can get a good yap out of.

Having always written about collaborative comedies, the idea of focusing
on one great man who was no longer around to answer back was a particular
stumbling block at first – although the intention was specifically to write
a 'History of *Hitchhiker*', the bond between Creator and Creation here
is so total as to make any attempt to differentiate history from biography
little short of pedantry. And who was I to pontificate on the personal life of
one of our greatest humorists and thinkers, a remarkable man I had always
venerated but never met – let alone insufferably assume the familiarity of
calling him 'Douglas'? A cat may look at a king, but there was a whole circuit
of psychological hurdles to clamber over here. Nonetheless, the idea of a
fresh exploration began to stick, as at least three distinct reasons for *The
Frood* to exist had become clear.

There was no doubt that any fresh *Hitchhiker* historian was going to be
standing on the shoulders of rather tall people, and so my first instincts
were to contact Gaiman, Webb and Simpson – the first was unavailable,
the second is sadly no longer with us, but Mike Simpson did kindly get in
touch, only to explain that he had long since hung up his spurs as unofficial
Adams expert, but I would be welcome to comb through his huge archive
of research, donated to the Science Fiction Library at the University of
Liverpool (where my exploration was expertly aided by Andy Sawyer, with
Lorna Goude and Kate Hawke). Although *Don't Panic, Wish You Were Here*
and *Hitchhiker* all have distinct lasting value to the committed Adams fan,
however, they left a surprising mass of grey area still to be coloured in.
The most obvious point was that much time had passed since the existing
books were written or updated, but added to that was that none of them
had really approached *Hitchhiker* from a doggedly comedic point of view
in accordance with Adams' original intentions, favouring literary or sci-fi
concerns, whereas I am strictly a comedy geek. Above all, it seemed to me
that nobody had actually attempted to tell the story of the creation of *The
Hitchhiker's Guide To The Galaxy* with any real chronological flow, due to
the thematic and time-scrambling temptations of Biography. Straightening
out the timeline shone such an utterly new light on this epic story, and on
the creation of a comedy classic, that there was no longer any doubt that

a more holistic approach to one of the greatest radio comedies of all time would be not only justifiable but welcome. It was with great excitement that I discovered that the then-nebulous entity known as 'The Douglas Adams Estate' tentatively agreed.

But then, with so much material already in existence, research was going to be by the lorry-load and, above all, how would the extended *Hitchhiker* family take to being bothered once again to regurgitate anecdotes possibly honed over a hundred sci-fi convention appearances? Early encouragement was given by John Lloyd, Jon Canter, Mary Allen, Stephen Fry and his ever-wonderful sister Jo Crocker but, as they all felt very much 'on record', the idea grew that this should be the first book on *Hitchhiker* to be specifically commented on by Douglas alone, from his lifetime of interviews, press junkets and chat-show appearances (albeit with a careful eye on his celebrated anecdote-sculpting, embroidery, and truth distortion, which always tended to be in the name of a laugh). The word went out to all that this new official book was an opportunity to get together around the metaphorical campfire and swap old tales of the super-sized, enthusiastic, inspiring friend they all missed, to clear any existing misapprehensions, and have a final say on the subject, for a generation at least. Of course I did not miss my opportunity to spend an evening in the pub with Martin Smith and Will Adams, to Skype with Andrew Marshall and be passed on to his friend Rob Grant to discuss *Hitchhiker* and *Red Dwarf* ... Otherwise, my life was now dedicated to getting up every morning to walk to my desk to try to write the story of a man who got up every morning and walked to his desk to try to write ... and so on.

Gaining official approval on paper was gratifying, but it was the personal thumbs-up from those carrying Douglas' torch that truly mattered. One of the most pleasant days in my career to date came when I was invited down to Stalbridge in Dorset by Douglas' family to have a gloriously cordial, sunny Sunday lunch reminiscent of something H. E. Bates would have dreamt up, in the company of The Frood's mother Janet Thrift, sister Sue Adams, brother James and sister-in-law Bronwen, plus the next generation, Ella, Max and Joe. James showed me around the very country lanes where Douglas had jogged, explained where the condemned mill that started it all once stood, and generally made it clear that, this time, they hoped for a book which would do their absent relative justice – and of course the same sentiments were expressed by Douglas' other sisters Jane and

Heather. Visiting the legendary Ed Victor's office inspired a different kind of anxiety, but thanks to his wonderfully helpful aide Maggie Phillips, my publisher, the eminent Trevor Dolby and I perched on a sofa's edge like Harry and Ron summoned to Dumbledore's office, and received a benevolent twinkle from Douglas' closest compadre which allowed the story to go ahead with a new-found confidence.

By this point, however, a fourth and overwhelmingly decisive reason for *The Frood* to be unleashed on the world had come along. Just a few years earlier, Polly Adams and her stepfather George Lloyd-Roberts had made the emotional decision to have a comprehensive clear-out, and deposited Douglas' entire paper archive with his old college at St. John's, where Special Collections Librarian Kathryn McKee was overseeing its careful preservation and organisation by the pleasingly named archivist Mandy Marvin – and I would be the first writer to be allowed access to this huge treasure trove, even gifted accommodation within the portals of St. John's itself. I had yet to recover from the honour of having Richard Curtis hand me an unproduced *Blackadder* script two years previously, but the experience of swanning around the *Shada*-inspiring antiquity of Cambridge, elbow-deep in *Hitchhiker* jokes and details that nobody had clapped eyes on for decades, private notebooks in adolescent handwriting and unexplored fantasies directly from the Frood's typewriter, was a whole new world of bedazzling privilege. Although I had made my own London pilgrimage, walking from Highgate Cemetery to Adams' Islington, I was also very lucky to be shown around 'Adams' Cambridge' by surely the incumbent Douglas Adams oracle, David Haddock, who continued to be utterly indispensable as an arbiter of accuracy for the narrative. My two trips eastwards added up to several days' intense harvesting of unpublished material, which all had to be meticulously scanned and transcribed, and although only a percentage of the most startling and relevant material has made it into this book, what you will find here will so entirely astonish even the most obsessive Adams fan that the archive provided by far the most conclusive reason for this fresh take on the *Hitchhiker* story. In the same year as *Hitchhiker* debuted, Richard Usborne edited a remarkable book called *Wodehouse At Work To The End*, looking respectfully over the shoulder of Douglas' humorist idol, and with this archival windfall *The Frood* could perform the same function.

And so the tale continued on to its tragic conclusion – my main fear being over-identifying with the Frood and risking the whooshing sound of my own deadlines. But then another hurdle presented itself: with no Douglas around to comment on the last thirteen years of busy *Hitchhiker* activity, who could take his place as our guide? It only seemed right that his closest friends and collaborators should finally get their say, and so further chats with Ed Victor, Robbie Stamp, and Dirk Maggs were utterly crucial in exploring the terrible concept of 'What Douglas Would Have Wanted'. But the most important person to talk to was, of course, Polly – despite being at uni only a short distance away, she was naturally snowed under with exam revision and worse, but when a window did open, getting to meet her in person was not a disappointment – and it gave me a chance to thank her for allowing all us *Hitchhiker* fans access to her father's private notes and rough drafts after all these years.

This book glories in astonishing coincidences – arguably part of the inter-connectedness of all things – but although, as any fan knows, *Hitchhiker* is never truly dormant, the timing of 2014's live *Hitchhiker* broadcast on Radio 4, literally during the last fortnight before a whooshing sound was headed my way, really would have made for improbable fiction. Having chronicled the creation and growth of *Hitchhiker* over four decades, suddenly I was there with the flesh-and-blood actors who had only been characters on the page hitherto. It was a jubilant but fraught schedule at the BBC Radio Theatre, so I barely got to say a hello to anyone at the time, but subsequent chats with Simon Jones, Susan Sheridan, Mark Wing-Davey, Samantha Béart, Toby Longworth, Geoff McGivern and Phil Pope really helped make the end of the story the celebration it needed to be – let alone meeting the diehard fans, particularly the hugely helpful Kevin Davies, and ZZ9 luminaries including Carrie Mowatt and Deborah Fishburn. One of the scariest issues with taking on the mantle of 'Official Adams Biographer' has of course been the potential for risking the 'infinite umbrage' of hardcore fans, but no gang could be more lovely and welcoming – it's well worth signing up to ZZ9, if you were in any doubt.

Dozens of other kindnesses allowed *The Frood* to end up in your hands, courtesy of Frank Bowles, Michael Bywater, Sue Freestone, Peter Gill, Jacqui Graham, Garth Jennings, Nicholas Joll, Darrell Maclaine-Jones, Jennifer Morgan, Peter Pann, Sean Sollé, Steven Sutton, plus the Preface team Trevor Dolby, Rose Tremlett, John Sugar, Phil Brown, Nick Austin and particularly my original editors, readers and encouragers, Humphrey Price and Tim Worthington. Plus, double acknowledgements go to James Thrift, Will Adams and Kevin Davies for photographic brilliance.

But in the end, the meeting of this deadline was down to me, the blinking cursor on the blank screen, and Douglas Adams. Among the many jaw-dropping discoveries in his private archive were numerous notes to himself, to stave off depression and remind him of what he was capable, and they could still give a struggling author a fillip decades later:

> Writing isn't so bad really when you get through the worry. Forget about the worry, just press on. Don't be embarrassed about the bad bits. Don't strain at them. Give yourself time, you can go back and do it again in the light of what you discover about the story later on. It's better to have pages and pages of material to work with and sift and maybe find an unexpected shape in that you can then craft and put to good use, rather than one manically reworked paragraph or sentence ... But writing can be good. You attack it, don't let it attack you. You can get pleasure out of it. You can certainly do very well for yourself with it ...!

The last point applies only to Douglas himself, of course, but I was grateful for his inadvertent pep talks, which helped *The Frood* finally take its place in the world, hopefully illuminating, entertaining and astonishing *Hitchhiker* fans all over the planet, over a decade after the infinitely unfair loss of the Creator himself.

And I am very thankful to say, after a year's intense nosiness in the Frood's life, that far from heading to the pet shop to buy a 'Douglas' to kick I have a deeper and stronger love for the Man and his Creation than ever before, which is as it should be.

I love deadlines – I love the screeching sound they make when you just about avoid crashing into them.

JEM ROBERTS, Bath, Summer 2014

APPENDICES

DNA TIMELINE

11/03/52	Douglas Noël Adams born to Christopher Adams and Janet née Donovan, Mill Rd Maternity Hospital, Cambridge, UK. The family soon move to London, where his sister Susan is born three years later.
1957	Janet divorces Christopher and takes DNA and Sue to live with her mother in Brentwood, Essex.
09/59	DNA enters Brentwood Prep School.
07/60	Christopher Adams marries Judith Stewart, née Robinson, who has two daughters, Rosemary and Karena. They have a daughter, Heather, in July 1962.
07/03/62	Frank Halford gives DNA 10/10 for an adventure story.
07/64	Janet marries Ronald Thrift, and moves to Dorset. They have a daughter, Jane, in August 1966, and a son, James, in June 1968.
23/01/65	First national publication, in *The Eagle*.
12/70	DNA leaves Brentwood School.
07/71	DNA travels around Europe with the aid of *The Hitchhiker's Guide to Europe* by Ken Welsh.
10/71	DNA arrives at St John's College, Cambridge, having won an Exhibition in English.
25/11/72	John Cleese interview published in *Varsity*.
14/06/73	*Several Poor Players Strutting & Fretting*, at the School of Pythagoras, St. John's.
15/11/73	*The Patter Of Tiny Minds* debuts.
13/01/74	*The Patter Of Tiny Minds* London debut at Bush Theatre.
06/74	DNA graduates with a BA in English Literature.
15/07/74	*Chox* London debut; DNA meets Graham Chapman.
06/11/74	*Cerberus* debuts at the Arts Theatre, Cambridge.
09/75	*So You Think You Feel Haddocky* debuts at Little Theatre, London.
10/01/76	*Out Of The Trees* is broadcast on BBC2.
07/06/76	*A Kick In The Stalls* debut.
08/76	*The Unpleasantness at Brodie's Close* debuts at the Edinburgh festival.

18/02/77	*The Hitchhiker's Guide To The Galaxy* verbally commissioned by Simon Brett.
04/04/77	DNA hands in pilot script for *THHGTTG*.
31/08/77	Full series of *THHGTTG* commissioned by the BBC.
08/03/78	The Primary Phase of the *THHGTTG* radio series begins on BBC Radio 4.
01/05/79	The first stage production of *THHGTTG* debuts at the ICA, London.
12/10/79	*THHGTTG* novel published by Pan.
11/79	First *THHGTTG* album available via mail order, reaching shops six months later.
05/01/80	The second theatrical adaptation of *THHGTTG* debuts at Theatr Clwyd, Mold.
21/01/80	The Secondary Phase of *THHGTTG* begins on BBC Radio 4, and runs for five days.
07/80	The disastrous theatrical adaptation of *THHGTTG* debuts at the Rainbow Theatre, London.
01/10/80	*The Restaurant at the End of the Universe* published by Pan.
05/01/81	*THHGTTG* BBC TV series begins.
08/82	*Life, The Universe and Everything* published by Pan.
05/83	DNA decamps to LA to begin work on *THHGTTG* movie.
11/11/83	*The Meaning of Liff* published by Pan/Faber & Faber.
10/84	*THHGTTG: The Adventure Game* published by Infocom.
11/84	*So Long, and Thanks for All the Fish* published by Pan.
06/85	Death of Christopher Adams.
07/85	Douglas and Jane travel to Madagascar with Mark Carwardine to find the aye-aye.
11/86	*The Utterly Utterly Merry Comic Relief Christmas Book* published by Collins.
06/87	*Dirk Gently's Holistic Detective Agency* published by Heinemann.
08/87	*Bureaucracy* published by Infocom.
10/87	*Don't Panic* by Neil Gaiman, first published by Titan Books.
10/88	*The Long Dark Tea-Time of the Soul* published by Heinemann.
10/89	*Last Chance to See* broadcast on BBC Radio 4.

20/09/90	*Hyperland* broadcast on BBC2.
10/90	*Last Chance to See* published by Pan.
10/90	*The Deeper Meaning of Liff* published by Faber & Faber.
25/11/91	DNA and Jane Belson married, London.
10/92	*Mostly Harmless* published by Heinemann
10/93	First DC Comics *THHGTTG* adaptation published.
22/06/94	Polly Jane Rocket Adams born.
11/10/94	*The Illustrated THHGTTG* published by Weidenfeld & Nicolson.
28/10/94	DNA joins Pink Floyd on stage at Earl's Court, London.
12/97	*Starship Titanic* by Terry Jones published by Pan.
04/98	*Starship Titanic* CD-ROM published by TDV.
04/01	*The Hitchhiker's Guide To The Future* broadcast by BBC Radio 4.
11/05/01	DNA dies of a heart attack, Santa Barbara, USA. He is cremated, with his towel, five days later.
25/05/01	The first annual Towel Day held around the world in Adams' memory.
03/02	*The Salmon of Doubt* published by Macmillan.
03/03	*Hitchhiker* by M. J. Simpson published by Coronet.
06/10/03	*Wish You Were Here* by Nick Webb published by Headline.
21/10/04	The Tertiary Phase of *THHGTTG* radio series begins on BBC Radio 4.
28/04/05	*THHGTTG* movie released in the UK, and the following day in the USA.
03/05/05	The Quandary and Quintessential Phases begin on BBC Radio 4.
12/10/09	*And Another Thing ...* by Eoin Colfer published by Penguin/Hyperion.
16/12/10	*Dirk Gently* TV series piloted, BBC4. A full series follows in March 2013.
12/06/12	The first *THHGTTG Radio Show Live* tour begins.
15/08/13	*Afterliff* published by Faber & Faber.
29/03/14	*THHGTTG* broadcast live on Radio 4 as part of 'Character Invasion Day'.

H2G2 DATABANK

Episode Guides, Bibliographies, Links

BOOKS: NOVELS, SCRIPTS & COMICS

The Hitchhiker's Guide To The Galaxy – Pan Books, 1979

The Restaurant at the End of the Universe – Pan Books, 1980

Life, The Universe and Everything – Pan Books, 1982

So Long, and Thanks For All The Fish – Pan Books, 1984

THHGTTG: The Original Radio Scripts – Pan, 1985

The Utterly Utterly Merry Comic Relief Christmas Book (with *Young Zaphod Plays It Safe* and *The Private Life of Genghis Khan*) – Fontana Press 1986

Mostly Harmless – Heinemann, 1992

THHGTTG, Restaurant, LUE – DC Comics, 1993, 1994, 1996

The Illustrated THHGTTG – Crown, 1994

And Another Thing … by Eoin Colfer – Penguin 2009

THHGTTG: Further Radio Scripts – Pan, 2012

RADIO, TELEVISION & FILM
THE HITCHHIKER'S GUIDE TO THE GALAXY – BBC Radio 4

PRIMARY PHASE (Rec. June, Nov–Dec '77)
Written by Douglas Adams (with John Lloyd, Fits 5–6). Produced by Simon Brett (Fit the 1st) and Geoffrey Perkins, with music by Paddy Kingsland.

Fit the 1st	08/03/78
Fit the 2nd	15/03/78
Fit the 3rd	22/03/78
Fit the 4th	29/03/78
Fit the 5th	05/04/78
Fit the 6th	12/04/78

CHRISTMAS SPECIAL (Rec. Dec '78)

Fit the 7th	24/12/78

SECONDARY PHASE (Rec. Jan '80)

Fit the 8th 21/01/80
Fit the 9th 22/01/80
Fit the 10th 23/01/80
Fit the 11th 24/01/80
Fit the 12th 25/01/80

The Book: Peter Jones; Arthur Dent: Simon Jones; Ford Prefect: Geoffrey McGivern; Prosser/Prostetnic Vogon Jeltz: Bill Wallis; Lady Cynthia Fitzmelton: Jo Kendall; The Barman: David Gooderson; Vogon Guard/Eddie the Computer: David Tate; Trillian: Susan Sheridan; Zaphod Beeblebrox: Mark Wing-Davey; Marvin the Paranoid Android: Stephen Moore; Slartibartfast: Richard Vernon; Bang Bang: Ray Hassett; Majikthise: Jonathan Adams; Vroomfondel/Shooty: Jim Broadbent; Frankie Mouse: Peter Hawkins; B-Ark Captain: David Jason; Number One: Jonathan Cecil; Number Two: Aubrey Woods; Marketing Girl: Beth Porter; Arcturan Number One: Bill Paterson; Roosta: Alan Ford; Gargravarr: Valentine Dyall; Nutrimat Machine: Leueen Willoughby; Zaphod Beeblebrox IV: Richard Goolden; The Wise Old Bird: John Le Mesurier; Lintilla: Rula Lenska; Hig Hurtenflurst: Marc Smith; Poodoo: Ken Campbell; Zarniwoop: Jonathan Pryce; Announcer: John Marsh.

STEAFEL PLUS – BBC Radio 4

(Presented by Sheila Steafel, with Simon Jones, sketch written by Douglas Adams. Broadcast 04/08/82)

THE LIGHT ENTERTAINMENT SHOW – BBC Radio 2

(Presented by Roy Hudd, with Simon Jones and Stephen Moore, sketch written by Tony Hare and Peter Hickey. Broadcast 03/10/82)

TERTIARY PHASE (Rec. Aug–Oct 2004)

Fit the 13th 21/09/04
Fit the 14th 28/09/04
Fit the 15th 05/10/04
Fit the 16th 12/10/04
Fit the 17th 19/10/04
Fit the 18th 26/10/04

QUANDARY & QUINTESSENTIAL PHASES (Rec. April–June 2005)

Fit the 19th   03/05/05
Fit the 20th   10/05/05
Fit the 21st   17/05/05
Fit the 22nd   24/05/05
Fit the 23rd   31/05/05
Fit the 24th   07/06/05
Fit the 25th   14/06/05
Fit the 26th   21/06/05

The Book: William Franklyn; Prostetnic Vogon Jeltz/Wowbagger: Toby
Longworth; Eddie the Computer: Roger Gregg; Slartibartfast: Richard
Griffiths; Zem the Mattress: Andy Taylor; Deodat: Bruce Hyman; Henry
Blofeld: Himself; Fred Trueman: Himself; Judiciary Pag/Russell: Rupert
Degas; Krikkit Man 1: Michael Fenton Stevens; Krikkit Man 2: Philip Pope;
Krikkit Man 3: Tom Maggs; Thor: Dominic Hawksley; Award Winner: Bob
Golding; Woman with Sydney Opera House Head: Joanna Lumley; Party
Doorman: Paul Wickens; Prak: Chris Langham; Hactar: Leslie Phillips; Rob
McKenna: Bill Paterson; Fenchurch: Jane Horrocks; Barman: Arthur Smith;
Vogon Guard: Bob Golding; Stewardess: Alison Pettitt; Hooker: Fiona
Carew; Vogon Helmsman: Michael Cule; Canis Pontiff: Chris Emmett; Raffle
Woman: June Whitfield; BT Operator: Ann Bryson; Jim: Simon Greenall;
Speaking Clock: Brian Cobby; Ecological Man: David Dixon; BBC Head
of LE: Geoffrey Perkins; Murray Bost Henson: Stephen Fry; East River
Creature: Jackie Mason; Wonko the Sane: Christian Slater; Tricia McMillan:
Sandra Dickinson; Nick Clarke: Himself; Charlotte Green: Herself; Peter
Donaldson: Himself; Sir Patrick Moore: Himself; Voice of the Bird: Rula
Lenska; Prophet: John Challis; Information Creature: Mitch Benn; Gail
Andrews: Lorelei King; Colin the Robot: Andrew Secombe; Old Man on
the Pole: Saeed Jaffrey; Smelly Photocopier Woman: Miriam Margolyes;
Random Dent: Samantha Béart; Old Thrashbarg: Griff Rhys Jones; The
Newsreader: Neil Sleat; Agrajag: Douglas Adams.
COMPLETE CD BOX SET RELEASED 2005

THE HITCHHIKER'S GUIDE TO THE GALAXY LIVE – BBC Radio 4

(Broadcast live from the BBC Radio Theatre, 10.15 a.m. Saturday 29 March 2014)

The Book: John Lloyd; Arthur Dent: Simon Jones; Ford Prefect: Geoffrey McGivern; Zaphod Beeblebrox: Mark Wing-Davey; Trillian: Susan Sheridan; Marvin: Stephen Moore (and Tom Maggs); Slartibartfast: Toby Longworth; Random: Samantha Béart; Max Quordlepleen: Andrew Secombe; Reg Nullify: Philip Pope; Announcer: Neil Sleat; Spot Effects: Ken Humphrey; Sound Production: Jerry Smith; Adapted and Directed by Dirk Maggs; Produced by David Morley. A Perfectly Normal Production.

THE HITCHHIKER'S GUIDE TO THE GALAXY – BBC1

(Written by Douglas Adams. Produced and directed by Alan Bell. Rec. March–July 1980, September 1980–January 1981)

Episode 1	05/01/81
Episode 2	12/01/81
Episode 3	19/01/81
Episode 4	26/01/81
Episode 5	02/02/81
Episode 6	09/02/81

The Book: Peter Jones; Arthur Dent: Simon Jones; Ford Prefect: David Dixon; Barman: Steve Conway; Prostetnic Vogon Jeltz: Martin Benson; Vogon Guard: Michael Cule; Trillian: Sandra Dickinson; Zaphod Beeblebrox: Mark Wing-Davey; Marvin: David Learner, Stephen Moore (voice); Gag Halfrunt: Gil Morris; Eddie the Computer: David Tate; Slartibartfast: Richard Vernon; Lunkwill/Loon-Quall: Antony Carrick; Fook/Phougg: Timothy Davies; Deep Thought: Valentine Dyall; Majikthise: David Leland; Vroomfondel: Charles McKeown; Bang Bang: Marc Smith; Shooty: Matt Zimmerman; Garkbit: Jack May; Hotblack Desiato: Barry Frank Warren; Bodyguard: Dave Prowse; Max Quordlepleen: Colin Jeavons; Dish of the Day: Peter Davison; The Great Prophet Zarquon: Colin Bennett; Number One: Matthew Scurfield; Number Three: Geoffrey Beevers; B-Ark Captain: Aubrey Morris; Marketing Girl: Beth Porter; Hairdresser: David Rowlands; Management Consultant: Jon Glover; Number Two: David

Neville; Naked Man On Beach: Douglas Adams.
RELEASED ON BBC DVD 2002

THE SOUTH BANK SHOW: DOUGLAS ADAMS – ITV
(Broadcast 05/01/92. Written by Douglas Adams. Edited by Melvyn Bragg)
The Book: Peter Jones; Arthur Dent: Simon Jones; Ford Prefect: David
Dixon; Marvin: Stephen Moore (voice); Electric Monk: Paul Shearer; Dirk
Gently: Michael Bywater.

THE MAKING OF THE HITCHHIKER'S GUIDE TO THE GALAXY
(Released on BBC Video 1993. Directed by Kevin Davies)
The Book: Peter Jones; Arthur Dent: Simon Jones; Ford Prefect: David
Dixon; Vogon: Michael Cule.

THE HITCHHIKER'S GUIDE TO THE GALAXY
(Screenplay by Douglas Adams and Karey Kirkpatrick. Directed by Garth
Jennings. Produced by Nick Goldsmith, Jay Roach, Roger Birnbaum,
Jonathan Glickman, Gary Barber. Executive Producer Robbie Stamp. UK
Release 28/04/05, US Release 29/04/05. Budget $45m. Box office $105m)
The Book: Stephen Fry; Arthur Dent: Martin Freeman; Ford Prefect: Mos
Def; Prosser: Steve Pemberton; Prostetnic Vogon Jeltz: Richard Griffiths;
Vogon Kwaltz: Ian McNiece; Trillian: Zooey Deschanel; Zaphod Beeblebrox:
Sam Rockwell; Marvin: Warwick Davis, Alan Rickman (voice); Eddie the
Computer: Thomas Lennon; Gag Halfrunt: Jason Schwartzman; Jin Jenz
Reporter: Kelly Macdonald; The Whale: Bill Bailey; Slartibartfast: Bill Nighy;
Questular Rontok: Anna Chancellor; Humma Kavula: John Malkovich;
Fook: Dominique Jackson; Lunkwill: Jack Stanley; Deep Thought: Helen
Mirren; Magrathean Video Recording: Simon Jones; Other Voices/Cameos:
Reece Shearsmith, Mark Gatiss, Edgar Wright, Garth Jennings, Zoe Kubaisi.
RELEASED ON BUENA VISTA DVD 2005

NOTABLE THEATRE PRODUCTIONS

THE HITCHHIKER'S GUIDE TO THE GALAXY – ICA THEATRE

(Adapted and directed by Ken Campbell, 1–9 May 1979)
Lithos & Terros: Cindy Oswin, Maya Sendalle; Arthur Dent: Chris Langham;
Ford Prefect: Richard Hope; Zaphod Beeblebrox: Mitch Davis/Stephen
Williams; Trillian: Sue Jones-Davis; Marvin: Russell Denton; Prosser: Roger
Sloman; Slartibartfast: Neil Cunningham.

THE HITCHHIKER'S GUIDE TO THE GALAXY – THEATR CLWYD

(Adapted and directed by Jonathan Petherbridge, 15 Jan–23 Feb 1980, and
numerous further productions)

THE HITCHHIKER'S GUIDE TO THE GALAXY – RAINBOW THEATRE

(Adapted and directed by Ken Campbell, July 1980)
The Book: Roger Blake; Arthur Dent: Kim Durham; Ford Prefect: David
Brett; Vogon Captain: Michael Cule; Trillian: Jude Alderson; Zaphod
Beeblebrox: John Terence/Nicolas d'Avirro; Marvin: David Learner;
Slartibartfast: Lewis Cowen; Deep Thought: James Castle; Barman: David
Atkinson; Benjy Mouse: Beverly Andrews.

THE HITCHHIKER'S GUIDE TO THE GALAXY RADIO SHOW LIVE – TOUR 2012/2013

(A Perfectly Normal Productions presentation, touring June–July 2012 and
September–October 2013)
The Book (narrator): Various; Arthur Dent: Simon Jones; Ford Prefect:
Geoffrey McGivern; Zaphod Beeblebrox: Mark Wing-Davey/Mitch
Benn; Trillian: Susan Sheridan; Marvin: Stephen Moore (and Tom
Maggs); Slartibartfast: Toby Longworth; Random: Samantha Béart; Max
Quordlepleen: Andrew Secombe; Reg Nullify: Philip Pope; Spot Effects:
Paul Weir/Ken Humphrey; Adapted and directed by Dirk Maggs.

ALBUMS & SINGLES

THE HITCHHIKER'S GUIDE TO THE GALAXY – Original Records, 1979 ORA042

THE RESTAURANT AT THE END OF THE UNIVERSE – Original Records, 1980 ORA054

The Book: Peter Jones; Arthur Dent: Simon Jones; Ford Prefect: Geoffrey McGivern; Zaphod Beeblebrox: Mark Wing-Davey; Trillian: Cindy Oswin; Marvin: Stephen Moore; Prosser: Bill Wallis; Eddie: David Tate; Slartibartfast: Richard Vernon; Deep Thought: Valentine Dyall; Garkbit: Anthony Sharpe; Max Quordlepleen: Roy Hudd; Vroomfondel: Jim Broadbent; Reg Nullify: Graham de Wilde; B-Ark Captain: Frank Middlemass; Number Two: Stephen Grief; Marketing Girl: Leueen Willoughby; Magrathean PA: Douglas Adams.

THHGTTG TV THEME MUSIC – JOURNEY OF THE SORCERER (Leadon) / REG NULLIFY IN CONCERT / DISASTER AREA: ONLY THE END OF THE WORLD AGAIN (Tim Souster / Douglas Adams) Original Records 1980 ABO5

MARVIN / METAL MAN (Adams/Moore/Sinclair) – Polydor 1981 POSP261

THE DOUBLE B-SIDE: REASONS TO BE MISERABLE / MARVIN I LOVE YOU (Adams/Moore/Sinclair) – Polydor 1981 POSP333

KLAUS KONIG – AT THE END OF THE UNIVERSE (Homage à Douglas Adams) – Enya, 1992 (Unofficial German jazz instrumental album inspired by *Hitchhiker*.)

THE HITCHHIKER'S GUIDE TO THE GALAXY OST – Hollywood Records, 2005

ZAPHOD BEEBLEBROX FOR PRESIDENT (Talbot/Hannan) Hollywood Records, 2005 (Unreleased movie track, available on YouTube.)

REASONS TO BE MISERABLE (HIS NAME IS MARVIN) – Hollywood Records, 2005

(Re-recorded version performed by Stephen Fry, available on download)

AUDIOBOOKS (Selected)

THE HITCHHIKER'S GUIDE TO THE GALAXY; THE RESTAURANT AT THE END OF THE UNIVERSE; LIFE, THE UNIVERSE AND EVERYTHING; SO LONG AND THANKS FOR ALL THE FISH – EMI Listen For Pleasure, 1981–1984

(Abridged talking books, read by Stephen Moore)

THE COMPLETE HITCHHIKER'S GUIDE TO THE GALAXY TRILOGY – Dove Audiobooks, 1994

(Unabridged talking books, read by Douglas Adams)

THHGTTG: DOUGLAS ADAMS LIVE IN CONCERT – Phoenix Audio/ TDV, 1999

(Selected readings by Douglas Adams, live at the Almeida Theatre, Islington, 1996)

THE COMPLETE HITCHHIKER'S GUIDE TO THE GALAXY TRILOGY – Random House Audio, 2005

(Unabridged talking books, the first read by Stephen Fry, the rest by Martin Freeman)

COMPUTER GAMES

THE HITCHHIKER'S GUIDE TO THE GALAXY – Infocom, 1984

(Written and programmed by Steve Meretzky and Douglas Adams)

THHGTTG: VOGON PLANET DESTRUCTOR – Starwave Mobile 2005

THHGTTG: ADVENTURE GAME – TKO Software 2005

TOWELS & TOYS (Selected)

- Original Eugen Beer towel, 1985, Rod Lord's 'Don't Panic' towel from Papillon Embroidery 2012, plus at least eight other towel designs from publicity drives, and unofficial merchandising.
- TV Series lead figurines: Arthur, Ford, Trillian, Zaphod, Marvin
- Movie 3" models – Arthur & Marvin, Jeltz & Zaphod, Kwaltz & Marvin

- Movie 6" action figures – Arthur, Zaphod, Marvin, Kwaltz, Jeltz
- Movie knitted plushes – Arthur, Ford, Trillian, Marvin, Zaphod
- Movie 10" Marvin roto action figure
- Movie Marvin Headknocker
- Movie Hitchhiker Survival Pack: Babel fish, towel, electronic thumb
- Movie Marvin's Gun replica (shoots sucker-darts)
- Movie POV Gun replica (Ltd. Edition)
- Movie paperweights, mugs, desk tidies, posters, tie-in books, shot glasses, T-shirts, etc.
- ZZ9 Fanclub Beeblebears, T-shirts, pendants, etc.

LIFF, DIRK GENTLY & OTHER BOOKS, PROGRAMMES & RELEASES FEATURING, WRITTEN OR INSPIRED BY DOUGLAS ADAMS (Selected)

The Meaning of Liff (with John Lloyd) – Pan, 1983

Dirk Gently's Holistic Detective Agency Heinemann, 1987

The Long Dark Tea-Time of the Soul – Heinemann, 1988

The Comic Relief Revue Book (contributor) – Penguin, 1989

The Deeper Meaning of Liff (with John Lloyd) – Pan, 1990

Last Chance To See – Pan, 1990

Douglas Adams's Starship Titanic (by Terry Jones) – Pan, 1997

OJRIL – The Completely Incomplete Graham Chapman (contributor) – Batsford, 1999

The Salmon of Doubt – Heinemann, 2002

Last Chance to See: In The Footsteps of Douglas Adams by Mark Carwardine – Collins, 2009

Shada (by Gareth Roberts) – BBC Books, 2012

Afterliff (by John Lloyd and Jon Canter) – Faber & Faber, 2013

City of Death (by Gareth Roberts, based on a story by David Fisher) – BBC Books, 2015

OH NO IT ISN'T – BBC Radio 4 (Contributor. Broadcast 30/08/74)

MONTY PYTHON – BBC2 ('Funny word' contributor. Broadcast 05/12/74)

OUT OF THE TREES – BBC2 (by Graham Chapman, Douglas Adams & Bernard McKenna. Broadcast 10/01/76)

THE BURKISS WAY – BBC Radio 4 (Contributor, episodes 11, 14, 18. Broadcast 12/01/77, 02/02/77, 02/03/77)

DOCTOR ON THE GO: 'For Your Own Good' – LWT (by Graham Chapman & Douglas Adams. Broadcast 20/02/77)

DOCTOR WHO: 'The Pirate Planet' – BBC1 (Written by Douglas Adams. Broadcast in four parts 20/09/78–21/10/78)

BLACK CINDERELLA TWO GOES EAST – BBC Radio 2 (Written by Clive Anderson & Rory McGrath. Produced by Douglas Adams. Broadcast 25/12/78)

DOCTOR SNUGGLES – ITV (Created by Jeffrey O'Kelly. Episode 7 'The Remarkable Fidgety River' and Episode 12 'The Great Disappearing Mystery' written by Douglas Adams & John Lloyd for Polyscope Productions, 1979)

DOCTOR WHO: 'City of Death' – BBC1 (Written by David Agnew, i.e. Douglas Adams. Broadcast in four parts 29/09/79–20/10/79)

DOCTOR WHO: 'Shada' – N/A (Written by Douglas Adams. Production abandoned 1979. Released on BBC Video 1992. Adapted into Big Finish Audio Drama and webcast animation, 2003)

IT MAKES ME LAUGH – BBC Radio 4 (Presented and written by Douglas Adams. Broadcast 19/07/81)

AN EVENING WITHOUT – Original Records, 1981 (Additional material)

BUREAUCRACY – Infocom, 1987 (Text adventure written by Douglas Adams, with Michael Bywater & others)

LAST CHANCE TO SEE – BBC Radio 4 (Written and presented by Douglas Adams & Mark Carwardine. Broadcast 04/10/89–08/11/89)

HYPERLAND – BBC2 (Written by and featuring Douglas Adams, with Tom Baker. Produced by Max Whitby. Broadcast 21/09/90)

LAST CHANCE TO SEE: CD-ROM – The Voyager Company, 1992 (Book and radio extracts, with photographs and notes)

DESERT ISLAND DISCS – BBC Radio 4 (Guest. Broadcast 06/02/94)

THE ASCENT OF MAN – BBC Horizons (Specially recorded introductions, June 1998)

STARSHIP TITANIC – TDV, 1998 (Videogame written by Douglas Adams, Michael Bywater, Neil Richards & others. Released on PC 10/02/98, Mac 25/03/99)

THE INTERNET: THE LAST BATTLEGROUND OF THE 20TH CENTURY – BBC Radio 4 (Written and presented by Douglas Adams. Broadcast in two parts, 01/09/99–08/09/99)

PETER JONES – A CELEBRATION BBC Radio 4 (Presented by Douglas Adams. Broadcast 18/07/00)

THE HITCHHIKER'S GUIDE TO THE FUTURE – BBC Radio 4 (Written and presented by Douglas Adams. Broadcast in four parts, 04/10/00–25/10/00)

DIRK GENTLY'S HOLISTIC DETECTIVE AGENCY – BBC Radio 4, THE LONG DARK TEA-TIME OF THE SOUL – BBC Radio 4 (Based on the books by Douglas Adams. Adapted and directed by Dirk Maggs. Broadcast in two series of six parts 03/10/07–07/11/07, and 02/10/08–06/11/08)

Dirk Gently: Harry Enfield; Richard MacDuff: Billy Boyd; Susan Way: Felicity Montagu; Professor Chronotis: Andrew Sachs; Detective Sergeant Gilks: Jim Carter; Janice Pearce: Olivia Colman; Michael Wenton-Weakes: Michael Fenton-Stevens; Gordon Way: Robert Duncan; The Electric Monk: Toby Longworth; Kate Schechter: Laurel Lefkow; Thor: Rupert Degas; Odin: Stephen Moore; Toe Rag: Michael Roberts; Elena: Sally Grace; Simon Draycott: Peter Davison; Cynthia Draycott: Jan Ravens, Neil Sharp: Philip Pope; Additional voices by Andrew Secombe, Jon Glover, Jeffrey Holland, Tamsin Heatley, Wayne Forester, John Fortune.
RELEASED ON BBC AUDIO 2007, 2008

LAST CHANCE TO SEE – BBC1 (Presented by Stephen Fry & Mark Carwardine, in tribute to Douglas Adams. Broadcast in five parts, 06/09/09–04/10/09. Also, follow-up *Return of the Rhino* broadcast on BBC2 31/10/10)
RELEASED ON DEMAND MEDIA DVD 2011, DIGITAL CLASSICS 2010

DIRK GENTLY – BBC4 (Inspired by the books by Douglas Adams, created and written by Howard Overman, produced by Chris Carey. Pilot broadcast 16/12/10, three episodes broadcast 06/03/12–20/03/12)
Dirk Gently: Steven Mangan; Richard MacDuff: Darren Boyd; Susan Harmison: Helen Baxendale; DI Gilks: Jason Watkins; Janice Pearce: Lisa Jackson; Gordon Way: Anthony Howell.
RELEASED ON ITV STUDIOS HOME ENTERTAINMENT DVD 2012

DIRK GENTLY: ORIGINAL TELEVISION SOUNDTRACK (by Daniel Pemberton. Released on Moviescore Media 2012)

BOOKS, PROGRAMMES & RELEASES ABOUT DOUGLAS ADAMS
(Selected)

Don't Panic by Neil Gaiman (and others) – Titan, 1985

The Pocket Essential Hitchhiker's Guide by M. J. Simpson – Pocket Essentials, 2001

Wish You Were Here by Nick Webb – Headline, 2003

Hitchhiker by M. J. Simpson – Coronet, 2003

The Making of THHGTTG by Robbie Stamp (ed) – Boxtree, 2005

The Anthology at the End of the Universe by Glenn Yeffeth (ed) – Benbella Books, 2005

The Science of THHGTTG by Michael Hanlon – Macmillan, 2005

The Rough Guide To THHGTTG by Marcus O'Dair – Rough Guides, 2009

Die Wissenschaft bei Douglas Adams by Alexander Pawlak – Wiley, 2010

42 by Peter Gill – Beautiful Books, 2011

I Was Douglas Adams' Flatmate by Andrew McGibbon (ed), Jon Canter – Faber & Faber, 2011

Philosophy & THHGTTG by Nicholas Joll (ed) – Palgrave Macmillan, 2012

PRIVATE PASSIONS: DOUGLAS ADAMS – BBC Radio 3, 13/09/97

THE GUIDE TO 20 YEARS' HITCHHIKING – BBC Radio 4, 05/03/98

BOOK CLUB: DOUGLAS ADAMS – BBC Radio 4, 02/01/00

OMNIBUS: THE MAN WHO BLEW UP THE WORLD – BBC1, 04/08/01

SO LONG & THANKS FOR ALL THE FISH – BBC Radio 4, 01/09/01

SIX CHARACTERS IN SEARCH OF AN ANSWER: ARTHUR DENT – BBC Radio 4, 09/07/02

THE BIG READ: THHGTTG, WITH SANJEEV BHASKAR – BBC1, 07/08/03

BBC7 25TH ANNIVERSARY TRIBUTE TO THHGTTG – BBC7, 02/03/03

DOUGLAS ADAMS AT THE BBC – BBC AUDIOBOOKS, 2004

INSIDE THHGTTG – BBC2, 07/05/05

THE DOCTOR AND DOUGLAS – BBC Radio 4, 02/04/10

THE MEANING OF LIFF AT 30 – BBC Radio 4, 28/02/13

FURTHER BIBLIOGRAPHY

Allen, Keith: *Grow Up*, Ebury, 2007; Chapman, Graham (and others): *A Liar's Autobiography Volume VI*, Methuen, 1990; Fielding, Helen: *Cause Celeb*, Picador, 1994; Hamilton, Paul, Peter Gordon, Dan Kieran: *How Very Interesting: Peter Cook, His Universe And All That Surrounds It*, Snowbooks, 2006; Hewison, Robert: *Footlights!*, Methuen Publishing, 1984; Hind, John: *The Comic Inquisition*, Virgin Books, 1991; McCabe, Bob: *The Life of Graham*, Orion, 2005; McCabe, Bob (ed): *The Pythons Autobiography by The Pythons*, Orion, 2003; Palin, Michael: *Diaries 1969–1979: The Python Years*, Weidenfeld & Nicolson, 2006; Perry, George: *The Life of Python*, Pavilion, 1994; Rhys Jones, Griff: *Semi-Detached*, Penguin, 2007; Russell, Mike: *Digging Holes In Popular Culture*, Oxbow Books, 2001; Sheckley, Robert: *Dimension of Miracles*, Granada Publishing, 1969; Vonnegut, Kurt: *The Sirens of Titan*, Millennium, 1990; Wilmut, Roger: *From Fringe to Flying Circus*, Eyre Methuen, 1980; Wodehouse, P. G.: *Sunset at Blandings*, Penguin, 2000

ARTICLES, FURTHER SOURCES

The Douglas Adams Estate and Preface Publishing would like to thank a number of newspapers, magazines and periodicals for numerous Adams quotes, including: *Doctor Who Magazine, Mostly Harmless, Penthouse, Personal Computer Magazine, SFX, Starburst, TV Zone, Variety, The Guardian, The Observer, The Independent, The Times, The Telegraph, The Daily Mail*. While every effort has been made to credit periodicals for quotes, the author and publishers would be happy to make any amendments in further editions.

LINKS

And Another Thing: 6of3.com; **BBC Hitchhiker**: bbc.co.uk/radio4/hitchhikers, bbc.co.uk/cult/hitchhikers; **Digital Biota Speech**: biota.org/people/douglasadams; **DNA Newsgroup**: alt.fan-douglas-adams; **Final Grandson of Wowbagger the Infinitely Prolonged**: wowbagger.com; **H2G2**: h2g2.com; **Hitchhiker Towels**: hhgttg.co.uk; **Hitchhiker Wiki**:

hitchhikers.wikia.com; **Life, DNA & H2G2**: douglasadams.eu; **Milliways Article**: waxy.org; **M. J. Simpson's Movie Review**: planetmagrathea.com/shortreview.html; **Official Douglas Adams**: douglasadams.com; **Perfectly Normal Productions**: perfectlynormal.net; **The Digital Village**: tdv.com; **The Hitchhiker's Guide To Towels**: towel.org.uk; **ZZ9 Fan Club**: zz9.org

UNPUBLISHED HITCHHIKER EXTRACTS

Primary sources: St. John's College Library,
Papers of Douglas Noël Adams.

Extracts from the archive are used with
grateful thanks to the Douglas Adams estate
and by permission of the Master and Fellows
of St. John's College, Cambridge.

1. THE HITCHHIKER'S GUIDE TO THE GALAXY
(Original Pitch)

A science fiction comedy adventure which roams freely round the universe of time and space, moving in and out of fantasy, jokes, satire, parallel universes and timewarps, following in the wake of two men who are researching the New Revised Edition of the Hitchhiker's Guide to the Galaxy. One of them is an extra-terrestrial who has spent several years on Earth incognito. When he first arrived the minimal research he had done suggested to him that the name Ford Prefect would be nicely inconspicuous. On discovering his error he later changed this to Ford L. Prefect in an attempt to repair the damage. His companion is Aleric B, an earthman, who is persuaded to join him on the project after his pride is rather stung by seeing the original edition of the Guide: in all its million micropages there is only a one-word entry describing the inhabitants of Earth: 'Harmless'. Their adventures are set against a Universe torn asunder by the frightful struggle between 'Mrs Rogers', a giant mega-computer who behaves (and talks) like a cross between the Queen and Margaret Thatcher and adopts a rather Jewish-motherly attitude towards the Universe which she sees as being her charge – and The Naughty One, who is a freak of nature, a fantastically intelligent but rather greasy Chinese Meal which sits in state on a grubby red and white checked tablecloth on its own artificial asteroid from which it generates most of the malevolent influences in the Universe.

The story starts on Earth. Aleric has known Ford for many years, but has not the faintest suspicion

that he is not a perfectly normal human being. Aleric
lives in a small flat over a village shop which is due
for demolition. As the programme opens we hear the
shopkeeper having a demolition sale, auctioning off
sticks of rhubarb, paper clips, everything he's got, in
fact. Ford arrives in the shop on his way up to see
Aleric and is compelled to buy five thousand paper
clips and a door before he can force his way through
the bargain-hungry mob of housewives. Aleric is
preparing for siege. He's resisted all the compulsory-
purchase orders and is now intending to resist the
bulldozers. Having fought the plans for the new bypass at every level up to and including the Houses of
Parliament there's nothing left to do but sweat it out.
Ford seems strangely preoccupied and unsympathetic and
keeps on trying to steer the conversation onto such
inappropriate topics as flying saucers and whatnot.
Aleric is exasperated, and when a man from the council
arrives with a couple of bulldozer-driving heavies in
tow, he sees that Ford is going to be no help in the
great confrontation and banishes him to the kitchen to
make coffee. Aleric's slanging match with the men who
want to knock his house down is interspersed with Ford
trying to get a word in edgeways and explain that after
all this time he is actually from an entirely different
planet, that he's about to leave and would be extremely
pleased if Aleric would care to accompany him. Aleric
finds himself apologising to the council man for having
such odd friends. The council man suggests that perhaps
they should go and talk in the site hut where he has
some documents etc., and no loonies claiming to be from
outer space.

   In the hut Aleric's attention is diverted whilst the
demolition ceremony is initiated. A local lady dignitary
makes a speech and swings a bottle of champagne against

the bulldozer as it moves in for the kill. When the crunch comes, Aleric hears it, of course, runs out shouting that he's been tricked and the world is a very naughty place. Suddenly the piercing scream of jets is heard in the sky and a fleet of flying saucers streak down towards them. As everyone flees in panic Ford appears and grabs Aleric, pulling him towards the saucers. At that moment an unearthly voice rings out through the air, announcing that on account of redevelopment of this sector of the galaxy and the need to build a new stargate by-pass through space, the Earth will unfortunately have to be demolished. There are a few appalled cries of protest, to which the voice answers that the plans have been on public view on a planet somewhere near Alpha Centauri for the last fifty years, so everyone's had plenty of time to lodge formal complaints, and it's far too late to start making a fuss now. He gives the order to demolish, and a low rumbling hum starts up, quickly mounting in intensity. Pandemonium, wind, thunder, shrieks, a devastating explosion, and finally silence.

* * *

Aleric wakes to find himself in the sick bay of a spaceship. Ford is with him. Time for explanations ... Aleric is staggered by it all, but insists on returning home, or at least the nearest equivalent - and soon, too - he doesn't want to miss 'Star Trek'.

2. THE DENTRASSI (Cut from *THHGTTG*)

The history of the Dentrassi is rather curious. They are directly descended from the medico-technocratic caste of the Rinnsool-White planet in the Fluuod star cloud a mere fifty parsecs from the Galactic centre. Rinnsool-White was a sparkling clean, chilly, tiresome planet which always looked to the first-time visitor as if it had only been created that morning. Walk down a main street and you see nothing but chilly vistas of stainless-steel health department offices and glass shops which mostly sold frozen food and toothpaste. The major achievements of Rinnsool-White lay in fields of atomic physics, ice-skating and, most of all, dentistry – a science which they developed to unsurpassed levels of technical sophistication and hygiene. Most of the population were of course miserable as sin, but had always assumed that this was a perfectly normal and healthy feature of any perfectly normal anally deranged guilt-ridden society. The race had been like this for so long that none of them could remember what it was they felt guilty about, which made them feel twice as guilty. This is, of course, a terrifyingly self-perpetuating and self-amplifying phenomenon, more so when you consider the fact that if you delved far enough back into the mists of the planet's history you would find that the whole process was started off by someone who had accidentally strangled a cat and couldn't bear to tell anyone about it.

The original Dentrassi were the highest caste on the planet and were all research dentists. They inhabited huge gleaming whiteglass tower blocks from which they would issue long and frightening lists of all the things

that had been newly discovered to be bad for the teeth.
This way they kept the entire population and themselves
in a state of perpetual terror. Long ago sweets were
banned, then alcohol, then meat, then some forms of sex,
then most forms of sex, smoking went early, breathing
through the mouth was frowned on, excess talking
caused plaque, even collecting antique vases was said
to give you gum cavities. This could not, of course, go
on forever, and in the end the day dawned when every
conceivable activity had been investigated and found
dentally damaging, and an ever-tauter terror afflicted
the Dentrassi - that they couldn't find anything to add
to the terrible list. The whole planet waited in a state
of frozen panic until one young Dentrassi struck the
coup de grace by coming up with the magical notion that
toothpaste was also bad for the teeth. At that point
something in the racial psyche snapped and the Dentrassi
were thrown into exile on a nearby primitive jungle
planet and told to rethink their lifestyle.

This they did. Within a generation they had become the
most hedonistic garlic-gummed good-time layabouts this
side of the Gorst Nebula. It's a great pity that they
hardly figure in the story at all.

3. ARTHUR'S REVERIE (Cut from *THHGTTG*)

Arthur listened for a short while, but being unable
to understand the vast majority of what Ford was
saying he retreated into a reverie. There is, he
thought as he trailed his fingers along the edge of an
incomprehensible computer bank, a fascination in pure
technology, in machines which unthinkingly turn events
into other events. Man comes naked into the world, and
after thousands of years of living in it, scratching
around for survival, he begins to notice that things
don't happen by accident but because instant by instant
they are obeying precise laws – physical laws. When a
drop of rain falls it does so because a certain volume of
air at a certain height contained a certain proportion
of water vapour which was acted upon by certain changes
of temperature and pressure with the result that water
was precipitated out. It falls at a rate of acceleration
governed by its own mass, by the mass of the planet it is
falling towards and modified precisely by the friction
of the air it is falling through. The raindrop is not
making it up as it goes along, it is being governed by
its puppet masters, the laws of physics.

Man notices this, and it occurs to him that he can take
a hand. If he can work out why certain things happen
in certain ways in certain conditions then he can make
them happen to order. He has noticed that water falls,
and then, by following the path of least resistance,
flows into channels, and eventually flows on down to
the sea. One day he realises that if he hangs an upright
wooden wheel in the flowing water, the wheel will turn.
If he then connects that wheel to two large stones in a
particular way the stones will turn. If he then puts his

corn between the two wheels he can grind it into flour
to make his bread with. If he simply put the corn in the
river he would lose the corn, and if he put the stones
in the river he would lose them. If he ignored the river
and the stones and put the corn straight in the oven he
would end up with something he could eat in the cinema
but not spread his butter on. If he ignored the whole lot
he would die of starvation.

Man finds these relationships absolutely fascinating,
and as the centuries pass he finds out more and more
about connecting the right thing to the right thing in
more and more complicated ways. He never actually makes
anything happen, he simply manipulates the paths of
least resistance through which the natural forces are
bound to flow. Then one day he builds something that has
so many things connected in such complicated ways to so
many other different things that he only has to press
a button and the whole lot launches itself straight out
into space. The neat thing about it is that thousands of
tons of metal are shooting up into the sky for exactly
the same fundamental reasons that a drop of rain is
falling out of it.

Arthur felt pleased with himself for this thought,
and for being part of a race, albeit extinct now, which
had through nothing but mental ingenuity learnt to
recognise and control the invisible forces around it.
In his reverie he reached out and pressed an invitingly
large red button on a nearby panel. The panel lit up
with the words "Please do not press this button again."
He shook himself.

4. MARVIN MEETS HIS DESTINY (*LUE* notes)

Marvin becomes somewhat of a celebrity in the galaxy, or at least a celebrated freak. He reacts to this as he reacts to everything else that happens to him – he hates it. People stop him in the street and say things like "Give us a grin, little robot, give us a little chuckle." He explains that to get his face to grin would take a good couple of hours in the workshop with a wrench.

In his new public role he is sometimes called upon to perform public functions. On one occasion he is asked to open a new hyperbridge designed to carry ion-buggies and freighters across the Southern Alpha Swamp of Squornshellous Zeta. He stands on the platform at the ceremony. He says "I declare this hapless cyberstructure open to the unthinking abuse of all who wantonly cross her," and presses the button. The entire fifty-mile bridge spontaneously folds up its glittering spans and sinks into the mire.

There is a moment of expensive silence. Marvin leaves under a cloud – but a man approaches him and remarks that it's an ill wind ... Marvin agrees that it probably is, and that he wouldn't be surprised to see some pretty sick fog coming in over the marshes as well.

But the man has a job for him. He must find a ship and take news of this catastrophic event to the Drubbers, who desperately need bad news of any kind. Puzzled as to what this can mean Marvin nevertheless agrees to do the task and sets off to the star where the Drubbers live, whoever or whatever they might be.

He has a very depressing trip. Sadly his ship is attacked by pirates, dishearteningly it runs out of fuel, and eventually it crash-lands dejectedly on the

world where the Drubbers live. It is the gloomiest world
Marvin has ever seen, and he feels immediately quite
at home. He meets a creature with a hangdog expression
who spends all day scratching in order that at the end
of the day he can go and tell his masters what it feels
like.

"What does it feel like?" asks Marvin.

"Wretched", replies the creature.

"And who are your masters?"

"The Drubbers."

"Ah", says Marvin, "I have some news for them."

"I hope it's bad", says the creature.

"It is", says Marvin, "extremely bad. And lots of it."

The creature is profoundly depressed by some of the
stories Marvin has to tell him, and says that they must
take them straight to the Drubbers themselves who will
greet the news with terrible groans and lamentations
and tears – in other words, with great appreciation.

He takes Marvin to the Chamber cave of the Drubbers,
and there, indeed, the Drubbers are.

This world is what California will one day turn into,
because of a dangerous excess of pleasure. The Drubbers
were originally the greatest of hedonists, continually
subjecting themselves to every form of pleasure they
could think of, and quite enjoying themselves thinking
up other forms as well. They got to the stage where
they were, as a race, so completely wired up that the
slightest additional nice thing that happened to any of
them would make them explode – literally explode. They
had, therefore, to start finding ways of making life
less pleasant for themselves just to survive.

And their lives are now the epitome of unpleasantness.
The cave which Marvin enters is cold and damp, and
utterly huge. Inside it is a vast three-foot-deep lake,
which is freezing cold, smelly, and full of irritants.

In this stand the Drubbers. They all stand in it
continually whilst it periodically rains or snows on
them. Bad music is played continually over a very bad-
quality P.A. system, and is continually interrupted by
news broadcasts telling of one terrible piece of news
after another. People are continually being brought in
to hurl abuse at them and hope that they don't have a
nice day. All this is necessary to stop them feeling good.
Occasionally something less than totally unpleasant
occurs to one of them, and they explode messily.
Procreation obviously causes them terrible problems, and
indeed, their race is therefore in constant danger of
extinction.

Marvin meets them and is impressed with their problem,
as they are with him.

The eventual upshot of their meeting is that they
are able to enter into a symbiotic relationship.
Marvin takes over as their mentor, their guru, and
with him constantly around talking to them, helping
them, explaining his philosophy, they find they are
eventually able to move out of their cold smelly lake,
back out into the wholesome air and start to live normal
lives.

Marvin, too, finds that he has at last found a purpose
in what, for the sake of something to call it, he calls
his life.

5. WOWBAGGER (Original *LUE* manuscript)

In the bar, Ford had decided that a little entertainment
was called for, and as it seemed that no one else had
realised this, it occurred to him that he should be the
one to provide it. To this end, he announced in a very
loud voice that the world was going to end on Thursday,
but not to worry, because he was going to sing a song to
cheer everybody up.

Reactions to this were varied, but none of them were
encouraging. Ford was not deterred by this, and said so.
He had played to worse audiences, he said, and cited by
way of example a rather rough night he had experienced
at the Evildrome Boozarama in a particularly sleazy
part of the city of Babgadura on the fourth planet out
from the star Xash 3, which when last seen, and he had
no reason to believe this had changed, was slap bang in
the centre of the Gagrakacka Mind Zones towards the
east of the Galaxy. Had anyone been there, he asked, and
added that he believed they hadn't. His audience were
getting restive at this point, so he reassured them that
he was getting very close now to the actual song, which
was in fact one he had learnt on the very night he was
attempting to interest them in. He then ducked off into
a quick digression on the subject of sex, being reminded,
as he explained, that it was also the first night on
which he had encountered Eccentrica Gallumbits, the
triple-breasted whore of Eroticon Six. With as much
delicacy and coherence as you could comfortably squeeze
on to the slide plate of an electron microscope he added
that the number of people who had survived an entire
night with the delectable Eccentrica — whose erogenous
zones, he explained, were reputed to start some four

miles from her actual body, and whose embraces were
frequently likened to an earthquake in a well filled
snake pit - was zero. He himself, he said, had managed
thirty minutes, which he would happily tell them all
about in extensive and graphic detail if it weren't for
the fact that he could sense they were so keen for the
song to begin.

It was a wild and tuneless yowl with principal
qualities of volume and length, and told of the exploits
of one of the Galaxy's great folk heroes, Wowbagger
Ultrajax. Wowbagger, it seems, had at some point early
in his eventful life stolen the great Quentulus Stone
of Firefrand from the Lajestic Vantrashell of Lob,
and so far from being thereby enabled to lead a life
of shameless luxury and hedonism, as he had hoped,
had been forced to spend the greater part of his time
fleeing the Silastic Armorfiends of Striterax as they
pursued him from world to world through the Radiation
Swamps of Cwulzenda, the Fire Mountains of Rita, the
Ice Storms of Varlengooten, the Gamma Caves of Carfrax
and so on. And when the Silastic Armorfiends flagged
in the chase, their places were taken by the Strenuous
Garfighters of Stug, and when they had had enough, the
Strangulous Stilletans of Haglavinda pursued Wowbagger
back through the Gamma Caves of Carfrax and the Ice
Storms of Varlengooten, until he began seriously to
regret that he had ever stolen the wretched Stone in
the first place. His vexation was increased by the fact
that the power for which the Quentulus Stone was famous
was that of bestowing eternal life on its owner, and it
was beginning to look as if he had an awful lot more of
this aggravating lifestyle to look forward to. He could
simply get rid of the Stone, but being now something
over three hundred thousand million years old he

couldn't help feeling that it would be an awful waste
of time if he were just to give up now. Added to which,
he would of course simply drop down dead if he lost the
stone, and he regarded this as a constant and annoying
temptation rather than an acceptable solution.

Ford's song to this effect was going down very badly
in the bar at Lord's cricket ground, and many people
left it before Ford was finally ejected.

One of these men walked past Arthur a minute or two
later and sparked off a moment's thought in Arthur's
mind.

The thought was this:

"I," thought Arthur, "am a rather special and
extraordinary person."

He had always felt appallingly ordinary before. How,
he thought, would this man passing him in the crowd (the
one from the bar) react if he knew the truth about this
person he was passing so casually?

He looked at the man critically. He was slight, middle-
aged, balding a little, a little grey, he was wearing
an over-tightly-fitting tracksuit presumably in an
effort to look younger than he was, and wore a haggard
expression. Mortgage problems, presumably. How would he
react if he knew that Arthur, perfectly ordinary-looking
Arthur Dent - ordinary except of course for the dressing
gown which was not really standard cricket-watching
wear but which was nevertheless less than exotic, veering
as it did more towards the overhomely side of odd rather
than the overexotic - how would this man, the one
standing next to him (Arthur was trying to keep a steady
grip on his ideas and failing - he'd had a lot to contend
with in recent months and often found that even in
quieter months, trying to marshal his thoughts was like
trying to herd bees with a whip) how would this adjacent
man react if he knew that Arthur was a time traveller?

The man glanced briefly at Arthur and then out at the field of play.

Arthur shook his head with a tiny indulgent smile. "If only you knew," he thought to himself. "If only you knew."

Arthur was now almost glowing with the secret knowledge of himself as space adventurer, time traveller, cave dweller, converser with pandimensional mice, in short all those things which a few hours previously had been the burden of his nightmares. And here he was, he thought, standing unnoticed in a crowd, conspicuous only for his matted beard and tatty dressing gown. He looked behind him for one last glance at the man in the tracksuit who had sparked off this thought, but he had disappeared.

"Oh well," thought Arthur. "Probably popped off for a cup of tea I shouldn't wonder," and, prompted by this speculation, suddenly felt the need of some tea himself.

The man in the tracksuit had disappeared because he was now running as fast as his poor exhausted three-hundred-thousand-million-year-old legs would carry him across the hidden pathways with which he was now sickeningly familiar in the radiation swamps of Cwulzenda. The stench of death and decay, the rancid swirling mist, the foul gaseous gurgles that echoed across the festering face of this bilious land, these were the things he knew. The freak effect of the Magic Moment Grade Three wave had temporarily washed him up on the temporospatial beach of St. John's Wood and had now returned him whence he had come.

He ran on, his feet slipping and squelching in the globbery slime, but more slowly now. The hideous shape which loomed suddenly out of the mist on his right was, he knew, the stump of a tree which marked the division of the paths through the mire. He could either go left

as he usually did, and hope to make the ten miles to the
military spaceport before the night closed in, or take
the right fork and try to seek refuge for the night in
the nearby village of the marsh mutants.

But his feet were running more slowly. He turned
and looked behind him. There, miles behind him in the
yellowish leaden sky, were the three red dots of the
Arduon tracker ships following him implacably as they
had done now for … for years.

He gasped the rancid air. St. John's Wood (he didn't
know it was called that) had been quite an experience
for him. He had just suddenly popped up there, in the
gentlemen's toilet as a matter of fact.

A little dazed, he had made use of facilities that had
for millennia been beyond his wildest dreams of luxury,
cleaned himself up, and walked out into what appeared
to be a bar of some sort where a drunken madman was
singing a song which told the story of his, Wowbagger's,
life.

This surprised him. There is no point in saying
anything more than that. Any attempt to express the
level of surprise he experienced at this point by saying
that he was as surprised as … as … as anything at all,
is doomed to failure, because from now on surprise
levels will be best measured by comparing them with how
surprised Wowbagger Ultrajax was on walking into this
strange bar and hearing a drunken Ford Prefect singing
a song about him. So, for instance, one would measure
Oedipus's surprise on meeting his mother at about 22 on
the Wowbagger Scale.

He sat down, rather heavily as it happened. He
listened. Numb bewilderment gripped him, which means
that on the Wowbagger scale he was calming down.

After a while, he walked out. There, on a field in
front of him, was being enacted what was, in his eyes,

one of the most ghoulish and grisly charades he had ever witnessed.

And then a strange, bedraggled and bearded man in a tattered gown had given him a strange, knowing smile, almost a leer, and Wowbagger had known that his time was come.

He was being softened up for hell.

Or maybe this was it already.

Either way, he knew what he had to do ...

6. MISTAKES (Attempted *LUE* beginning)

Before time began, a lot of things happened that hardly bear talking about, though apparently somebody has a message about it somewhere.

This story starts a little later than that. It is based in this Galaxy, the one we all know and love, with its millions of suns, its strange and wonderful planets, its eerie moons, its asteroids, its comets, its gas clouds and dust clouds and its immensity of coldness and darkness.

It affects, however, the entire Universe.

Just occasionally it should be remembered that this Galaxy is just one of infinite millions, but then it should be forgotten again, because it's hard for the mind to stagger around with that kind of knowledge in it.

Since this Galaxy began, vast civilisations have risen and fallen, risen and fallen, risen and fallen so often that it's quite tempting to think that life in the Galaxy must be a) something akin to seasick – space sick, time sick, history sick or some such thing – and b) stupid.

When you get down to street level, however, you realise that the phrase "life in the Galaxy" is pretty meaningless, since it describes billions of separate short-lived beings, all of whom have for some vicious reason been programmed to be incapable of learning from each other's mistakes.

Here is a very simple example at street level.

The street is a cold but busy one in a city called New York on a recently demolished planet that hardly anybody has heard of, and nobody likes.

A man is walking along it. What happens to him has happened before to others and will happen again. He walks past a site where an extremely tall building is being put up in the place of another extremely tall building which has just been pulled down (an explanation of why this happens would only confuse matters at this point).

As he passes, a small tool falls from high up in the scaffolding with which the building is surrounded and buries itself snugly into his skull. This has the effect of bringing his life, with all its memories, its loves, its hard-won battles, its instructive defeats, its rewards, its disappointments – in short, his entire experience – to an abrupt end. The last thing the man sees before his personal light is shut off is a sign on the scaffolding which says 'We Apologise For The Inconvenience.'

From across the street a woman – the man's mate – sees this happen. Failing to learn from the incident that the Universe in general and New York in particular is a randomly dangerous place, she runs pointlessly to his aid and has her own life, with all its experience, brought to an end by a yellow taxi cab whose driver would never apologise for anything. The cab driver was only there at that point because he was completely lost in one of the most rationally laid-out cities on the Earth, but that, again, is another purely local problem.

This story is about a much much larger problem, but strangely enough it does come to involve this otherwise unheard-of and harmless planet in rather a curious way, and the reason why nobody likes it.

It also involves a large number of mistakes ...

7. FINTLEWOODLEWIX (Attempted *LUE* beginning)

Reason notwithstanding, the Universe continues unabated. On millions of planets throughout the Galaxy new dreams are being dreamt, new hopes are hoped, and new days continue to dawn, despite the terrible failure rate.

On the planet Ramtad Efta the Lirteenth, Ramtad Efta, after whom the planet had reluctantly been named, sat and brooded. Things hadn't worked out quite as he'd wished and he didn't know why. That, for the moment, is his problem. It will become a problem of more general interest later.

On the planet Erglefall Sandwijhaven a new government had just been elected, pledged to oppose, rout and undo utterly all that the previous government had set out to do. This involved moving the entire population of the planet back out of the sea, cutting off their fins and learning about bricks again, but no one seemed to mind. They just kept their fins somewhere they knew they could find them after the next election.

On the planet Fintlewoodlewix, later renamed the Earth, nothing so exciting was happening ...

8. ARTHUR'S NIGHTMARE (Original *LUE* manuscript)

In the beginning (of this story) was the word. In fact
it wasn't really a word as such, and it wasn't really
the beginning, because the word, or whatever it was, was
preceded by a few slight snuffling noises, some vague
murmuring, a little muttering and grumbling and then a
short silent pause. And darkness covered the face of the
land.

The word, when it came, was a terrible scream, an
appallingly deafening, throat-tearing scream. One
of those ghastly screams that make your skin try to
clamber off the top of your head, a deafening bellow
of fear, misery and astonishment. It was followed by
a resumption of the silence, only this time it was a
ringing and rather surprised silence. It happened most
mornings ...

And the word, if not exactly void, was certainly
without form. No one who heard such a scream would ever
attempt to spell it, it would have been impossible to
break it down into any recognisable phonemes without a
great deal of sophisticated measuring equipment and a
very large research grant, neither of which were even
remotely available at this particular time and place.

But the sense was quite clear. Something very very
nasty had just occurred to the speaker, something which
shocked them to their very soul, and they wished to
indicate that he/she/it had just been through some
kind of experience that they would happily have done
without.

And the next thing that happened was that there was
light. There was, it should be stressed, absolutely no
causal connection between these events. First there was
the word, then there was light. This is not to deny the

implicit interconnectedness of all things, but just to
say that the light was due along at about that time
anyway.

It was sunrise. The sun rose creepingly over the hills.
The sun which was rising was an unregarded yellow one
lying in the uncharted backwaters of the unfashionable
end of the Western spiral arm of the Galaxy.

The hills over which it was rising were those of an
utterly insignificant little blue-green planet whose
ape-descended life forms have recently died out to be
replaced by a race of people who would one day invent
the digital watch, and then perish shortly afterwards
when their world was unexpectedly demolished to make
way for a hyperspace bypass.

Several billion trillion tons of super-hot exploding
hydrogen nuclei rose slowly into view above the grey
watery horizon, though, this being an autumn morning of
the grisly kind, their appearance was that of a small
ball, cold, and damp with mist. This breaking dawn was
cold and foggy, and if you were standing there in the
middle of it you could be forgiven for thinking that
the dew that morning must have fallen with a sickening
wet thud. If you were standing there you could be
forgiven for thinking a lot of things, prime amongst
which would probably be the thought that you'd much
rather be somewhere else, and this as it turns out is not
insignificant ...

A small unidentified furry animal of phenomenally
low intelligence peered out at the hazy ball of the sun
from behind a little tuft of grass and its nose twitched
in fear and astonishment. It could not remember ever
having seen anything so appallingly strange before.
This was not because it had spent its life underground,
or was naturally nocturnal in its habits, but because,
as has already been mentioned, it was phenomenally

unintelligent. The events of the previous day, and the
day before that, and so on, had now entirely slipped
from its mind. The reason why it was an unidentified
small furry animal is that it didn't last far enough
along the path of evolution ever to acquire a name. It
died out because it was completely incapable of coping
with all the surprises that came its way every day of
its bemused life ...

The sun continued its long haul up the sky. The small
rat-like creature scampered over the ground weaving
to the left and right in the way that small rat-like
creatures traditionally do, ducked into the mouth of a
small cave into which the light of common day was now
beginning to make its way, scurried in alarm over the
motionless form of a body that was lying huddled in the
corner, wriggled rapidly down a crack in the rock, and
never appeared in any work of literature ever again.

If you had been standing there with a Dream Descry-
O-Mat or a Hope Homer – and this in itself is pretty
unlikely, because anyone rich enough to own either or
both of these ludicrously expensive pieces of flash
equipment would probably pay good money not to be
standing there with them – you would detect just one
dream in the vicinity.

The nightmare.

The cave's interior was damp and dark and smelt in
that pungent way which suddenly makes you realise that
your nostrils go far deeper back into your skull than
you normally suppose. Its walls were slimy. It was cold.

It was, nevertheless, the cave which the man called
home until he could think of a better name for it, or
find a better cave.

He lay in it, not knowing for the moment where he was,
huddled in a corner, shivering. The terrible yell had
shocked him out of a deep sleep, and he felt shaken and

411

dizzy with a nasty blur where his mind should be, as if
he had been walking in his sleep and had tripped and
sprained his brain. He didn't dare to open his eyes, even
to move, until he had some idea of what to expect...

His nightmare, it seemed, had, like most nightmares, a
fairly straightforward beginning.

It began with a house. His house.

He knew it. Its shape, the texture of its brick, the
worn threads of its carpet, all came vividly to mind.
But the nightmare was shaking it, like a bear shaking
a house in a tree, the walls cracked and strained, dust
clattered from them. It was being demolished.

Suddenly he knew where he must be, or at least he
could make a very straightforward guess.

He must be in a small Spanish hotel, he decided. That
was it. He could remember getting the brochure and
suspecting that it would be a bit dismal in the off-
season. He must have gone.

Or there must have been an accident, he had been
hurt, hit on the head maybe. That was it. He must be in
hospital with amnesia. Hospital! That would explain the
cry, of course, he thought to himself. You always hear
cries like that in hospital, they're full of people in
pain, waking up to discover they've had the wrong arm or
leg lopped off, people encountering their first National
Health Service meal, or, if they're in the private wing,
their first non-National Health Service meal bill. He
breathed a sigh of relief. That's where he must be, he
thought. He was with BUPA. He had paid his subscription.
He relaxed.

His fingers felt down beside him for the edge of his
bed. They encountered rock, rough, earthy rock, and a
small muddy puddle. He panicked. In his mind he flipped
furiously through his bank statements - disconnected
gobbets of his memory were now leaping back at him -

he must have paid, he was sure he had, he'd made out
a standing order, for heaven's sake … His fingers
scrabbled desperately for the hard steel of the bed
frame, the crispness of white sheets, but he could find
neither amongst the mud. Where was he? Who was he?

In his mind was growing the dark suspicion that the
answers, when he found them, would not be enjoyable.

He tried to calm himself, to focus his mind back on
his nightmare. What had happened after his house got
demolished? The Earth got demolished. He looked for the
symbolism in that, couldn't find any and struggled to
recall other images.

Who had yelled?

He felt himself falling, dizzily, spiralling downwards.
He gripped the stone fiercely, but it seemed to spin with
him. The idea came to him again that the Earth had been
destroyed and he fought it off. He grabbed a handful of
mud. This is the Earth, he insisted to himself, this is
earth, this.

Ford Prefect. A face, a name he knew. Ford would make
it come right. A memory came to him of Ford standing at
a bar, wild-eyed, claiming to be from another planet.
That seemed plausible.

Then his mind threw up another image, that of Ford
not standing at a bar, but he dismissed it as too far-
fetched.

The plink plink plink of dripping water chipped at
his mind. The cold which afflicted his face, hands and
feet began to extend inwards and grasp at his heart.
Again, he felt a terrible aloneness as his mind began
relentlessly to assail him with images of the Earth
being demolished, of men with two heads, of a giant
spaceship shaped like a running shoe, of a man telling
him he designed Norway, of … Tricia McMillan, of a
restaurant at the end of the Universe (wasn't that in

Chelsea ...?) of dust, rubble, explosions, stars, of coffins full of frozen hairdressers ...

The continuing plink plink plink of the water dripping in the darkness made him think rather hard at this point, and with relief, he came up with a theory to account for everything so far.

He hadn't woken up yet. That was it. He was still dreaming. That was why he seemed to be lying in a cold wet dark cave. Silly him. He laughed.

For some reason his laugh came out as a thin scratchy rasp, and he suddenly realised that his throat was rough, sore and aching.

He tried to speak but he couldn't. He put his hand up to his throat and was startled by the thickly matted damp beard it encountered. He rubbed his larynx. He tried to make a quiet humming noise but his throat was too sore. It was numb with hoarseness.

Suddenly, without warning, it was back. All his early life, just like that. It dropped back into place with a sort of mental plop. Memories of his childhood, his parents, his first home, his first school, his friends, his adolescence, his girlfriends, a few trips abroad, university, his life in London, his move to ... with his memories came a shocking realisation.

He had obviously led an appallingly dull life. The memories were like the Christmas parcel which arrives in late November and on December 25th turns out to contain handkerchiefs. That might explain why he had such an extraordinary and bizarre dream – some sort of compensation mechanism might be at work deep in his subconscious.

It was at that moment that he finally managed to work out who it was that had screamed.

The man's name was Arthur Dent.

9. THE CONSULTANT (Original *LUE* manuscript)

On prehistoric Earth a cloud descended.

This was such extraordinary behaviour for a cloud that for a second or two Arthur didn't know how to react, so he didn't. Then, slowly, carefully, millimetre by millimetre, he opened his mouth and gazed at it. A few seconds later again he said "haaaaa" and "waaaaa" and, finally, "hooooo."

Ford Prefect was staring earnestly in the opposite direction at the time, but hearing Arthur's remarks and detecting little sense in them, he turned round and therefore witnessed the phenomenon for himself.

The cloud had parked itself (if that is the right word for what it had done – there is no commonly accepted expression since no cloud had ever done anything like it before) about a hundred yards from them. They looked up at the sky. The sun shone out of it perfectly innocently. It was alone. There were no clouds scudding about it, or anywhere near it, or anywhere at all from one horizon to the other. There was no escaping the fact that the cloud now stationed in the field in front of them was the same one that had been hanging in the sky all morning.

It was a large, fluffy cumulonimbus of the archetypal kind, such as one might see on a weather chart, or a child's painting, or a chocolate-box top – almost anywhere in fact other than parked in a field.

It was white and peculiarly attractive. Ford and Arthur realised that it must be attractive because they discovered that slowly, wonderingly, they were walking towards it.

As they approached, it seemed gradually to change its aspect – no longer white, but grey, no longer fluffy, but sheer, a sheer cliff face of swirling grey mist and

smoke that darkened the air around it. The more Arthur
walked towards it, the more he became aware that the
tiny hairs on the back of his neck were trying to stay
behind.

And it was becoming clear that as well as standing in
the field there were other significant ways in which it
differed from the standard fluffy cumulonimbus cloud.
It had, for instance, lights in it. Nothing you could
focus on, nothing you could single out with your eye and
say that here was a yellow, red or green light, but there
were lights in it. And patterns, shapes, evanescent,
swirling in the mist, numbers, symbols dancing dizzily
invisible, beyond the grip of vision, but nonetheless
subliminally there.

And it seemed to want them to come in.

They paused and looked around them. Behind them lay
the hills, the trees, the grassy fields, quietly getting
on with looking peaceful and unconcerned. In front of
them lay this cloud that wanted them to come in.

Having nothing pressing to keep them outside beyond
a vague sense of self-preservation, they shrugged and
walked into the mist.

The first unexpected thing about it was that it was
hollow. The mist was simply a wall, three, maybe four feet
deep. They walked through it and emerged into the second
unexpected thing, which was some kind of sand-covered
arena, an oval area about one hundred yards across at its
widest point and circumscribed simply by the wall of grey
mist which was open at the top to the blue sky.

The third and fourth unexpected things were sitting
on top of each other.

The one was a man, and the thing on which he was
sitting motionlessly seemed to be some kind of horse.
Arthur didn't look too carefully in case he found
that it wasn't a horse and that he didn't like what it

actually was. For the moment "some kind of horse" lurked
steadily in the lower periphery of his vision, which was
otherwise wholly occupied with its master.

The man was one of the most terrifying things that
either of them had ever seen, given that neither of them
had dared to look closely at the horse.

He was dressed in black. His boots were black, his
leggings were black, his belt was black with little black
studs, his loose black tunic was black, his gloves were
black, the medallion round his neck was black. If you'd
met him at a discotheque you would have laughed, but the
blackness of his eyes was appalling.

The face in which they were set was hard and cold,
yet smooth and strangely beautiful. A large-scale bust
of him would have passed unnoticed on Easter Island, at
least unless the sculptor had somehow managed to capture
the expression in the black appalling eyes. That would
have set it firmly apart, because the expression in them
was a devastating shock to all who saw it.

It was love.

It was huge, passionate, insatiable love.

And as one saw the love in those eyes, one prayed
fervently, desperately, from the bottom of one's quaking
heart that one never, ever got to meet whomever or
whatever it was he was in love with.

He sat very still, gazing not at them, but slightly
above and through them.

A breath of wind slightly lifted the front lock of his
hair, then thought better of it, replaced it with respect
exactly as it had been before and hurried off in search
of a few leaves to rustle instead.

Seconds ticked by.

The horse pawed the ground in a broody sort of way as
if there were a lot of evil things it was keen to get on
with elsewhere.

When finally they looked down at the horse they were deeply disturbed by it. Even Ford Prefect, who had once proved that he could quell an Algolian Suntiger with a look, provided that look was fuelled by a good half-bottle of Ol' Janx Spirit, shuddered.

Exactly why it would have been hard to say. It wasn't just the sheer scale and muscle of the beast, it wasn't just the evil sheen of its magnificent hide, it wasn't just the smallness of its black eyes, the redness of its wet and flaring nostrils, the brilliant whiteness of its fearsome teeth, the gleaming blackness of the prongs with which its harness was studded, or the ugly images on the small television monitors ranged along its neck. It was just the vague feeling that this was a horse on a morning out from hell.

The silence was becoming unbearable, and Ford steeled himself to break it.

"..." he said, and then cleared his throat and started again. "Just who are you and what are you doing here?" he said at last. As a piece of bravado it didn't quite work. It was too loud at the beginning, too quiet in the middle, and then much too loud again at the end.

The man looked down at him and waited an impressive number of seconds before replying. When he did reply, his voice was deep. It rolled like thunder in a distant valley.

He said, "And who are you and what are you doing here?"

Ford was startled. He experienced a keen sense of disappointment. After all the build-up, he thought, this was not the stuff of great conversations. Someone who looks like this and sits on a horse like that, he thought, should have a better line in discourse. Emboldened by the sense of anti-climax, he said exactly that, and waited.

And waited.

The man waited.

The horse flicked its tail idly, though not at a fly. There were no flies anywhere in its vicinity. Any fly who came anywhere near a horse like that would have to be out of its tiny ectomorphic skull.

The silence continued, and it became uncomfortably apparent that the man did actually want an answer to his question. His eyes settled on them with the effect of a couple of vultures settling on somebody who's only just started to become aware of feeling a little ill.

"OK," said Ford. "OK," he blustered. "OK, my name's Ford Prefect, this is Arthur Dent, OK?"

He rolled his shoulders in what he hoped was a pugnacious manner, but clearly it wasn't so he stopped again. He hopped from foot to foot, but the horse glanced at him briefly so he stopped that too. He was not getting the better of this conversation, and all he'd done so far was introduce himself.

"And," he shouted, "as to what we are doing here, just don't ask! I mean, look at the place! You can't. You've got your zarking cloud in the way, but take it from me. We are here because we are stranded, and that is all. Stranded, stuck, marooned in this primeval festering dump of a pit that a flea wouldn't thank you for leaving it in."

Arthur bridled slightly at this description of what was, after all, his own beloved home world, tired though he was of being stuck in its prehistoric past without tea or newspapers. However, he let it pass.

"We are not," Ford thundered on, "doing anything. We are merely being here. With a few ancillary activities such as hating every minute of it. And we wandered into your zarking cloud because it was in the zarking way. Anything else you want to know, or shall I just keep shouting at random?"

The man leaned forward slightly. A tiny smile lurked near his mouth but never quite reached it. He patted his horse's neck and cuffed it lightly behind the ear - something that anybody else would have deserved a medal for.

"So am I right," he said at last, "in thinking that you feel you ought not to be here?"

Ford stared at him. "Congratulations," he said, "you got it."

This attempt at facetiousness seemed to go down particularly badly with the horse. The man calmed it with another gentle pat.

"If you feel that you are in the wrong place," he said to them quietly, "you should have contacted me sooner."

This stumped them. They looked at each other and then back at him.

"We didn't contact you," said Ford.

"No," said the man, with the air of one who is pursuing a higher chain of logic than any that might be apparent from his conversation, "you didn't."

"So?" said Ford. The man patted the horse again.

"So," he said. He glanced into the encircling wall of mist, but not, apparently, at anything in particular. Certainly not anything enlightening.

"We don't even know who you are," said Arthur.

"I am a Consultant in these matters," he said.

"Ah, I see," said Arthur, in the hope that Ford might know what he was talking about.

"What are you talking about?" said Ford. "What matters?"

"Everything," said the Consultant, "Life, the Universe ..." he shrugged, "with particular reference to the problem of Where Things Ought To Be. That is my special field."

Ford took a deep breath. The Consultant held up a hand as if to stop them saying "What do you mean by ..." etc.,

and they waited. Then they saw that in his hand was a
piece of paper. He handed it to them!

"What is it?" he said.

Ford looked at it, turned it over, looked at the other
side, turned it back again.

"It's a piece of paper," he said. Arthur examined it
and agreed. It had a few squiggles and marks on it, but
nothing that meant anything to either of them. The only
odd thing about it was the way it had appeared in his
hand out of thin air.

"Not magic," said the Consultant, "hyperinfra-
structuraltempethatonic transference."

With a sudden swift movement he dismounted and stood
in front of them.

"I pulled it out of a different point in time and
space," he said, "or rather the same point if you accept
the view that all points in time and space are equal and
simultaneous. I don't myself, but then I know a great
deal more about it than anyone else." He smiled. That is
to say, he executed a facial manoeuvre that would have
been a smile on anybody else's face. Its actual effect was
to make Arthur's stomach lurch.

The Consultant took the piece of paper from him and
held it up.

"Tell me where you think it ought to be," he said.

"I think," said Arthur to Ford, "I may take a little
walk. Give me a shout if anything intelligible happens."

The Consultant restrained him gently but firmly.

"Tell me," he said, "where."

"Now look," said Ford, "you said something about
getting us out of here ..."

"I said something about Where Things Ought To Be,"
said the Consultant, "which is a tricky matter requiring
infinite skill and judgement. Fortunately I have them.
Take this piece of paper."

"What,' said Ford in exasperation, "is so important
about this wretched piece of paper?"

"Nothing," said the Consultant, with another of
the smiles which had played such havoc with Arthur's
digestive system, which had already had a tough time
that morning coping with the overcooked rabbit, "not
here. Here it is perfectly harmless. I suppose you could
cut your finger on the edge, but ..." He shrugged.

"But?"

"I plucked it out of space-time. I can put it back just
as easily, anywhere, anywhen. If I put it - as I can,
now, like that -" he flicked his fingers and the paper
was gone, "into the wrong person's pocket on one of the
planets of the Allied Republics of Gognagamma ..."

"Gogna ...?"

"Gognagamma. Another Galaxy, you wouldn't know it -
then I can guarantee you that within hours five hundred
and thirty-seven thousand billion people would be dead.
The apparently meaningless symbols on it are the secret
firing codes for their entire nuclear arsenal. If I put
it there now, and you were still to be standing here
in a few billion years' time, then the tiny pinprick of
light you would see in that corner of the sky would be
Gognagamma, signing off. If, however, I were to collect
two hundred and forty-nine of these -" he turned his
hand round to show them that in fact he still had the
paper held between his knuckles like a conjuror, "and
took them to a redemption centre on Langaba III, only
thirty light years from here, I could get a free pop-up
toaster. Tempting, eh?"

Arthur goggled.

"Why?" said Ford. "What is it?"

"A bill for roof repairs."

"A bi ..."

"... 11 for roof repairs, yes. Addressed to one Frob

Gronta, an amphibious life form in financial trouble
in the Minor Magellenic Clouds. I'm afraid he killed
himself when he saw it. The shock sent his son into a
mental hospital where he later met a female amphibian
with similar emotional difficulties. Together they
composed the greatest comic operas their world had ever
known. Transformed the cultural life of a generation."

Arthur nodded wisely to himself, realised after a
while that this wasn't getting him anywhere and decided
that he would say "What?" after all.

"I said something about Where Things Ought To Be,"
said the Consultant. "This piece of paper first, then
you. There are things you should understand. To you this
is a meaningless, harmless piece of paper. It has a few
meaningless symbols on it. But we live in an infinite
Universe. At least, you do. I live nearby."

"Wh …"

"Skip it. In an infinite Universe there are infinite
possibilities. Yes?"

"Yes, OK," said Ford irritably.

"And therefore an infinite number of things this piece
of paper can mean, yes?"

"Yes," said Ford again.

"And what it means depends on where it is. Yes?"

"Could you just assume," said Ford, "that whatever you
say, we agree?"

"For instance, there is a world on which this piece
of paper is legal currency," continued the Consultant.
"I know, I've been there. Only once, the food is shocking.
But this piece of paper would buy you an awful lot of
it. It would buy you friends, power, beautiful houses,
anything you wanted, assuming you actually wanted to
be there which you wouldn't because the food is so bad …"
He frowned slightly into the distance. "Where do you
think this piece of paper ought to be?"

Arthur felt there was some kind of spell going on
and felt dizzy with either that or bewilderment, or
maybe with the sheer fear of this strange tall hawk-
like figure standing inexplicably over them with the
blackness of hell in his eyes, the sun behind his thin
head and a scrappy piece of paper in his hand to which
he seemed to attach inordinate importance.

He wiped his hand across his forehead and took a deep
breath.

"Honestly," he said, "I don't know. And I can't really
pretend to understand what you're talking about."

Ford gestured that he went along with Arthur. Ford
shrugged. Arthur shrugged. Their shoulders collided.
They had nothing to say. Arthur wondered if he should
mention that the horse seemed to be eating the sand, but
decided not to.

"On Sagyavan Alpha," continued the Consultant,
"this piece of paper is the death warrant of an
innocent and good man. I could put it there and he
would die. Like that." He made a graphic gesture.
"The people would be incensed. They would rise and
overthrow their government, which has committed every
possible crime of tyranny – except for this one – and
as a result millions of people would lead free and
happy lives which would otherwise have been denied
them. On Pelphonicos this paper would undoubtedly be
recognised as the missing masterpiece by their greatest
artist …"

"Yes, we begin to get the idea," said Ford. There are
times when it's best just to go along with things.

"So you see the complexity of the matter," said
the Consultant, "the skill and judgement that the
disposition of objects requires, if Life is to have
meaning."

"Er, yeah," said Ford.

"So where," asked the Consultant, "do you think this piece of paper Ought To Be?"

"Er, yeah," said Ford on the grounds that the last time he had said it it seemed to get by without trouble. He had been seized by a sudden urge to start jumping in and out of lakes again. This time he thought he might be an olive. Arthur simply mumbled non-committally a mumble that he had developed years ago as a child, for use in history lessons. He had practised it into a tape recorder for hours till he was certain that it sounded equally and simultaneously as much like, or unlike, "1066" as it did "Schleswig-Holstein." He had never expected to need it again, and was startled and pleased to discover it popping up now and making itself useful.

"Good," said the Consultant unexpectedly, "you shall have it."

With a movement too swift for Arthur to deflect he advanced on him with the piece of paper, and unexpectedly pushed it into the pocket of his dressing gown. Arthur stood amazed.

"What in God's name am I supposed to do with it?" he wittered.

The close physical presence of the man was terrifying. His height – he was very tall – his thinness, his ... hookedness, the fearsomeness of his eyes, the fact that he was standing with the sun directly behind his head, all contributed to an effect which Arthur was later to describe in the diary he came to keep of these events, first as "evil" (which he crossed out), then as "overpowering" (which he crossed out), then as "psychically pungent" (which he crossed out with a thin, reluctant line) and finally as "indescribable".

"What do you mean," said the Consultant in a voice like a mighty river flowing into a blast furnace, "by God? There isn't a God."

425

"Ah, is that so," said Arthur, in the most uncontroversial voice he could muster. "I'd often wondered."

"Well, you can stop wondering now," hissed the Consultant, "because there isn't one."

"Right," said Arthur, "right." He stuck his hands jauntily into his pockets and looked about him. He regretted looking about him because the first thing his eyes fell upon was the horse. It seemed to have little flames coming out of its nostrils. He looked hurriedly back at the Consultant. "Right," he said again.

"Cold fact!" shouted the Consultant.

"Cold fact," agreed Arthur.

"Nasty things happen, nice things happen. Not many, but they do. People should just get on and make the best. Yes?"

"Can you just assume," said Arthur tactfully, "that anything you say, I agree? With you all the way."

"I!" snapped the Consultant. "I give it meaning, if it has one. A phony bill for roof repairs! Ha! I'm the one! I cause pain, trouble. Only the bad things give life meaning, make it grow, you see that?"

"I, er ... well, that is to say ..."

"But not any more. I give up. He can have it back."

"I'm sure you're right."

"And people comfort themselves with the idea of a God! Pathetic, weak, woolly-minded idiots. Too weak to face up to reality. God! What a stupid idea!"

He turned and fixed his eyes on Arthur and on Ford.

"If there is such a thing as a God," he said advancing on them, "may he strike me down where I stand!"

Out of a clear blue sky a bolt of lightning hit him squarely in the back of the neck.

"Now, I don't want you jumping to any conclusions," he said, and collapsed in a smoking heap.

"Did that just happen?" said Ford. Arthur nodded
wordlessly.

The horse flashed them a moody look. It pawed the
ground. It moved away and slowly circled back. It began
to approach them. It broke into an easy trot, and then
into a canter. They turned and ran.

The wall of cloud was about a hundred yards behind
them, a seething writhing mass of smoke. They ran, they
stumbled, they staggered across the sand, the sound
of hooves drumming in their ears. They ran till they
thought their hearts would burst, ran into the cloud,
clawed their way panting, gasping and crying through
it, and emerged on the other side in the middle of Lord's
Cricket Ground towards the end of the last test of the
Australian Series in the year 198-, with England needing
only twenty-eight runs to win.

* * *

"Yes, that was a surprise," said Arthur Dent many
years later. His diary had been published. It caused a
considerable stir throughout the Universe, a Universe
much changed from the one we know now, because of the
intervening passage of the Magic Moment Grade One ...

It made Arthur something of a celebrity, and though
he resisted this and preferred to spend the latter part
of his life in quiet seclusion in the small cottage he
built for himself in the shadow of his beloved monastery
of Mon, he was often visited there by historians,
journalists and students, and sometimes the just plain
curious who were prepared to go that far off the beaten
track to look at somebody whose life had been lived so
far from life's safety rails.

Arthur continued to claim that he hadn't really
done anything, that he was more differed from than

differing, more happened to than happening, that his
life had been governed by the principle of Where Things
Ought To Be, but eventually he agreed to record a series
of interviews. These are recorded on five tapes stored
in the Quantum History Department of the University of
New Maximegalon.

The tape shows him as a man in perhaps his early
sixties, hair grey now and thinning. His face is worn
and lined by a life of almost continual astonishment and
worry, but softened now by philosophy and herbal cream,
both supplied by the monks of Mon.

As he speaks, his voice is soft and kindly, and faintly
in the background can be heard from over the monastery
walls the serene sound of the monastery choir. They sing
of the ineluctability of this, the inconsequence of that,
the incomprehensibility of the other, the importance of
believing it all, and the futility of worrying about any
of it.

Tape three begins with Dent saying, "Yes, that was
a surprise," and this is in answer to the question at
the end of tape two, which refers to the unexpected
materialisation at Lord's cricket ground.

At another point on the tape, Arthur Dent claims
that if he holds his head very still for a while he can
understand how and why it all happened.

10. ARTHUR'S DIARY (Original *LUE* manuscript)

FIRST EXTRACT FROM ARTHUR DENT'S DIARY.

Slartibartfast has suggested that as he thinks I seem
to have a certain amount of difficulty in comprehending
what he regards as simple basic ideas, I ought perhaps to
keep a diary of events and sort them out for myself at
my leisure.

I don't think I have trouble comprehending things.
I don't understand what he means by that. I would say
this, however, that events seem to have a great deal of
trouble in laying themselves out in ways that make sense
to me.

However, I will keep a diary, and this is me starting
it. I'm using some sort of pen which I'm told is the
height of scientific sophistication, but it irritates the
hell out of me. Every time I pause for more than five
seconds, thinking about what to write next, the pen just
goes ahead and writes a word anyway, selected on the
basis of what it thinks I'm thinking, and that's supposed
to get the ball rolling for me. Well, it doesn't, it just,
as I say, irritates the hell out of me.

Tea. There, it's just done it. That was the pen, not me.
Admittedly, I could do with a cup.

I'm writing this as fast as I can, so that I don't
get interrupted by the pen, so if some of it seems
superfluous or off the point or, as in that previous
phrase, tautological, that'll be the reason. I'm just
keeping writing whilst I try to gather up the strength
required to describe exactly what happened at the end
of that extraordinary Test Match, and just getting
my writing wrist moving smoothly is having a kind of
welcome soothing effect. You will notice that I have not
put a date at the top of this page. I say "you" assuming

429

that anybody is ever going to read this, and indeed
assuming that there is going to be anybody by whom it
could be read - anybody at all, if what Slartibartfast
tells me is true, which I can scarcely credit.

I don't know what the matter with old Slarts is, he's
not his old self at all. He tells me he's become the Vice-
President of an organisation called the Campaign for
Real Time and keeps pushing leaflets at me. I'd better
read one soon, if only to shut him up. He says he felt
he ought to do something useful in his old age and keeps
on muttering about something his mother told him when
he was a small boy, which is something I find a little
hard to visualise. It was, apparently, quite a long time
ago. The five-million-year sleep he'd just woken up
from when last I met him was apparently not his first.
Anyway, what his mother said, apparently, was that he
should leave the Universe the way he found it, and that,
he says, is a tall order. I can imagine.

Dates. Ah, that in fact was the pen being useful for
once and reminding me that I completely forgot what I
set out to explain in the last paragraph. I haven't put
the date at the top of this page for two reasons. One
is the insistence of Slartibartfast, because he says, in
his capacity as VP of CAMTIM (the Campaign for Real
Time) that if this document were to fall into the hands
of someone in the past it would only cause more of the
sort of problems he's trying to sort out, and the other
is that I don't know what it is. At present time of
writing we (I will explain exactly who "we" comprises
in a minute) are ... wait till I check this out ... we are
apparently moving paratangentially across a radian
subarc of the Deep Time field, so you tell me what the
date is. Ah, we've arrived somewhere, I'll have to stop
for the moment.

SECOND EXTRACT FROM ARTHUR DENT'S DIARY.

Deep breath. Looking back at the previous entry in
this journal I'm a bit surprised by the lightness of its
tone, but then I don't think things had really sunk in.
Perhaps Slarts is right about me. Perhaps Ford is right
about me. I hope not, he's a great deal ruder. Either way,
it's time I began to lay out the facts.

England won the Test Match. It may seem inconsequential,
but they did. It did. (Is England "it" or "they"? Oh, get
on with it.) The match ended with another smacking six,
right into the crowd, and the crowd went wild, stormed
the pitch and did all that sort of thing. Slartibartfast
reacted to this like a mammoth staring out of a block
of ice, and I really began to think that he must be
an Australian supporter, though it seemed a little
unlikely.

There then followed a little ceremony — I gather this
is (was) a new thing, not previously done, and probably
designed to make the whole business better television.
The Ashes were presented to the captain of the English
team there on the field. The TV companies didn't know it
at this point, but they were in for some very very good
television indeed ...

I think something's happening, I'll have to st

11. INTER-SPECIES LOVE (Original *LUE* manuscript)

So far, there has been very little description in this
narrative of the relationship between Zaphod Beeblebrox
and Trillian, and there is a reason for this. They are,
strictly speaking, of different species. Anyone who needs
any further explanation should consult the Imperial
Galactic Law Statute 161251/110352, which covers what
it calls Unnatural Practices. The Statute is, frankly,
repressive, and falls into three separate sections. The
first is astonishingly long and graphic and describes
exactly what the Statute means by "Unnatural Practices".
The second section is, by contrast, extremely brief and
defines exactly how much of this sort of thing anyone
else is allowed to describe in a published work. The
third section deals with penalties for contravening
section two and is, if anything, even longer and more
graphic than section one.

This is a relatively recent statute. Astonishingly
enough (until you think it through) it was actually
conceived and made into law during the Presidency of
Zaphod Beeblebrox himself. The reason why this is, on
the face of it, astonishing is that in all other respects
Zaphod's Presidency was the most decadent in history. The
reason why it ceases to be astonishing when you think it
through is this:

Zaphod is widely thought to have written most of
section one himself. The statute as a whole

(a) is pure pornography,

(b) outlaws all other pornography,

(c) is therefore the only book in the Galactic History
of publishing to have outsold that wholly remarkable
book, The Hitch Hiker's Guide to the Galaxy.

432

Because of an inexplicable computer malfunction there is no one who can say for certain where the revenue from the sales of this statute ended up, but, equally, there is no one who can't guess.

12. THE ASSUMPTION OF SAINT ZALABAD (*MH* notes)

In the worlds beyond the Great Moosop of Rhontoid they were celebrating the Feast of the Assumption of Saint Zalabad, and all was going sensationally well.

Zalabad had been a great and popular king, and had assumed that everyone would like to have a huge feast at his expense every year for no better reason than that it would be a terrifically good time for all concerned, and his Assumption had proved to be entirely correct.

So correct, in fact, that after his death his people made him a saint. They hadn't had any saints before, and thought that having one who was just plain good-hearted would be a tremendously good start. There were grumbles, of course, there always are. There were those who said that you couldn't have a proper religion that wasn't based on some acts of senseless brutality that everyone could torture themselves about, and maybe a few other people while they were at it – but everyone was just kind to these people till they shut up.

This afternoon was one of singing and dancing in the streets and nearly everyone was having fun.

Swept up in the cheerful celebrating crowds was Arthur Dent. The ship he was travelling on had made an unscheduled stopover, and while he had been moping around the spaceport bookstall he reflected that in spite of the rapid march of progress, spaceports were even duller than airports used to be. Railway stations were duller than seaports used to be, airports were duller than railway stations used to be, and spaceports were duller than airports used to be – even Birmingham airport (Birmingham in the Sublime Rosterox of Hawsqaja, beyond the Balastras of the Seven Binjis).

As Arthur was hanging around someone came up and did

something so pointlessly nice to him that he thought he'd
better go and have a look at what kind of world he had
landed on.

"Er, thank you," he said, and stepped out into the sun.

"Have a drink!"

"Thanks ..."

"Some fruit!"

He had rarely had such a thoroughly delightful
afternoon, and it was only marred towards the end
by the sudden sight of a depressingly familiar shape
walking up the thronged streets towards him - if
walking is a word that adequately describes the sort of
dreary cybernetic trudge the figure affected. Arthur
tried in vain to duck out of sight in the crowd.

Something odd whizzed over his head, but when he
looked up a few minutes later, though everyone else
in the crowd was looking past him, the morbid heap of
misbegotten metal he was trying to avoid was standing in
front of him, gazing at him with calm contempt.

"Oh, er, Marvin, hello," said Arthur, "how something or
other to see you, what's the word I want? Nice. How nice
to see you, so to speak. Yes."

Marvin continued to gaze at him.

One of the great drawbacks, Arthur reflected, with
this business of being able to whizz backwards and
forwards in time as everyone seemed to be doing in
today's (or yesterday's, or tomorrow's or next week's - it
hardly made any difference any more) modern galaxy was
that, even though you may have solemnly ministered at
somebody's deathbed one week, that was no guarantee that
you weren't going to have to engage them in pleasant
chit-chat the next.

His last encounter with the robot had concluded with
Arthur laying his terminally rusted remains to rest
in the dust of the planet Sevorbeupstry, trying hard

435

to keep the words "Good riddance" from popping into his brain the whole time.

"So, er, how have you been, then?" he asked.

"Quiet, obedient and desperate," said Marvin.

"Well, sorry to hear that," said Arthur. "Good heavens, is that the time? I mustn't keep you. Terrible crowds for the festival, eh?"

Arthur tried to keep a tight grip on his goodwill, but it was like throttling a fish.

"This business about saving your life," said Marvin dully, "I don't suppose you'll want to mention that. Heigh ho. On I go."

(In order to be able to make Zalabad a saint they have to have a proper religion, which means it must be properly based on something nasty having happened, without which goodness can have no meaning. Merely being good and kind and pleasant is all very well in its place, but it's hardly religious is it? Hardly fervent.

They are all getting ready for the great guilt. Maybe they are handing out Anti-Guilt T-shirts.)

13. BAGGY THE RUNCH (*MH* notes)

The history of the Hitchhiker's Guide to the Galaxy is one of vision, idealism, struggle, passion, greed, success, failure, and enormously long lunch breaks.

The earliest origins of the Guide are now lost in the mists of time (for other and more curious theories about where they are lost see below) but most of the surviving stories speak of a founding editor called Baggy the Runch.

The story of Baggy the Runch is a very instructive one. Baggy the Runch was born on the remotest of frontier planets, beyond the reach of even the most powerful rock-video relay stations, which had been reached by the last straggling pioneers of the Third and Last Great Outpush who had spent over twenty years' hard travel getting there. It was called Nowwhat and was very good for being cold and wet on, and one of the few planets in the Galaxy to have its own motto, which goes like this: "Even travelling despondently is better than arriving here."

The major activities on Nowwhat consisted of catching, skinning and eating Nowwhattian boghogs, and only the skinning was in any way easy. There was a lot of shivering too, that was very popular on Nowwhat, largely because the Nowwhattian boghog fur skins were unaccountably thin ...

It was into a world of this kind that Baggy was born, and almost instantly abandoned, with nothing to his name but his name – Baggy the Runch. His parents had thought to do this one little thing for him: if he could cope with a name like that, they argued, he could cope with anything. But it was not to be. He wanted to let his parents know about the names that he in turn

had thought of for them. With a name like that, he
discovered that he couldn't cope with being introduced
to people and therefore never had any friends who might
have helped him cope with some of the other things in
life, like the cold, the wet and loquacious boghogs. So
he ran off into the swamps where he was brought up,
incredibly painfully, by boghogs. The result of this was
that now no one could bear to be introduced to him, and
so his isolation was complete. His life was, therefore,
thoroughly miserable.

One day Baggy the Runch was sloshing around aimlessly
in a field near Nowwhat's grim little spaceport when he
came across a discarded copy of the Hitchhiker's Guide to
the Galaxy lying in a puddle. He picked it up and turned
it over and over, staring at it in astonishment. Here was
something he could hold over his head to keep the rain
off!

Anyone who thinks that a plastic book some six inches
by four inches would not keep off a great deal of rain
simply has no idea how much rain there was on Nowwhat.

Picture, then, a wretched little savage boy sitting
shivering in a puddle holding the key to the Galaxy two
inches above his head. Continue to picture it, because
the scene is about to change.

(He left the planet at the first opportunity,
smuggling himself aboard the ship of an itinerant
thermal-underwear trader who had made a fortune by
following the pioneer settler routes after a well-judged
interval of years.)

14. GALACTIVID (*MH* notes)

One morning in May the world woke up to the most
extraordinary news. That is to say that England woke
up to it. In other parts of the world they were going to
bed or having lunch, but in all cases, it was the most
extraordinary news.

The news was that an alien intelligence had been
monitoring our civilisation for many years, and not
only that, but they had also been taping 'The Liver
Birds' and 'Are You Being Served?' and syndicating
them throughout the galaxy without paying a penny in
royalties.

The news broke because a rival TV network operating
out of Mintakam, which is the fourth star in the
constellation of Orion, arrived in their starships to
put in a counter-bid for the next 'Liver Birds' series
and were aghast to discover first of all that there
were no plans for doing any more, and secondly that
Galactivid (the company that had been putting out the
shows up to now) had been doing it scot free.

It was hard to say who was the most astonished, the
people of Earth who had long imagined themselves to be
alone in a Universe of unimaginable size and grandeur,
created especially for them to occupy one minute corner
of, or the small purple executives from Cosmicpix who
realised they'd been had.

A junior executive from BBC Enterprises took them to
the hospitality suite and entertained them by asking
what kind of journey they had had and was trying to
find some ice ...

15. LAJAWAG (*MH* notes)

Many moving tales are told of people who have consulted
that entirely astonishing work of reference, The
Hitchhiker's Guide to the Galaxy, and had their lives
changed for ever by it. How many of these changes are
for the better is of course a matter of constant and
often acrimonious debate.

No one enjoyed a nice spot of acrimony in his debate
more than Lajawag Bunkwot, one of the most enterprising
editors in the Guide's long, illustrious and frequently
blameless history. He claimed that the Guide was the
greatest boon ever bestowed on creation, and when he
claimed something, it stayed claimed.

"The Hitchhiker's Guide to the Galaxy", claimed
Lajawag (this was part of his statement to the Galactic
Intriguing Incidents Squad) "has been, without question,
one of the greatest boons ever bestowed on a lucky
creation by its creator, if there is one, and if there
isn't, well, blind chance is a terribly clever thing, isn't
it, particularly working all those orbits. It's as much
as I can do to park my jet scooter. May I go now, please,
officer?"

THE RING PULL

Dirk Gently's Holistic Detective Agency

DIRK GENTLY'S HOLISTIC DETECTIVE AGENCY is a brand new novel I'm working on at the moment which is *nothing at all* to do with **The Hitch Hiker's Guide to the Galaxy.**

It's a kind of ghost-horror-detective-time-travel-romantic comedy epic and is largely concerned with mud, music, and Quantum mechanics - you get the idea. It's being published in Britain by *Heinneman* and in the USA by *Simon and Schuster*. It should be out about the middle of next year with a sequel to follow a year later.

On September 29th this year, Heinneman are publishing a four-in-one hard back volume of all the **Hitch Hiker** books, for which I have written a new and unhelpful introduction.

The Utterly Utterly Merry Comic Relief Christmas Book.

I hope you've heard of **Comic Relief** by now, which is a group of comedy writers and performers working to raise money for Ethiopia and the Sudan. You'll probably remember **Living Doll** by *Cliff Richard and the Young Ones*, which was a #1 hit earlier this year - that was a **Comic Relief** project. I've been compiling a **Comic Relief** book for Christmas, which includes new material from **The Young Ones, Spitting Image,** an **Adrian Mole** story from Sue Townsend, more **Heroic Failures** from Stephen Pile, more **Man's Best Friend,** more **Meaning of Liff** from John Lloyd and myself, a **Hitch Hiker** story, and other short story collaborations by Terry Jones, Graham Chapman and myself. All the money is going to charity, and you *have* to buy it.

Bureaucracy.

This is a new computer game I've collaborated with games designers at Infocom on. The game involves you in a bewildering series of adventures from your own home to the depths of the African jungle, but the object of the game is simply to get your bank to acknowledge a change of address card. This should be available at the beginning of 1987.

The Hitch Hiker Interactive CD.
The what? You may well ask. This is an entirely new medium that hasn't even reached the market yet. The end result should be a kind of cross between the best aspects of the radio series, the tv series, and the computer game.

The Hitch Hiker Movie.
Who knows? You know as much as I do. Every time I ask I'm told it's about to happen. I've given up asking.

Last Chance to See...

During the next year I'm embarking on a number of wildlife expeditions with zoologist Mark Carwardine to search out some of the world's rarest animals. The plan is to do a radio series and a book based on on the trips. I hope that one of these will be the first radio programme to be recorded entirely underwater in stereo.

THERE'S NOTHING
INTERESTING ON THIS PAGE
AT ALL.

LIST OF ILLUSTRATIONS

Pages 4 and 5: Selection of book covers: © William Heinemann, © Tor
  Books/Pan Macmillan, © 2008 Editorial Anagrama, © 1992 Harmony
  Books, © 2010 Pearl Publishing, © 1981 John Books Ltd, The Folio
  Society edition of *The Hitchhiker's Guide to the Galaxy*, illustrated by
  Jonathan Burton and introduced by Terry Jones, is available from www.
  foliosociety.com, The Folio Society edition of *The Restaurant at the End
  of the Universe*, illustrated by Jonathan Burton and introduced by Adam
  Roberts, is available from www.foliosociety.com

Page 6: *The Illustrated Hitchhiker's Guide to the Galaxy* cast photo ©
  Weidenfeld & Nicolson; DC Comic adaptation © DC Comics

Page 7: Trillian and Marvin © Photos 12/Alamy; Ford, Arthur and Zaphod ©
  AF Archive/Alamy; knitted toys courtesy of NECA

Page 8: Douglas Adams © Corbis; Douglas Adams' grave is author's own
  photograph

QUOTATIONS IN THE TEXT

And Another Thing… by Eoin Colfer, Penguin. Copyright
   © Eoin Colfer, 2009

Dimension of Miracles by Robert Sheckley, Granada Publishing.
   Copyright © Robert Sheckley, 1969

Doctor Snuggles, TV series. Copyright © ITV

Doctor Who, TV series. Copyright © BBC

Douglas Adams' Starship Titanic by Terry Jones, Pan Macmillan.
   Copyright © Terry Jones, 1997

Life, The Universe and Everything by Douglas Adams, Pan Macmillan.
   Copyright © Douglas Adams, 1982

Monty Python's Flying Circus, TV series. Copyright © BBC

Mostly Harmless by Douglas Adams, William Heinemann.
   Copyright © Douglas Adams, 1992

Oh No It Isn't, TV series. Copyright © BBC

So Long, and Thanks for All the Fish by Douglas Adams, Pan Macmillan.
   Copyright © Douglas Adams, 1984

The Burkiss Way, TV series. Copyright © BBC

The Hitchhiker's Guide to the Galaxy by Douglas Adams, Pan Macmillan.
   Copyright © Douglas Adams, 1979

The Hitchhiker's Guide to the Galaxy, movie script. Copyright
   © Disney, 2005

The Hitchhiker's Guide to the Galaxy, TV series. Copyright © BBC

The Hitchhiker's Guide to the Galaxy: The Original Radio Scripts, Pan
   Macmillan. Copyright © Douglas Adams, 1986

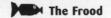

The Lavishingly Tooled Smith & Jones Instant Coffee Table Book by
Griff Rhys Jones, Rory McGrath and Clive Anderson, Fontana.
Copyright © 1986

The Restaurant at the End of the Universe by Douglas Adams,
Pan Macmillan. Copyright © Douglas Adams, 1980

The South Bank Show, TV series. Copyright © BBC

The Week Ending, TV series. Copyright © BBC

INDEX

DNA indicates Douglas Noël Adams.

and 16, 18, 19, 20, 25–6, 51, 53, 57–61, 63, 67, 75–6, 78, 81, 84, 85, 89, 90, 91–2, 110, 150, 151, 157, 163, 167, 193, 202, 204, 216, 244, 254, 256, 292, 295, 300, 303, 307, 308, 363; science, love of 10, 12, 24–5, 69, 264, 286, 296, 297, 298, 315, 316–17; scuba-diving, love of 224, 228, 304; technology and *see* **technology and;** wealth and 156–9; writing, struggles with 79, 80, 85–6, 93, 109, 121, 133, 139, 140–1, 147, 149, 156, 158, 161–3, 176–8, 193, 202–9, 210–11, 216–17, 231, 236–41, 242, 243, 251, 252, 253, 254, 257, 258, 262–3, 265–6, 271–9, 290, 292, 306, 309, 319, 367–9

childhood and schooldays: animals and 13; birth 9–10, 372; Cambridge, gains place at 26–7; childhood 11–27; comics, love of 16–18; *A Dissertation on the Task of Writing a Poem on a Candle and an Account of Some of the Difficulties Thereto Pertaining* 23–4; *Doctor Which* (comic episode of *Doctor Who*), writes 19, 23; family ancestry/background 10–11, 57; first writing 15–17; guitar playing 22–3, 28, 35, 146, 164–5, 285; hitchhiking/travelling 27–30, 33, 64, 180; Jobs 27, 37–8; letter to *Eagle* comic (first published writing) 17; *Monty Python's Flying Circus*, love of 25–6; music, love of 20–3, 28, 94–5; parents split, life after ('shuttlecock kid') 12–13; piano playing 22; radio programmes, love of 18–19; reading 16–17; religion

and 14, 26–7, 28; schooldays 13–27 *see also under individual school name;* short story in *Eagle* comic 18, 372

conservation work: gorilla charities, supports 260, 261, 285; *Last Chance To See* 248, 253, 258, 259, 260–2, 270, 309, 317, 359–60, 373, 374, 383, 384; *Last Chance To See* (Fry & Carwardine), inspires 344, 385; Madagascar trip to track down the aye-aye 245, 247–8, 373; Save The Rhino and 261, 345, 358; White Rhino appeal and 286

death 312–13, 314–21, 327, 374; cremation 318; Highgate Cemetery, ashes at 319, 367; memorial service, St-Martins-in-the-Fields 318–19; 60th Birthday celebrated, 2012 351

finances: accountant losses tax savings 253–4; acting and 40; comedy sketch writing and 44, 78–9; conservation projects and 261, 301; Duncan Terrace house and 253; *The Hitchhiker's Guide to the Galaxy* and 101, 117, 129, 131, 134, 146, 152, 156–9, 198–9, 224, 242, 247, 252, 253–4, 283, 360; holidays and 64; jobs and 27, 37–8, 48–50, 57, 65, 79, 89, 108, 272; lack of money within family during childhood 11–12, 13; public speaking and 264; wealth, effect upon life of 156–9

health: back problems 80; death from heart attack 312–13, 314–21, 327, 374; high blood pressure 297; breaks pelvis 37–8; exercise 80, 85, 103, 107, 236, 297, 312; smoking